PROUST
MANN
JOYCE

in the Modernist Context

GERALD GILLESPIE

PROUST
MANN
JOYCE

in the Modernist Context

SECOND EDITION

The Catholic University of America Press
WASHINGTON, D.C.

The paper used in this publication meets the minimum requirements of
American National Standards for Information Science—Permanence
of Paper for Printed Library Materials,

ANSI Z39.48–1984.

∞

The Library of Congress has catalogued the original edition as follows:

Gillespie, Gerald Ernest Paul, 1933–

Proust, Mann, Joyce in the modernist context / Gerald Gillespie.

p. cm.

Includes bibliographical references and index.

ISBN 0-8132-1350-9 (clothbound : alk. paper)

1. European fiction—19th century—History and criticism.   2. European
fiction—20th century—History and criticism.   3. Proust, Marcel, 1871–
1922—Criticism and interpretation.   4. Mann, Thomas, 1875–1955—
Criticism and interpretation.   5. Joyce, James, 1882–1941—Criticism
and interpretation.   I. Title.

PN3499 .G55 2003

809.3'04—dc21

2002151657

ISBN: 978-0-8132-1788-8 (pbk: alk paper)

CONTENTS

Contents

PREFACE TO THE SECOND EDITION

The gratifying critical response to my book has encouraged me to prepare the augmented paperback edition you now hold. I have been mindful of three points communicated in several reviews and privately. Some readers wished for a more expansive title, explicitly adding on one or more of their favorite authors important in the implicitly plural "context" alongside my triumvirate. Variants such as "Proust, Mann, Joyce, Kafka, Woolf as Modernist Artists" and "Proust, Mann, Joyce, et al. in Modernist Contexts" once figured among the many choices I had originally considered. However, to resurrect any scrapped alternative now, so it seemed to me, would be a confusing change. Other readers wished for somewhat more attention to the work of important modernists reaching into or past World War II, which was a primary boundary, even though chapter fourteen looked well beyond it. Some readers urged me to expand upon several of the most important features of modernist prose fiction as of the mid-twentieth century. The entirely new chapter fifteen seeks to meet this desire for a statement about at least part of the lasting legacy.

Chapter fifteen devotes attention to the later work of Joyce and Mann who survived the heyday of modernism and were a potent factor at mid-century. It serves both to refocus on the three preeminent figures named in the book's title and to celebrate special moments in which they rose to insights that, in the final analysis, are spiritual triumphs. This alone would suffice to earn them an honored place in twentieth-century literature and to establish an indebtedness of future generations to them for their inspiring example. My selection is minimal by virtue of limitations on space and is meant only to encourage fellow readers to gather their own sets of favorite moments.

The interest in my named key authors and their contemporaries of the multifarious context has hardly abated since the original fourteen chapters went to press late in 2003 in anticipation of Bloomsday 100. Doing a paperback edition affords an opportunity to add a few desirable enhancements. This has meant being able to offer readers some select supplementary pointers to interesting work published in the opening years of

Preface to the Second Edition

the new millennium on core issues with which *Proust, Mann, Joyce in the Modernist Context* is concerned. Several of the chapters have been expanded to give more weight to such topics, among others, as contributions of New World authors to the larger context, and the important relationship between film and literature in the twentieth century. A suggestion made in the original preface bears repeating here. The number of superb writers was so large in the twentieth century, it stands to reason that some readers will be more curious about certain contemporaries or immediate successors only noted cursorily in this book. They should consult the index as a helpful resource to trace connections which regrettably I must forgo pursuing.

I salute the staff of the Green Library at Stanford University for their always generous assistance and wish to express special thanks to David McGonagle, director of the Catholic University of America Press, and his team for their support of this effort.

PREFACE TO THE FIRST EDITION

I have not written this book with the aim of imposing yet another theory of modernism; rather, its chapters have grown from the pleasures of reading key authors and my interest in principal themes they developed. Three discoveries accompanied this reading experience. First, I felt general dissatisfaction with theories of modernism propounded in recent decades, especially those that isolated only certain habits and currents as constituting a "breaking point" in literary culture, in disregard of the actual profusion of relevant but "nonconforming" creative expression. Second, I found that I was enjoying a considerable number of authors of the past few decades who began to be described as "postmodernist," yet I sensed no disjuncture in such a degree as many "believing" postmodernists proclaimed. Nor had my addiction to modernist authors dampened my appreciation of great writing from preceding centuries. Likewise, my interest in newer trends in film and television, the electronic revolution, and more did not displace older loves in the realms of music, painting, theater, opera, and other arts. Third, I felt disappointed by the unrelenting attack on literary art at large on the part of many fellow academics who were pouring their energies into internecine cultural warfare.

I realized that Marcel Proust's narrator figure in *A la recherche du temps perdu* (In Search of Lost Time) made much greater sense to me when he meditated on the way successive generations of pundits, increasingly journalistic in their habits, exaggerated faddishness as innovation during the birth of modernism itself in order to be fashion leaders, while ignoring the deeper rhythms and logic of culture. Also clear to me was that I felt a kinship with Joyce in resisting any inhibition about bringing into my own spiritual and aesthetic life whatever the ages offered (as paltry as my own capacity for absorption might be). And I knew as a "felt reality" (to borrow John Barth's phrase) that my readerly existence would indeed grow bleak if the principle of "erotic irony," as Mann formulated it, did not keep alive what he perceived as the beneficent humanistic code that had emerged from long centuries of striving.

Preface to the First Edition

Attempts to reinstate the great metanarrative that Goethe had glimpsed in *Faust: Eine Tragödie* sometimes wore a comic as well as a grave face. Although I admired Rilke's use of Picasso's paintings in the opening pages of *Die Aufzeichnungen des Malte Laurids Brigge* (The Notebooks of Malte Laurids Brigge, 1910) and Gide's use of Nietzschean paradigms in *L'immoraliste* (The Immoralist, 1902) such appreciation did not inhibit me from putting my Erasmian-Rabelaisian glasses back on in a different hour to laugh with Proust and Joyce and Mann over the human comedy. The young twentieth century was manifestly and lavishly rich in talent, and as I came of age moving into its second half, it never occurred to me to confine myself to worshipping in only one of the sectarian chapels of such an endless cathedral. Though sometimes the world took on the qualities of an ambiguous labyrinth in the works of the great novelists, they also perceived larger patterns that suggested a cathedral-like realm.

Thus readers who engage with me in this "conversation"—about a number of works of fiction, the fine arts, and cinema produced mainly in the first half of the twentieth century, and some further moments from the second half—should expect neither a unifying theory nor a refusal to adopt prickly critical terminology, such as the generic label "postmodern," that has become entrenched more or less as standard dictionary items by the start of our new millennium. I feel no doctrinaire obligation when using common vocabulary created in part by persons of quite doctrinaire persuasions.

Because of its avowedly personal and eclectic approach, I want to say a few words about how various readers might take up this book. Many chapters, especially in part one, offer "pretexts" and "contexts" of modernism; others, especially in part two, move into "posttexts" of modernism. Some chapters concentrate on one or more of the title authors, whereas some treat Proust or Mann or Joyce alongside other modernists. The point of such diachronic and/or synchronic mixtures is to suggest, in abbreviation, that there are multiple legitimate ways to contextualize these authors' works. The purpose is not to posit a supreme triumvirate of modernism in splendid isolation. But that may not be congenial for the devoted Joyceans, or Proustians, or Mannians who are eager mainly to get to the matter concerning their favorite. Contextualization may be annoying too for avid students of modernism who are not very interested in seeing how certain phenomena connect with past moments in literature—not to speak of those readers who believe that modernism is a special realm in itself and who only want to cross-check their particular view against those details I select here from prime modernist works.

I hope that the following indications can serve as a kind of nonprescriptive road map for continuing the stroll in the labyrinth and making whatever deviations or loops may suit a particular reader. The general introduction ("A Stroll in the Labyrinth") and the selective synthesizing coda ("By Way of Conclusion") are not the only "bookends." The opening and closing chapters ("The Spaces of Truth and Cathedral Window Light" and "Structures of the Self and Narrative") form a large bracket around the the dozen chapters numbered from two to thirteen. These bracketing chapters, one and fourteen, have historical introductory sections—and the reader can choose not to start at their beginnings but instead from the modernist threshold in each case. Appropriate to chapter fourteen is that it carries us forward to various "posttexts" that seem natural consequences of the immediately preceding modernist moments.

Some readers may eventually want to circle back and note how chapter five ("Ironic Realism and the Foundational Romance") has a similar division, the "pretexts" and "contexts" of its first section being followed by the "posttexts" of its second. But, then, chapter eight, which is focused on Joyce, and chapter twelve, which is focused on the trio Proust, Joyce, and Mann, both introduce important pretexts. The book's division, between part one ("Modernist Moments and Spaces") and part two ("Metamorphosis, Play, and the Laws of Life"), does not effect an exclusive generic segregation of chapters. True, part one deals across the board with modernist forms and themes, while part two focuses mainly on Proust and/or Mann and/or Joyce. Yet parts one and two are "cross-contaminating" to a large extent insofar as chapters under either shift between narrower and broader focalization. For example, chapter two ("Epiphany") summons the three title authors to serve as chief examples, while chapter thirteen ("The Haunted Narrator") brings in several other writers, so that there is no neat partition that locates Proust, Mann, and Joyce in their own fenced suburb. The principal ground movement that, I hope, justifies the sequence of the closing chapters is the book's general drift, finally, toward "posttexts" of modernism.

I do not intend my suggestions of variant ways of reading within and across the actual chapters to resemble a mind-game, although that is a possibility that any reader could easily hit upon. Often enough, in actual works of art, pretexts obtrude everywhere as elements of a construed present, as heritage that an author (re-)adopts into the category of context, whether the author likes or dislikes what is cited or used. If we attempt to subtract all the pretexts from context, we can scarcely retain any sense of a complex work. With the passage of time, what is initially perceived as a posttext becomes yet another instance of renewal of context. A posttext too deals by necessity with preceding contexts, those configurations that literary history tries to wrestle into some order of temporal perspectivism. This book has avoided the exercise of compulsively stripping out pretexts in order to monumentalize a theoretical stance vis-à-vis Proust, Mann, and Joyce. Of course, admittedly, the act of following certain strands into and out of works by the title authors amounts to a critical stance in its own right. The point is that any reader is free to disregard these filaments if a stripped-down pursuit of motifs as used by a particular author is his or her priority.

All of the above being said, part one comprises preponderantly a set of studies of ways of seeing the world, formal habits, and themes in modernism at large, whereas part two comprises more heavily a set of studies dedicated to the principal writers named in the main title. Together these parts show them as woven into and reciprocally as coproducers of the "modernist context." Just as each of the chapters of part one could be expanded into distinct monographic subjects, so could each of the great writers of part two be the subject of a vast array of monographs. This book implements neither of those options, which are the usual choices of most critics and perfectly legitimate in themselves. Instead, the chapters here have a general drift that I trust is appropriate to the inner tendency of the major narratives on which the stature of Proust, Mann, and Joyce rests.

Their works evidence an epic impulse, a need to take account of the complexity of the world, at least in representative samplings. They record plenty of error, suffering, and anguish as intrinsic to the human experience. But in the final analysis their encyclopedic drive leads them to create a choral hymn to the beauty and mystery of existence in the condition of time. They attempt to reconstitute meaning on a scale that explicitly acknowledges an evolved standard for measuring values. In moving toward the "posttexts" which the closing "bracket" (chapter fourteen) brings, I trust that the reader will not have forgotten the new luminosity, the illumination craved by artists that the opening "bracket" (chapter one) introduces.

ACKNOWLEDGMENTS

I owe thanks to several learned societies, as well as several publications and their editors, for permission to use in whole or part papers of mine that have previously appeared in periodicals, congress proceedings, or collective volumes. I am grateful to the Brazilian Comparative Literature Association, the British Comparative Literature Association, the Greek Society for General and Comparative Literature, the International Comparative Literature Association, the Sahitya Akademi of India, and the South African Society for General Literary Studies; likewise to the journals *Comparative Criticism, Literator, New Comparison, Prism(s),* and *The Comparatist;* as well as to the editors of the following volumes: *Comparative Literary History as Discourse; Countercurrents: On the Primacy of Texts in Literary Criticism; Limites; Narrative Ironies; Nature: Literature and Its Otherness; Parodia, pastiche, mimetismo; Reflection and Action: Essays on the German Bildungsroman; Sensus Communis: Contemporary Trends in Comparative Literature;* and *Sinn und Symbol.*

I would like to thank the outside readers for the Catholic University of America Press whose learned advice was very instructive. While I have benefited greatly from their suggestions, naturally they bear no responsibility for my lapses. By their own enthusiasms, my students at Stanford University, the University of East Anglia, and the University of Munich have lent encouragement for the interests pursued in these pages. This book could not have reached press without the expert help of Katarina Kivel and Pat Welch in retyping and formatting its chapters.

PROUST
MANN
JOYCE

in the Modernist Context

A Stroll in the Labyrinth

Each of the three luminous names—Proust, Mann, Joyce—in the title of this book conjures a universe in itself. Exploring these universes with their own galaxies has delighted generations of readers and challenged the most resourceful of hermeneuts. After decades of commentary on their lives, works, and times, much of it "classic" in its own right, it is obvious that no comparative study can aspire to do more than to highlight some symptomatic affinities, while acknowledging crucial differences, among authors of such individual complexity.[1] The foolhardiness of attempting to situate these accomplished storytellers as modernists is even more apparent in the face of two facts of cultural history. First, for many purposes one could concentrate on other major writers instead, for example, on Gide, or Woolf, or Kafka, as anchors holding important fields of reference in place pertinent to the modernist context; indeed, this study will consider a number of other authors who helped create the larger context for modernism either as forerunners or as contemporaries. Second, from the late 1960s to the early 1990s, a host of critics and theoreticians have subjected "modernism" to a prolonged hostile interrogation. As has been typical of new critical currents in past contestatory episodes of Western literature (e.g., in romanticism), the critical camp of self-designated rejectors and deconstructors of "modernism" not only have sought to redefine and thus to control our reception of modernist values and traits, but have also extensively coopted important repertorial materials of modernist literature.[2] Many of the attackers have thought

1. Works published in the 1980s and 1990s by Garland, such as Michael Palencia-Roth, *Myth and the Modern Novel: García Márquez, Mann, and Joyce* (New York, 1987), William Carpenter, *Death and Marriage: Structural Metaphors for the Work of Art in Joyce and Mallarmé* (New York, 1988), and Hilary Clark, *The Fictional Encyclopedia: Joyce, Pound, and Sollers* (New York, 1990), have shown the way for a variety of comparative investigations with crosscultural scope and holistic perspective.

2. Joyce obviously provides the best materials for redefinition as postmodern; Mann seems unassimilable for such purposes. An example of efforts to coopt modernists by distorting their express opinions, and by reducing a complex vision into bizarre caricature,

Introduction

of themselves as participating in a "postmodern" transformation of consciousness and culture. What now further complicates my task is the evident collapse of "postmodernism" in the early 1990s, even though many of its effects linger and some certainly will leave a permanent trace.

This book will not attempt to prophesy by shaping an answer to the question, What will the ostensible passing of modernism and of postmodernism in turn portend? For a comprehensive historical coverage of the latter "tendency," "movement," or "period," readers can consult the collaborative volume *International Postmodernism* and Virgil Nemoianu's important fresh assessment of contemporary debates over the "postmodern" condition in *Postmodernism and Cultural Identities.*[3] The persisting issues concerning relationships and shifts between modernism and postmodernism are also revisited in the recent two-part collaborative volume *Modernism,* along with a host of other topics and perspectives.[4] I will take up briefly only the general proposition of whether it is necessary to accept the terms of the late twentieth-century attack on modernism or whether other terms have the advantage of greater adequacy. My approach by necessity will suggest a partial, indirect view of our contemporary scene, but commentary on postmodernism is not a chief matter here. I trust the several chapters of this book will make my admiration for the modern "epic" writers as unambiguous as possible. If the principal modern poets were my central subject, a comparable admiration would prevail, with a number of specific reservations too. My own sense of the achievement and lasting worth of Proust, Mann, and Joyce has not diminished but grown over the course of five decades of rereading them and has contributed to my enjoyment of many writers of recent decades down to the present. Much of the finest literature from World War II to the recent fin-de-siècle on several continents seems to me to fit comfortably alongside these earlier masters, and while I can appreciate efforts to

---

is Margaret E. Gray, *Postmodern Proust* (Philadelphia: University of Pennsylvania Press, 1992). Gray imposes a straitjacket of "undecidable ambiguities" on *A la recherche* to arrive at the implausible view that, at every level of narration, a supposed "'écriture féminine' dissolves imposed differences of genre and gender, dissolving the possibility of representation itself" (112).

3. *International Postmodernism: Theory and Literary Practice,* ed. Hans Bertens and Douwe Fokkema (Philadelphia: John Benjamins, 1997). Virgil Nemoianu, *Postmodernism and Cultural Identities: Conflicts and Coexistence* (Washington, D.C.: The Catholic University of America Press, 2010). Still helpful for contextualizing aspects and waves of twentieth-century literature is Matei Calinescu, *Five Faces of Modernity: Modernism, Avant-garde, Decadence, Kitsch, Postmodernism* (Bloomington: Indiana University Press, 1977).

4. *Modernism,* ed. Astradur Eysteinsson and Vivian Liska, 2 vols. (Philadelphia: John Benjamins, 2007).

segregate modern and postmodern traits as a formalistic exercise, I feel no urge at all to condemn more recent works that do not appear to participate wholeheartedly in some version of a postmodern aesthetic. As Michal Valdez Moses has argued in *The Novel and the Globalization of Culture*, there are powerful reasons in world literary development why the aggregate of superior imaginative writing worldwide, including much that often is labeled "postmodern," makes good sense as a continuum from the efforts of European and Euro-American modernism at large.[5]

At least since the Renaissance, paradigm shifts in European and Euro-American literature have exhibited broad similarities in the way they unfold. I believe this proposition applies quite distinctly in the case of postmodernism. No paradigm shift of the past five centuries has ever been so all-powerful as to sweep away virtually every vestige of form and content in a rival cultural worldview or the accrued collection of writing and reading habits within the complex, variegated, polycentric, and enormous cultural supersystem that, in retrospect, for convenience, we today call "Western." One of the familiar means employed in the creation of a critical framework to set apart a new generation or tendency has been to reverse or displace many key traits and values of the predecessor generation or rival tendency, while selectively coopting certain materials. If there is no collective label under which the attributes of the older or rival orientation are grouped, a pejorative marker usually is invented or evolves. Once a general label has emerged and is well established, it can function as a badge of prestige; and negative labels can readily be converted into positive ones. Often a style term—sometimes transposed from another art medium—serves to bundle aspects of form and worldview in a constellation of literary works.

Classic examples include the invention and use of the term "baroque" by Enlightenment critics to overturn a wide array of artistic practices and of supposed ideological defects of the seventeenth century. Although the pejorative sense has recurred a number of times right into the late twentieth century, eventually "baroque" has settled down, alongside "mannerist" and more localized terms (e.g., "metaphysical" in British literature) as a more neutral cover term for certain phenomena of the late Renaissance and has acquired a positive aura in connection with major artists like Bernini, Cervantes, Donne, and Bach. Another example is the undermining of the term "Enlightenment" by romantic critics ea-

5. Michael Valdez Moses, *The Novel and the Globalization of Culture* (Durham, N.C.: Duke University Press, 1995).

ger to counter the spiritual impoverishment that its excessive rationalism supposedly promoted and/or to coopt and supersede Enlightenment
claims of revolutionary leadership in the saga of human development—a
claim that the Enlightenment had earlier taken over as a conscious revival of Renaissance aspirations. In these instances, each contestatory new
wave did gradually acquire a name setting it apart. Postmodernism bears
a clear family resemblance in its zeal to displace or supersede modernism. However, the peculiar echo effect of the supersessional umbrella label, internalizing modernism while ostensibly passing beyond it ("post-
"), suggests that some further distinct term—and a separation of some
new aesthetic and ethos from two conjoint varieties of modernism—may
yet evolve.

A specific illustration: The journal *boundary 2* started some forty
years ago explicitly as an organ of postmodernism. A key article entitled "The Detective and the Boundary" in its inaugural issue (1972) by
its founding editor William V. Spanos serves to illustrate many attitudes
symptomatic of the rejection of modernism.[6] The contradictions inherent in this earlier act of rejection have reached hypertrophy in several
lines of critical theory of the past three decades. Spanos's opening definition, omitting the crucial figure Thomas Mann, covers the main ground
of this view:

> The literary revolution called Modernism that took place at the end of
> the nineteenth century in reaction against the European middle class
> ethos and reached its apogee in the works of such writers as Marcel
> Proust, Stéphane Mallarmé, W. B. Yeats, Ezra Pound, James Joyce,
> T. S. Eliot, and Virginia Woolf—and in the New Criticism—was, ideo-
> logically, a revolt against the Western humanistic tradition and, aes-
> thetically, against the "Aristotelian" tradition. (Spanos 147)

The opening paragraph further claims that as of World War II, with
the rise of existentialism "as mode of consciousness, the 'anti-Aristote-
lianism' of the modernist movement underwent a metamorphosis so
profound" that a "'postmodernism'" separated from earlier "Symbolist
modernism." Paragraph 2 goes on to stipulate that symbolist modernism
privileged "poetry" over "prose" in its search for

> a language that achieves an autonomous and something like autotelic
> status. On the level of mimesis, Symbolist anti-Aristotelianism consti-

6. William V. Spanos, "The Detective and the Boundary: Some Notes on Postmodern
Literary Imgination," *boundary 2* 1, no. 1 (1972): 147–68.

A Stroll in the Labyrinth

tuted a rejection of the primacy of linear and temporal plot in favor of the simultaneity of "spatial form." (Spanos 148)

I do not agree that the major modernists—even in their acts of challenging simplistic linear and teleological thinking—were engaged in a sustained rejection of Western humanism. Indeed, I believe quite the opposite; but here is not the place to enter into the counterargument, which the ensuing chapters make implicitly and explicitly. The crucial turn comes when Spanos argues that, in contrast, "in partial reaction against [this] refusal of historicity," the refusal of the postmodern imagination

> to fulfill causally oriented expectations, to create fictions (and in extreme cases, sentences) with beginnings, middles, and ends—has its source, not so much in an aesthetic as in an existential critique of the traditional Western view of man in the world, especially as it has been formulated by positivistic science and disseminated by the vested interests of the modern—technological—City. (Spanos 148)

Here for his own purposes Spanos combines two major insights of the early twentieth century that have been elaborated elsewhere without pejorative implication after World War II: the topic of spatialization, rekindled, for example, by Joseph Frank,[7] and the topic of an underpinning narrative structure in Western consciousness expounded notably by Frank Kermode and Northrop Frye.[8] In Spanos's version, however, we encounter the principal postmodernist charge against modernism: that in the aggregate it permitted an epochal failure or committed an inner metaphysical crime, whether because of negligent absorption in its own escapist vision or because of a simultaneously both necessary and perverse disguised will to power (a charge that Michel Foucault, among others, asserted against literature in general).[9] This failure postmodernist enthusiasts have variously castigated as a devious evasion of "history" or as a betrayal of Being. Neo-Marxian coopters of postmodernism favor emphasizing the first charge; crypto-essentialist existentialists favor the second; but, naturally, mixtures of accusatory style abound drawing

7. Joseph Frank, *The Widening Gyre: Crisis and Mastery in Modern Literature* (New Brunswick, N.J.: Rutgers University Press, 1965); see esp. ch. 1, "Spatial Form in Modern Literature," 3–62, first published in *Sewanee Review* 53, nos. 2–4 (1945).
8. Frank Kermode, *The Sense of an Ending: Studies in the Theory of Fiction* (New York: Oxford University Press, 1967). Northrop Frye, *The Great Code: The Bible and Literature* (New York: Harcourt Brace Jovanovich, 1982).
9. Michel Foucault, *Les mots et les choses: Une archéologie des sciences humaines* (Paris: Gallimard, 1966); *L'archéologie du savoir* (Paris: Gallimard, 1969).

on both charges. In "The Detective and the Boundary," Spanos appeals specifically to Heideggerian categories in order to tie the two aspects of failure together and to indict modernist art as complicit in the evasion of dread, uncertainty, discontinuity, and absurdity by the positivistic mind. Although in passing he concedes that, "as a whole, scientists and psychologists no longer are inclined to view existence in this rigidly positivistic and deterministic way, it is nevertheless this structure of consciousness" that supposedly permeates both the masses of "the modern technological City and of the political executors of its will" (Spanos 151). On the one hand, the Western habit of teleological thinking is suspect because it is grounded on religious metanarrative, although the Marxian version of a plot line to history escapes explicit condemnation. On the other hand, Western artists are rebuked for what Frank (without pejorative intent) has summed up as "the transformation of the historical imagination into myth."[10]

Several characteristics of this outlook merit more extended attention than is possible in this "introduction." Let me begin with an indispensable ingredient: it is helpful to note that Spanos's reliance on the model of a population base of the urban industrial age whose "will" is expressed through a political superstructure parallels the general framework of a number of influential theories that commingle Marxian and Freudian suppositions, such as Fredric Jameson's *The Political Unconsciousness: Narrative as Socially Symbolic Act*.[11] Henri Ellenberger has shown convincingly in *The Discovery of the Unconscious* that both the Marxian and the Freudian views of identity formation invoke a tripartite structure of psychological relationship whereby the "ego" is suspended in a field of tension between a natural (biological or material) foundation and a societal (imposed or inculcated) superstructure and that their paradigms bear striking resemblance to the model advanced by romantic psychology.[12] The formalistic analogies between the Marxian and Freudian sense of the constructed, fictional nature of identity—variations on the dominant nineteenth-century model rooted in romantic science of the early 1800s—are so pronounced that one would expect their eventual fusion, as indeed occurs in the Frankfurt School, most notably in the later work

---

10. Frank, *The Widening Gyre*, 60.
   11. Fredric Jameson, *The Political Unconsciousness: Narrative as Socially Symbolic Act* (London: Methuen, 1981).
   12. Henri F. Ellenberger, *The Discovery of the Unconscious: The History and Evolution of Dynamic Psychiatry* (New York: Basic Books, 1970).

of Herbert Marcuse.[13] Needless to say, the general propositions of "deconstruction" depend on the concept of the existence of a "constructed" consciousness. Beyond the linguistic turn ushered in by Lévi-Strauss, literary structuralism (in its own "poststructuralist" aftermath) provided aspirant deconstructors with the tools to build almost any supposed linguistic-societal model they wanted as an object to dismantle and expose in its pernicious operation.

In a retrospective statement in the volume *International Postmodernism*, Spanos has rejected the Jamesonian line, expressed in works such as *Postmodernism; or, The Cultural Logic of Late Capitalism*, and has revalorized existentialist consciousness of an epochal crisis as the genuine postmodern core.[14] However, upon the twentieth anniversary of *boundary 2* and its move to Duke University, the successor editor Paul Bové changed its lead epigraph to emphasize sociological interests, in keeping with the increasingly neo-Marxian direction in its contents. The offerings of *boundary 2* slowly converged to a noticeable extent with the virtually coeval journal *New Literary History*, although the latter has shown greater openness to a variety of newer directions in literary theory. It is important to remember that many participants in the older spectrum of postmodernism—among others, existentialists expecting some kind of transformational *kairos* or entrance into a cultural apocalypse, proclaimers of the "body," followers of DeManian and Derridean deconstruction, cultural relativists, and an assortment of antinomians—were not originally identified explicitly with neo-Marxian positions.

In my estimation, the self-refashioning of *boundary 2* reflects the broader and longer term drift that has meanwhile carried into neo-Marxian symbiosis many who aspire to participate in postmodernizing discourse. Darío Fernández-Morera has examined this phenomenon in the U.S. academy in some detail[15]—and I believe the U.S. situation can stand extensively for aspects of the European, although local resistances to cultual degradation often have been stronger outside the United States.

---

13. See, e.g., Herbert Marcuse, "Repressive Tolerance," in *A Critique of Pure Tolerance*, ed. Herbert Marcuse, Robert P. Wolff, and Barrington Moore Jr. (Boston: Beacon Press, 1965); and Theodor W. Adorno, "Freudian Theory and the Pattern of Fascist Propaganda," in *The Essential Frankfurt School Reader*, ed. Andrew Arato and Eike Gebhardt (New York: Urizen Books, 1978).

14. William V. Spanos, "Rethinking the Postmodernity of the Discourse of Postmodernism," in *International Postmodernism*, 65–74; Fredric Jameson, *Postmodernism; or, The Cultural Logic of Late Capitalism* (Durham, N.C.: Duke University Press, 1991).

15. Darío Fernández-Morera, *American Academia and the Survival of Marxist Ideas* (New York: Praeger, 1996).

Introduction

The movement from "literary studies" to "cultural studies" offers many analogies to this general drift. But there are also contrarian signs. New historicism has begun to manifest a cleavage between those who explicitly espouse neo-Marxian thought and others who wish to exploit new lines of analysis instrumentally, while retaining literature as their primary object and without endorsing the Marxian worldview. A fundamentally anti-European bias has dominated postcolonial studies ever since nativist experts in the variety of cultures succumbed to the neo-Marxian attraction, but a new significant block of non-Marxian scholars may well emerge once again in this area too, even though the old- and new-style Marxians entrenched in the academy currently hope to shut out any new voices. Deconstructionist denunciations of the hegemony of the European metaphysical tradition and of its latter-day offshoots in the natural and social sciences greatly facilitated approximation to neo-Marxian tenets on the part of a host of academic critics. Though it may be a sad spectacle, today it comes as no surprise that a streak of vulgar Marxism tainted the newer work of a once "strong" relativist philosopher like the late Richard Rorty,[16] or that an esteemed founding figure of deconstructionism like the late Jacques Derrida turned into an apologist for the uncovered fascist sentiments of the young Paul DeMan and began for a while to take on neo-Marxian coloration in his rhetoric.

It is not conducive to a careful evaluation of individual authors that a number of contemporary critics apply virtually formulaic general critiques to whole blocks of modernists. Among the blatant contradictions that arise is the spectacle of today's essentially neoformalist theoreticians accusing modernist writers of deviance and failure because of their formalistic experiments as artists in the earlier twentieth century. A striking illustration of this unhelpful practice is Hayden White's sweeping statement derivative from Jameson: "The abandonment of normal narrativity by modernist writers, therefore, was the expression on the level of form of the rejection of historical reality. And since fascism was based on a similar rejection of historical reality and a flight into purely formalistic political solutions for social contradictions, modernism could be seen as the expression in literature of fascism in politics."[17] But as Vir-

---

16. E.g.: Richard Rorty, *Contingency, Irony, and Solidarity* (Cambridge, U.K.: Cambridge University Press, 1989).

17. Hayden White, *Figural Realism: Studies in the Mimesis Effect* (Baltimore: Johns Hopkins University Press, 1999), 22. White's own extreme formalistic approach to both literature and history as an encounter with tropes and rhetorical devices goes far beyond the Aristotelian heuristic description of modes in Northrop Frye's *The Anatomy of Criticism: Four*

gil Nemoianu demonstrates in a searching essay, this sort of statement as made here by White simply cannot stand up to the evidence.[18] Hostility to formalism as politically suspect has been pervasive throughout the twentieth century in many systems and movements, including rightist ones. Nemoianu senses a coutervailing desire to escape from complexity and exercise minute control, and sees as a constant operating in our world "that hostility to the subtleties of formalist literary practice and critical analysis derives from this desperate yearning for simplicity."[19]

Much has been and will yet be written about the moral inadequacy and intellectual failure widespread in the loose collection of trends in "cultural studies" that extensively have elected to seek shelter under the umbrella idea of being "postmodern." But my purpose here is not to engage in the current debate in this regard. As I trust will emerge from relevant places in my book, I do not believe modernism represented any monolithic view of history. Bolshevism, fascism, and Nazism—the three most successful totalitarian revolutions in Europe—rose as specters overlapping the prime time of modernism. They tended to divert attention from the ongoing development of the Western liberal ethos, the crisis and death of which they stridently proclaimed. Some prominent modernist writers died early enough and did not have to face the worst, while some managed to push the oncoming nightmare out of their work and life; some were disturbed, baffled, confused in some degree as the modern world seemed to go crazy; some were momentarily, others permanently seduced by the promise of a radical cure or transformation of society; some sought to cope actively with the menace inherent in the totalitarian appeal itself. Besides positions taken by many concerned artists, there were plenty of explicit warnings raised by philosophers such as Julien Benda in 1927 and José Ortega y Gasset in 1930 regarding the spiritual and cultural roots of epochal disorder.[20] Ezra Pound's disgust over what he perceived as dangerous, degenerate developments in West-

---

Essays (Princeton, N.J.: Princeton University Press, 1957). The fact that White rationalizes his programmatic avoidance of any "final" engagement with values of profound concern to serious writers like Proust, Mann, and Joyce must eventually raise the hermeneutic suspicion that he himself, rather than the major modernist storytellers, may be nolens-volens confused with respect to twentieth-century fascism.

18. Virgil Nemoianu, "Hating and Loving Aesthetic Formalism: Some Reasons," *Modern Language Quarterly* 61 (2000): 41–57.

19. Nemoianu, "Hating and Loving Aesthetic Formalism," 54.

20. Julien Benda, *La trahison des clercs,* intro. André Lwoff and René Étiemble (Paris: Editions Grasset et Fasquelle, 1975); José Ortega y Gasset, *La rebelión de las masas,* intro. Thomas Mermall (Madrid: Editorial Castalia, 1998).

Introduction

ern culture was an important factor impelling him momentarily into a real betrayal of that culture; and such betrayals, whose motivation is often well documented, reach from before the youth of Paul DeMan down to the present day. It is an ongoing story, and understanding the multistranded plot line involves more than citing a few selected notorious examples. I have commented elsewhere on the fact that a great mainstream tradition of ethical realism flowed alongside modernism all the way.[21] Similarly, I have commented elsewhere on the importance of discriminating the range of cultural and philosophical views in twentieth-century literature that shadowed and interlaced with modernism—for example, cultural conservatism, fascism, communism, existentialism, vitalist, anarchic, nihilist and mystical strains, and apophatic writing.[22]

Even John Harrison's otherwise helpful study of English-speaking writers entitled *The Reactionaries* is, in my view, too indiscriminate in commingling quite different cases.[23] It is also defective because it omits even a rudimentary illustration of the fact that innumerable left-wing authors of the modernist period were temporarily or permanently drawn toward or into the totalitarian sphere—one thinks, for example, of important cases like that of G. B. Shaw, who was attracted to strongman figures out of a desire for forcing social changes through, but who finally drew back ashamed in the face of dictatorial brutality in his own times. In *Modernism in the Second World War*, Keith Alldritt offers a more nuanced analysis of several English-speaking poets and shows not only how their experience did sometimes constructively modify their view but also how proponents of quite diverse social philosophies, covering the gamut from conservative to communist, could share crucial modernist tenets and habits—proving to Alldritt that modernism actually overarched and transcended the serious ideological divide.[24] The most careful analysis of mixtures of, and contrasts between, moral confusion about and resistance to totalitarian appeals in the English-speaking world during

21. Gerald Gillespie, "The Ethical Burden of Realism in the Modern Novel: From *Uncle Tom's Cabin* to *I Am Charlotte Simmons*," in *Komparatistik als Humanwissenschaft: Festschrift zum 65. Geburtstag von Manfred Schmeling*, ed. Monika Schmitz-Emans et al. (Würzburg: Königshausen & Neumann, 2008), 343–51.

22. Gerald Gillespie, "Internal Liminalities, Transcultural Complexities: Expanding Frontiers for Comparative Literature," in *Old Margins and New Centers: The Legacy of European Literatures in a Globalized Age* (Bruxelles: Presses Interuniversitaires Européennes, forthcoming).

23. John R. Harrison, *The Reactionaries: Yeats, Lewis, Pound, Eliot, Lawrence. A Study of the Anti-Democratic Intelligentsia* (New York: Schocken Books, 1967).

24. Keith Alldritt, *Modernism in the Second World War: The Later Poetry of Ezra Pound, T. S. Eliot, Basil Bunting, and Hugh MacDiarmid* (New York: Peter Lang, 1989).

the first two-thirds of the twentieth century is Peter E. Firchow's *Strange Meetings: Anglo-German Literary Encounters from 1910 to 1960*.[25] As Firchow documents, even during the cold war period very few of the prominent British leftists ever achieved anything more than a grudging admission of having been self-blinding concerning the actual horrors perpetrated by Soviet totalitarianism and the menace it represented to the world, at least as serious as fascism and nazism. Comparably inglorious is the record of a considerable number of French intellectuals as late as the 1970s in their attitudes regarding the reality of the Maoist Cultural Revolution, as exemplified, for example, by members of the Tel Quel group.[26] Among novelists and essayists, works by Aldous Huxley, George Orwell, E. M. Forster, and other representatives of that special British strain of modern humanists in the first half of the twentieth century eloquently testify to a capacity in literary modernism to perceive and to resist totalitarian impulses. John Dos Passos and Ernest Hemingway could be cited among prominent North American authors who felt the urgency of engagement to protect a liberal heritage against antidemocratic powers.

The partial and sometimes then collective surrender of specific societies to totalitarian impulses is certainly not attributable to modernism per se even in a more endangered territory such as Germany in the aftermath of World War I. There the reading public could turn for guidance to the rapidly evolving, powerful insights of Thomas Mann and the already formed liberal-democratic views of his older brother, Heinrich. In crucial essays such as "Von deutscher Republik" (The German Republic, 1922), Thomas Mann set forth the compelling reasons why a defeated Germany should embrace the historic opportunity of joining the politically more advanced Western democracies, of becoming modern in a more general sense. His great warning novel *Der Zauberberg* (The Magic Mountain, 1924), set in the years approaching World War I, plumbed the sickness of his era that threatened another devastating explosion; and his novella *Mario und der Zauberer* (Mario and the Magician, 1930), set in fascist Italy, heralded the deadly German form of evil incarnate in Hitler. In the 1930s, the German novelist reached out to other prominent European artists and intellectuals such as André Gide and Sigmund Freud.

25. Peter Edgerly Firchow, *Strange Meetings: Anglo-German Literary Encounters from 1910 to 1960* (Washington, D.C.: The Catholic University of America Press, 2008).

26. See Eric Hayot, *Chinese Dreams: Pound, Brecht, Tel Quel* (Ann Arbor: University of Michigan Press, 2004); and my commentary in *Chinese Literature: Essays, Articles, Reviews* 27 (2005): 173–76.

Introduction

To fight the Nazis Mann summoned enormous energies in old age as a leader of the exile community. His *Joseph* tetralogy (1932–1942) mobilizes the deep anthropological foundation of European thought for the modern struggle as he perceived it going into World War II, while the novel *Doktor Faustus* (1945) probes the bitter necessity for the total defeat of what Germany had become as an outlaw nation because of the Nazis. Mann's personal political progression, blending his early cultural conservatism eventually with respect for the liberal tradition of the advanced democracies and a brand of democratic socialism, traced a pathway that the German nation tragically failed to pursue in the Hitler period. Unreconstructed Marxist writers like Bertold Brecht who after World War II tolerated actual police states like the (so-named) German Democratic Republic cut very poor figures by comparison.

Mann's vigorous shift into an active political role was intertwined with his development as a cultural analyst and essayist. The thorough integration of cultural analysis already characterizes his brilliant first novel *Buddenbrooks* (1901), and this capacity attains formidable proportions in *Der Zauberberg*, which appeared two years after publication of the completed version of Joyce's *Ulysses* and the death of Proust. For all their differences, Mann's major novels and Proust's series *A la recherche du temps perdu* (In Search of Lost Time, 1913–1927) perform certain strikingly analogous tasks insofar as they incorporate thorough examination of the cultural roots, operative impulses, and contemporary directions of their respective cultures and situate Germany and France in the larger European scene. Of course, the same holds for *Ulysses* with respect to Joyce's detailed commentary on the relationship of Ireland to Europe and the world. A wealth of passages and sections in Proust's first and second volumes, *Du côté de chez Swann* (Swann's Way, 1913) and *A l'ombre des jeunes filles en fleur* (Within a Budding Grove, 1919) are, in effect, skillfully fictionalized essays that carry us through the development of the arts and critical thought in the second half of the nineteenth and into the twentieth century. Proust re-creates the unfolding of modernism as a lived experience for a keen observer of the age such as he himself was. His lead narrator's commentary includes, among other things, notice of transformations wrought by new technologies such as electric lighting and cinema, the metamorphosis of social classes (viewing mainly the bourgeoisie and upper crust), and the shiftings of political sentiments and power. The final (posthumously published) volume *Le temps retrouvé* (Time Regained, 1927) offers a deep psychohistorical analysis of the horrendous conflict unleashed in World War I and explores the strangeness of the world altered by violence and death, yet its survival in metamorphosis. Proust's relatively early death spared him, like Rilke and Kafka, any direct witness of the totalitarian triumph of the early twentieth century, but we can surmise where he would have stood, since the narrator of *A la recherche* (in harmony with the author's personal views) forcefully sympathizes with the cause of Dreyfus and evidences a finely nuanced modern liberal humanism.

Joyce's programmatic decision to maintain the authenticity of his art by freeing it from subservience to partisan political messages goes back to his student days in Dublin when, notoriously, he refused to back chauvinist proclamations of national liberation. Yet his earlier works such as "The Dead" (1907) and *A Portrait of the Artist as a Young Man* (1916) evidence a passionate interest in the Irish liberator hero Parnell, while in *Ulysses* Stephen Dedalus thrills at the thought of Moses, a sublime liberator of his people and refounder of their culture. The theme of a struggle for genuine, creative freedom against political and religious imperialism runs throughout *Ulysses*. In contrast to Proust and Mann, Joyce's social vision focused quite readily on the life conditions and mentalities of the lower middle classes and the ordinary urban population. His cosmopolitan love for the richness of European culture and history at large never dulled his personal response to specific realities of his own times, nor tempered his profound iconoclasm. Perhaps no figure among the modernists seems closer to the spirit of Rabelais as a joyous advocate for human renewal. In addition, by temperament more than ideological conviction, Joyce was a socialist, but one clearly not favoring the use of force to compel supposedly better behavior. Joyce's disdain for the modern dictators is recorded, as is his distancing himself from their foolish supporters like Pound as World War II was brewing. As critics such as Dominic Manganiello and Trevor Williams have argued in detail, a more careful reading of Joyce's fictions yields a myriad of reflections on societal and political situations.[27] Even *Finnegans Wake* (1939) is enjoying fresh attention as a source of such contemporary references. I believe Mann merits first place in the specific category of antifascist fiction, although he is equalled or outstripped by the younger George Orwell. But Simon Carnell arrives at a plausible affirmative answer to the question posed by his

---

27. Dominic Manganiello, *Joyce's Politics* (Boston: Routledge & Kegan Paul, 1980); Trevor L. Williams, *Reading Joyce Politically* (Gainesville: University Press of Florida, 1997).

Introduction

article, *"Finnegans Wake:* 'The Most Formidable Anti-Fascist Book Produced between the Two Wars?'"[28]

In *Joyce, Race, and Empire,* Vincent John Cheng expatiates on the remarkable breadth of Joycean observations formed from the peculiar vantage point of an exile from a colonized nation.[29] More recent investigations of Kafka's fictions in the light of biographical materials—for example, John Zilcosky's study of *Kafka's Travels: Exoticism, Colonialism, and the Traffic of Writing*—indicate that the Prague writer too was keenly interested in what was happening to diverse peoples as a result of colonization and modern trade and travel.[30] The intricacies of Kafka's outsider-insider position are only one set of such cultural complications of great importance because of the way they bear on the remarkable innovations in narrative consciousness in modern fiction. Proust was part Jewish (through his mother, née Jeanne Weil), was acquainted with many Jews, and included a variety of Jewish characters in *A la recherche.* Uninhibited by any fear of appearing to be anti-Semitic, he could examine particular roles, foibles, and strengths of these characters both as individuals and social types. Mann married into a prominent Jewish family, enjoyed the friendship of many Jewish artists and intellectuals throughout his life, and treated Jewish figures in a number of his works, daring like Proust to touch on controversial aspects of Jewish identity in the German context. With the *Joseph* tetralogy, deliberately countering the Nazis' perverse myth making, Mann thematized the foundational role of the Jews in the evolution of religious consciousness. Through an openly declared spiritual affinity with the Jews, Joyce developed an analogous capacity to explore a Jewish side to European identity and to appreciate minority cultures in relation to majority or dominant strains. What is impressive in Proust, Mann, Joyce, and a number of other fine modernist storytellers are their keen eye for particular human phenomena, genuine concern for humane values, and large-minded historical vision.

This would amount to a contradiction by definition, if we were to accept the postmodernist dictum that modernism "evaded" history and existential contingency. A more careful consideration of the evidence, how-

---

28. Simon Carnell, *"Finnegans Wake:* The Most Formidable Anti-Fascist Book Produced between the Two Wars," *"Finnegans Wake": "teems of times": European Joyce Studies* 4 (1994): 139–63.

29. Vincent John Cheng, *Joyce, Race, and Empire* (Cambridge, U.K.: Cambridge University Press, 1995).

30. John Zilcosky, *Kafka's Travels: Exoticism, Colonialism, and the Traffic of Writing* (New York: Palgrave/St. Martin's Press, 2002).

ever, will bear out that, far from affirming a positivistic sense of history, the great modernist novelists were engaged in a profound examination of the question and problem of time, a challenge they knew could not be evaded. After his youthful start as a cultural conservative, Mann became an inspirational activist in history in his own time. As an international figure, he thus posed a natural challenge to the aspirations of many on the Left. Many maligners refused to believe in his conversion to democracy because his allegiance was to a Western brand rooted in the history of such imperial nations as Great Britain, France, and the Netherlands. As noted, Proust fared better at the hands of critics by dying soon after World War I and Joyce by coming from a small, neutral nation and appearing for a long while to be unclassifiable. Yet Proust, Mann, and Joyce shared a fascination for testing the nature of time and of human experience in the condition of time. All three demonstrated a remarkable ability to frame the metaphysical challenge that being in time posed. Thus they had an effect on the public mind that was as lasting, if not more lasting, than the theorizing by contemporary philosophers and psychologists whom they digested or to whom they bore spiritual affinities; in many instances, they and the "official" savants were drawing on common earlier sources. It is no exaggeration to say the discoveries about time, which Proust, Mann, and Joyce were able to formulate and convey as felt realities, became the basis for the altered time sense of the twentieth century.[31]

In addition, no generation of artists since the romantics contributed so decisively to the psychological deepening of anthropology and to the formation of a new psychohistorical sensibility. With good reason, Mann took pride in having been at least a coexplorer of the human psyche, if not well in advance of leading professional analysts like Freud. Joyce from early on acted as a conscious iconoclastic venturer into the amazing virtual infinity of the psyche and, with as good reason as Mann, he never felt himself to be less than a pioneer. The names of Freud and Jung may not appear explicitly in Proust's huge novel, but Schopenhauer,

---

31. Especially valuable for its critical diachronic command of modernism in a larger historical framework, as well as for its overview of questions about time explained in major modernist authors, is Ricardo J. Quinones, *Mapping Literary Modernism: Time and Development* (Princeton, N.J.: Princeton University Press, 1985). Ulrich Karthaus, "Der Zauberberg—ein Zeitroman (Zeit, Geschichte, Mythos)," *Deutsche Vierteljahrsschrift für Literaturwissenschaft und Geistesgeschichte* 44 (1970): 269–305, helped set a positive direction regarding "time" in Mannian studies. Julia Kristeva, *Time and Sense: Proust and the Experience of Literature*, trans. Ross Guberman (New York: Columbia University Press, 1996), is a superior synthesis, amplifying her *Proust and the Sense of Time*, trans. Stephen Bann (London: Faber & Faber, 1993).

Nietzsche, and Bergson figure as direct references. Certain fictional lead characters within the works of Joyce, Mann, and Proust—notably Stephen Dedalus, Hans Castorp, and Marcel—as well as the highest narrative voice framing them, wrestle with the nature of time and of the psyche "as"—that is, on behalf of—the experiencing human subject. In capacious retrospect from the threshold of our new millenium, this interrogation of time is a colossal achievement—a standard that challenges, awes, intimidates, but also inspires those in its shadow.

If we gather Mann, Proust, and Joyce into an aggregate and consider how powerful is their historical knowledge, what diachronic depth and synchronic density it exhibits, and how dogged is their refusal to take standard answers in searching the human record for clues and patterns, we can scarcely conclude that these literary artists are less subtle and informed than their critics. In a book concentrating on English-language authors, Michael Tratner has argued more reasonably that the great modernists, whether nominally left-wing or right-wing in political terms, saw themselves as artists who were "subversive" of a self-exhausted nineteenth-century order, and that they succeeded in creating on a deeper level a real engagement with the rise of the masses and a challenge by collectivist impulses.[32] Hence it amounts to blaming the messenger when partisan critics attribute to this "team" some large share of guilt or responsibility for considering negative thematics abroad in their age, such as the possibility of a collapse of European order, or of virtually apocalyptic alteration. It is equally perverse to level this charge in reverse, by claiming that modernist authors of their caliber were wrongfully seeking to reconstitute a collapsed world order, to rescue a sick civilization that should be permitted or forced to die and give way.

Joyce directly confronted the problem of cultural decadence and subordination in the case of his own people and sought to demonstrate the act of creative defiance, when the mind throws off the crushing burden of history and failed imperial authority. Proust and Mann looked unflinchingly at the terrifying phenomena of World War I, and Mann again faced the horror of the reinstated apocalypse of World War II. The multifaceted question of European decadence, which so many thinkers such as Nietzsche and Spengler posited in the late nineteenth and early twentieth century, was one that the great modernists could not ignore and, in fact, integrated into their respective visions of life. To fault them for do-

32. Michael Tratner, *Modernism and Mass Politics: Joyce, Woolf, Eliot, Yeats* (Stanford, Calif.: Stanford University Press, 1995).

ing so amounts to blatant disregard for their achievement in raising such issues to consciousness in art. As John B. Foster has shown, all major modernist novelists were post-Nietzschean in some significant degree and considered his among other critiques of cultural "lateness"[33]—but the evidence is abundant that they exercized their right to affirm values that they regarded as transcending even the form of the world they thought was passing.

Some critics may qualify as delusional the joy of great storytellers in attributing meaning to the human experience; but there is no scope to deny the powerful presence of such affirmation in their total oeuvre. Proust, Joyce, and Mann were constitutionally unable to join the treacherous clerks of whom Julien Benda has spoken. Extraordinary in their collective achievement is the extent to which they succeeded in restoring ludic suppleness in the search for answers. Their powers of synthesis were unparalleled since the great romantic and nineteenth-century "unsystematic" philosophers, and as a consequence they figure among the most important "universalizing" novelists since the high and late Renaissance (e.g., Rabelais, Cervantes).

Malcom Bradbury's excellent book, *The Modern World: Ten Great Writers* (written in conjunction with a BBC television series with the same title), profiles mainly novelists and dramatists.[34] Of the ten featured writers (Dostoevsky, Ibsen, Conrad, Mann, Proust, Joyce, Eliot, Pirandello, Woolf, Kafka), only one is principally a poet, although Bradbury's "Introduction" considers a wider array including key poets like Pound and the rise of postimpressionist art, among other symptomatic phenomena. Moreover, Bradbury hedges with the phrase "modern world" and feels no compunction about reaching back into the second half of the nineteenth century for significant impulses. I sympathize with this broader approach, which I relate to a less doctrinaire and "Proustian" sense of literary history. I am mindful that I could have gathered clusters of important poets to make the transition from symbolism to modernism— Mallarmé, Rimbaud, George, Yeats, Pound, Eliot, Rilke, Trakl, Guillén, Valéry, Saint-John Perse, Benn, Pessoa, Ungaretti, Stevens, and more would have been very congenial for such purposes, and to me personally as a reader. The choice of several great novelists over dramatists or poets is an economy that testifies more to the extraordinary richness of the

33. John Burt Foster, *Heirs to Dionysus: A Nietzschean Current in Literary Modernism* (Princeton, N.J.: Princeton University Press, 1981).
34. Malcolm Bradbury, *The Modern World: Ten Great Writers* (New York: Penguin Books, 1988).

period than to a disregard of other claims. And in the case of the novel, a less parsimonious selection could have included many more authors from Flaubert to Svevo and beyond than are considered here.

There is some justification in seeing the figures central in this book, Proust, Mann, and even Joyce, not as radical asserters of modernism throughout their writings, but rather as transitional to "hard-core" modernism, at least in certain moments of their art. This may be the natural result, however, of the scope of their larger fictions. If our habit is to focus on smaller works of the early twentieth century that exhibit fragmentariness, indeterminacy, rupture, and so forth, we will tend not to see the appearance of such features within the encompassing complexity of the works of Proust, Mann, and Joyce—sometimes on a far bigger scale of execution than is possible in works that have abandoned any concomitant aspiration to be encyclopedic. Proust, Mann, and Joyce may offer us vital insights into the breakup of an older world picture and its representational norms, but they do so without losing track of the powerful structuring realities that inform contemporary life and refuse to disappear for the convenience of new theorizing. The strongest efforts to separate them from the "true" exponents of modernism most frequently have been made by critics who privilege concepts of epochal rupture and indeterminacy as a more valid response to a shattered world picture—a break they perceive surfacing principally in poetry and painting.[35] The noted comparatist Anna Balakian reembraced this general thesis in a searching chapter entitled "Problems of Modernism" in one of her last books, *Snowflake* (1994).[36] She attributed to outmoded "habit and respect" calling "Joyce, Yeats, Thomas Mann, Proust, and others of their generation" modern. She hoped literary historians would eventually invent a due classification to replace the "provisional" label and separate them from the artists representing a decentered, decontrolled universe and experimenting with techniques such as montage, collage, abrogation of time through discontinuity, and more.

Radical models of wide import did appear in literature of the early nineteenth century, for example, as already mentioned, Goethe's epical or cosmic drama *Faust* 1 and 2. As several chapters in this book will illustrate, it is obvious why various proponents of the primacy of one po-

35. Marjorie Perloff, *The Poetics of Indeterminacy: Rimbaud to Cage* (Princeton, N.J.: Princeton University Press, 1981).

36. Anna Balakian, *The Snowflake on the Belfry: Dogma and Disquietude in the Critical Arena* (Bloomington and Indianapolis: Indiana University Press, 1994).

larity in modernist literary art—where techniques such as random or abstract assemblage, a sense of indeterminacy, and so forth are domi-nant—would seize on Joyce's *Wake* and aspects of *Ulysses* and attempt to segregate these works in a special class. But in so doing, as I hope to show, critics must disregard analogies in a number of other novels of high modernism that merit more considered attention. It is true that in comparison to the innovations in romantic fiction soon after Sterne, there was no sudden rupture in the major narrative modes of the later nineteenth century. The city, as the new focal site of modernist attention, and a source of images and ideas for experimentation, indeed appears in poetry from Baudelaire onward with a distinct intensity and acquires dazzling attributes in Rimbaud. The naturalism of Zola promotes a com-bination of pathological analysis and dystopic vision. But in general it is the social drama of the modern city at various levels that becomes more central in the work of a host of major novelists beyond Balzac and Dick-ens, such as Galdós, James, Fontane, Wharton, and Döblin, who repre-sent urban modernity more broadly.

The concept of an epochal crisis in the second half of the nineteenth century often is couched in the terms of realist fiction—for example, through the depiction of historical disjunction as in Flaubert's *L'éducation sentimentale* (Sentimental Education, 1869) or in terms of pseudorealist pathologies as in Mann's *Buddenbrooks* (1901). Earlier prevalent assump-tions about art being an "imitation" of nature or mimesis were gradu-ally displaced because of a number of forces. Besides the already men-tioned displacement of nature or the land by the city, psychological discoveries altered the way of treating experiencers who appear in fic-tions; simultaneously, the liberation of myth from any controlling reli-gious dogma, underway since the Renaissance, became pervasive and provided a field of reference in its own right. Anthropology and histori-cism rose together, but romanticism had meanwhile suggested radical new ways of regarding myth and history as interrelated. Thus, while an-thropology and history initially buttressed a "scientific" analytical view of the human race, by the fin-de-siècle neoromantic currents challenged positivistic doctrine. The novelists Proust, Mann, and Joyce arrived on the scene at a propitious juncture to be the beneficiaries of a liberation from secular realist doctrines about myth, and to enjoy this dispensa-tion without the need either to participate in neoromantic defiance of realism or to renounce the anthropological insights into myth making accumulated since the Renaissance. Thus into the bargain they regained the capacity to be open again to the sacred as an ineluctable discovery.

These same novelists absorbed the presence and effects of the newer technologies and media of modernism—they witnessed the inroads of electric lights, the telephone, the radio, the underground, and the airplane, as these were added to railroads, photography, the steamboat, the telegraph, and transoceanic cable lines, the host of new technologies that accelerated the alteration of the conditions of life in the nineteenth century.[37] While sometimes the rapidly developing urban world is narrated in forms that seem traditional, the disturbing, energizing effect often is felt as in Mann's tour-de-force portrayal of the nineteenth century from Goethe to Bismarck in *Buddenbrooks*. Even cinema initially adapted its main narrative procedures from nineteenth-century literature, but it did so during a time of the breaking up of the hard surfaces of reality, when the impressionists had begun reconceiving the nature of painting and psychological impressionism was flourishing in fiction. The union of deeper impulses of narrative and film in the first three decades of the twentieth century is part of the bigger history of modernist fiction, and Mann, Joyce, and Woolf were among those keenly aware of the new medium.[38] Older narrative materials and forms—for example, the ongoing world-girdling story of colonization, the bildungsroman as a means to profile individual participation in the world, and so forth—naturally live on as storytelling means, even though they may actually be revolutionized in structural terms, as, for example, in the early case of Mann's novella about "education" *Tonio Kröger*. Older frameworks for understanding forces and dynamics in world development—for example, the habit of cultural mapping inherited from the Renaissance—are prolonged by modernism through their reapplication. The search for the special purposes of art—its capacity to open our eyes and minds—appears in new configurations of epiphany, privileged moments characteristic of modernist prose. Today we take for granted the expectation of arrival at privi-

37. In *The Proustian Quest* (New York: New York University Press, 1992), William C. Carter demonstrates in impressive detail two powerful impulses intertwined in Proust's work: his genuine fascination for modern technology and media, and his moral insights into human error, suffering, and loss and the concomitant need for spiritual striving. Carter shows how these constitute a nexus in Marcel's relationship to Albertine.

38. Roger Shattuck, *Proust's Binoculars: A Study of Memory, Time, and Recognition in "À la recherche du temps perdu"* (Princeton, N.J.: Princeton University Press, 1962; paperback, 1983), is instructive in showing the artistic unity born of Proust's multidimensional "optics," spatializtion of time experience, and technique of building toward "privileged moments." Shattuck (49–83) distinguishes three principles of vision—the "cinematographic," the "montage," and the "stereoscopic"—out of whose interplay the eventual possibility of "simultaneity" and the powerful coda of *Le temps retrouvé* emerge.

leged moments in a "Proustian" universe or a "Mannian" or a "Joycean" one; but going through such processes in fiction was an important new aesthetic experience in the young twentieth century.

This book looks at selective instances of what modernism questioned, challenged, rethought, reexplored—for example, personal versus collective identity, the laws of history and time, the nature of cultural evolution, the processes of reproduction of cultural forms that brought about new "periods" of European life, and new growth of cultures as in the New World. Modernism—in picking up the task from romanticism— broached the question of alienation as a pervasive spiritual malaise of our new era. But modernism also reaffirmed values in spite of the seeming threat of relativity and absurdity.[39] Among the great modernist novels that therefore most interest me here are those that juxtapose a foundational picture of the human estate with the most terrifying existential encounters—with the grim horror of mass violence in World War I (coda to *Der Zauberberg*, final volume of *A la recherche*), with the bloody core of a mindless nature, with the numbing possibility that God is dead. But these same works reveal miracles that defy ordinary understanding—life and love being a prime miracle to Joyce, the beauty of moral and artistic achievement being such for Proust, and the story of the human spirit a miracle in progress for Mann. For all their remarkable distinctness of mind as literary creators, Proust, Mann, and Joyce returned again and again to a sacramental sense of things. That is their broader foundation.

These chief authors wrote works of encyclopedic girth because they were cosmic builders, with an inner eye yearning finally to behold the artifice of eternity. My endeavor is to approach without unseemly abruptness the new visionary capacity in modernism they helped to establish. I hope that my "prelude" in the opening chapter will also serve to suggest what I cannot follow in more detail, without neglecting my main subject matter: the natural processes of sharing across genres and media. In the same spirit, the aim of my "coda" is to withdraw from the "postmodern" scene by suggesting, again, that certain predispositions eventually become generalized throughout the arts and that as heirs we share in onmoving cultural streams in multiple ways. I trust that this too comes into view in a "Proustian" optic.

39. Patrick Brunel, *Le rire de Proust* (Paris: Honoré Champion, 1997), examines the many aspects of playfulness, self-deprecation by the narrator, comic mimesis, and comic fantasy in *A la recherche,* and makes a powerful case that Proust's "laughter" serves as a defense against the danger of disdain for humanity—a view that brings Proust closer to the humoristic Joyce (not mentioned).

PART ONE

MODERNIST
MOMENTS
AND
SPACES

I   THE SPACES OF TRUTH AND
CATHEDRAL WINDOW LIGHT

---

1. *The Romantic Prelude*

The metaphor of being "at the window" serves as the final chapter title of Roger Cardinal's *Figures of Reality* (1981) to characterize the core of European poetic consciousness during the larger period that stretches roughly from romanticism through the twentieth century.[1] Appreciation of the modernist experience or sense of being in the presence of such light is indeed enhanced if we examine its romantic roots.

Among its many themes, the opening monologue of the scene "Night" in *Faust* I (1808) reminds us of the drive of Renaissance aspirations to break through the encumbrance of a decaying medieval tradition. Goethe has Faust, the discontented savant, think of his gothic study with its books and research apparatus as a prison that separates him from vital nature (lines 398ff.): "Woe, am I stuck in this dungeon still? / Cursed dank hole in the wall; / where even heaven's gentle light passes / murkily through stained glass."[2] These lines, originally composed around the mid-1770s and preserving the storm-and-stress flavor of the *Urfaust,* bring together two images that were an abundant source of metaphor throughout the romantic era.

One image, the figurative "dungeon," invokes the medieval castle or church as the container of dark forces, motives, or secrets, as the focus of a curse, an association popularized by eighteenth-century gothicism. Romantic authors were attracted to the ambivalence inherent in the church and the castle as repositories of a special illumination, as we see, for example, in Byron's "Elegy on Newstead Abbey" (1807).[3] Having explored

---

1. Roger Cardinal, *Figures of Reality* (Totowa, N.J.: Barnes & Noble, 1981).

2. Johann Wolfgang von Goethe, *Die Faustdichtungen: Urfaust, Faust, ein Fragment, Faust, eine Tragödie,* ed. Ernst Beutler (Zürich: Artemis-Verlag, 1950).—"Weh! steck ich in dem Kerker noch? / Verfluchtes dumpfes Mauerloch, / Wo selbst das liebe Himmelslicht / Trüb durch gemalte Scheiben bricht!"

3. Lord George Gordon Byron, *The Poems and Dramas of Lord Byron* (New York: Arundel, n.d.).

both negative and positive memory entombed in this "dark pile" (line 17), Byron ends by jibing at modern pomp and at the shallow fad of creating artificial ruins and "romantic" landscapes (an outgrowth of the very fascination exhibited in his own poem), yet strikes a final pose of secret atunement with the ruins as a fatal man. Readers of the age widely understood Goethe's wayward experiencer, who yearns for the moonlight outside, yet abandons his beloved in an actual dungeon, as someone of this type.

The other image, the window, is a favorite romantic symbol of the transactional membrane between self and world. The window marks the existence of otherness and a beyond to which the self is attracted. In John Keats's poem "The Eve of St. Agnes" (1820), the ballad-style narrative moves from the wintry church—where the "sweet Virgin's picture" and "Music's golden tongue" posit hope for "the scultptur'd dead [. . .], Emprisoned in black, purgatorial rails" (strophes 1–3)—into Madeline's bedchamber as into a most precious chapel within the medieval castle. There Porphyro, at first concealed, witnesses her prayer as she is bathed in the magic light transmitted through the stained glass window that unites the organic and the supernatural realms (strophes 24 and 25).[4] This illumination of the beloved as an embodied paradise not only sanctifies the ensuing bridal night, but empowers the couple to escape from the castle as from a potential hell, fleeing forever into the "elfin-storm from faery land" (strophe 39). Natural and poetic truth have redemptively penetrated the depths of gothic night through the window.

The elder Goethe expatiated on the idea of the work of art as a simultaneous mediation and reception of divine light in an untitled poem of the year 1826, which I render here in prose: "Poems are stained glass windows! / If one looks into the church from the marketplace, everything there is dark and gloomy; / and this is just how it looks to Mr. Philistine. / He may well be irritated and remain irritated his life long. / But do just once come inside! / Greet the holy chapel, / and everything suddenly is colorfully bright, / history and adornment radiate in a trice, a noble illumination has its significant effect. / This will be of value to you children of God. / Be edified and rejoice your eyes."[5]

4. John Keats and Percey Bysshe Shelley, *Complete Poetical Works* (New York: Random House, n.d.).

5. "Gedichte sind gemalte Fensterscheiben! / Sieht man vom Markt in die Kirche hinein, / Da ist alles dunkel und düster; / Und so sieht's auch der Herr Philister. / Der mag denn wohl verdrießlich sein / Und lebenslang verdrießlich bleiben. // Kommt aber nur einmal herein! / Begrüßt die heilige Kapelle; / Da ist's auf einmal farbig helle, /

The Spaces of Truth and Cathedral Window Light

The term "stained glass windows" that states the primary thing that poems are has the transparency about which the poet is speaking. The poem interposes itself as both means and end; the light of the work of art, its aesthetic illusion (Schein), constitutes a realm in itself. While it would be rewarding to dwell here on Goethe's concept of the symbol, more pertinent to my argument is the complex spatialization of the experience. Not only are we invited into a larger structure ("church"); once inside, we discover an enclosed smaller structure ("chapel"). This makes explicit our initial awareness that the church is a dedicated space—in effect, a chapel in the metaphoric temple of the world.

Within the chapel, as within the church, religious images are resplendent in their supratemporal sense and tell of a past that reaches into the present. The structure (church, chapel) contains artifacts that in their turn embody meanings. Edification flows out of the delight to which we open our eyes, once our eyes function in sympathetic attunement to the holy light of the cosmos by being transmitters of the light of art. The eyes as instruments of the mind become, once again, the traditional windows in the emblematic temple of our own being. That lingering sense descends from older meditative poetry—a familiar example in the English tradition is George Herbert's poem, "The Windows" (published in *The Temple*, 1633).[6]

Novalis dramatically internalized this space of discovery or revelation in *Heinrich von Ofterdingen*.[7] Left as a fragment in 1800, this novel is ostensibly set in the Middle Ages before humanity's secondary fall in history, a fall marked by the Reformation and the Enlightenment, which supposedly dimmed the power of faith and poetry. In chapter 5, the quester knight, Heinrich, learns the ethos of mining by which Novalis transcribes the noble task of high romanticism. Heinrich personally descends by labyrinthine ways into the underground where his dreamlike movement in a mysterious cathedral-like immensity[8] is both an exploration and a synthesis. He encounters secrets touching the world and the self: a multiplicity of geological, evolutionary, historical, and psychologi-

---

Geschicht' und Zierat glänzt in Schnelle, / Bedeutend wirkt ein edler Schein. / Dies wird euch Kindern Gottes taugen, / Erbaut euch und ergetzt die Augen."

6. The poet opens with a striking emblem: "Lord, how can man preach Thy eternal word? / He is a brittle crazie glasse; / Yet in Thy temple Thou dost him afford / This glorious and transcendent place, / To be a window through Thy grace" (George Herbert, *The Poems of George Herbert*, ed. Arthur Waugh [London: Oxford University Press, 1952]).

7. Novalis (Friedrich von Hardenberg), *Hymen an die Nachts; Heinrich von Ofterdingen* (Munich: Wilhelm Goldmann Verlag, n.d.).

8. "erhabenen Münster" (Novalis, *Hymnen* [. . .] *Ofterdingen*, 92).

cal factors and potentialities. Just before Heinrich meets the hermit in the cave, Novalis repeats the equation between the interior realm of the psyche and the natural magic of the nocturnal realm, that night which so haunts Faust in part I of Goethe's play. Novalis fervently believes in the rightness of the inner illumination. A unifying synaesthesia supports not only the analogies between the night and organic psychic spaces, but also the perception of the developmental process as if it is both underway and completed. The entry into the space of the experiencing self—here through a tapestry door—is also the discovery of a complex structure for which Novalis's image too is a cathedral. In short, Novalis conjoins the thematics of anamnesis and of the self. They become the medium and the space of recollection in a manner that anticipates the Proustian method.

Ottilie's solitary church visit depicted in part 2, chapters 2 and 3, of Goethe's *Die Wahlverwandtschaften* (Elective Affinities, 1809)[9] is another example of the imagery of dedicated space that conveys simultaneously a character's personal inner illumination and the suprapersonal truth of art. Ottilie is already virtually enshrined in the restored side-chapel and looking down as if from heaven because the young artist has intuitively painted variations of her face in his murals (JA 21.159); she is an authentic Germanic type, recurring "after a disappeared golden age, after a paradise lost" (JA 21.154)[10] toward which the medievalizing present aspires. Overwhelmed by the restored, reconsecrated space, which is both strange and familiar to her, Ottilie soon connects her own rediscovery of this sacred environment on the eve of Eduard's birthday with the realization of the necessity of loss. She inwardly accepts death, turning like the sunflower depicted in the chapel toward heaven (JA 21.162). Goethe's description emphasizes her stepping through the chapel door into an unexpected radiance that is the objective correlative of her personal epiphany. It is a space bathed by the light of a stained glass window:

> A solemn many-colored light fell through the gracefully composed panes of the single, high stained-glass window. The whole space acquired an unfamiliar quality and induced a peculiar mood. The beauty of the vaulting and the walls was heightened by the decorative de-

9. Johann Wolfgang von Goethe, *Die Wahlverwandschaften*, ed. Franz Muncker, Jubliäumsausgabe 21 (Stuttgart and Berlin: Cotta, 1809). Hereafter cited as JA, 21 with page number.

10. "nach einem verschwundenen goldenen Zeitalter, nach einem verlorenen Paradiese" (JA, 21.154).

sign of the floor, paved with specially shaped bricks which were joined by mortar to form a beautiful pattern. The Architect had had these bricks as well as the stained glass prepared in secret and was able to assemble everything in a short time.[11]

Afterwards, in analogy to her own alienation upon crossing into another realm, she records in her journal her thoughts about the strange destiny of the modern artist who must be exiled from his own gifts to mankind, his own constructs or acts of mediation:

> His works abandon him [. . .]. How often he devotes his whole mind and inclination to bring forth spaces from which he by necessity is excluded. [. . .] In places of worship he draws a line between himself and the holy of holies; he is no longer allowed to ascend the steps whose foundation he has laid for the heart-lifting celebration, just as the goldsmith reveres only from a distance the monstrance whose enamel and precious stones he has duly set together.[12]

Ottilie's mind is filled with the imagery of death and rebirth; she yearns for the emergence of "the inner light"[13] and, though still on earth, in her spirit actually already waits in heaven to greet her friends (JA 21.163f.).

The negative interpretation of this symbolic interior realm in high romanticism, in direct contradiction to Novalis, already appears at the opening of vigil 4 in the anonymous *Nachtwachen von Bonaventura* (Night Watches of Bonaventura, 1804).[14] There the church, borrowed whole from horrific gothicism, is enshrouded in the paralyzing enchantment of night; its windows are occluded, inoperative, ignored. When the

---

11. "Durch das einzige hohe Fenster fiel ein ernstes buntes Licht herein: denn es war von farbigen Gläsern anmutig zusammengesetzt. Das Ganze erhielt dadurch einen fremden Ton und bereitete zu einer eigenen Stimmung. Die Schönheit des Gewölbes und der Wände ward duch die Zierde des Fußbodens erhöht, der aus besonders geformten, nach einem schönen Muster gelegten, durch eine gegossene Gipsfläche verbundenen Ziegelsteinen bestand. Diese sowohl als die farbigen Scheiben hatte der Architekt heimlich bereiten lassen, und konnte nun in kurzer Zeit alles zusammenfügen" (JA, 21.161).

12. "[. . .] Seine Werke verlassen ihn [. . .]. Wie oft wendet er seinen ganzen Geist, seine ganze Neigung auf, um Räume hervorzubringen, von denen er sich selbst ausschließen muß. [. . .] In den Tempeln zieht er eine Grenze zwischen sich und dem Allerheiligsten; er darf die Stufen nich mehr betreten, die er zur herzerhebenden Feierlichkeit gründete, so wie der Goldschmied die Monstranz nur von fern anbetet, deren Schmelz und Edelsteine er zusammengeordnet hat [. . .]" (JA, 21.162f.).

13. "das innere Licht" (JA, 21.163).

14. Anonymous (August Klingemann), *Die Nachtwachen des Bonaventura: The Night-Watches of Bonaventura*, ed. and trans. Gerald Gillespie (Edinburgh, U.K.: Edinburgh University Press, 1972; bilingual).

strange narrator Kreuzgang takes up his perch "in the old Gothic cathe-dral,"[15] in order to witness such matters as the Oedipal ragings of Don Juan, he situates himself in the church as if within the subjective, iron-ic, theatrical space of an imagination divorcing itself from the world and self-destructing in the process. Whenever some residual value appears as a last glimmering—for instance, the death of a freethinker surround-ed by his adoring family in vigil 1—the watchman peers into the interior space of the scene as into a chapel-like subspace. In this novel the met-aphor of internalized space embraces all aspects of mankind's divorce from nature and the inexorable retreat into and captivity in the self and mind. Art does not escape the curse, as we repeatedly learn. Bonaventura elevates to an aesthetic antiprinciple the discovery that the internally il-luminated drama of the human mind is spectral and phantasmagorical. The opening words of the final vigil stress the colorlessness of the con-demning and condemned entropic mind as it plunges into nothingness.

When Stendhal allows us, with Julien Sorel, to intrude behind the scenes during the church celebration honoring the king in *Le rouge et le noir* (The Red and the Black, 1831), the inner spaces of ecclesiastical power exhibit only such a deceptive, base, theatrical light. The dandyish, unctuous young bishop practices hieratical poses before a mirror in a chamber whose gothic windows are ominously walled up.[16] A surviving, remote inner sanctum, the magnificent old gothic chapel ablaze with candlelight, is reserved by church authorities only for show, for a coup de théâtre to dazzle the susceptible ladies of rich families (108). Julien sens-es that, in effect, there are no windows, only occlusion and entrapment.

The great romantic painter Caspar David Friedrich is one of the most insistent thematizers of the window as a boundary between selfhood and otherness. He is also one of the most important artists who links mod-ern consciousness in the individual subject, facing windows, doors, and gates, with collective cultural experience. The painting *Frauengestalt im Atelierfenster des Künstlers* (Female Figure in the Window of the Artist's Studio, ca. 1818), by allowing us viewers, like the implied artist, to gaze over her shoulder from the inside toward the partly intimated outside realm, exhibits Friedrich's characteristic mode of romantic irony. This internally replicated, self-conscious framing of the act of observing the world attains a new degree of complication in *Die Kreidefelsen auf Rügen*

15. "in dem alten gotischen Dome" (*Nachtwachen*, 58).
16. Stendhal (Henri Beyle), *Le rouge et le noir*, ed. Henri Martineau (Paris: Garnier, 1957), 103.

The Spaces of Truth and Cathedral Window Light

(The Chalk Cliffs at Rügen, 1818–1819) where the viewer of the painting gazes through a bony aperture in nature at the sea, as into the infinite, while internal figures on the chalk cliffs in the work engage in three different modes of seeing. Pictures of fenestrated or gated walls through which we look, like the implicit artist, constitute another large category of Friedrich's works.

The import of self-aware vision is spelled out more fully in *Klosterhof im Schnee* (Cloister Courtyard in the Snow, 1819), which depicts a procession of tiny robed figures passing through a gothic gate and entering into the empty space of a ruined church, as if for some commemoration. All that remains of the church are the high glassless windows of the apse, and we gaze through them at the same muted rose tone (a promise of rebirth?) in the winter clouds visible also through the blasted trees that internally frame the remnant. The surrounding snowy cemetery brings home powerfully the truth of the winter trope. But since, in sympathy, we are invited to pass through the gate and to stare through the empty windows, we quickly arrive at the realization that the physical tokens of the death of religion have been transmuted in our mediating spirits into a new kind of truth. The outer structures of faith from an earlier age are now internalized in the mind that must face the reality of the historical situation and look through it. The humble clerics in this painting or in the similar *Abtei im Eichwald* (Abbey in the Oak Wood, 1809) suggest the collective heroism of those persisting in their belief. This complex understanding is present, though veiled, in *Winterlandschaft mit Ruine des Klosters Eldena* (Winter Landscape with Ruin of the Eldena Cloister, 1808) where a bent solitary figure passes in a wintry landscape before the shards of fenestrated church walls—a figure as noble in isolation as is the tiny internal viewer of the infinite in *Mönch am Meer* (Monk on the Seashore, 1810–1811). There can be no mistaking the moral rightness of romantic consciousness in such late Friedrich works as *Eule in gotischem Fenster* (Owl in Gothic Window, 1836), where the emblematic bird of wisdom and the night stares at us in challenge from a ruined church window, or the mellower *Der Träumer* (The Dreamer, 1835), depicting a solitary man reading in the frame of a ruined church window beyond which nature emits a roseate and golden glow, sunset or sunrise.

2. Toward the Fin-de-Siècle

Hawthorne's artist novel, *The Marble Faun* (1860), establishes in fulsome detail the kind of late romantic consciousness that will nourish symbolism and modernism.[17] The New England author uses to full advantage a well-established literary fascination for Rome and Italy. The interaction of the sculptor Kenyon and the painter Hilda, the American protagonists, with Donatello, the young Italian nobleman of ancient lineage, and the mysterious Miriam, constitutes, among other things, an exploration of cultural development. As they discuss or enact, and the narrator interposes his own insights into, aspects of the Judaic, Catholic, Protestant, and humanist heritages, the plot line acquires connections that reach back through romanticism and the Renaissance over the Middle Ages to our ancient classical and Oriental roots. In the gothic depths of the catacombs and ruins of Rome, as in the regions, cityscapes, buildings, and artworks of Italy everywhere, reside forces that are historical, psychological, and archetypal: these the novel evokes and examines, continuing a heritage ingrained since the Renaissance and modified and enriched in romanticism.

In canto 4 of *Childe Harold's Pilgrimage* (1818), for example, Byron exercises the license to contemplate Rome as a grand key to the story of European man. In so doing Byron dwells on two of the most important Roman temples, both of which later figure in *The Marble Faun*. One, the Pantheon, stands as the monument that still conveys to the modern pilgrim the great inspiration of ancient civilization, whose pietas, decorum, and virtus are apprehended as the light entering its eyelike aperture. Despite the extra allure the surviving pagan holy place might be expected to possess for Byron, he goes on in *Childe Harold* to devote seven full stanzas instead to praise of "the vast and wondrous dome" (stanza 153) of St. Peter's, a grandeur that causes the mind to grow "colossal" (stanza 155), to rise through the cathedral's "gigantic elegance" toward a harmony "all musical in its immensities" (stanza 156). Initially the "Outshining and o'erwhelming edifice / Fools our fond gaze"; but gradually "growing with its growth, we thus dilate / Our spirits to the size of that they contemplate" (stanza 158).[18] The achievement of the daring Renaissance mind embodied in St. Peter's overshadows for Byron any lesser, negative association the cathedral has as the supreme basilica of Catholicism.

Although couched in a more strictly Protestant framework, Haw-

17. Nathaniel Hawthorne, *Novels: "Fanshawe," "The Scarlet Letter," "The House of the Seven Gables," "The Blithedale Romance," "The Marble Fawn,"* ed. William Charvat, Roy Harvey Pearce, et al. (Columbus: Ohio State University Press, 1982). Passages from *The Marble Faun* will henceforth be cited in the text with the abbreviation MF and the page number.

18. George Gordon Lord Byron, *The Poetical Works of Lord Byron* (London: Oxford University Press, 1921), 247–48.

thorne's treatment of St. Peter's, elaborated in chapters 36 to 39 of *The Marble Faun*, is just as complex as Byron's. Plunged into sorrow through knowledge of her friends' desperate crime, Hilda unbeknownst inspires a painter who secretly captures her "forlorn gaze," similar, so the Roman connoisseurs judge, to that in "the portrait of Beatrice Cenci" (MF 1127). Of course, this identification is sufficient for the reader who reads by the somber light of Shelley's tragedy (1819). Though the daughter of New England Puritans, Hilda instinctively begins praying to the Virgin Mary, the "humanized" archetype of "Divine Womanhood" (MF 1128). Restlessly wandering the galleries and churches of Rome, she now has the capacity to perceive the conflict between the sensual and the spiritual in the great masters, ambiguities in the works making up the long European heritage; yet also to feel poignantly the rare "hallowed work of genius" (MF 1134) amid the plethora of commonplace, deconsecrated art. It is during this travail that Hilda experiences the awesome spaces of St. Peter's. In chapter 39, entitled "The World's Cathedral," trembling on the brink of conversion, she has recourse to the confessional. In the preceding chapter entitled "Altars and Incense," Hawthorne pays an ambivalent romantic tribute to Catholicism's all-encompassing aesthetics that appeals to the whole range of sensibility, including our weaknesses. The introductory image for the mediational role of the Catholic system is that of cathedral window light:

> It supplies a multitude of external forms, in which the spiritual may be clothed and manifested; it has many painted windows, as it were, through which the celestial sunshine, else disregarded, may make itself gloriously perceptible in visions of beauty and splendor. (MF 1138)

In this chapter's prelude the narrator takes us into the glowing sacral interior, under the lofty arches, within the space of apotheosis that the churches of Rome collectively constitute; and Hilda makes the familiar progression through these, by way of the "Pantheon, under the round opening in the Dome," to the unsurpassable "grandeur of this mighty Cathedral" (MF 1141). At first St. Peter's "stands in its own way"; and Hilda clings to her own "childish vision," until by repeated visits she discovers—in the words of the narrator—"that the Cathedral has gradually extended itself over the whole compass of your idea; it covers all the site of your visionary temple, and has room for its cloudy pinnacles beneath the Dome" (MF 1142f.). Before re-creating Hilda's breakthrough experience of the "comprehensive, majestic symbol" (MF 1143), the narrator prepares us with a statement that pertains equally to our own experience of Hawthorne's entire book: "it is only by this fragmentary process that you get an idea of the Cathedral" (MF 1142).

Before we witness Hilda's arrival at an epiphanic turning point, Hawthorne conducts us on a larger journey through the cultural topography of Italy under the guidance of the sculptor Kenyon who, starting in the "grand frame-work of the Apennines" (MF 1029), combines an actual tour of art appreciation with his mission to aid the guilt-stricken Donatello and Miriam, and thereby Hilda too. The wanderer Kenyon is our representative expert in this celebration of the romance of art; he interprets the evidence of the human story throughout the ages in Italy and even savors wine in accordance with the romantic thesis of recollection. In probing the archaic origins of Monte Beni, he senses that the local "wine of the Golden Age" unmistakably pertains to a whole range of human acts that underlie the emergence into civilization: "There was a deliciousness in it that eluded analysis, and—like whatever else is superlatively good— was perhaps better appreciated in the memory than by present consciousness" (MF 1037). Unlike Donatello, who is still struggling to comprehend his fall from natural grace, Kenyon can see the glorious Italian landscape unfolding to the horizon, studded with cities, "the seats and nurseries of early Art" (MF 1065). He draws strength reading "a page of heaven and a page of earth spread wide open before us," something "only expressible by such grand hieroglyphics as these around us" (MF 1066). Kenyon's experience of the sublime of the greater world at sunset, a sublime understood to embrace all the time layers in the mind of its beholder, recapitulates with narrative amplitude the romantic meditation such as practiced by Shelley in "Lines Written among the Euganean Hills" (1818).

The interpenetration of all things and of "the mind which feeds this verse / Peopling the lone universe" (lines 318–19)—to use Shelley's words —actually has already occurred in Kenyon, and thus his understanding preconditions the step-by-step exploration of that immense canvas of culture over time in the company of Donatello, his pupil and patient.[19] The narrator, suspecting the life of a people "becomes fascinating either in the poet's imagination or the painter's eye" when they "are waning to decay and ruin" (MF 1098), is implicated in his character's act of recollection. The narrator's authoritative discussion of the complexities embodied in the particular places and monuments blends into Kenyon's.

19. Percey Bysshe Shelley, *The Poetical Works of Shelley*, ed. Newell F. Ford (Boston: Houghton Mifflin, 1975), 371.

The Spaces of Truth and Cathedral Window Light

Chapter 33, entitled "Pictured Windows," then fully internalizes the exploration. In the "forgotten edifices" of ancient towns we see the ghostly centuries piled up. But within the gothic cathedrals and churches, the spirit of history is emitted as a glow of art for those still wanting to see. Especially in the stained-glass windows of gothic churches, the mind experiences its own act of recognition, because

> the light, which falls merely on the outside of other pictures, is here interfused throughout the work; it illuminates the design, and invests it with living radiance; and, in requital, the unfading colors transmute the common daylight into a miracle of richness and glory, in its passage through the heavenly substance of the blessed and angelic shapes, which throng the arch window. (MF 1104)

Kenyon, agreeing with the awakening Donatello on the horror of spiritual opacity, speculates that the punishment of unresolved sin may be "that it shall insulate the sinner from all sweet society by rendering him impermeable to light, and therefore unrecognizable in the abode of heavenly simplicity and truth" (MF 1105). Just as Goethe says in his poem that starts, "Poems are stained glass windows,"[20] Kenyon and Donatello find the windows dreary outside: "That miracle of radiant art, thus viewed, was nothing better than an incomprehensible obscurity, without a gleam of beauty to induce the beholder to attempt unravelling it" (MF 1107).

These lessons prepare for the reversal when, in chapter 34, Hawthorne makes the entire market square of Perugia, under real daylight, into the sacral space of restored community. The cathedral suddenly recurs as the world and history through whose chapels we journey. Kenyon has been changed inwardly by his own charitable mission and new experiences, as we learn in chapter 43, where he wanders through "vast ranges of apartments" past centuries of the "treasures and marvels of antique art" in the Vatican. He is modern man walking through time represented in frozen images. Significant is his progress beyond the merit of the Apollo Belvedere to the "terrible magnificence" and "sad moral" of the Laokoon group (MF 1178f.). The metaphor of the church window appears in the narrator's paraphrase of Kenyon's thoughts about the nobler forms: "Being of so cold and pure a substance, and most deriving their vitality more from thought than passion, they require to be seen through a perfectly transparent medium" (MF 1178).

Kenyon seeks farther through the obelisques, pyramids, monuments,

20. "Gedichte sind gemalte Fensterscheiben."

and other markers of the Roman Campagna, which seem to reveal the universal sickness and depravity of the present as against eternity; this landscape of tombs and dishonored graves pictures the modern spiritual struggle against death. But eventually he happens upon and unearths the "long-buried hands," and soon more parts of a statue that rivals the Venus de' Medici, the feminine analogy to the Apollo Belvedere; and instantly he makes the connection: "I seek for Hilda and find a marble woman!" (MF 1206). "It is," the narrator confirms, "one of the few works of antique sculpture in which we recognize Womanhood, and that, moreover, without prejudice to its divinity" (MF 1207). With the bridal token, a bracelet that is like the eye of the Pantheon, Hawthorne invites us in the novel's closing page to look through his book's intertwined double plot, while considering the immemorial relationship of Miriam-Donatello and that of the modern American artist couple Hilda-Kenyon, as through a magic glass. We gaze through the multiple facets of the symbol as through the transparency of the church window.

Hawthorne brings us for brief previews into the forgotten cultural realm that a fellow New Englander, Henry Adams, revisits in his book *Mont-Saint-Michel and Chartres* in 1904, celebrating the glorious reemergence of the feminine in the interior sanctuary of the great medieval churches ("Astarte, Isis, Demeter, Aphrodite, and the last and greatest deity of all, the Virgin" [198]).[21] The year 1904 is, of course, the year in which, in his novel *Ulysses* (1922), Joyce places the visit of the father and son questers, Bloom and Dedalus, to the queenly precinct. The time of Hawthorne's novel is that of the passionate work of restoration of great French cathedrals undertaken by the architect and author Eugène-Emmanuel Viollet-le-Duc (1814–1879). If the trajectory from Hawthorne to Adams and Proust represents one line of revaluation, a second line emphasizes the displacement of the church at the heart of the city. Edward Engelberg has argued convincingly that, from the mid-nineteenth century into modernism, major novelists often "feminized" the cathedral. Concomitant with their recognition that a collapse of faith had voided churches of their once enormous symbolic powers, writers used cathedral scenes ironically as sites of erotic encounter or suggestion, as well as to imply "a counterpoint between bourgeois reality" and an "outworn creed."[22] He examines how Flaubert's cathedral at Rouen in *Madame Bovary* (1857),

21. Henry Adams, *Mont-Saint-Michel and Chartres* (Boston: Houghton Mifflin, 1930).
22. Edward Engelberg, "The Displaced Cathedral in Flaubert, James, Lawrence and Kafka," *Arcadia* 21 (1986): 246.

The Spaces of Truth and Cathedral Window Light

James's Notre Dame in *The Ambassadors* (1903), Lawrence's Lincoln cathedral in *The Rainbow* (1915), and Kafka's Prague cathedral in *Der Prozeß* (The Trial, 1925)[23] serve to link the lofty and the banal, to contrast an older communal bonding and moral imperative with the tawdry individual rebellion and sexuality of the present, although in the case of Kafka the church retains its authority against the all-too-human protagonist.

3. The Symbolist Heritage

Major symbolist and postsymbolist poets recognized the importance of this same disjuncture that had conditioned the status of modern consciousness. José-Maria de Hérédia's *Les trophées* (The Trophies, 1893) exemplifies the historical dimension.[24] The poem "Vitrail" ("Church Window") that just precedes "Epiphanie" ("Epiphany") in this collection presents the "window" of its title as an intersection of planes of time, viewpoints, and viewers who are implicated in the mysterious image and its light. The word "Today"[25] with which the sestina opens reinforces the temporal framing that the first quatrain establishes with the verb tense of line 1: "This window has seen dames and lords of might, / Sparkling with gold, with azure, flame and nacre, / Bow down before the altar of their Maker / The pride of crest and hood to sacred right, / [. . .]."[26] The reader too is paradoxically captured. The unnamed poetic mind has implicitly already involved the reader in the permanent stare of the entombed nobility who repose in the church in the roseate glow, themselves having meanwhile become part of the image of the Middle Ages that remains to us, as the closing tercet states: "All voiceless, deaf and motionless are they, / Whose eyes of stone look on the window nigh, / Yet cannot see its rose that blooms always."[27] Building upon romantic recollection and anticipating Proust, Hérédia savors the insight that, in a certain sense, the participants of the lived Middle Ages could not truly know their own essence in the immediacy of experience so well as they embody it for us in a monumental permanence of their images and

23. Franz Kafka, *Der Prozeß*, ed. Max Brod (Frankfürt: S. Fischer Verlag, 1953).
24. José-Maria de Hérédia, *Les trophées*, ed. W. N. Inee (London: Athlone Press, 1979).
25. "Aujourd'hui."
26. "Cette verrière a vu dames et hauts barons / Étincelants d'azur, d'or, de flamme et de nacre, / Incliner, sous la dextre auguste qui consacre, / L'orgueil de leurs cimiers et de leurs chaperons: [. . .]."
27. José-Maria de Hérédia, *Sonnets from "The Trophies" of José-Maria de Hérédia*, trans. Edward Robeson Taylor, 5th ed. (San Francisco: Taylor, Nash & Taylor, 1913), 93.—"Ils gisent là sans voix, sans geste et sans ouie, / Et de leurs yeux de pierre ils regardent sans voir / La rose du vitrail toujours épanouie."

that we are privileged to bear witness to their beauty, once it is mediated.

The title of the collection *Les trophées* should be taken literally, because Hérédia is displaying the rich exotic booty, the glimpses that poetic recollection saves from oblivion. As viewings from a multitude of perspectives, together the sonnets gradually suggest an ultimate, ungraspable symbol: the deeper mystery of the unfolding of Western consciousness. Hérédia divides his "trophies" into subcycles that follow, and reconstitute, the developmental outline already familiar as the deep structure of civilization in Hawthorne's *The Marble Faun* and many another nineteenth-century work that aspires to an "epic" understanding of our past. The poem "Vitrail" opens the subcycle of "Le Moyen Age et la Renaissance" (The Middle Ages and the Renaissance), which closes in an exotic evocation of the decadence of the dream empire of the early modern period. Other poets will make other specific choices of materials in the twentieth century in reapproaching this kind of grand recapitulation. But, in essence, Ezra Pound's *Cantos* (1925ff.) reinstate more fulsomely the nineteenth-century universalizing survey of the human pathway such as Hérédia attempted in fewer, finer slices.

The subcycles "Romancero" (Book of Romance) and "Les Conquérants de l'Or" (Conquistadors) explore the drama of the expansion of the European system to the New World, the extraordinary surge of energies that, in the final analysis, faces the same inexorable limits of death and decay as do all other human enterprises. Hérédia celebrates the coming into existence of the matrix to which he owes his own being as a son of the Caribbean. Long before such cultural exiles as Alejo Carpentier, Hérédia here sketches in verse the foundational romance that will be such an important genre in the Latin American novel of the second half of the twentieth century. Traveling back and forth between the Old and the New Worlds and back and forth perspectivally in history implies movement around the elusive symbol—and also movement through the mediating "window" that finally proves to be invisible, or only knowable in the emptied frame or art. That is all we are promised in the poem "L'oubli" ("Oblivion") opening *Les trophées,* as the first quatrain states: "The Temple's ruins all the headland strew, / Upon whose tawny height brass heroes wane, / With marble goddesses, whose glory vain / The lonely grass shrouds tenderly from view."[28]

28. Hérédia, *Sonnets from "The Trophies,"* 5.—"Le temple est en ruine au haut du promontoire. / Et la Mort a mêlé, dans ce fauve terrain, / Les Déesses de marbre et les Héros d'airain / Dont l'herbe solitaire ensevelit la gloire."

The Spaces of Truth and Cathedral Window Light

Hérédia's formal substitution of the ruined temple for the church—a pictorial example of the latter as emptied form would be Friedrich's painting of a ruined abbey amid oaks[29]—is far from a neoclassical gesture after romanticism; it draws upon a fundamental sensibility enunciated in Stéphane Mallarmé's early poems gathered in 1866 under the title *Parnasse contemporain* (Contemporary Parnassus). Mallarmé's poet is faced with his own decrepitude, the evidence of eternity, the threat of the void, "The insensibility of the blue [sky] and the stones" ("Sadness of Summer," 1864); he seeks a direction out of the sterility of his own awareness and the limits of exhausted nature, but the question remains "Whither to flee in this futile and perverse revolt?" ("Azure," 1864); nonetheless, the heart cannot forswear its yearning for the Baudelairean voyage of discovery "seeking an exotic nature" ("Sea Breeze," 1864).[30] In this well-known context, Mallarmé's "window" is the emptied framing that haunts us; however, the negative force of space defined by the framing reveals a positive insight acquired.

This paradox has a special poignancy in Mallarmé's "Les fenêtres" (The Windows, 1863) since the poem's protagonist is a sick old man who, through the hospital windows, fastens upon the virginal luminosity outside. Robert Cohn (1991) has argued persuasively that the "drunken" viewer rediscovers the "mother" as the primal channel and attachment.[31] The first-person voice is torn by the questions that recognition of his yearning raises, but despite his alienation he associates his destiny with this childlike thirst as of strophe 7. The window of birth and nourishment becomes a surface, the mirror, simultaneously, the spectral moment of self-recognition, of transformation, of restoration, of recollection—the glass of "art" or "mysticity." In rough prose, lines 28–32 read:

> In their glass, bathed by eternal dews, which the chaste morning of the Infinite gilds, I look and see myself an angel! and I die, and I love—whether that window-pane be art or be mysticity—to be reborn bearing my dream in diadem, to an anterior heaven where Beauty blossoms.[32]

29. *Die Abtei im Eichwald.*

30. "L'insensibilité de l'azur et des pierres" ("Tristesse d'été"); "Où fuir dans la revolte inutile et perverse?" ("L'azur"); "pour une exotique nature" ("Brise marine"). Stéphane Mallarmé, *Oeuvres complètes*, ed. Henri Mondor and G. Jean-Aubry (Paris: Gallimard, 1945).

31. Robert G. Cohn, "'Les fenêtres' de Mallarmé," in *Vues sur Mallarmé* (Paris: Nizet, 1991), 29–37.

32. "Dans leur verre, lavé d'éternelles rosées, / Que dore le matin chaste de l'Infini / Je me mire et me vois ange! et je meurs, et j'aime / —Que la vitre soit l'art, soit la mysticité—

But caught below in the impure, the Self ("Moi") is the swan that ago-nizes over whether to break the crystalline surface and take flight, fear-ful of an eternal Icarian fall. In the death-conditioned vision of this sym-bolist swan, we can hear resonating the deathsong of the romantic swan. For example, in Clemens Brentano's "Schwanenlied" (Swan Song, pub-lished 1811), so admired by Hölderlin, the poetic bird recognizes and blesses life "between dawn and dusk," as the seasons rush past and while its head is plunging into the waters of baptism and death as into a mirror. At the moment of passionate understanding, it realizes it is fro-zen into the winter ice and its own plumage betokens the deathly purity of snow and stars.

The relationship between "mirror" and "window" interests poets throughout the longer period marked by the succession of romantic, symbolist, and modernist sensibilities. Rilke, an inheritor through both the German and the French traditions, is especially attracted to the pos-sibilities for combining or bridging motific materials.[33] The abandoned sacral or private space as a simile for the poetic self and as the medium for recollection is frequent in his early lyrics, for example, in the opening line of the pieces gathered in 1896 under the title *Traumgekrönt* (Dream-crowned): "My heart is like the forgotten chapel" (SRZ 1.75).[34] The typi-cal romantic room and window of the experiencing-poetizing subject ap-pear in such poems as "Am Rande der Nacht" in the collection *Das Buch der Bilder* ("On the Edge of Night," Book of Images, 1900), while "Letzter Abend" in *Neue Gedichte* ("Final Evening," New Poems, 1906) adds the motif of the internal mirror and enlarges the room into an androgynous intersubjective space, the boundary between inner world and outer na-ture still being the traditional window (SRZ 1.400, 521). In "Casabianca" in *Advent* (1897), the poet recognizes that communion still occurs even though to the forgetful world the church windows are "hollow" (strophe 2): "Forgotten saints dwell / there lonely in the altar's sanctuary: / Eve-ning hands in crowns to them / through hollow windows" (SRZ 1.119).[35]

As they will be for Proust, in *Das Buch vom mönchischen Leben* (Book

---

/ A renaître portant mon rêve en diademe, / Au ciel antérieur où fleurit la Beauté!" (lines 28–32).

33. Rainer Maria Rilke, *Sämtliche Werke*, ed. Ruth Sieber-Rilke and Ernst Zinn, 3 vols. (Wiesbaden: Insel-Verlag, 1955–1966). Hereafter cited as SRZ with volume and page num-bers.

34. "Mein Herz gleicht der vergessenen Kapelle" (SRZ, 1.75).

35. "Vergessene Heilige wohnen / dort einsam im Altarschrein: / der Abend reicht ih-nen Kronen / durch hohle Fenster hinein." (SRZ, 1.119).

of Monastic Life, 1899) churches for Rilke are a species of fading music, "in their climbing heavenward / like harps, sounding consolations" (SRZ 1.289).[36] In *Das Buch von der Armut und vom Tode* (Book of Poverty and Death, 1903), the humblest space can be in correspondence to that authentic embodiment: "The poorman's house is like an altar shrine" (SRZ 1.362).[37] In "Die Kathedrale" (The Cathedral) in his *Neue Gedichte* (New Poems, 1907), Rilke suddenly feels confronted by the mysterious life story of the churches that, as sacramental embodiment, seem so out of place in the quotidian town, almost out of time despite their surviving material features (lines 23–27): "Birth was there in these underpinnings, / and power and impetus in this rearing, / and love everywhere as wine and bread, / and the portals full of plaints of love" (SRZ 1.498).[38]

The paired poems "Adam" and "Eva" of *Der neuen Gedichte anderer Teil* (New Poems, part 2, 1908) return to the examination of the gentler aspect of the Middle Ages. Our First Parents (as archetypes) occupy a surprising position "above" us (as beholders) despite the Fall. Yet they appear respectively startled and proud (Adam), and uprooted, yearning, and recollective (Eve). They are in an awkward relation to the great rose window, estranged but close to that very symbol they embody—on our behalf, and like us. The unidentified voice of the poem speaks with authority and analytical externality that adds to the irony of discovering the latent glory of the window. In effect, we have happened upon the protagonists of an educational wandering after the fortunate Fall. It is an arrival at a steep place, where pausing, we, as our First Parents, are discomfited by our exile and yet determined to see it through. The avatars Adam and Eve, being "roses" in conformity with Christ and Mary, dizzyingly ascend into the rose of the window.

Several poems following "Die Kathedrale" in *Neue Gedichte*—"Das Portal" (The Portal), "Die Fensterrose" (The Rose Window), "Das Kapital" (The Capital), "Gott im Mittelalter" (God in the Middle Ages)— examine aspects of the structure bearing on the nature of the too demanding deity revealed thereby. The sonnet "Die Fensterrose" (The Rose Window) glimpses the terrifying mystery of the symbol. In rough prose, it can be translated as:

36. "in ihrem Steigen und Erstehen / als Harfen, tönende Vertröster" (SRZ, 1.289).
37. "Des Armen Haus ist wie ein Altarschrein" (SRZ, 1.362).
38. "Da war Geburt in diesen Unterlagen, / Und Kraft und Andrang war in diesem Ragen / und Liebe überall wie Wein und Brot, / und die Portale voller Liebesklagen" (SRZ, 1.498).

In there: The languid tread of their paws a stillness which almost disconcerts you; and then, suddenly, how one of the cats takes the look of it wandering back and forth violently into its great eye;—that look which, as if seized in a vortex's gyre, swims a little while and then submerges and has lost any knowledge of itself, when this eye, apparently at rest, opens and slams itself shut with tumult and rips the gaze right into the red blood: Thus once upon a time out of dark being the cathedrals' great rose windows plucked a heart and ripped it into God.[39] (SRZ 1.501)

The human glance is drawn into an abyss on high when the window as a catlike eye suddenly tears and devours the beholder. Our selfhood is annihilated in the sudden sacrificial moment. This is, on the one hand, a savage rendering as in mystical poetry; the final tercet interprets medieval total dedication to God as being engulfed in the Redeemer-Victim's blood at the heart of the rose. The moment bears resemblance, on the other hand, to the realization of the dangerous attraction toward the divine that results in the poet's being blasted by his presumption. In Hölderlin's poetry, the chastened hubristic "priest" plummets to earth. Here the narrating voice moves within a symbolist perspectival network of associations. It returns suddenly from the rose as the frightening eye, the power of which has been evoked, to the real ground of the street, to the normal terrain of history from which, nowadays, we look at cathedral rose windows.

Rilke's late French poems, gathered in the cycles *Les roses* (Roses) and *Les fenêtres* (Windows), delicately fuse the architectonic window and the organic window of symbolism in order to allow the transmuted spaces of self and art to flow in and out of each other and of the natural estate.[40] The taproots nourishing these cycles go deep into the soil of romantic literature. The rose reclaims its universality, standing both for the organic realm as "a fragrant labyrinth" and for the psychological realm as "this love-space," which flow together as one. The rose incarnates the mystery

39. "Da drin: das träge Treten ihrer Tatzen / eine Stille, die dich fast verwirrt; / und wie dann plötzlich eine von den Katzen / den Blick an ihr, der hin und wieder irrt, // gewaltsam in ihr großes Auge nimmt.— / den Blick, der, wie von eines Wirbels Kreis / ergriffen eine kleine Weile schwimmt / und dann versinkt und nichts mehr von sich weiß, // wenn dieses Auge, welches scheinbar ruht, / sich auftut und zusammenschlägt mit Tosen / und ihn hineinreißt ins rote Blut—: // So griffen einstmals aus dem Dunkelsein // der Kathedralen große Fensterrosen / ein Herz und rissen es in Gott hinein" (SRZ, 1.501).
40. Rainer Maria Rilke, *The Complete French Poems of Rainer Maria Rilke*, trans. A. Poulin Jr. (Saint Paul, Minn.: Graywolf Press, 1986); page references after P refer to this bilingual edition.

of our pilgrimage as children of Adam and Eve; it is the "rose infinitely holding the fall."[41] Even God, appearing as Self, looks out of the window at the roses in the garden: "God, while looking out the window, / keeps house."[42] Like the flesh, ours or that of the rose, the poem envelops and determines the space of the mystery with a symbolist theatrical gesture as "curtain, / vestment of the void!"[43]

4. Modernist Narrative

Beyond episodic nuclei around which chapters may cohere, the first complex order of epiphany in narrative fiction is that associated with an aesthete or artist as in *A rebours, Tonio Kröger, Portrait of the Artist as a Young Man,* or *A la recherche du temps perdu.* There are innumerable instances when as privileged listeners we hear Proust's (as yet unnamed) narrator in *Du côté de chez Swann* (Swann's Way), the first book of *A la recherche du temps perdu,* recount specific moments of aesthetic breakthrough based on his own experiences. Among the analogies proffered on page 1 for the "work" we are entering is the famous equation: "a church, a quartet, the rivalry of Francis I and Charles V."[44] In a striking reversion to an older model, Proust reinvokes the positive imagery of cathedral window light. Even though he uses the danger-laden romantic motif of the magic lantern or internal projection, he combines the romantic room as the interior space of the subject with the window as the metaphor of mediation. This promise of meaningful correspondences offsets the evident malaise of the experiencing subject. In the overture passages of the Combray section of *Swann's Way* the narrating voice recollects early moments in the development of his own imagination during childhood. The stories projected by magic lantern to amuse him both alleviate and aggravate his awareness of separation within, and alienation from, his own mental space:

> At Combray, as every afternoon ended, long before the time when I should have to go to bed and lie there, unsleeping, far from my mother and grandmother, my bedroom became the fixed point on which my melancholy and anxious thoughts were centered. Someone had indeed

41. "l'odorante labyrinthe" (P, 6–7); "cet espace d'amour" (P, 4–5); "rose qui infiniment possède la perte" (P, 8–9).

42. "Dieu, en regardant par la fenêtre, / fait la maison" (P, 163).

43. "rideau, / robe du vide!" (P, 36–37).

44. "une église, un quatuor, la rivalité de François Ier et de Charles Quint" (Marcel Proust, *A la recherche du temps perdu,* 4 vols., ed. Jean-Yves Tadié, vol. 1, *Du côté de chez Swann; A l'ombre des jeunes filles en fleur* [Paris: Gallimard, 1987], 1:3; hereafter cited as R 1).

had the happy idea of giving me, to distract me on evenings when I seemed abnormally wretched, a magic lantern, which used to be set on top of my lamp while we waited for dinner-time to come; and, after the fashion of the master-builders and glass painters of gothic days, it substituted for the opaqueness of my walls an impalpable iridescence, supernatural phenomena of many colours, in which legends were depicted as on a shifting and transitory window. But my sorrows were only increased thereby, because this mere change of lighting was enough to destroy the familiar impression I had of my room, thanks to which, save for the torture of going to bed, it had become quite endurable. Now I no longer recognised it, and felt uneasy in it, as in a room in some hotel or chalet, in a place where I had just arrived by train for the first time.[45]

The master image of the church and the church window is a guarantor once again of the inherent correspondence between the revelations of form in the organic realm, in the psyche, and in art. This is made abundantly clear in the famous episode in the Combray section when, as a boy, the narrator glimpses Gilberte amid the hawthorns. The progression over synesthetic-musical bridges builds to several epiphanic peaks that are resolved and muted in the irony of the aged narrator's recollection of how the power of his imagination converted the color of Gilberte's eyes from black to his childhood ideal, blue. Here Proust also picks up and carries forward the romantic and symbolist theme in blue, as part of the elaborate chromatics of his novel. At one point the divine light of the Easter season—the ruling trope of the Combray section—is experienced as being transmitted through the blossoms as if pouring in through the windows of a church:

45. Marcel Proust, *Remembrance of Things Past*, vol. 1: *Swann's Way; Within a Budding Grove*, trans. C. K. Scott Moncrieff and Terence Kilmartin (New York: Random House, 1981), 1.9, 109–10.—"À Combray, tous les jours dès la fin de l'après-midi, longtemps avant le moment où il faudrait me mettre au lit et rester, sans dormir, loin de ma mère et de ma grand-mère, ma chambre à coucher redevenait le point fixe et douloureux de mes préoccupations. On avait bien inventé, pour me distraire les soirs où on me trouvait l'air trop malheureux, de me donner une lanterne magique dont, en attendant l'heure du dîner, on coiffait ma lampe; et, à l'instar des premiers architectes et maîtres verriers de l'âge gothique, elle substituait à l'opacité des murs d'impalpables irisations, de surnaturelles apparitions multicolores, où des légendes étaient dépeintes comme dans un vitrail vacillant et momentané. Mais ma tristesse n'en était qu'accaru, parce que rien que le changement d'éclairage détruisait l'habitude que j'avais de ma chambre et grâce à quoi, sauf le supplice du coucher, elle m'était devenue supportable. Maintenant je ne la reconnaissais plus et j'y étais inquiet, comme dans une chambre d'hôtel ou de châlet où je fusse arrivé pour la première fois en descendant de chemin de fer" (R, 1.3).

The hedge resembled a series of chapels, whose walls were no longer visible under the mountains of flowers that were heaped upon their altars; while beneath them the sun cast a checkered light upon the ground, as though it had just passed through a stained-glass window; and their scent swept over me, as unctuous, as circumscribed in its range, as though I had been standing before the Lady-altar, and the flowers, themselves adorned also, held out each its little bunch of glittering stamens with an absentminded air, delicate radiating veins in the flamboyant style like those which, in the church, framed the stairway to the rood-loft or the mullions of windows and blossomed out into the fleshy whiteness of strawberry-flowers.[46]

Onto the correspondences inhering in the structures of organic nature, art, and the mind, gradually we superimpose the patterns discovered in history. Toward the end of the Combray section, for example, the narrator (Marcel) recalls, through the virtually time-liberated optic of an indefinite later moment, the overwhelming vision of Mme de Guermantes in the church, her aristocratic eyes emitting "a flood of blue light"[47] like cathedral windows. We are privy not just to a recollection of the complex process by which Marcel integrated all his prior knowledge and imaginings about her with the human actuality of the person and the occasion, but to a recollection of an epiphany occurring in a context that is effectively unlocked by that epiphany. Through Marcel we submit to the spell and totality of a ritual that marks and qualifies biological and social time: the wedding mass. We are further initiated into a living and dying structure, the church at Combray that houses the meaning of his vision in many forms, including entire works of art therein, and which is a point of "lyrical" precipitation in the recollected experience when Marcel recognizes his attraction to the duchess. His youthful interpretation of her gesture of tenderness, first associated synesthetically with the light, cloth, and flowers that produce "an epidemis of light"[48] flows over into an overt critical insight, a mature reference to instances where the arts

46. Proust, *Remembrance*, 150—"La haie formait comme une suite de chapelles qui disparaissaient sous la jonchée de leurs fleurs amoncellées en reposoir; au-dessus d'elles, le soleil posait à terre un quadrillage de clarté, comme s'il venait de traverser une verrière; leur parfum s'étendait aussi onctueux, aussi délimité en sa forme que si j'eusse été devant l'autel de la Vièrge, et les fleurs, aussi parées, tenaient chacune d'un air distrait son etincelant bouquet d'étamines, fines et rayonnantes nervures de style flamboyant comme celles qui à l'église ajouraient la rampe du jube ou les meneaux du vitrail et qui s'épanouissaient en blanche chair de fleur de fraisier" (R, 1:138).
47. "flot de lumière bleue" (R, 1.175).
48. "un épiderme de lumière" (R, 1.176).

as complex structures ("certain pages of Lohengrin, certain paintings by Carpaccio, [. . .] Baudelaire")[49] have synesthetically bridged the realms.

We can see in painting too at the turn of the century just how thoroughly the church window and its light have pervaded French art by offering an attractive metaphorical capacity. The work of Odilon Redon illustrates this. In his *Le jour* (The Day, 1891), we gaze out of a mournful dark interior through a barred window at the trunk section of the tree of life outside. His *Le liseur* (The Reader, 1892) thematizes how a high window admits illumination into the inner space where it shines upon and is radiating forth from a book that his own teacher reads—in a setting probably influenced by Albrecht Dürer's picture of Saint Jerome in his study. In *La fenêtre* (The Window, ca. 1894) a figure, hands clasped on face in wonder, kneels in interior darkness by a barred window in the shape of a church window through which radiates an indefinite luminous vision. In *Vitrail-Beatrice* (Beatrice Window, 1895) the organic and spiritual fold together in Dante's beloved caught like a saint's effigy in a stained glass window. The many idealized heads and figures in magical color by Redon from the 1890s onward—for example, *Sita* (1892), *Orphée* (1903), *Buddha* (1905), and *Hommage à Gauguin* (1906)—could readily also be integrated into a window, as is the head with profuse flowers in another work entitled *La fenêtre* (1907).

The many pastels and oils by Redon carrying the label "window" in the first decade of the new century cover the gamut from direct representation of a historical church window from within the church, to figures in holy scenes in his own manner, to virtually abstract flowering framed within architecturally distinct gothic church windows. Robert Delaunay's *Fenêtre* (Window, ca. 1912–1913) demonstrates the possibility of summing up this great romantic-symbolist tradition in a modernist vein. Delaunay's cubist window is simultaneously the abstractly reconceived total image of an entire cathedral, which, as if liberated from its own structural materials, seems to soar like a rocket in the direction given by, and within, a gothic arch as if it is window transcendent. Even though Walter Gropius wanted to ban the history of architecture from the curriculum, the Bauhaus manifesto of 1919 carries a woodcut image of a gothic cathedral for the sake of its ascendant abstract lines. The "cathedral" has become iconic for a more comprehensive cultural idea and thus it can serve to represent the modernist reinvocation of the (often

49. Proust, *Remembrance*, 194.—"certaines pages de Lohengrin, certaines peintures de Carpaccio, [. . .] Baudelaire" (R, 1.176).

medievalizing) romantic respect for the union of aesthetics and crafts-manship. Not as something to imitate, but as a symbol, the cathedral is congenial to the Bauhaus program to bring painting, sculpture, architec-ture, decoration, and design together.

It is indicative of its status that even the avowedly antiromantic writer William Dean Howells is able to exploit the space illuminated by cathe-dral window light for swift characterization of a complex set of cultural and psychological understandings. In part 1, chapter 8, of his novel *A Hazard of New Fortunes* (1890), the American couple, the Marches, mo-mentarily step out of the morning rush of New York City into Grace Ca-thedral, whose architecture, though imitative, they nonetheless admit to be "beautiful." As a narrated moment, their immersion is brief, and it can be kept to a few pen strokes because the cluster of associations is so well established:

> Rapt far from New York, if not from earth, in the dim richness of the painted light, the hallowed music took them with a solemn ecstasy; the aerial, aspiring Gothic forms seemed to lift them heavenward. They came out reluctant into the dazzle and bustle of the street, with a feeling that they were too good for it, which they confessed to each other with whimsical consciousness.[50]

Reader escapism too is held in check by the virtual shorthand citation of the basics. The pause to acknowledge the spell of the place is also a chance to recognize being situated beyond romanticism:

> "But no matter how consecrated we feel now," he said, "we mustn't for-get that we went into the church for precisely the same reason that we went into the Vienna Cafe for breakfast—to gratify an aesthetic sense, to renew the faded pleasure of travel for a moment, to get back to the Europe of our youth. It was a purely pagan impulse, Isabel, and we'd better own it."[51]

In drawing the geocultural coordinates, Howells not only confirms that the wholesome realism of the Marches is the successor to the re-ligious sentiment embodied in the church. He also indicates that the contemporary United States, though schooled by older Europe, has sub-sumed, critiqued, and incorporated the various lessons in a modern form; the United States is now the scene of the vital action.

50. William Dean Howells, *A Hazard of New Fortunes* (New York: New American Li-brary, 1965).
51. Howells, *A Hazard of New Fortunes*, 47.

One generation later, back in old Europe in chapter 9 of Franz Kafka's novel *Der Prozeß* (The Trial, 1925), Josef K. is exploring what at first appears to be an empty, dank cathedral while waiting to show it to a never-to-arrive Italian business client as a tourist attraction. He strains to see pictures and emblems by the faint light of lamps including his pocket torch, when mysteriously a vester motions him toward a pulpit from which a priest, who turns out to be the prison chaplain, preaches an accusatory sermon at him. The episode is replete with glimpses of traditional imagery that modernist readers, unlike obdurate K., can scarcely resist acknowledging.

As chapter thirteen, "The Haunted Narrator before the Gate," will treat at greater length, Kafka's cathedral gradually reveals itself to contain the lost complexity that the protagonist has representatively forgotten. That complexity permeates, but is also subsumed by, the mind of the outer narrator who probes the metamorphosed condition of K.'s mind. Internalized in Kafka's cathedral chapter are many representations on chapel walls only dimly perceived by Joseph K. and the great midrashic exchange between the prison chaplain who expounds the parable of the "gate of the Law" with K. as maladroit and resistant interlocutor. In the parable, the radiance of God shines forth through the "gate" into an interior darkness that bears remarkable resemblance to the darkness in which the human subject is caught. If the entire cathedral chapter functions like a stained glass window (paradoxically, in spite, or because, of the expressed theme that the cathedral's windows are occluded), the reader, with his or her particular nature, remains beyond K. as the challenged perceiver who must relate to the light.

Several general conclusions can be drawn from the modernist paintings and narratives examined above. Each tends to thematize some aspect of the symbolist response to a threatening loss of cultural and sacral values. The artist's sense of being "haunted" by hidden or receding meaning tends to reinstantiate what has been lost, at least in a preliminary gesture. Rilke establishes a new secular position as an ontological existentialist in respectfully acknowledging (like Hérédia) the cultural forms that once flourished as expressions of life's genuine mystery and of the human spirit; he moves from keen observation of these to reverential acceptance of supreme symbols taken from "ordinary" life in extraordinary condensation, thereby providing us with reconstituted sacraments. In contrast, Kafka elevates "forgetting," the experience of separation from the sacred, on one level, seemingly, its collapse, to a central place in his art; the reader remains "haunted," even "paranoiac," but unendingly driven to interpretation. The great question becomes whether, by negation too, the sacred persists. Proust carries us beyond this existential and spiritual wounding (Mallarmé's "glaive sûr" in "L'azur") to completion of the symbolist goal of "recollection" (Baudelaire's "receuillement"). He accepts the historical evidence—already noted by the romantics—for the time process in which the complex expressions of the human desire for the sacred are inexorably involved; he depicts that need as a permanent attribute of human existence; and he recuperates the sacramental correspondence between the laws of life and human striving. In Proust, nature's light and that of cathedral windows ultimately merge in the same space of truth.[52]

52. Roger Shattuck, *Proust's Way: A Field Guide to "In Search of Lost Time"* (New York: W. W. Norton, 2001), if not the finest, is certainly unexcelled as a general introduction to all aspects of the novel: the character of its author, its genesis, its ground plan and main themes, its meticulous layering of observations, and more. Shattuck argues against the standard view that the principle of memory is paramount in *Search*. I concur with Shattuck's finding (justifiably restated from his earlier work) that Proust integrates modes of vision associated with modern technologies. I differ, however, in finding that Proust also restores a holistic sense, achieving a vision informed by an awareness of the sacred. The dimension of the sacred emerges from moments when Proust's narrator integrates personal-experiential and cultural memory. Robert Fraser, *Proust and the Victorians: The Lamp of Memory* (London: Macmillan, 1994), observes how much the French novelist absorbed of the Victorian sense of moral illumination through cultural recovery of values. One of the better comparative studies of the factor of memory is Suzanne Nalbantian, *Aesthetic Autobiography: From Life to Art in Marcel Proust, James Joyce, Virginia Woolf, and Anaïs Nin* (New York: St. Martin's Press, 1994).

2 EPIPHANY

Applicability of a Modernist Term

Discussions of epiphany as an important twentieth-century literary device habitually revert to the key passages in the never completed novel *Stephen Hero* (begun 1904) where Joyce has his protagonist artist adapt the religious term to literary purposes. There is the "fragment of colloquy" whose "triviality made [Stephen] think of collecting many such moments together in a book of epiphanies. By an epiphany he meant a sudden spiritual manifestation, whether in the vulgarity of speech or of gesture or in a memorable phase of the mind itself." And Stephen explains to Cranly that he has suddenly recognized even "the clock of the Ballast Office [. . .] an item in the catalog of Dublin's street furniture" as an "epiphany": "Imagine my glimpse at that clock as the gropings of a spiritual eye which seeks to adjust the vision to an exact focus. The moment the focus is reached the object is epiphanised."[1] Yet neither the enlarged edition (1974) of the *Princeton Encyclopedia of Poetry and Poetics* nor the reprinted fourth edition (1981) of the *Oxford Companion to English Literature* granted separate treatment to the modernist term "epiphany," perhaps out of the belief that its application is too narrowly circumscribed by its association with the aesthetics of its chief propounder, Joyce.[2]

But as William T. Noon has cautioned, we should not take Stephen's more limited point of view in place of Joyce's larger poetic framework and development "in the direction of symbolic transformation" of reality; the "Joycean epiphany expands thus in symbolic dimensions in proportion as it concentrates its radiance in verbal signs which exist not in isolation but in combinations of patterned sense and sound."[3] And as Mor-

1. James Joyce, *Stephen Hero*, ed. John J. Slocum and Herbert Cahoon, rev. ed. (London: Jonathan Cape, 1956), 216.

2. Zack Bowen underscores its persisting attraction for Joycean scholarship in "Joyce and the Epiphany Concept: A New Approach," *Journal of Modern Literature* 9 (1981–1982): 103–14.

3. William T. Noon, S.J., *Joyce and Acquinas* (New Haven, Conn.: Yale University Press, 1957), 65, 69, in the seminal fourth chapter titled after Joyce, "How Culious an Epiphany."

ris Beja has shown, the term is also pertinent to a fuller understanding of a wide range of great British and American authors, and he extends it to Proust and Kafka as well.[4] I hope to underscore that "epiphany" can indeed serve the broader purpose in comparative criticism of marking an intersection of certain key traits in the narrative fiction of many notable European writers. Unmistakable by the end of the 1920s in works by Proust, Joyce, Mann, and Woolf is an ability to build toward climactic moments elaborately synthesized out of elements, which, taken in more obvious, smaller constellations, have the character of postromantic prose poems, essaylike meditations, or dramatic fragments. The ways such "epiphanic" junctures are structured reflect the absorption of several further important lessons: the techniques of impressionism, symbolist "depersonalization" and "evocation," and the emerging psychological ideas of the era of Freud and Jung, as well as the experience of the Wagnerian leitmotif, photography, and cinema.

Thus, aspects of the modernist epiphany can be and have been described as pertaining to more than one artistic current of the ending nineteenth century; and, accordingly, restrictive "purist" approaches are useful only to help us reach the more difficult terrain where we see how established technical capacities subserve this new mode. Beja points to the use of epiphany as something shared by the less traditional writers both in the short story and in the novel, and he cites as the most significant underlying trends "the fascination of twentieth-century novelists with psychology and the subjective processes of the mind" and "the invasion of the novel by the characteristics, techniques, and standards of poetry."[5] In an age of "uneasy disillusion with religion" and "equally great loss of faith in reason," the literary epiphany, through "instantaneous, intuitive illumination," can readily assume the thematic role of discovering a pattern in the besetting trivia, while epiphany is simultaneously a valuable technical device liberating an author from such conventional barriers as chronology, genre, objectivity, and point of view. That is why epiphany so often appears in conjunction with stream of consciousness, space and time montage, discontinuity and incongruity, authorially orchestrated irony, symbolic design and synthesis—in short, with the characteristic methods, tropes, and thematics of the novel in the age of psychology well described by Leon Edel and Robert Humphrey in the

4. Morris Beja, *Epiphany in the Modern Novel* (Seattle: University of Washington Press, 1971).
5. Beja, *Epiphany,* 21f.

1950s.[6] The rise of a postromantic, antirealistic reappreciation of the role of memory, intuition, and the psychological relativity of time in relation to perception and knowledge is corroborated through innumerable references by major artists to the relevance of philosophers such as Arthur Schopenhauer (1788–1860) and Henri Bergson (1859–1941).

It is necessary to distinguish between the availability of newer techniques for rendering perception and the uses to which these were put in the longer run by modernist artists who ceased to be bound by the doctrines therewith connected. For instance, by applying a narrower standard for impressionism as the description of moments that are witnessed by an inherently passive observer or authorial voice but without any significant story interest in the perceiving subject, John William Mains excludes virtually all complex poetry and fiction a priori as "expressionism, symbolism, autobiography, lyricism." Precisely because "the epiphany technique concentrates on some object or event within a story and attempts to make it contain or climax the story's meaning," so Mains argues, even if the result is merely to focus diffused elements of a story as Joyce does with the gold coin in "Two Gallants," that means moving toward symbolism. Works such as James's *The Golden Bowl* (1904), Woolf's *The Waves* (1931), Joyce's "The Dead" (1907), and Lawrence's *The Rainbow* (1915) are distinctly symbolist because in them "systematic recurrence of some event, feeling or object insistently suggests a deeper-than-surface meaning, or [. . .] the author uses universally significant (archetypal) elements in conspicuous places."[7] Manns's meticulous exclusionary discriminations do provide excellent starting points for considering why the epiphany, at first so closely associated in Joyce's practice with the forms of the short story and the novella, could be expanded as a major device in his and other major novels of the early twentieth century.

By 1800, romantic practice and theory had endowed the fragment, the novella, and the novel with new generic potential that carried well into the next century. Novalis's *Hymnen an die Nacht* (Hymns to the Night, 1800) illustrate the romantic clustering of fragmentary utterances in freely associative lyrical narrations and meditations and the development of leitmotifs toward dramatic culminations not governed by conventional time. The organizing principle of the stricter novella from around 1800

6. Leon Edel, *The Modern Psychological Novel* (New York: Grove Press, 1955); Robert Humphrey, *Stream of Consciousness in the Modern Novel* (Berkeley and Los Angeles: University of California Press, 1958).

7. John William Mains, "Literary Impressionism: A Study in Definitions" (Ph.D. diss., University of Washington, 1978), 6, 103, 106.

was a central symbol or symbolic system, while the plot usually pivoted around a revealing incident[8] or turn of events,[9] but the novella too could employ dream structures as in Tieck's "Der blonde Eckbert" (Blond Eckbert, 1797) or Eichendorff's "Das Marmorbild" (The Marble Statue, 1819).[10] With his passive hero who moves through dreamlike symbolic encounters in *Heinrich von Ofterdingen* (1800), Novalis hoped to free the novel as well to be a vehicle for transcending the limits of reality. Ralph Freedman, among others, has located in romantic fiction the antecedents of what he terms the modern "lyrical novel."[11] As mentioned, Beja similarly identifies invading "poetry" as a constituent of the epiphany in narrative prose and describes the quest for synthesis in Eliot's poetry as its aesthetic analogue in the modern lyric.[12]

Beyond the direct example of romantic writing, Huysmans's *A rebours* (Against Nature, 1883) demonstrated how to reemploy the prose-poem and essayistic fragment as constitutive elements of a new kind of modern antinaturalistic novel. Huysmans's protagonist aesthete Des Esseintes, directly inspired by Baudelaire and Mallarmé, recognizes how attributes of "form, aroma, color, quality, vividness, object or being,"[13] which otherwise deployed might support impressionistic realism, can be brought into relation in the mind of the reader so as to reveal in concert, sometimes through the synthesizing agency of a single key term "once he had penetrated the symbol, [. . .] a general effect."[14] Des Esseintes meditates on creating a symbolist narrative out of prose-poems, "a novel concentrated in a few phrases, which would contain the triply distilled juice of hundreds of pages usually employed to establish the setting, to sketch the characters, to cram together the supporting incidental observations and minor details."[15] By its very nature it would demand of its readership an elitist collaboration: "[T]he novel thus conceived, thus condensed

8. "eine unerhörte Begebenheit" (Goethe).
9. "Wendepunkt" (Tieck).
10. On the discrimination of novella form in the nineteenth century, see Gerald Gillespie, "Novella, Nouvelle, Novelle, Short Novel? A Review of Terms," *Neophilologus* 51 (1967): 117–27, 225–30.
11. Ralph Freedman, *The Lyrical Novel: Studies in Hermann Hesse, André Gide, and Virginia Woolf* (Princeton, N.J.: Princeton University Press, 1963), ch. 1 and 2. The territory is already sketched by Edel in *The Modern Psychological Novel*, e.g., ch. 10: "The Novel as Poem."
12. Beja, *Epiphany*, 66–69.
13. "la forme, le parfum, la couleur, la qualité, l'éclat, l'objet ou l'être" (Joris-Karl Huysmans, *A rebours*, in *Oeuvres complètes* [Geneva: Slatkine, 1972], 7.298; hereafter cited as *A rebours*).
14. "dès qu'il avait pénétré le symbole, [. . .] un ensemble" (*A rebours*, 298).
15. "un roman concentré en quelques phrases qui contiendrait le suc cohobé des cen-

in a page or two, would become a communion of thought between a magician author and an ideal reader."[16] As is obvious by this point in Huysmans's book, the story of Des Esseintes's exploration of and struggle with decadence is actually being told through an interconnecting of fragments of greater length and complexity than a literalist reading of this incapsulated model of the novel would lead us to expect. In other words, the prose-poem has already been subordinated in practice by Huysmans to a new purpose toward the conception of which Des Esseintes suggestively gropes.

The tooth-pulling scene in chapter 4 of *A rebours* illustrates the resultant epiphany-like structure. The impressionistic selection of salient "real" clinical details might well have underpinned merely a grim nineteenth-century naturalism did the episode not operate through a double register. On one level, it directly exhibits the horror of actual existence without mitigation; but, on another level, it resonates with insights that great religious thinkers and major artists have imparted to the reader both explicitly, through intermittent fragments reflecting the workings of the protagonist's mind, and implicitly, through connections thereby excited in the reader's mind. Huysmans draws an unspoken bizarre and ironic comparison between the protagonist's hellish recollection of that operation and his discovery, after his revery, that his jewel-studded pet turtle has died because it is unable to support such denaturing luxury. This epiphany not only links disparate matters in a minor dramatic climax but prepares the ground for the long excursus on the art of Moreau, Luyken, Dürer, Delacroix, Redon, Goya, and others and the Salomé figure in chapter 5, and it still resonates in Des Esseintes's encounter with a Salomé-like succuba who is unmasked as, among other things, the pox and syphilis in his nightmare of chapter 8. That is, an early epiphany proves to support thematics that will emerge further on, and the novel's ongoing clarifying re-examination is focused through resolving symbols that at first are masked; for Des Esseintes's grotesquely separated part in chapter 4 ("a blue tooth from which gore dangled")[17] already suggests the severed head of John the Baptist that Salomé craves in chapter 5.

There are many striking similarities of subordinated impressionistic detail in the episode of the fatal extraction of Thomas Buddenbrook's

---

taines de pages toujours employées à établir le milieu, à dessiner les caractères, à entasser à l'appui les observations et les menus faits" (*A rebours*, 301f.).

16. "Le roman ainsi conçu, ainsi condensé en une page ou deux, deviendrait une communion de pensée entre un magique écrivain et un idéal lecteur [. . .]" (*A rebours*, 302).

17. "une dent bleue où pendait du rouge" (*A rebours*, 77).

tooth, a climax that concentrates all the pain latent in the long submerged, now remembered teachings of Schopenhauer in part 10 of *Buddenbrooks* (1901). The young novelist Thomas Mann, though still writing ostensibly as a clinical naturalist, deftly introduces the epiphanic process with ironic double focus: we experience, on the one hand, a character's rebirth of consciousness and, on the other hand, a confluence of key leitmotifs in the authorial system. The tacit compositional principle is Wagnerian, while the framework of guiding ideas is Nietzschean.[18] One of the chief distinctions between Thomas's crisis of consciousness in the novel *Buddenbrooks* and the climaxes in the early novella *Tonio Kröger* (1903) is that in the latter the central protagonist is an artist figure contemplating life. Tonio is destined from childhood to probe the meaning of such leitmotif signs as his crossed Northern and Southern attributes, and to witness out of time, notably at the dance seen again years later in Scandinavia after the storm, the typology in which he himself is caught. This epiphany, his deeper recognition undergirding the artistic commitment in his letter to a fellow artist at the end, bears resemblance to the helpless knowledge of Gabriel through whose artistic imagination within Joyce's "The Dead" we obtain a double focus illuminating the mystery of passion.

Even these few examples from narrative fiction suggest the extent to which minor generic shifts will determine the kind of illumination of, or insight into, the world, character, or self. In the following contrast, we can observe an analogous effect of minimal changes in the inner contours of poems, which, under a loose definition, belong to descriptive impressionism. Charles Leconte de Lisle's vision of great African creatures in his poem "Les éléphants" (1862)—simultaneously, the evocation of a privileged moment and an instance of painterly, though exotic, impressionism—demonstrates their thingliness. Rilke then captures a different variety of thingliness in a more familiar urban setting in the poem "Das Karussell (Jardin du Luxembourg)" (The Carousel [Luxembourg Garden], 1908), in which the reduced representation of the same creature, now expressly part of a human artifice, recurs provocatively as a key color and sound motif ("And now and then a white elephant").[19] While, on the surface, the human story too seems relegated to the equalizing painterly chromatics (e.g., "red lion," "blue girl"),[20] the observer's

18. Cf. my commentary in this regard in my discussion of John Burt Foster's book, *Heirs to Dionysos: A Nietzschean Current in Literary Modernism* (Princeton, N.J.: Princeton University Press, 1981), in *Comparative Literature* 37 (1985): 85–90.

19. "Und dann und wann ein weißer Elefant."

20. "roter Löwe," "blaues Mädchen," etc.

voice ironically frames the vision by turns of phrase that undercut the moment as it might appear to childlike watchers or captivated children (e.g., "before it sets," "just as in the woods, only that"),[21] and reaches an essentially metaphysical insight and also a poetological self-commentary ("this breathless blind play").[22] In both of these poems the implicit observing intelligence still appears to maintain the impressionist propriety of gazing at a neutral object-in-time as Monet does in his famous series of paintings of the cathedral of Rouen under different kinds of light. Rilke, however, writes as if he presupposes the evocation of the dispersonalized "symbol" as a step in grasping its secret.

Rilke follows the symbolist moment when the linkage occurs between the principles of evocation and epiphany. A case in point is Leconte de l'Isle's disciple, José-Maria de Hérédia, who expressly gives the title "Epiphanie" to a sonnet evoking the journey of the Magi as they travel forever "in the old images" in the luminosity of cathedral windows.[23] He may have inspired T. S. Eliot's more dramatic narrative poem "The Journey of the Magi" (1927), and Joyce, who knew the symbolists well, may have found epiphany to be a useful term for his own purposes. Be that as it may, Hérédia's aesthetic intention is clear from the poem "Vitrail" (Window) that just precedes "Epiphanie" in *Les trophées* (The Trophies, 1893). The "window" is an intersection of planes of time, views, viewpoints, and viewers who are implicated in the mysterious image. The word "Aujourd'hui" (Today) with which the sestina opens reinforces the implicit framing of line 1 ("Cette verrière a vu [. . .] " [This glass has seen (. . .)]) of the sonnet. As was noted in chapter one, the reader is paradoxically captured—along with the poetic mind whose vision has implicity involved him—in the permanent deathly stare of the entombed nobility who repose in the church in the roseate glow, having meanwhile become part of the image of the Middle Ages that remains to us ("[. . .] they gaze without seeing the rose of the stained glass window—ever radiant").[24]

21. "eh es untergeht," "ganz wie im Wald, nur daß," etc.

22. "dieses atemlose blinde Spiel"; preceding passages in "Das Karussell" cited from Rainer Maria Rilke, *Sämtliche Werke*, 6 vols., ed. Ruth Sieber-Rilke and Ernst Zinn (Weisbaden: Insel-Verlag, 1955–1966), 1.530f.

23. "dans les vieilles images" (cited from *Poésies complètes de José-Maria Hérédia: Les trophées, sonnets et poèmes divers* [Paris: Librairie Alphonse Lemerre, 1924; rpt., Geneva: Slatkine, 1979], 98; hereafter cited as *Les trophées*).

24. ". . . ils regardent sans voir / La rose du vitrail toujours épanouie" (*Les trophées*, 97). One of the earliest and most suggestive linkings of such symbolist window imagery, special "lights," and "the woven fabric of [. . .] texts, the miraculous filters" with Joyce's epiphanies is by Robert G. Cohn in *The Writer's Way in France* (Philadelphia: University of Pennsylvania Press, 1960), 207ff.

Epiphany

In literature, the structured mental experience of epiphany may involve minimally the capture or establishment of some image, but the latent or overt drama of epiphany in fiction fits into a more comprehensive narrative frame and the containing artwork aspires to an integrity higher than the truth or falsity of revelations attained by characters who may be present as experiencing subjects. Hence, as Zack Bowen notes, while the epiphanies of artist figures are not neccessarily more reliable gauges of truth than those of other characters in Joyce's works, such protagonists, with their inherent creative tension and developed imaginative craftmanship, provide a special opportunity for concentrated narrative synthesis. Stephen's celebrated vision of the girl on the beach at the end of *A Portrait of the Artist as a Young Man* (1916) is such an instance. Joyce depicts the coalescence of Stephen's aesthetic ideas and creative capacity in a moment when the protagonist can fleetingly glimpse his own experience with the objectivity of a demiurgic playwright:

> So Stephen is led to describe the artistic process of epiphany-making. The three forms in the hierarchy of values regarding epiphanic—lyric, epic, and dramatic—deal with the artist's concept and image of himself: "the lyrical form, the form wherein the artist presents his image in immediate relation to himself; the epical form, the form wherein he presents his image in mediate relation to himself and others; (and) the dramatic form, the form wherein he presents his image in immediate relations to others."[25]

This specific hierarchical scheme advanced by Stephen, even if it is just one thread for Joyce—other novelists have their own variations— nonetheless demonstrated why the epiphany could be developed into an elaborate narrative procedure. Beyond episodic nuclei around which chapters may cohere, the first complex order of epiphany in narrative fiction is that associated with the mental life of an aesthete or artist.

There are innumerable instances when as priviledged listeners we hear Proust's (as yet unnamed) narrator in *Swann's Way* recount specific moments of aesthetic breakthrough based on his own experiences. Toward the end of the Combray section, for example, the narrator (Marcel) recalls, through the virtually time-liberated optic of an indefinite later moment, the overwhelming vision of Mme de Guermantes in the church. We are privy not just to a recollection of the complex process by which Marcel integrated all his prior knowledge and imaginings about

---

25. Bowen, "Joyce and the Epiphany Concepts," 111.

her with the human actuality of the person and the occasion, but to a recollection of an epiphany occurring in a context that is effectively unlocked by this epiphany. Through Marcel we submit to the spell and totality of a ritual that marks, but qualifies, biological and social time, the wedding mass; we are further initiated into a living, and dying structure, the church at Combray that houses the meaning of his vision in many forms, including entire works of art therein that incorporate the strata of time focused by his epiphany. There is a point of "lyrical" precipitation in the recollected experience when Marcel recognizes his attraction to the duchess. His youthful interpretation of her gesture of tenderness, first associated synesthetically with the light, cloth, and flowers that produce "a bloom of luminosity" (SLT 1.251)[26] flows over into an overt critical insight, a mature reference to instances where the arts—"certain pages of Lohengrin, certain paintings by Carpaccio, [. . .] Baudelaire" (SLT 1.251)[27]—have synesthetically bridged the realms.

This intrusion of the implicitly aged narrator functions like a punctuation mark separating the recollected internal event from an immediately following, second stage of awareness for young Marcel that results in a conscious, successful effort to shape, through art, a realization of an epiphany. The happenings in the church—which for the reader effectively reach an epiphanic climax—function in the faintly traced plot line as a formative stimulus for Marcel to cross a boundary in life. He starts to pursue the secret of impressions that arrest his attention, and one day, fascinated by the towers of Martinville, after glimpsing them over again, he attempts to capture the experience of sudden insight—an epiphany not unlike Stephen's encounter with the clock of the Ballast Office—in a descriptive fragment. Comparable to the focusing of a spiritual eye is the moment of partial unveiling:

> And presently their outlines and their sunlit surfaces, as though they had been a sort of rind, peeled away; something of what they had concealed from me became apparent; a thought came into my mind which had not existed for me a moment earlier, framing itself in words in my

26. Illustrative passages are deliberately repeated here from chapter one. English citations, indicated by SLT with volume and page number, follow Marcel Proust, *In Search of Lost Time*, trans. by C. K. Scott Moncrieff and Terence Kilmartin, rev. by D. J. Enright (New York: Modern Library, 1998). Citations from the French, indicated by R with volume and page number, follow the Pléiade edition: Marcel Proust, *A la recherche du temps perdu*, ed. Jean-Yves Tadié (Paris: Gallimard, 1987). The original reads: "une épiderme de lumière" (R, 1.176).

27. "certaines pages de Lohengrin, certaines peintures de Carpaccio, [. . .] Baudelaire" (R, 1.176).

head; and the pleasure which the first sight of them had given me was so greatly enhanced that, overpowered by a sort of intoxication, I could no longer think of anything else. (SLT 1.255)[28]

The second complex order of epiphany is constituted when the point of view of such a guiding protagonist is relativized. This occurs when the Stephen of *Portrait* becomes one of several principal voices and points of view alongside Bloom's and Molly's in *Ulysses,* and because Joyce employs a wide range of divergent techniques of narration, a multiplicity of styles, and a vast network of correlated motifs, symbols, settings, and allusions to art, religion, and mythology in this polyphonic composition. Proust too ultimately subordinates his own "portrait of the artist as a young man" to the larger rhythms and aims of his *roman fleuve.*

Among the radical generic shifts, we must instantly regress from the "overture" of *Swann's Way,* the dreamlike meditation spoken by a troubled mature mind, into the childhood at Combray evoked in dream, then again emerge from it into the insomniac bleakness of middle age, but in order to share with the unnamed narrator the crucial mature epiphany, his tasting of the sacramental "piece of madeleine soaked in her decoction of lime-blossom" (SLT 1.64),[29] which, by triggering involuntary memory, permanently and luxuriantly evokes for him and for us the vision of Easter at Combray and of growing up. But upon arrival with this self-examining first-person voice at a significant youthful boundary of creative response, and before we see the formation of a budding author completed in the recovered memory of Combray, Proust startles us by shifting without explanation and in medias res to "Un amour de Swann" (Swann in Love, part 2 of *Swann's Way*), that is, to an exemplary Flaubert-like narration in the third person. In virtual fact, with our implicit acquiescence, the hypothetical artist has disappeared behind his own omniscient voice in postepiphanic clarity into the perfected nineteenth-century genre and only the revealed existence of Swann at a critical juncture in Swann's life remains.

In Proust, the individual attainment of insight, even that of the narrator as an authorial persona, is woven into an elaborate tapestry of leit-

28. "Bientôt leurs lignes et leurs surfaces ensoleillées, comme elles avaient été une sorte d'écorcé, se dechirèrent, un peu de ce qui m'était caché en elles m'apparut, j'eus une pensée qui n'existait pas pour moi l'instant avant, qui se formula en mots dans ma tête, et le plaisir que m'avait fait tout à l'heure éprouver leur vue s'en trouva tellement accru que, pris d'une sorte d'ivresse, je ne pus plus penser à autre chose" (R, 1.178f.).
29. "morceau de madeleine trempé dans le tilleul" (R, 1.47).

motifs. In the symphonic composition of *A la recherche*, the epiphany attaches and reattaches the individual mind to the binding threads of a traditional tropology. Thus the metaphor of the lime tea and the madeleine is both conclusive and prefatory, both a rediscovery of the sacramental mystery of incarnation and a disclosure of the potent trope of spring. Proust's use of tropological guideposts from the religious calendar—"the only true holidays, the holy days of religion"—is abundantly evident in the celebrated passages where Marcel, amid the hawthornes "as though I had been standing before the Lady-altar," encounters the "pink one" (SLT 1.194–96) and experiences the arresting vision of Gilberte as a little girl whose black eyes he can only see as blue.[30] Here the narrator's irony gently mutes the epiphany; we are never really permitted to lapse into forgetting that the anachronism, only apparent, springs from the fact that memory, following the liberating insight, must inherently be channeled through the recollecting, hence mature, mind. Finally, among other supreme acts of anamnesis in *Swann's Way*, the representative aspects of the feminine—for example, the triad of the witchlike old woman reading the paper, young Gilberte, and Odette as queen strolling through the park—become copresent with the realized system of the tropes; childhood days and spring are enfolded in elegiac summation; and the influence of art, for example, Bergotte's, is no longer separable from other factors in the narrator's individuation or in Proust's motific and temporal cross-cutting and fusion of images at the close.

With open reference to its own master tropes and compositional aims, the coda of the first book decisively shifts into the autumnal mood:

> That complexity of the Bois de Boulogne which makes it an artificial place and, in the zoological or mythological sense of the word, a Garden, came to me again this year [. . .] the transformation scene of autumn [. . .] the time of year at which the Bois de Boulogne displays more separate characteristics, assembles more distinct elements in a composite whole than any other. (SLT 1.598–600)[31]

The Bois, combining the topoi of "wood" (labyrinth) and "garden," the narrator clearly envisions as man's reconstruction of nature also into a

---

30. "ces seules vraies fêtes que sont les fêtes religieuses"; "devant l'autel de la Vierge"; "épine rose" (R, 1.136–37). "Epine rose" is literally "rose hawthorne."

31. "Cette complexité du Bois de Boulogne qui en fait un lieu factice et, dans le sense zoologique ou mythologique du mot, un Jardin, je l'ai retrouvée cette année [. . .] spectacle de l'automne [. . .] où le Bois de Boulogne trahit le plus d'essences diverses et juxtapose le plus de parties distinctes en un assemblage composite" (R, 1.414–15).

social artifice, and as such this large model of the artwork both reveals and copes with the thematized threat of "absence," the loss of magic and meaning. This grandly orchestrated coda imitates at large the epiphanic process of spiritual refocusing in a multitude of preparatory and cumulatively contributory moments. The only anticipatory instance of an epiphany of relatively comparable complexity is the long segment on Swann's torment during the evening at the Saint-Euvertes' told in the third person. Insights from all the arts crowded into Swann's mind and, after a series of preliminary peaks, are brought into resolving focus by his new attunement to "the little phrase from Vinteuil's sonata" (SLT 1.490).[32] Elsewhere the orchestration of epiphany ordinarily does not greatly exceed in complexity the scale of specific channels or approaches in art being discovered by Marcel—for example, the alteration of his perceptions anticipating, yet enhanced by his interest in, the painter Elstir's impressionism in *A l'ombre des jeunes filles en fleurs* (Within a Budding Grove), the second volume of *A la recherche.*

But Proust believes that disparate single instances of epiphany must eventually also bear some relation to the total effect of a masterwork. Because so many characters in his *roman fleuve* are depicted as sharing wittingly or unwittingly in some fashion in the experience of key, representative expressions in art—most notable, perhaps, is the Vinteuil phrase—artworks gain an extraordinary historical and ontological status, which in turn is reflected in their romanesque value in Proust's plotting of his novel. The metaphor of the crossroads is already latent in Paris, with its modern Étoile and other intersections, before the narrator discovers them; Paris is a warren of intersections, a crossroads of crossroads. Like persons and societies, artworks are "real" intersections in time, and we could legitimately apply to them what Proust says about the gathering or resolving function of Mademoiselle de Saint-Loup through whom at last the ways of Swann and the Guermantes join:

> Was she not—are not, indeed, the majority of human beings?—like one of those star-shaped crossroads in a forest where roads converge that have come, in the forest as in our lives, from the most diverse quarters? Numerous for me were the roads which led to Mlle de Saint-Loup and which radiated around her. (SLT 6.502)[33]

32. "la petite phrase de la sonate de Vinteuil" (R, 1.339).
33. "Comme la plupart des êtres, d'ailleurs, n'était-elle pas comme sont dans les forêts les 'étoiles' des carrefours où viennent converger des routes venues, pour notre vie aussi,

Two basic tendencies of "superepiphanic" progression, which often work in tandem, are the convergence into nodular junctures (Proust's "star-shaped crossroads" [SLT 6.502])[34] and the cumulative cross-referencing of consciousness and points of view. An outstanding example of the first kind of progression is Woolf's experiment in *To the Lighthouse* (1927) with its final convergence of the going and of the completed painting that incorporates the going. The joint undertaking of the surviving members of the Ramsey family synchronizes with Lily's achievement of her vision, both in the work of art she creates and in her personal realization of the truth behind the enigma of the dead Mrs. Ramsey, upon whom, as Erich Auerbach has said, "the content of all the various consciousness" in the novel, including Mrs. Ramsey's own, is directed. Woolf accomplishes the natural evolution of the novel from "the unipersonal subjective method" to the "multipersonal method with synthesis as its aim"; "the exterior events have lost their hegemony, they serve to release and interpret inner events."[35] I would add that the convergence in the final symbolic situation and the haunting presence of the central symbol of the lighthouse throughout combine to bring Woolf's novel very close to the novella form. This effect is all the more enhanced by the involution of time (nominally at least ten years) into an archetypal present whose fullness contains also what is only apparently absent. We experience this through the trope of the summer holiday—here as the time of going to the lighthouse across the feminine waters. Even though Woolf's novel *Orlando, a Biography* (1928) clearly embraces many centuries in the evolutionary time of the human spirit, these are glimpsed as a continum that is yielded by the transformations undergone by its androgynous title figure, and the discovery process that carries us to the mysterious night scene and reunion, culminating at the stroke of midnight on "Thursday the eleventh of October, Nineteen Hundred and Twentyeight," so powerfully ties all events to a core symbolism that this book too resembles a novella.[36] Thus, although ostensibly we might associate the evolutionary paradigm with Joyce's through-composed parody of centuries of English writing in the "Oxen of the Sun" chapter in

des points les plus différents? Elles étaient nombreuses pour moi, celles qui aboutissaient à Mlle de Saint-Loup et qui rayonnaient autour d'elle" (R, 4.606).

34. "étoiles des carrefours."

35. Erich Auerbach, *Mimesis: The Representation of Reality in Western Literature*, trans. Willard R. Trask (Princeton, N.J.: Princeton University Press, 1953), 536.

36. Virginia Woolf, *Orlando, a Biography* (New York: Harcourt, Brace, 1928), 329; these are the very final words.

Epiphany

Ulysses, Orlando is in certain respects, despite all the many differences, closer formalistically to Mann's *Der Tod in Venedig* (Death in Venice), the pseudobiographical novella of that ambivalent representative of the Western ethos, Gustav Achenbach.

I have stressed two phenomena often associated with the complex constellation of epiphany: the relativizing of the role of the internal experiencer and/or the expansion of an educational protagonist into an encyclopedic vehicle for important insights that the author seeks to configure. In either case, the novelist tends to shift some or most of the epiphanic work onto an ideal competent reader, or to seek a qualitative reinstatement of myth, or to wrest from mutable language a triumph of poetic vision as ecphrasis. Innumerable illustrations of a transference to the reader beckon, but I shall cite here one that happens simultaneously to demonstrate the widespread modernist awareness of the new medium of film. In chapter 5 of *Der Zauberberg* (The Magic Mountain, 1924), the ironizing authorial voice, taking us along with Hans Castorp into the actually and aptly named "Bioskop-Theater," and giving trenchant details about the shows and spectator reactions, analyzes the all-too-human appeal of cinema "constructed [. . .] to cater to the innermost desires of an onlooking international civilization" (MM 317).[37] But then, quite suddenly, we are conducted through a startlingly compact montage of cinematic newsreels and documentaries that exhibit the mental and cultural strata of actual diverse peoples on many continents, who for the most part unconscious of the global pattern of human existence are hurtling toward a catastrophe at the start of the twentieth century. This ghostly revelation, that fades out with the word "Ende," is already available to, and is principally consumed within, the endangered West; but implicitly only the reader awakened to the meaning of dream by the naked display of dreaming—not the mesmerized viewers—truly sees the "Phantom."[38]

Comparable is the montage rendering Bloom's vision in which the bestial horror of the "murderers of the sun" is transcended to reveal the glorious archetype of the queen of heaven and thus the father. To be-

37. See chapter six, "Cinematic Narration in the Modernist Novel." English citations, indicated by MM and pagination, are from Thomas Mann, *The Magic Mountain*, trans. H. T. Lowe-Porter (New York: Modern Library, 1952). German citations, indicated by Zb and pagination, are from Thomas Mann, *Der Zauberberg: Roman* (Frankfurt: Fischer Taschenbuch Verlag, 1987). The original German reads here: "hergestellt, aus sympathischer Vertrautheit mit den geheimen Wünschen der zuschauenden internationalen Zivilisation" (Zb, 335).
38. Thomas Mann, Zb, 336.

gin with, the passage belongs in the flow of the above-mentioned parody of stages in the evolution of English through which Joyce chooses to
narrate the "Oxen of the Sun" chapter, set in the maternity ward where
the birth of Mrs. Purefoy's child is awaited. Although the tenor of the vision as a kind of projected reading of Bloom's imagination accords with
Bloom's sentiments, the part is, of course, primarily a linguistic and motivic tour de force. Though shot through with narrative irony, it nonetheless has the serious purposes of enabling a joint climax of the parodied
styles and "a myriad metamorphoses of symbols"—but the reader senses that he or she shares this more immediately with the hidden author,
rather than attains to it through the experiencing character.[39]

The famous "Snow" section of chapter 6 in *The Magic Mountain* illustrates the movement to and fro between a more directly authorial discourse, as in Mann's meditative overtures to chapters 6 and 7, and discourse effected through the intermediation of an educational protagonist
who serves as the chief encyclopedic vehicle. In the "Snow" episode it is
primarily the sheer adventure of the penetration by Castorp, "our son of
civilization," into "the uncanny" (MM 477)[40] that grips the reader's attention.[41] But since the immediately recognizable ground pattern is the entry by a quester into a dangerous wilderness or realm of enchantment as
in a romance (or, by analogy, a Wagnerian opera), and since Mann quite
openly comments on the thematics of the symbolic drama into which we
are being drawn, we can scarcely miss the interplay of supporting leitmotifs and newly compounded allusions, while the narration is fluctuating
over reportage, authorial reconstruction of Castorp's thoughts, indirect
speech, and fragments of direct quotation. With the juxtaposition and
blending of elements from various temporal zones of life experience, and
sometimes through associational techniques familiar in Freudian psychology, Mann creates a modern counterpart to romantic dream structures with a transcendent symbolism. The measure of his success is the
culmination of the "Snow" episode, Castorp's famous epiphany, when he
"remembers" the crucial evolutionary moment of ancient culture.

I am not concerned here with the relative importance of artistic ri-
valries and influences (e.g., Renaissance paintings, Goethe's treatment
of myth, Hoffmann's fantasies on art, Wagner's compositions), or of
ideas from anthropology and the philosophy of history (e.g., Bachofen's,

39. James Joyce, *Ulysses* (New York: Vintage Books, 1961), 414.
40. "das Kind der Zivilisation"; "das Unheimliche" (Zb, 503, 506).
41. The adventure proper starts from page 500 of *Der Zauberberg*.

Nietzsche's), in Mann's portrayal of this complex act of anamnesis, but rather with its artistic structure. Eventually released by the Dionysian sacramental potion ("Portwein") Castorp's mind floats in a synthesis of home sights, odors, and sounds that "literally" become opera music and through this he arrives ecstatically in the blue realm of the sacred Mediterranean.[42] There he witnesses the dignity of emergent civilization and his gaze is directed by a John the Baptist-Hermes figure to the temple at its core. Having passed the female figures enshrined there (Demeter and Persephone), Castorp penetrates to the inner chamber where he glimpses the horror of the witches dismembering and devouring a child—a sight that jolts him out of the arms of death into a momentary new level of wakeful dreaming more lucid than conscious life. Castorp's dream combines both Freudian and Jungian features; for example, the witches curse anachronistically in the dialect of his Northern homeland, yet his is a communal dream retrieved from the depths of the Western mind:

> Now I know that it is not out of our single souls we dream. We dream anonymously and communally, if each after his own fashion. The great soul of which we are a part may dream through us, in our manner of dreaming, its own secret dreams, of its youth, its hope, its joy and peace—and its blood sacrifice. (MM 495)[43]

We share his illumination that the myth of the earth mother contains the horror of the mindless cycle of nature, but that, by building the temple to house the sacred mystery, a consciousness acquires form, and there is a beginning of meaning: "And from love and goodness alone can form come" (MM 496).[44] This epiphany impels Castorp to conceive his own affirmation, "a dream poem of humanity" (MM 496),[45] and to oppose love to death. The "Snow" episode expansively recapitulates much of the technique of rendering archetypal dreaming earlier seen in the novella *Death in Venice*. Of course, the positive outcome for Castorp is quite different from that for Aschenbach, from whose vivid Apollonian reveries the counterpart Aphroditean glory is conspiciously missing,

---

42. The passage into the epiphanic vision starts on 516.

43. "Man träumt nicht nur aus eigener Seele, möcht' ich sagen, man träumt anonym und gemeinsam, wenn auch auf eigene Art. Die große Seele, von der du nur ein Teilchen, träumt wohl mal durch dich, auf deine Art, von Dingen, die sie heimlich immer träumt,—von ihrer Jugend, ihrer Hoffnung, ihrem Glück und Frieden . . . und ihrem Blutmahl" (Zb, 521).

44. "Auch Form ist nur aus Liebe und Güte" (Zb, 523). I have slightly modified Lowe-Porter's English.

45. "ein Traumgedicht vom Menschen" (Zb, 523).

until a primordial feminine emerges with the maenads in his orgiastic dream shortly before his death. Dionysos revenges himself on the representative Western intellectual when Aschenbach fatefully retrieves the deeper meaning of his own classical heritage from such long forgotten readings as Euripides' *Bacchae*.

The omnipresence of mythological allusions and the outright reinvocation of myth in modern fiction exhibit, among other things, the thirst for a poetic language that will inevitably conduct toward or virtually in itself constitutes epiphany. Limits of space forbid entering into a therewith connected third order of complex epiphany that sometimes occurs as modernist ecphrasis. Following the lead of Noon, Raymond Prier has shown how already in *Ulysses* Joyce engages in radical linguistic innovation to rival the archaic style:

> to destroy the horizontal more superficial nature of modern prose style, and to deepen the vertical, "meaningful" nature of his own. [. . .] The "secret" of the [archaic] style is unconscious non-horizontal repetition, a piling up of language that both reveals and induces a particular psychological, temporal condition.[46]

In the case of Joyce, at least, we observe a writer who strives for far more than the spatialization of consciousness in ironic signs when he helps us leave history and reenter myth through our experience of the symbolic structure of words.[47]

46. Raymond A. Prier, "Joyce's Linguistic Imitation of Homer: The 'Cyclops Episode' and the Radical Appearance of the Catalogue Style," *Neohelicon* 14, no. 1 (1988): 39–66.

47. Michael Davidson examines the problematical concept of narrative spatialization from a hermeneutic perspective in an article on "Ekphrasis and the Postmodern Painter Poem," *Journal of Aesthetics and Art Criticism* 42 (1983): 69–79. There have been careful attempts to see a potentially postmodern tendency that springs out of Joyce's comic genius and linguistic experimentation—e.g., Pierre Vitoux, "L'esthétique de Joyce: De l'épiphanie à la déconstruction de l'objet," *Cahiers Victoriens et Edouardiens* 14 (1981): 89–101. Nonetheless, as Prier argues, we still need a better distinction between Western hyposyntactic spatialization (and I would add "mere" poetologically self-referential "deconstructive" writing), on the one hand, and Joycean linguistic ecphrasis, on the other. Meanwhile, the spread of the term "epiphany," with a concomitant widening of its semantic field in the later twentieth century, is evident from articles extending it, above all, to novella and short story writers—e.g., Lee B. Jennings, "Keller's Epiphanies," *German Quarterly* 55 (1982): 316–23, or Efraim Sicher, "Art as Metaphor, Epiphany, and Aesthetic Statement: The Short Stories of Isaak Babel," *Modern Language Review* 77 (1982): 387–96.

3 THE PLACE OF
FIN-DE-SIÈCLE NATURE

This older fin-de-siècle coincided with the apogee of modern European imperialism. The effects of several centuries of detailed encounters and symbioses with non-European peoples and places complicated even further the context in which the diverse range of European nature could be comprehended. The imperialist climax occurred in tandem with profound alterations in the structures of living and their evaluation, especially in the more rapidly industrializing and urbanizing parts of Western Europe. Any adequate answer to "where" nature was situated around 1900 requires looking into a host of rival views about the man-nature relationship, and these many interlaced, often contradictory, attitudes are our actual heritage from the European experience.

Therefore, I ask you to think of my cluster of examples drawn from literature as expressions actually surrounded by the city-, town- and landscapes of the times, and as expressions interactive with scientific and social thought, as well as with the other arts. It was during the period spanning from the work of the poet Charles Baudelaire at midcentury to that of the sociologist Georg Simmel[1] at the turn of the century that European attention shifted decisively from wild and rural nature as a model to the urban realm, and away from an Enlightenment view of the individual protagonist acting in society toward an anthropological-psychological interest in interior mental structures. The historically intertwined literary moments of naturalism and symbolism in the last decades of the nineteenth century can be pulled apart analytically, but due respect for their inherent ambivalence obligates us to see them again as aspects of a contest among inconsistencies sometimes reciprocal and asymmetrical.

Actual citizens who happened to be devoted to positivistic and ma-

1. Georg Simmel, "Die Großstädte und das Geistesleben" (Big Cities and the Life of the Mind), in *Aufsätze und Abhandlungen 1901–1908*, Bd. 1., ed. Rüdiger Kramme and Angela and Otthein Rammstedt (*Gesamtausgabe*, ed. Otthein Rammstedt, Bd. 8) (Frankfurt: Suhrkamp, 1995), 116–31. Originally published in the volume *Die Großstadt, Jahrbuch der Gehe-Stiftung zu Dresden* 9 (1903): 185–206.

terialist views of nature—who regarded nature as something requiring mainly good social goals and management—walked, in those days of naturalism and symbolism, past the controversial new impressionist paintings on the walls of avant-garde galleries and ate lunch with acquaintances who were reading books in which the hard surfaces of reality were dissolving into that flux of impressions so powerfully evoked by Walter Pater in the famous conclusion to *Studies in the History of the Renaissance* in 1873. Pater suppressed his conclusion in the second edition retitled *The Renaissance: Studies in Art and Poetry* (1877) out of concern for how it might affect the young, but restored it with slight changes in the third edition (1888). Its relevance justifies pausing a moment to sample Pater's sense of a general breakup of an objective external order in art:

> Or if we begin with the inward whirl of thought and feeling, the whirlpool is still more rapid, the flame more eager and devouring. There is no longer the gradual darkening of the eye and fading of color from the wall,—the movement of the shoreside, where the water flows down indeed, though in apparent rest—but the race of the mid-stream, a drift of momentary acts of sight and passion and thought. At first sight experience seems to bury us under a flood of external objects, pressing upon us with a sharp and importunate reality, calling us out of ourselves in a thousand forms of action. But when reflection begins to act upon those objects they are dissipated under its influence; the cohesive force seems suspended like a trick of magic; each object is loosed into a group of impressions—color, odor, texture—in the mind of the observer. And if we continue to dwell in thought on this world, not of objects in the solidity with which language invests them, but of impressions unstable, flickering, inconsistent, which burn and are extinguished with our consciousness of them, it contracts still further; the whole scope of observation is dwarfed to the narrow chamber of the individual mind.[2]

Clearly, these insights posed a serious challenge to materialist views of nature. That they were not incompatible with a tough-minded recognition of biological groundedness is evident when we turn to the contemporaneous philosopher Friedrich Nietzsche. In 1872 in *Die Geburt der Tragödie aus dem Geiste der Musik* (The Birth of Tragedy Out of the Spirit

2. Walter Pater, *Walter Pater: Three Major Texts ("The Renaissance," "Appreciations" and "Imaginary Portraits")*, ed. William E. Buckler (New York: New York University Press, 1986), 218.

of Music) Nietzsche proposed that twinned principles manifested themselves in the actions of the human psyche: a Dionysian impulsion expressing the "effusion of the unconscious will" and an Apollonian drive to shape, define, and transfigure.[3] In this revision of the great romantic atheist Arthur Schopenhauer, "the glorious Apollonian illusion, [. . .] the image, the concept, the ethical teaching and the sympathetic emotion [. . .] tears man from his orgiastic self-annihilation and hides the universality of the Dionysian process from him" (Birth 128).[4] It is crucial that Nietzsche abandons formulating the operation of the inexorable laws of life either in Hegelian idealist-historicist or in materialist-sensationalist terms, and instead envisions process and flux as having a deep structure determined by the unconscious. Now "music is the real idea of the world, drama"—that is, tragic myth—"is but the reflection of this idea" (Birth 129).[5]

These two examples must suffice for the moment to indicate a direction in thought and literary expression that flourishes around 1900: the approach to nature as a sometimes deceptive surface beneath whose phenomena one discerns elusive pattern-making forces in action. But, as its solidity dissolved, where did that older nature relocate itself to? What happened to that part free and savage, part beneficent and domesticated nature so prevalent at the time of the American and French Revolutions—that is, of a cresting organicist faith in the great chain of being and in the therein embedded human sentiments; what became of that nature that once represented the nurturing source of an eventually achievable earthly paradise? During the intense industrialization and urbanization of the nineteenth century, such a nature more broadly conceived indeed continued to occupy its traditional roles, but it also began to invade new hosts. It withdrew into the construct of the park in the metropolitan territories and receded into the remoter exterior and exotic zones opened by European imperialism. It turned into esoteric and

3. Friedrich Nietzsche, *"The Birth of Tragedy" and "The Case of Wagner,"* trans. Walter Kaufmann (New York: Vintage Books, 1967), 128; hereafter cited as Birth. "Ergusse des unbewussten Willens" (*Die Geburt der Tragödie aus dem Geiste der Musik,* in Nietzsche, *Werke,* ed. Giorgio Colli and Mazzino Montinari, vol. 3, part 1 [New York: Walter de Gruyter, 1972], 133).
4. "jene herrliche apollinische Täuschung"; [Mit der ungeheuren Wucht] "des Bildes, des Begriffs, der esthetischen Lehre, der sympathischen Erregung reisst das Apollinische den Menschen aus seiner orgiastischen Selbstvernichtung empor und täuscht ihn über die Allgemeinheit des dionysischen Vorganges hinweg" (Geburt, 133).
5. "die Musik ist die eigentliche Idee der Welt, das Drama nur ein Abglanz dieser Idee" (Geburt, 134).

interior precincts of culture and literature within the confines of brash nineteenth-century economic and social development. The city itself was discovered to be the new heightened or lowered nature, and the literary feminization of urban existence in place of nature completed the reevaluation. Nature also intruded everywhere in urban consciousness in the form of inextinguishable primary myths, and by century's end nature was widely held to exert its powers out of the unconscious, out of its supposed bastion in the psyche. Let us now consider seriatim specific illustrations of these cardinal aspects of literature's nature.

Monographic treatments such as those by Chadwick and Thacker[6] will convince those as yet unfamiliar with the rich cultural history of parks just how long and complex it is. The arts and crafts of classical villa gardens and the poetic and cosmological sense of paradise embodied in ancient garden culture were preserved by the medieval monastic establishments and bequeathed to the Renaissance. The prestige of the park in the eighteenth century is unimaginable without the innumerable earlier gardens of poetry as in Boccaccio and Petrarch, and of love as in the *Roman de la rose,* or without the Academy garden from Socrates and Cicero to Ficino, and Renaissance attempts to represent an ideal cosmos through parks and urban restoration. By a natural process of transference, princely parks gradually came into the broader public domain. In an early instance, Charles I opened Hyde Park to his subjects to cultivate their goodwill in 1635. Thriving cities grew out around great princely pleasure grounds in early modern Europe and eventually incorporated them as a treasured part of the urban core, such as Munich filled in around the so-named English Garden, which the American-born Benjamin Thompson proposed as a "people's park" to Karl Theodor of Bavaria in the great revolutionary year 1789. By the mid-nineteenth century, the idea had taken firm hold that a major metropolis required impressive parks to affirm its world rank, to afford the elegant classes a splendid backdrop for social parading, and to grant the urban population at large access to salubrious air and recreation. Thus, in the 1850s, Baron Georges Eugène Haussmann, as prefect of Paris, undertook the enormous task of reordering the present-day Bois de Boulogne as just such a city park. In the same decade, despite many political problems, the authorities of New York managed to acquire and redesign the huge rectangular area in

6. George F. Chadwick, *The Park and the Town: Public Landscape in the Nineteenth and Twentieth Centuries* (New York and Washington, D.C.: Praeger, 1966); Christopher Thacker, *The History of Gardens* (Berkeley and Los Angeles: University of California Press, 1979).

Manhattan that became Central Park. Four million foreign and domestic visitors were counted by 1863, eleven million by 1871. By the fin-de-siècle, parks captured, managed, and internalized nature for urban life, whether in the shape of absorbed, formerly princely precincts or as daring new creations of the bourgeois age itself.

Below I shall take up the relevance of the park as a wilderness preserve set within larger nature, external to the city but meant for the edification of civilized people. This concept appeared in the American movement to create national parks, the first of which was the remote Yellowstone National Park established in 1872. A more immediate issue is the way in which the city usurped the place of nature in the nineteenth century, or, seen from a contrary perspective, how nature infiltrated and subverted the city. Since I treat this tendency at greater length in the following chapter, some of the directly pertinent points can be summed up briefly here. In the poetry of Charles Baudelaire, as criticism has long since noted, the city takes on what was formerly nature's broader role as the primary scene of human experience. Older categories such as the idyll and the pastoral are transposed onto the city and commingled with recognition of its geometrical, mechanical, and relentless aspects and of the deformation of Rousseauesque natural or Schillerian naive man in it. In the resultant new aesthetic, the postromantic epistemological status of the self gets linked to that of the city. Baudelaire's Paris is the simultaneously dystopic and intoxicant showplace where human frustration and desire are juxtaposed. The metropolis is recognized in *Les fleurs du mal* (Flowers of Evil, 1857) as a complex sign system that, on the one hand, proffers bafflement, in its guise as a labyrinthine hell, site of the diseased, criminal, demonic, and uncanny; and, on the other hand, constitutes a spectacle, a form of inspiration, a veritable drug. Spelled out with dazzling intensity in the poetry of Arthur Rimbaud, and eventually revisited by the German expressionists, is the interplay between the degradation, strangeness, and repressiveness of the city and the monstrous consequences of its energy, a source of a new kind of beauty. Rimbaud explicitly connects this energy to the savage power in alien peoples beyond the edges of decadent Europe and senses it boiling below the civilized surface in the European underclasses.

Quite familiar too for their reintroduction of savage and unreliable nature into orderly metropolitan Europe are all those stories of adventure set either in the New World that Europeans had extensively settled or in yet remoter, untamable colonial hinterlands where European sway necessarily has ceded to otherness. Two of Arthur Conan Doyle's tales, *A Study in Scarlet* and *The Sign of Four* (both 1887), illustrate the theme of an interpenetration of center and periphery, while also exhibiting the mutual generic contamination among such popular nineteenth-century forms as the detective fiction, the romance, and the historical fiction.[7] In *A Study in Scarlet*, the Victorian gentleman Dr. John H. Watson, retired from military service in India, first introduces us to that eccentric hermeneut Sherlock Holmes and the science of deduction whereby, in the literary tradition of Edgar Allan Poe's Dupin in Paris, he reads the phenomenal surface of London and investigates the operation and source of forces and motivations that threaten British civilization. If the closer half of the narrated action is located in the imperial capital, the other half occurs mainly in the bleak high desert and mountains of the United States in the new Mormon country. We also glimpse the intermediate settled territory from Ohio to the East Coast, in the course of a tale of inhuman fanaticism versus redemptive love. The backwash of evil into London from Europeans who have gone wrong on the savage frontier is checked by "our detective police forces," so that the case "will serve as a lesson to all foreigners that they will do wisely to settle their feuds at home, and not to carry them on to British soil" (Study/Sign 130–31). This is one of the general teachings of Bram Stoker's *Dracula* (1897), when a vampire from the semi-European fringe country of Transylvania, that horror of invading otherness, crosses the watery *cordon sanitaire* and threatens to pollute the very blood of the heartland. In *The Sign of Four*, lucre from the city of Agra, "a great place swarming with fanatics and fierce devil-worshippers of all sorts" (Study/Sign 233), is the evil that poisons the hearts of British military men and reaches back over a lifetime from the exotic perilous edges of empire into the home country. The embittered, wily Jonathan Small, returning to the island of his birth with his loyal alter ego Tonga, a "little Andaman Islander [. . .] as venomous as a young snake" (Study/Sign 248), exhibits the deformation that lurks in waiting when nature as otherness overwhelms civilized people.

The fin-de-siècle and the years up to World War I offer so many instances of this center/periphery theme and inner/outer displacements of nature's power that I shall cite just a few more reminders. Among the many juxtapositions in George Villiers de l'Isle-Adam's decadent symbolist play *Axel* (première 1894) are the protagonists' luxury of mind,

7. Arthur Conan Doyle, *"A Study in Scarlet" and "The Sign of Four"* (New York: Berkeley Books, 1975); cited as Study/Sign.

means, and cultural heritage and the primordial Black Forest wilderness wherein, in Axel's castle, as in a Grail castle, the innermost treasure and power reside. In *Heart of Darkness* (1902), Joseph Conrad's aged narrator Marlow, one evening on a barge on the Thames in the heart of London, tells of penetrating into the forbidding African jungle on the great Congo River and there discovering that the exemplary exponent of the European civilizing mission, the apologist for imperialism, Kurtz, has regressed into primordial savagery. Kurtz's consort is an African woman with queenly attributes. With pointed irony, Conrad has an unnamed listener as the frame narrator mentally summon the historical memory of the moment when Roman imperial forces disembarked on the Thames to face the ferocious ancient Britons led by their warrior queen.

The terror and power at the heart of things is always out there, and emerges inexorably. It is into that borne of the maternal and unconscious that the desperate, but all-too-human, modern man Borg steers at the conclusion of August Strindberg's novel *I Havsbandet* (By the Open Sea, 1890). Symbolically at Christmas like the young Werther before him, though desirous of Promethean achievement, Borg sets "out towards the new Christmas star, out over the sea, the mother of all, in whose womb the first spark of life was lit, the inexhaustible well of fertility and love, life's source, and life's enemy."[8] Luxuriant tangles of vegetation, ornate fin-de-siècle decors, and equally luxuriant literary associations in the interior narration by the aptly named Desiderio Moriar dominate Gabriele D'Annunzio's tale *Leda senza cigno* (Leda without Swan, 1913). This linguistic and environmental hypertrophy suggests the mysterious attraction of suicide for the passionate Leda. The narrator's consciousness of being on the edge of the infinite oceanic expresses her essence in the final lines:

> The canals, the sand banks, the dunes, the long thin spits, the thrusting promotories, the low undergrowth, all the internal lines went in accord with the line of the ocean's horizon, obeying a rhythm of sublime perfection granted to man only during the hour that follows his passing. In a silence the same as perfect nudity, the beauty of the Occident lay there supine. (Nocturne 214)[9]

8. August Strindberg, *By the Open Sea,* trans. Mary Sandbach (London: Secker & Warburg, 1984), 185.—"Ut mot den nya julstjärnan gick färden, ut över havet, allmodren, ut vars sköte livets första gnista tändes, fruktsamhetens, kärlekens outtömliga brunn, livets ursprung and livets fiende" (*I Havsbandet,* in August Strindberg, *Skrifter,* 14 vols. [Stockholm: Albert Bonniers Förlag, 1946–1953], 2.343).

9. Gabriele D'Annunzio, *"Nocturne" and "Five Tales of Love and Death,"* trans. Ray-

The reference at the end of D'Annunzio's story to the ontological and existential condition of Europe as a late, ripe civilization ready to be ravaged by nature's power is unmistakable. It is at this kind of edge, now on the Lido beach, that Thomas Mann places us, with Aschenbach, in *Death in Venice* in the same year.

Not only does Mann firmly calibrate his fin-de-siècle novel *Buddenbrooks* (1901) by events in the political and economic development of nineteenth-century Germany much as, a generation earlier, Gustave Flaubert's *L'éducation sentimentale* (Sentimental Education, 1869) referenced phenomena attending the axial year 1848 in Paris. Nature too is emblematic and palimpsestial like the rest of geocultural space that affects the Buddenbrook family. They do not fully comprehend the power residing in nature that seemingly has been incorporated into the city under human management. Hence in book 1, chapter 1, the family church, the gothic pile of St. Mary's, long since Protestant, sits on the hill called Mount Jerusalem, while in chapter 10, neoclassical order and romantic sensibility are visibly present as inherited options of the Goethean period in the form of an actual French and an English-style garden. In book 10, chapter 7, the ocean depths ominously yield up secret life and symbolic sacrificial creatures to what appears a dead wintry surface at a seasonal turning of time both for the doomed family and for the rising German nation of the Bismarkian period. The novelist simultaneously allows Wagnerian musicality to reign in the unfolding of the epochal story, but he exercises a Nietzschean analysis of the antilife consequences when, following the repression of Dionysian energy, it surges forth in the family as supposedly it erupts in late nineteenth-century culture in bodily and mental sickness. Mann conjures the sort of commingled terror and awe and yearning that many fin-de-siècle artists felt toward nature.

We encounter this full-blown conflict a decade earlier, in Knut Hamsun's symbolist detective novel *Mysterier* (Mysteries, 1892)—one of the many notable ancestors of the so-called postmodern metaphysical genre.[10] An unnamed outer narrator observes Nagel, the interloping investigator and soon frequent interior narrator, who arrives in garish fau-

mond Rosenthal (Marlboro, Vt.: Marlboro Press, 1988), 214.—"I canali, i banchi, le dune, le lunghe lingue sottili, i capi protesi, le macchie basse, tutte le interne linee secondavano quella dell'orizzonte oceanico, per obbedire a un ritmo di perfezione sublime non consentito agli uomini se non nella sola ora che seque il transito. In un silenzio eguale alla nudità perfetta, la bellezza dell'Occidente stava supina" (Gabriele d'Annunzio, *La Leda senza cigno*, ed. Ezio Raimondi and Niva Lorenzi, 2 vols. [Milan: Arnaldo Mondadori Editore, 1989], 2.940).

10. Knut Hamsun, *Mysteries*, trans. Gerry Bothmer (New York: Carroll & Graf, 1971).

vist attire in a picturesque Norwegian town on a fjord as the midsummer festival approaches. We readers come to suspect Nagel is himself some sort of fraud, regardless of whether he hallucinates about or sometimes has real insights into the criminality that he detects beneath the masks of the local populace. At times a euphoric sense of the world fills him as if he is perceiving a cosmic music, "—God turning his treadmill" (Bothmer 64).[11] At times existential nausea wells up, and he deems "people in general, love, life—all a hoax" (Bothmer 284).[12] The nagging conviction that "life was an unfathomable misery" (Bothmer 245)[13] deprives him of any lasting romantic bliss; his manic states can be suddenly superseded by wild dread, and he is "possessed by that vague, mysterious fear that he was approaching a catastrophe" (Bothmer 334).[14] Nagel resembles the unnamed narrator in Poe's vignette "The Man of the Crowd" (1842) who stalks interesting human specimens in their urban haunts but desists in one instance out of anxiety, as if choosing to abort a promising detective investigation. Nagel confides: "I have a habit of roaming streets, following people; sometimes I choose an individual to follow from afar to see where he ends up. At night in a large city it can be fascinating and lead to fantastic encounters" (Bothmer 319–20).[15] Reciprocally, he suffers from fear of being stalked:

> For instance, when walking up a flight of stairs, he sometimes caught himself looking around to see if someone was following him. Why? Perhaps because he sensed a mysterious essence which so-called science was too obtuse and too insensitive to perceive, an essence emanating from an invisible power—the supernatural making itself manifest. (Bothmer 159)[16]

The original Norwegian wording of quotations is drawn from Knut Hamsun, *Mysterier* (Gyldendal: Norsk Førlag, 1992).

11. "Gud, der traadte sit Hjul" (*Mysterier,* 93).

12. "alle Mennesker og Kaerligheden og Livet er Bedrag" (*Mysterier,* 439).

13. "Livet var ganske ubegribeligt elendigt" (*Mysterier,* 382).

14. "Og Angsten vilde ikke forlade ham, denne dumpe og hemmelige Fornemmelse af, at han befandt sig i Naerheden af en Fare, en Ulykke, slap ham ikke" (*Mysterier,* 508).

15. "Jeg driver nu og da omkring i Gaderne, jeg ser paa Mennesker, udvaelger mig en enkelt Person, som jeg forfølger i Frastand og ser, hvor han endelig blir af tilslut; jeg skyr ikke at gaa lige ind i Huse og opad Trapper forat se, hvor han blir af tilslut. Om Naetterne i store Byer er dette overmaade interessant og kan føre én ind i de maerkeligste Bekendtskaber" (*Mysterier,* 489).

16. "ofte kunde han ikke gaa opad en Trappe for Eksempel, uden at vende sig om for hvert Skridt forat se, om der ikke skulde vaere nogen bag ham. Hvad var det? Ja, hvad det var! Noget mystisk noget, noget saelsomt, som den stakkels 'alvidende' Videnskab var for firkantet og for grov til at fatte, et Pust af enusynlig Magt, en Paavirkning af Livets blinde

The novel finally destabilizes our confidence as readers and induces in us a Nagel-like paranoia about our own world. A defeated Nagel finally obeys the call of the mysterious lady who, in his imagination or actually, committed suicide by drowning at San Francisco. When he enters the sea and death, taking with him the inner data of his efforts as detective, his essentially symbolist suspicion of "an essence emanating from an invisible power—the supernatural making itself manifest"—permeates our own acts of interpretation as readers. Cumulatively we share in his failure to assert his own merits in the midst of philistine pillars of the community; to solve the case of the probable murder of Karlsen; to cope with the Midget, the probable archvillain (unless possibly he is after all a grotesque saint); to fathom the cruel pride of the beautiful Dagny; to redeem the misused Martha; and to grasp the magic and terror that lurks in the idyllic setting. Like the Baudelairean or Platenesque beauty that kills, nature now excites a sense of horror. One of the humiliating ironies consists in our awareness that, if, as Nagel believes, the perfect crime is an "exception" to banal reality, our inability to decide whether a genuine crime has occurred alters our confidence in our world: "I'd like someone to find me a single exception—if there is one! For instance, I'd like to see a carefully planned crime, something to make one sit up and take notice" (Bothmer 65–66).[17] We cofailures cannot detect a meaningful crime either, and so we cannot know for certain whether nature is indeed a nightmare or a channel to superreality.

In noting the hints of Dagney's cruel pride in *Mysteries*, we approach, once more, from the angle of obsession with the femme fatale, that major thematic cluster of the second half of the nineteenth century: the feminization of the city, which is pictured as a relentless organism, by analogy to the lure and cruelty of life. As mentioned, the double identification of Paris with woman and death occurs in Baudelaire, but this identification draws its appeal from a familiar postromantic tradition. The contest between a seductive and castrating feminine life force and a puny masculine sense of moral order is provocatively uneven in Prosper Mérimée's novella *Carmen* (1845); Georges Bizet's opera version (first performed 1875) popularizes this lesson well into modernism; and Leopold von Sacher-Masoch modifies the relationship only slightly in his in-

---

Kraefter" (*Mysterier*, 249–50). Note: The Norweigian terms translated as "supernatural" by Bothmer are more literally "life's blind forces."

17. "Giv os hid for Eksempel en udviklet Forbrydelse, en fremragende Synd!" (*Mysterier*, 95).

fluential novel *Venus im Pelz* (Venus in Furs, 1870) by allowing the cruel mortal heroine Wanda too finally to be victimized by the very power of irresistible, tyrannical life she incarnates vis-à-vis her male slave Gregor-Severin. In his Salomé paintings of the 1870s, Gustave Moreau captures the struggle between the feminine natural principle, as the voluptuous dancer, and the male spiritual principle epitomized in John the Baptist. Spirit, in good Schopenauerian fashion, finally separates from the body in Moreau's paintings in the form of the severed head of John the Baptist. Odilon Redon continues the theme of the freed head in his paintings and adds the related seeing and warning eye in his paintings which drifts over the threshold of the nineteenth into the twentieth century. Joris-Karl Huysmans directly incorporates Moreau's work as an excitant for the fevered imagination of the decadent aesthete Des Esseintes in the novel *A rebours* (Against Nature, 1884), who flees the crushing and threatening banality of modern life and struggles to create an artificial paradise in its place. Des Esseintes's nightmares link sexual bondage, castration, the threat of venereal disease, the cultural crapulence of morally tainted modern France, and the horror of Paris as a modern hell.

Cultural historians like Phillippe Jullian[18] and Bram Dijkstra[19] have so thoroughly chronicled the appearance of hordes of seductive, diseased, perverse, and/or castrating females in European painting and literature of the 1890s and 1900s—the nymphs, sirens, sphinxes, whores, vampires, maenads, chimeras, the strong Judiths, Salomés, Circes, and others—that I can therefore limit myself here to underscoring that these threatening excitements flourished most particularly in conjunction with the climactic transformation of the modernist city. They invaded the city increasingly while the new technologies (railroad, streetcar, telephone, electric lighting, movies, radio, etc.) were charging it with superabundant and, as often as not, with liberating energies. Whether as outright detectives, critic-poets, or merely curious observers, a rich variety of hermeneut-flaneurs in the footsteps of Poe's Dupin, such as Joyce's Dedalus, Rilke's Brigge, and Mann's Aschenbach, explore this hyped-up metropolitan showplace and directly or indirectly discover that the modern European city is still Babylon. In its aggregate it is an uncaring liv-

18. Philippe Jullian, *Dreamers of Decadence: Symbolist Painters of the 1890s*, trans. Robert Baldick (New York and Washington, D.C.: Praeger, 1971); originally published as *Esthètes et magiciens* (Paris: Librairie Académique Perrin, 1969).

19. Bram Dijkstra, *Idols of Perversity: Fantasies of Feminine Evil in Fin-de-Siècle Culture* (New York: Oxford University Press, 1986).

ing body that has been reproducing its own dying cells down through the ages. If we take 1913 once again as a date of reference, we find, for instance, that a cabalistic metaphor of the city as love's body is spun through Joyce's *Ulysses;* that the underlying mother swamp and Dionysian music subvert the Apollonian superstructure of civic virtue and classic form in Mann's *Death in Venice;* and that the resourceful vamp Odette de Crécy snares for her own life purposes the title figure of Proust's *Swann's Way.*

To be sure, Proust represents a more generous strain of the modernist vision in which the anxiety-laden fin-de-siècle clichés about the feminine and nature are all made subordinate to a larger analysis and appreciation. Proust's grand coda drawing together all the themes of *Swann's Way* presents one of the most brilliant sustained examinations of the relationship among the many aspects and stages in the feminine role, the metamorphoses of nature, and the education of the human soul. The recapitulation occurs during a moody autumn in the guise of the elderly male narrator's recollection of his teenage emotions in the company of Odette, whom he evokes as the eventually triumphant society matron, Madame Swann, strolling through the Bois de Boulogne. While the meditating narrator moves in memory through the entire register of seasonal tropes associated with her manifestations, he celebrates Odette's permanent or archetypal reality as it has appeared at that height of life when, wrapped in furs against the cold, she was the veritable Venus to her Paris. Simultaneously, Proust's narrator celebrates the Bois de Boulogne in the complexity of its interwoven moods as the eternal *locus amoenus.* It is the human and poetic construct, the attempt to fuse city and park in an artificial paradise. This magnificent and expensive wish fulfillment of return to the Garden of Eden is simultaneously a gesture of urban humanity that reveals that necessarily death is part of the story. In his coda of 1913, by associating the poetic act of recollection with the cultural construct of the urban park, Proust suggests what Yeats fifteen years later, in his poem "Sailing to Byzantium," terms "the artifice of eternity"—that is, art as the supreme, authentic human response to mere nature.

My remaining principal categories, myth and psychology, have constantly obtruded during the foregoing sketch of places into which newer literature was relocating older nature around 1900. Little wonder that it is difficult to hold myth and psychology apart in cultural history at the modernist threshold once we pause to recall the extraordinary importance of theories of myth and the psyche from the Renaissance onward in reshaping both the human sciences and the arts. Those who wish to verify how relatively shallow most modernist and postmodernist efforts in these domains are in relation to the vast accrued work of recent centuries can have recourse to such broad-gauged accounts as Feldman and Richardson's *The Rise of Modern Mythology 1680–1860*[20] and Ellenberger's *The Discovery of the Unconscious: The History and Evolution of Dynamic Psychiatry*.[21] While the European and Euro-American worlds have continued to evolve in longer range terms within the channels of their complex Judeo-Christian tradition and its accommodations with rationalism and science, it is no exaggeration to say that, by 1900, the fascination for myth and for the catalogued residue of centuries of comparative religion have effectively, and perhaps with finality, displaced or replaced interest in the older core religion on the part of the European élites and thoroughly saturated their audiences.

I shall not attempt to survey the full variety of approaches to myth crowding the nineteenth century; rather, I want to focus on a perennial confrontation recurring in the general opposition between the Enlightenment and romanticism that the fin-de-siècle recycles and bequeaths to modernism. If myths were explanatory products of an archaic or inspired imagination, the question already arose in antiquity why they often contained a mixture of "reasonable" and "unreasonable" elements and to what extent various moments in the "aesthetic" re-creation of myths reflected "historic" matter or a "romantic" penchant of the human mind. The Renaissance revived the debate sparked by the Greek philosopher Euhemerus (316 B.C.) over whether a deterioration of language and memory accounted for many features of myth, and whether an improvement of human understanding and a gradual revision of obscured mythological sources were attainable. By and large, older rationalists and nineteenth-century positivists favored seeing in myths distortions of once actual historical legacies or of earlier attempts to grasp natural forces and events, distortions that resulted from religious belief and cult origins, but sometimes simply from accidental erroneous linkages of resemblances or through cross-cultural borrowings from some other originating center where insights had been concretized. The rationalist-positivist stream also frequently posited a common basis in the human

20. Burton Feldman and Robert Richardson, *The Rise of Modern Mythology, 1680–1860* (Bloomington: Indiana University Press, 1972).

21. Henri F. Ellenberger, *The Discovery of the Unconscious: The History and Evolution of Dynamic Psychiatry* (New York: Basic Books, 1970).

mind for generating myths. Because the romantics shared many of these notions and the etiological passion of humanism, they, like the major Renaissance poets, tended to prize mythological expression as part of a *prisca theologia* or its deep psychological equivalent, however much obscured or subject to yet further unfoldings. But in reaction to the Enlightenment's presumed overbearing prejudices, the romantics preferred such older allegorical embodiments of moral, religious, philosophical, and natural truths to arid modern analysis.

Three proclivities distinguished the romantic revision or rejection of European rationalism. One was the overturning of the Enlightenment distinction between myth as outmoded and history as scientific. The second was the recognition of imaginative creativity and reception down to the present as intrinsically a form of renewed participation in mythmaking. The third was the subjectivist revolution that located in the individual and in the collective psyche the motor driving the continuous reshaping of worldviews. Great Renaissance poets, often leaning on then-contemporaneous anthropologists, made daring use of perceived structural relationships among pagan and Christian paradigms and suggested their relevance to possible psychomachias or world-developmental progressions. The romantics went further by openly assimilating figures, images, and stories of the Middle Ages, the Renaissance, and their own times as further mythologems produced by, and manifesting the operation of, deeper forces. In a broader account, the complicating factor that many nineteenth-century thinkers transformed the romantic approach into one or another pseudoscientific teaching would require attention— for example, G. F. W. Hegel's dialectics of history, Karl Marx's dialectical materialism, and so forth. Likewise it would be appropriate to consider the crucial contribution of older European Neoplatonism to idealism at the romantic turn. We find the essential romantic propositions regarding the inner relatedness of nature and the human mind, as the latter discovers its own powers and destiny, in Percy Bysshe Shelley's poem "Mont Blanc" (1817), as in these illustrative lines:

> The secret strength of things,
> Which governs thought, and to the infinite dome
> Of heaven is as a law, inhabits thee!
>
> (lines 138–41)[22]

---

22. Percy Bysshe Shelley, *The Poetical Works of Shelley*, ed. Newell F. Ford (Boston: Houghton Mifflin, 1975).

The Place of Fin-de-Siècle Nature

Quite striking is the multiple reference of "thee"—to Mont Blanc as synecdoche for evolutionary nature, for time in process, thus for humanity in its larger destiny, the poet as vessel, his reader, and so forth. The crucial point about the conjunction of myth and psychology after 1800 is that the two fields have constantly intersected, and the subjectivist turn enabled the fusion between the subject matters of mind and nature. Thus, myth and psychology constitute by 1900 that single master nexus afterward so characteristic of twentieth-century habits for understanding the man-nature relationship and of habits persisting beyond our own recent fin-de-siècle into the twenty-first century.

Doubtlessly a hundred years hence students of cultural history will reconfirm today's surmise that post-Einsteinian physics and cosmology, the unfolding of particle and wave theory, and the impact of electronic media have meanwhile been the newer undergirding platform that started rising from modernism proper. But my goal here is to sketch where the older climaxing master nexus interlocked with this future we are just living through. It was essential that postromantic writers took up as a felt reality the understanding that the great archetypal creations of early modern and rationalist Europe were genuinely mythological in a profound way which allowed us to contrast and align them with those of antiquity and early Christian times. For example, we see this, in *Ender/ Eller* (Either/Or, 1843), in Søren Kierkegaard's reappreciation of the early modern Don Juan legend and his acceptance of the romantic virtual divinization of Mozart as the genius who brought the myth to its destined culmination, so that it now is capable of haunting us as a kind of latter-day revelation. And, clearly, what the mythological patterns feed to us in the (post)modern condition is the (post)romantic psychological discovery of our human condition, our conflicted "double" (subjective and somatic) nature with its perplexing choices. When they are popularized, European neomythological concretizations seem almost inevitably to gather into themselves one or another set of the vulgar sociological biases or passions of their age. For example, we find the romantic habit of mirroring the ancient primary myths of tragic human self-definition in works such as Richard Wagner's four-part cosmic music drama *Der Ring des Nibelungen* (The Ring of the Nibelung, started in 1844), which interprets the Oedipus story in terms of a cleansing epochal catastrophe when alienated feeling reasserts its rights against the repressive power of the state.

The purpose of these abbreviated illustrations is not primarily to recall that such romantics as Ludwig Tieck and E. T. A. Hoffmann had already established the modern Don Juan and Mozart theses prior to Kierkegaard, or that by the first decade of the nineteenth century Friedrich Hölderlin and others had already propounded the idea that the Oedipus legend signaled in antiquity a deep transformation of consciousness and institutions relevant to the modern revolutionary era. Rather, the point is that—after the romantics and by the fin-de-siècle of 1900—there is no significant turning back possible from the ever more firmly entrenched habit of treating myths as concretizations in which, supposedly, "true" or "deeper" nature is encapsulated, and of categorizing psychological patterns and processes in terms of myth. Like so many of his predecessor psychologists and anthropologists of the nineteenth century, Sigmund Freud finds that myth labels provide a useful shorthand for identifying aspects of the psyche, especially those nodular manifestations thereof that he terms complexes. His junior Carl Gustav Jung represents a continuing revivification of the European willingness to take serious consideration of non-European mythic and religious phenomena, to see these in relation not just to ancient but to later European spiritual and cultural responses to life. Jung is just one small part of the general anthropological expansionism of Europeans and Euro-Americans at the modernist threshold. The anthropological fascination has its parallel in postimpressionist painters like Paul Gauguin and Pablo Picasso who reach out to the so-called primitive strata of African, Asian, and Pacific art, as well as back to the ancient Mediterranean, and who are legion after 1900.

There is clearly a powerful antirealist tendency that appears in much of this artistic attention to a formerly exotic exterior beyond modern Europe and in the simultaneous resituating of the modern psyche on the surface of an abyss that opens into an interior of nature. All this was happening while—in their offices and their laboratories just around the next corner—various social philosophers and scientists, still upholding the doctrine of progress, doggedly insisted our task was to place nature under better management. That other main theme of the turn-of-the-century would require and merit a chapter in its own right. Worth citing at length here as a vision that discovers an unscientific alternate reality, not compatible with Western optimism about nature, is August Strindberg's famous preface to *Ett Drömspel* (A Dream Play, 1901), which exploits Hindu myth. I shall excerpt just a few telling phrases in reminder:

> I have in this dream play sought to imitate the incoherent but ostensibly logical form of our dreams. [. . .] The characters split, double, multiply, condense, float apart, coalesce. But one mind stands over and

above them all, the mind of the dreamer; and for him there are no secrets, no inconsistencies, no scruples, no laws. He does not condemn,
does not acquit; he only narrates the story.[23]

Strindberg's "dream play" is part of the relocation of the effective
core of nature into the underground life of the psyche during the fin-de-
siècle, plainly in evidence in works resistant to the excesses of intellectu-
alism and science such as Henri Bergson's *Essai sur les données immédi-
ates de la conscience* (The Immediate Elements of Consciousness, 1889).
But in Freud's *Die Traumdeutung* (Interpretation of Dreams, 1900), of
course, we already have a renewed attempt to command this realm once
again as the positivists aspired to do, to tighten the focus onto pathologies of the mind with ameliorative objectives.

A prime example of the earlier literary struggle in the later nineteenth century hovering between fascination, on the one hand, for the
perplexingly interfaced doubleness of inner-outer nature, and on the other, for scientific control over the secret source of disturbances that erupt
into our social realm, is Benito Pérez Galdós's novella *La sombra* (The
Shadow, 1870) published in the South at the same time as Leopold von
Sacher-Masoch's *Venus im Pelz* (Venus in Furs) in the North. Galdós's
story features a sophisticated gentleman detective as narrator who conducts us through his therapeutic investigation into the strange case
of an unreconstructed romantic recluse, Anselmo (namesake of Cervantes's "curious impertinent" in *Don Quixote*). This odd contemporary
of the later nineteenth century, so we eventually learn, in youth actually caused his wife's death out of his own sexual fear, but has repressed
this traumatic knowledge for many years. The connection between the
mythological heritage and the psychological reality is exhibited in the voluptuous painting collection of ancient subjects left to the mentally disturbed Anselmo by his father. In a series of bizarre encounters, Anselmo was threatened by the ancient Paris who stepped out of his picture
on the wall as a figment of the artistic imagination and became a force
in Anselmo's own home, just as Don Juan has been such a force steadily
on the Spanish scene. The concomitant social dimension intrudes as we

23. August Strindberg, *A Dream Play*, in *Selected Plays*, trans. Evert Sprinchorn (Minneapolis: University of Minnesota Press, 1986), 215.—"[. . .] sökt härma drömmens osam-
manhängande men skenbart logiska form. [. . .] Personerna klyvas, fördubblas, dubbleras,
dunsta av, förtätas, flyta ut, samlas. Men ett medvetande står över alla, det är drömmarens;
för det finns inga hemligheter, ingen inkonsekvens, inga skrupler, ingen lag. Han dömer
icke, frisäger icke, endast relaterar" (August Strindberg, *Samlade Skrifter*, 55 vols. [Stock-
holm: Albert Bonniers, 1912–1921], 36.215).

recognize that, unlike Anselmo, his actual, contemporary Spanish society accepts the complex double standards that any accommodation with real nature dictates. The success of the narrator's scientific reconstruction leads him to predict confidently that some day, by using positivistic approaches to the human story, the human sciences will increasingly be able to explain all past and present mental and spiritual phenomena.

The unresolved contest between and among various pessimistic and optimistic, mechanistic and organic, deterministic and morphological, idealist and materialist, spiritual and scientific, and other ways of situating nature lends an exhilarating zigzag texture to the aggregate of European literature around 1900. The reach for a new synthesis that is evident in fin-de-siècle crosscurrents still lingers into our times.

With such creative profusion, it is difficult to fix more than a few points of reference. There is a sense of dignity emanating from the mythic foundations of Europe in works such as the inaugural volume of James Frazer's *The Golden Bough* (1890); and analysts such as Jessie L. Weston in *The Legends of the Wagner Drama: Studies in Mythology and Romance* (1896) do not hesitate to subject any part of the literary tradition, even the very latest, to poetic anthropologizing. Using a Nietzschean optic but profiling the inner narrator's experience as if in French neoclassicistic tragedy, André Gide exploits the emblematic environments of Europe and North Africa in his novel *L'immoraliste* (The Immoralist, 1902) to exhibit the stark confrontation with primordial forces that erupt from depths underlying the surface rational order of the modern urban world as much as they manifest themselves in the processes of nature. In *Buddenbrooks* (1901), Thomas Mann confronts the possibility that perhaps all we can know is what myth reveals about nature and mind and language in any age. The encyclopedic range of Joyce's *Ulysses*, set in the year 1904 in the city of Dublin, allows the conflicted status and place of a nature that is thoroughly fused with the city to be exhibited exemplarily as our principal living space.

In an important review of the completed novel in 1922, Mary Colum argued justifiably that the complex, disparate structures and linguistic modes of *Ulysses* reveal the inroads of modern science; a scientific drive seems to be overwhelming and conquering literature as hitherto known.[24] In *El tema de nuestro tiempo* (The Modern Theme, 1938), José Ortega y Gasset pointed out, as World War II was erupting, that "the the-

24. Mary Colum, review of *Ulysses*, *The Freeman*, 19 July 1922.

ory of Einstein is a marvelous proof of the harmonious multiplicity of all possible points of view. If the idea is extended to morals and aesthetics, we shall come to experience history and life in a new way."[25] In effect, Colum and Ortega anticipated what critics of our own recently passed end-of-a-century, such as Stephen Kern in *The Culture of Time and Space, 1880–1918*, would still say in retrospect about the brave new world after 1900: "Thus the [. . .] most innovative novelists of the period transformed the stage of modern literature from a series of fixed settings of homogenous space into a multitude of qualitatively different spaces that varied with the shifting moods and perspectives of human consciousness."[26] In Kern's critical assessment we can still hear echoes of Pater's awareness of the breakup of solid nature that occurred in both literature and painting in the time of symbolism and impressionism—despite the efforts of the naturalists to construct a more readily graspable nature.[27]

But, in fact, from the start, other readers of Joyce could fasten with equal justification upon the persistence of master complexes of myth in *Ulysses*, and upon pervasive metaphors that comprehensively shaped our appreciation of the disparate, even particulate, and sometimes seemingly indeterminate matter in it. For example, fellow novelist Henry Miller recognized that "In *Ulysses* Joyce gives us the complete identification of the artist with the tomb in which he buries himself";[28] and the ruling cabalistic understanding of nature's and the city's, love's and the text's, bodies in *Ulysses* has been exposited in ample, convincing detail by such a fine scholar as Jackson I. Cope.[29] We simply cannot pull apart the scientific, thingly, and bodily references in this novel nor sunder them from the warp and woof of mythic and spiritual heritage without doing violence to the whole vision. Thus, to this extent, Joyce's work can demon-

25. Ortega y Gasset, *The Modern Theme*, trans. James Cleugh (New York: Harper & Row, 1961), 143.

26. Stephen Kern, *The Culture of Time and Space, 1880–1918* (Cambridge, Mass.: Harvard University Press, 1983), 149.

27. Retrospective appreciations today of the different order of complexity that modernist novelists brought about in nodular or clustered narrative webs include the almost numberless evaluations of more responsive critical theories about narration that appeared at the midpoint between modernism and its current epigones. An example would be the growth of interest in Mikhail Bakhtin rising about fifty years after his innovative work on concepts such as the chronotrope, heterglossia, etc. In this connection, see Stacy Burton, "Bakhtin, Temporality, and Modern Narrative: Writing 'the Whole Triumphant Murderous Unstoppable Chute,'" *Comparative Literature* 48 (1996): 39–64.

28. Henry Miller, "The Universe of Death," in *The Best of Henry Miller* (London: Heinemann, 1960), 207.

29. Jackson I. Cope, *Joyce's Cities: Archaeologies of the Soul* (Baltimore: Johns Hopkins University Press, 1981).

strate to us how the historical juncture of realism, naturalism, impressionism, and symbolism—the problematic tensions of which appear in Émile Zola's *Roman expérimental* (Experimental Novel) in the 1880s—results in the possibility for a new complex symbolic system, a system diverse enough to permit literature to retain all aspects of the interface between external and internal nature, a way to talk both about nature as knowable through surface phenomena and about nature as what human beings experience: a felt reality and a reality comprehending their own mysterious inner core.

As of the fin-de-siècle, the "where" that nature was at was not an "either/or" but a "both/and" location. This is the intersection that great writers crisscross with excitement around 1900 and before World War II.[30]

30. Many current "postmodernist" commentators who think of themselves as "theorizing" modernism seem constrained to mediate events in modernist art—a new dispensation they want to possess but also claim to supersede—only by indirection via theorist avatars who represent their own role-image (the superior "critical" mind). Meanwhile more direct engagement with the works of a major figure like Joyce has resulted in stellar years of literary scholarship in the 1980s, 1990s, and 2000s. It is to be hoped that efforts of the latter sort will help clear the way for more serious attention to what has been occurring around 2000 that is distinct from the constellation that dawned after 1900. Among many hopeful signs of openness to possible interrelations of science and the arts in "our" fin-de-siècle was the inaugural issue—concerning "Chaos in the Humanities"—of *Synthesis* founded by the late critic and novelist Patrick Brady (*Synthesis: An Interdisciplinary Journal* 1, no. 1 [Knoxville, Tenn.: New Paradigm Press, 1995]).

4   PRIME COORDINATES IN MODERNIST

CULTURAL MAPPINGS

European inner- and outer-directed cultural mapping were emblematized around 1300 in two Italian contemporaries, the Florentine Dante, celebrated for his spiritual journey, and the Venetian Polo, famed for his travels as far as Cathay. Prince Henry the Navigator of Portugal was already leading the thrust out into world oceans in the early 1400s that eventually would displace the Mediterranean in importance as the center of the European trading world. By the mid-sixteenth century, Cortes's companion Diaz del Castillo recounted the *Historia verdadera de la conquista de la Nueva España* (True History of the Conquest of New Spain, 1568 ff.; published postumously 1632); after midcentury, Camões sang the epic of the newly founded Portuguese world empire in *Os Lusiadas* (The Lusitanians, 1572), and Hakluyt chronicled *The Principal Navigations, Voyages, and Discoveries of the English Nation* (1598–1600). These markers suffice to remind us that only an analysis on the scale of Fernand Braudel's trilogy *Civilization and Capitalism, 15th–18th Century* (1979ff.) could furnish the adequate background for my topic.

Nonetheless, it is a reasonable foreshortening to cite the broad historical consensus on four main factors that combined after 1450 to give a lasting stamp to European cultural mappings. First, there was the concern to defend the southwestern and southeastern borders of European civilization against Islamic power. Second, humanist savants and artists established a new appreciation not only of the pagan Greeks and Romans, but also of the ancient Egyptian, Semitic, and Oriental worlds with which the Greco-Roman heritage was interlaced. Third, the success of Protestantism reinforced awareness that significant economic and innovative energies had shifted northward and westward toward the Atlantic littoral. And fourth, ongoing Renaissance exploration and colonization meant that Europeans would inevitably reorder perceived cultural space on the grandiose scale indicated by their own ventures. By the seventeenth century, on the basis of older lore and newer reports accruing from far journeys, anthropologists such as Kircher in *Oedipus Aegyptia-cus* (Egyptian Oedipus, 1652ff.) attempted to integrate the non-European peoples of the several continents alongside the Europeans in a better rea-soned universal history. In many strands reaching down to modernism, for example, from Aphra Behn's *Oroonoko* (1688), over Herman Mel-ville's *Typee* (1846), to Joseph Conrad's *Heart of Darkness* (1902), we can trace the ever deepening contribution of European eyewitnesses in far-away realms to the imaginative absorption of cultural differences.

I have commented elsewhere on the ways that European writers of-ten carried an assumed opposition between "earlier" and "later" forms of consciousness, internalized within themselves, and superimposed such paradigmatic distinctions on remote places and new homelands (René de Chateaubriand) outside Europe.[1] Eventually, enough authors were born in colonies that had evolved into new nations so that the experience of witnessing transformation right at the edge of contact between cultures could give way to an understanding that indeed some new human pol-ity had emerged that was not European but post-European, an epical mo-ment of creating a home (James Fenimore Cooper). A major conceptual breakthrough occurred when writers from the active rim of outshoots of Europe began to apply the lessons garnered by anthropology over sever-al centuries. Starting from an extra-European vantage point, they could critique both the European myth of the noble savage and the neomy-thology of brave new worlds like the United States (Herman Melville). On the threshold of modernism, the fresh enjoyment of discovering re-mote, relatively unspoiled "earlier" worlds was still possible, and some European writers of adventurous character managed to arrive just at what soon, in retrospect, appeared to be the last moment of such worlds in their authentic ambience (Robert Louis Stevenson). The painter and writer Gauguin, who had childhood roots in the New World, is emblem-atic of many tormented Europeans who never managed to find satisfac-tion in their quest to discover an unspoiled, non-European home. This frustrated search itself became an important new myth of modernism. The circular logic in being "too late," doomed to failure because of the rapid penetration of European ways, could serve like a perpetual motion machine to generate disappointment abroad as well as at home. It was a

---

1. See my chapter "In Search of the Noble Savage: Some Romantic Cases," in *Echoland: Readings from Humanism to Postmodernism* (Brussels: Presses Interuniversitaires Européen-nes, 2006), 244–52, illustrating the "naive/sentimental" dichotomy from the late eigh-teenth to the early twentieth century.

perfect extension of the Rousseauesque prejudice: the belief that Europeans were inherently spoiled by their own supposed progress and success. In many respects, this bias has outweighed the countervailing anxiety that sprang up in the New World as people of European background wondered whether the savage principle might subvert the civilizing principle. This anxiety has persisted at least since the famous treatise *Facundo o civilización y barbarie* (Facundo; or, Civilization and Barbarism, 1845) by Domingo Faustino Sarmiento, an important reformer president of Argentina (1868–1874). The works and letters of D. H. Lawrence during his period of living in New Mexico and Mexico reflect a rich ambivalence dealing with these themes of cultural opposition. Three-quarters of a century after Lawrence, these themes still percolate in the general discourse of the New World and provide staple materials for fields like postcolonial studies.

But I propose to focus here on the "internal" self-mapping of Europe that persisted against the background of these innumerable encounters around the globe, a European self-reassessment that continued despite the implication of an eventual decentering of Europe itself, and not just of the older Mediterranean core. The Renaissance pattern of religious divisions and of nations and their presumed antecedents defined the prime coordinates of a "Western" civilization up to World War I. Encyclopedic novels and romances of the sixteenth and seventeenth centuries, such as Rabelais's *Gargantua and Pantagruel* (1532ff.), Spenser's *The Faerie Queene* (1589ff.), Barclay's *Argenis* (1621), and Lohenstein's *Arminius* (1679–1680), while usually privileging one modern nation as providentially destined for greatness, treated Europe as a polysystem transected by a southeast-to-northwest developmental axis along which a great multipartite tradition was flowing in stages from antiquity to modernity. Enlightenment writers such as Pope and Voltaire, who regarded themselves as heirs of the Renaissance, saw this time line in terms of a dialectic of contending barbarian and civilizing impulses, while Herder's rival organicist view of history stressed the interplay of Hebrew and Hellene attributes as well as indigenous folkways in European development. The basics are contained in Herder's early travel journal of 1769 postulating two major flows that correlate roughly with a northwesterly extension of Oriental cultural influence and an initially northerly movement of the Indo-Germanic peoples who then impinge upon and blend into the mainstream of civilization:

Modernist Moments and Spaces

I see two streams, one out of the Orient, over Greece and Italy, that
has been softly sinking into southeast Europe, and also has invented
a soft southern religion, a poetry of the imagination, a music, art, decency, knowledge of the eastern South. The second stream goes over
the North from Asia to Europe; from there it overflows the former.[2]

Variations upon these often intertwined humanist and organicist dialectics of the Enlightenment recurred in romantic and nineteenth-
century thought in dazzling profusion—for example, to pick a few figures at random, in Hölderlin, Novalis, Heine, Coleridge, Nerval, and Arnold. Since a variety of novelists—for example, Scott in *Ivanhoe* (1819),
Disraeli in *Coningsby* (1844), Eliot in *Daniel Deronda* (1874–1876), Hawthorne in *The Marble Faun* (1860)—dealt with the theme of a Jewish
or an Oriental component in Western culture, Joyce's uses of Bloom in
Ulysses must be seen as continuing a rich tradition.[3]

The idea of a general Orient-to-Europe or southeast-to-northwest vector of culture had acquired great complexity as both a territorial and a
temporal developmental reference by the late nineteenth century. In section 21 of *The Birth of Tragedy,* Nietzsche can situate the transitory miracle of the Greek "Golden Age" on the accepted geocultural map, confident that his readers will be familiar with the coordinates:

Placed between India and Rome, and pushed toward a seductive choice,
the Greeks succeeded in inventing a third form, in classical purity—to
be sure, one they did not long use themselves, but one that precisely for
that reason gained immortality.[4]

2. My translation of the passage: "[. . .] so sehe ich zwei Ströme, von denen der eine
aus Orient, über Griechenland und Italien sich ins südliche Europa sanft senkt, und auch
eine sanfte, südliche Religion, eine Poesie der Einbildungskraft, eine Musik, Kunst, Sitt-
samkeit, Wissenschaft des östlichen Südens erfunden hat. Der zweite Strom geht über
Norden von Asien nach Europa; von da überströmt er jenen" (Johann Gottfried Herder,
Journal meiner Reise im Jahr 1769 [Journal of My Journey in the Year 1769], reprinted in
Sturm und Drang: Eine Auswahl theoretischer Texte, ed. Erich Löwenthal [Heidelberg: Lambert Schneider, 1972], 297).
3. On the development of discourse concerning such polarities as Hebrew-Hellene and
Oriental-European, see Joachim Dyck, *Athen und Jerusalem: Die Tradition der argumenta-
tiven Verknüpfung von Bibel und Poesie im 17. und 18. Jahrhundert* (Munich: Beck, 1977), and
E. S. Shaffer, *"Kubla Khan" and The Fall of Jerusalem: The Mythological School in Biblical
Criticism and Secular Literature, 1770–1880* (New York: Cambridge University Press, 1975).
4. Friedrich Nietzsche, *"The Birth of Tragedy" and "The Case of Wagner,"* trans. and ed.
Walter Kaufmann (New York: Vintage Books, 1967), 125. The original text reads: "Zwisch-
en Indien und Rom hingestellt und zu verführerischer Wahl gedrängt, ist es den Griech-
en gelungen, in classischer Reinheit eine dritte Form hinzuzuerfinden, freilich nicht zu
langem eigenen Gebrauche, aber eben darum für die Unsterblichkeit" (*Die Geburt der
Tragödie,* in *Nietzsche: Werke,* ed. Giorgio Colli and Mazzino Montinari [New York: Walter
de Gruyter, 1972], 3.1.129).

To illustrate this proposition, it is worthwhile to dwell at more length on the example of the Swiss writer Conrad Ferdinand Meyer who, in his historical novellas set in different eras and different parts of Europe, anticipates the sorts of mapping that Mann, Gide, D. H. Lawrence, and others will engage in under the influence of Meyer's contemporary Nietzsche. Typical is Meyer's at-times melodramatic *Die Versuchung des Pescara* (The Tempting of Pescara, 1887), which seeks to identify the constituent tensions of a polyform Europe in the aftermath of the battle of Pavia in 1525. The novella treats an axial juncture when, as incidental consequences of hegemonistic warfare between the great states of that time, Spain and France, the unification of Italy was thwarted, the revolutionary passions of Protestantism erupting in the German north were not curbed, and the power of imperial Spain crested. A work of art obtruding at the story's opening manifests the cultural doubleness of Renaissance Italy, scene of the action and surrogate for Europe at large. This recent picture, hung over the desk of Milan's ineffectual ruler Francesco Sforza, is divided between a recessive, pale Christ and strong-toothed, lusty eaters of the loaves and fishes. That is, if we read the immediate implication, humanism is now ascendant in Italy, and older Christianity is waning. Gradually the field of reference deepens, and later in the story we go with Pescara to view a painting in progress that depicts the lancing of Christ on the cross. Unbeknownst to those who seek to steer Pescara for political ends—such as to scourge heresy throughout Europe on behalf of the Inquisition and Spain, or to become the princely champion for Italian independence of whom Machiavelli dreams—the charismatic, victorious field marshal of the imperial forces is meanwhile stoically dying of his lance wound suffered at Pavia. On a mysterious level, he identifies with the sacrificial heroism of Christ and strives to exit from history as a just and honorable person, a participant capable of judging that European political realities and Renaissance Italy's "perverse and fantastical" streak will thwart Italy's cultural unification.[5] Pescara is conscious of two souls warring in him, "one Spanish and one Italian," and he has come to abhor what contemporary imperial Spain represents as a way for Europe or the world: "Still, this Spanish empire, whose gloom is spreading with lurid smoke on both sides of the sea, fills me with horror: Slaves

---

5. Conrad Ferdinand Meyer, *The Tempting of Pescara*, trans. Clara Bell (New York: W. S. Gottsberger, 1890; rpt., New York: Howard Fertig, 1975), 162; hereafter cited as *Pescara*. The original wording is "willkürlich und phantastisch" *(Die Versuchung des Pescara*, ed. Alfred Zäch, in *Sämmtliche Werke: Historisch-kritische Ausgabe,* ed. Hans Zeller and Alfred Zäch [Bern: Benteli-Verlag, 1962], 13.259; hereafter cited as *Versuchung).*

and executioners. [. . .] Your Italy, with all its sins, is human" (*Pescara* 151–52).[6]

The poetess Vittoria Colonna, Pescara's warm-hearted wife, thus works for a sublime earthly role for him that cannot be realized. In the episode of her embassy to the pope, Meyer makes it clear that she fuses all layers of *pietas* from antiquity, over the Middle Ages, to the humanist epoch. Vittoria embodies the sustaining nurture of her nation and the crucial feminine balance in deep culture. For example, her advocacy of the human claims of Julia, who has been wronged by the field marshal's nephew Del Guasto, parallels Pescara's own approach to resolving complex dilemmas in European high politics of the day. The spectacle of Spanish world empire, of "foreign invaders and high-handed adventurers who were appropriating both the Old and New Worlds," disturbs Vittoria at a deep level and shakes the Ghibelline loyalties traditional in her family. She rejects Charles V, though she knows he himself is not by birth Spanish, for his Spanish role. In her thoughts he represents an anti-European principle: "Why was the youthful emperor king of that reprobate nation [Spain!] in whose veins ran the blood of Moors and who had poisoned Italy with the race of Borgia" (*Pescara* 48).[7]

In juxtaposing the senior and junior couples in a subtle chiasmus, Meyer suggests what Italy (or Europe) is and can be. Del Guasto's mixed German and Spanish blood betokens a blending of North and South; he exhibits the infusion of barbaric vitality, but also the threat of dehumanizing harshness that needs tempering. Wholly consumed by love, blue-eyed Julia, the granddaughter of the wise Moorish doctor Numa Dati, connects the feminine and the European to their eastern roots. Vittoria, the proud descendant of the ancient Romans, lives on as poetry and as the disappointed Italian nation shall; while the sung hero Pescara, half-Italian and half-Spanish, bows out as a ritual victim whose passing hints at the historical divorce between Spanish and Italian affairs in the cards. His last dying act exemplifies spiritual courage and depth in the longer Judeo-Christian heritage; the choice he makes also associates the maturity of the Renaissance with the liberal tendencies that the northwesterly

---

6. "Dieses spaniche Weltreich aber, das in blutroten Wolken austeigt jenseits und diesseits des Meeres, erfüllt mich mit Grauen: Sklaven und Henker. [. . .] Dein verderbtes Italien aber ist wenigstens menschlich" (*Versuchung*, 253).

7. "fremden Räuber und hochfahrenden Abenteurer, welche die neue und die alte Erde zusammen erbeuteten"; "Warum war der junge Kaiser zugleich der König dieser ruchlosen Nation, in deren Adern maurisches Blut floß und die Italien mit ihren Borjas vergiftet hatte?" (*Versuchung*, 183).

thrust of European culture will advance. Caught between his desire to re-
habilitate the bungling Italian Sforza and the sinister demands of the fa-
natic Spaniard Monclada, Pescara convenes an imperial military tribunal
consisting of himself, his ally Charles de Bourbon, and the Spanish general Leyva. The Italian side of Pescara votes with the sympathetic, though
renegade, French prince, against the Spanish, in order to enable the
meaningful survival of Milan, the future focal point of Italian liberalism.
The compass swings about decisively, the needle pointing northwestward
from Italy over France. The Italian-French line, the axis preferred by British humanists, crosses and checks the alternate German-Spanish line.

Readers of the Swiss romantic realist Meyer are well prepared for fiction written more immediately under the influence of Nietzsche. Gide's
critical essay on Nietzsche in 1899 signals the widening influence of the
latter's psychologically grounded theory that overturns both the prevalent Western idea of progress and any merely reflexive, sentimental questioning of it, such as in the works of Rousseau. Nietzsche confronts
the Europeans, as heirs of a belief in historical progress and in translation of mandate; he confronts them with the paradoxical question of
how they could revise the Western sense of values, including the idea
of progress, without ceasing to be European. The protagonist of Gide's
novel L'immoraliste (The Immoralist, 1902), the wealthy scholar Michel,
exemplifies Nietzsche's category of Greek and Western overdevelopment
that reaches dangerous hypertrophy in theoretical man, who is alienated from life through his Apollonian excess.[8] Michel's secular asceticism
(like Gide's) is derivative from the stern Huguenot morals of his mother's family, but the competent reader after 1900 cannot fail to note that,
symptomatically, this French savant is attracted to the study of Phrygian
religious cults, to the neglected Dionysian polarity. Michel denies the
passions through an arranged marriage with his cousin Marceline, who
as a feminine alter ego enables initial stages of narcissistic mirroring.
A trip to Africa confronts him with an intensity of sensation in the desert landscape that endangers his stability, but the experience of his own
resulting illness makes him aware of the connection between his wife
Marceline's own eventual sickness and her religious sentiment, and between his own life denial and the aridity of modern science. Michel's
excesses when he experiences Dionysian liberation reveal a new form of

8. Cf. the treatment of Gide's novel by John B. Foster, *Heirs to Dionysus: A Nietzschean
Current in Literary Modernism* (Princeton, N.J.: Princeton University Press, 1981).

imbalance. His new desire to do research on the Goths reinstates the ancient reciprocal attraction between northern barbarians and the South, and the compass of the narrative once again points northward. The novel grows troubled as Michel's Dionysian joyousness overlaps with his surrender to the primitive, to criminality, and to homosexual inclinations. While fear of his own drift undercuts his transformation, Michel's symbolic plunge into a pool on the Amalfi coast affirms the existential leap he has made, his Dionysian baptism. As we move back northwestward, it is into the perplexing ambivalence of Michel's retreat to his estate in Normandy. There, as the novel closes, he attempts to balance Apollonian strength of mind and Dionysian richness of instinct. But we are uncertain of the outcome, because Michel succumbs to conniving in lower class criminality. Any higher control appears forfeited.

Thomas Mann's reaction to Nietzsche dates from slightly earlier than Gide's and by 1899 was tempered by rediscovering Nietzsche's master, Schopenhauer. Like Gide, Mann exploits elements from his own family and cultural background to establish, in the novel *Buddenbrooks* (1901), polarities that recur in all his later work: in broad outline, an interplay of masculine, Northern, and Protestant traits as against feminine, Southern, and Catholic ones. It is probable that some influence also was exerted by the Berlin novelist Theodor Fontane, who toward the close of the nineteenth century, in works like *Effi Briest* (1894–1895) and *Schach von Wuthenow* (1882), clearly maps the geocultural and developmental position of Germany as a culture caught between East and West, as well as between North and South. Fontane alludes to archaic layers of Germanness, reaching into rural hinterlands and rooted before the Protestant-Catholic split, and connects older Christianity with the pagan past. If Berlin is the transactional center of the Fontane compass, it opens upon a Balto-Slavic East and a Scandinavian North as into ambivalences and mysteries of deeper identity, but these are balanced by the pull of the progressive West and the comforting old knowledge of the warm South. The reminder of archaic rites haunts his pages. Hence readers of Fontane can be expected to be primed for such moments as the following daydream in Mann's jocoserious treatment of the young bourgeois engineer from Hamburg. In *The Magic Mountain* (1924), Hans Castorp first absorbs the lessons taught by the Apollonian champion, the liberal humanist Settembrini. But then he is ineluctably smitten by the antithetical Dionysian emissary, Clavdia Chauchat. This hot cat (Chauchat) on a cold Swiss roof is depicted thus on Mann's cultural compass:

But what—or who—was it that drew down the other side of the scales, when weighed over against patriotism, belles-lettres, and the dignity of man? It was—Clavdia Chauchat, "Kirghiz"-eyed, "relaxed," and tainted within; when he thought of her (though thinking is far too tame a word to characerize the impulse that turned all his being in her direction), it was as though he were sitting again in his boat on the lake in Holstein, looking with dazzled eyes from the glassy daylight of the western shore to the mist and moonbeams that wrapped the eastern heavens.[9]

The peaks of Switzerland in the seven years leading up to World War I are the focal point where Hans, the inexperienced engineer from bourgeois Hamburg, situated to the European progressive northwest, gathers important strands of the story of millennia that reveals his primordial kinship with the ancient world of the South and the East, a story that finally recedes into obscure cosmic origins. The compass needle at this axial center of modern Europe in Switzerland quivers with every mention of the contending forces, which are now internalized in the civilization. Jerusalem Hill and the gothic pile of St. Mary's in the Protestant Hanseatic city where the Buddenbrooks reside remind us, in the opening pages of that novel in 1901, that the central point of transactions is always inscribed upon a developmental palimpsest that we can project onto the compass.

In 1913, in *Death in Venice*, the geocultural intersection is the place where Wagner, the slave to and king of music, expired. Venice is transparently another boundary between Apollonian and Dionysian realms. The relevant map is suggested in the historian Aschenbach's walk by the neo-Byzantine mortuary at the North Cemetery in Munich. In fact, a herald of the mysterious divinity Dionysus appears, prompting Aschenbach's fleeting daydream of a crouching tiger in a tropical swampland. After a lifetime of intellectual exertions, he is attracted to the Mediter-

9. I follow the translation by H. T. Lowe-Porter, *The Magic Mountain* (New York: Modern Library, 1952), 160. The original passage reads: "Was oder wer aber befand sich auf dieser anderen, dem Patriotismus, der Menschenwürde und der schönen Literatur entgegengesetzten Seite, wohin Hans Castorp sein Sinnen und Betreiben nun wieder lenken zu dürfen glaubte? Dort befand sich . . . Clavdia Chauchat,—schlaff, würmstichig und kirgisenäugig; und indem Hans Castorp ihrer gedachte (übrigens ist 'gedenken' ein allzu gezügelter Ausdruck für seine Art, sich ihr innerlich zuzuwenden), war es ihm wieder, als säße er im Kahn auf jenem holsteinischen See und blickte aus der glasigen Tageshelle des westlichen Ufers vexierten und geblendeten Auges hinüber in die nebeldurchsponnene Mondnacht der östlichen Himmel" (*Der Zauberberg* [Frankfurt: Fischer Taschenbuch Verlag, 1987], 170).

ranean realm, to Venice as a crossroads of the Apollonian West (with its obsession for form, and classical love of plastic arts and plastic language), and of the Dionysian East (the world of passion, and of music as a direct expression of the "will"). Steadily, the unidentified narrator widens the scope of the intra-European model, linking it to a bigger world picture—the disease in the fetid underside of Venice breaks loose when cholera finds its way literally from India, the land of Dionysus's emblematic tiger, over the trade routes, to Venice. In a major crisis when the authorities seek to deny the menace, only the representative from the furthest rim of the northwestward movement of civilization has the will and capacity to tell the truth. An English official informs Aschenbach of the peril, but Aschenbach, slipping into his terminal thralldom to Dionysus, chooses to conceal what he has discovered. By 1935, in a talk entitled "Europe Beware," Mann is actively playing the real-life role of this responsible, westward-trending Hesperian, as he helps to rally the developed democracies against the age's social plague: the regressive barbarism of the spreading totalitarian revolution.

It is a natural step for the ironist Mann to move from his epic mode of narration into discursive prose as an essayist who advocates values in an evolving system. As Campbell has pointed out, Joyce narrates his *Ulysses* (1922) in a quite different mode, the dramatic, which is congenial to his stricter aesthetic code of art for art's sake and avoidance of political involvement. But the fact that, with Joyce, we behold all the elements of the human world in action does not diminish his connection with the encyclopedic-humoristic tradition. Joyce is certainly not inhibited in pursuit of one of its chief aims: a fuller mapping of the human universe. Through their varying degrees of conscious and unconscious participation in archetypes, Joyce objectifies in his major, minor, and peripheral characters the human aggregate that recapitulates the eternal story of humanity.[10] One ground pattern of the relationship between Leopold Bloom and Stephen Dedalus is the boundary and overlay of ancient Semitic experience and rawer European energy. The symbiosis expressed in Joyce's slogan "Jewgreek, Greekjew" plays with the more solemn Victorian discussion of the Hebrew and Hellene components in the Judeo-Christian world in order to repristinate our appreciation of them. This Bloomian-Dedalian bonding has its countless variations—for example,

10. An example of the new global reach of appreciation of myth, congenial to Joycean universality in fiction, is Joseph Campbell, *The Hero with a Thousand Faces,* 2nd ed. (Princeton, N.J.: Princeton University Press, 1968).

in the dialectic that has existed since time immemorial between Ireland, as a sustaining and/or corrupted mother, and the invading father, who wounds and/or engenders new life, and in the child who is the restarting or revalidation of the story. Our wandering through the labyrinth of Dublin with its denizens reinstates the map of the Odyssean quest. For Joyce, it is a quest that can occur anywhere; thus it is implicit in the life and works of myriad-minded Shakespeare into whom Bloom, Stephen, and all the questers merge.[11]

Like Mann, though far more radical than Mann in his antirealist experiments, Joyce reaches out to a remarkable repertory of world cultures for the materials bearing on the interaction of the civilized and barbarian, and other polarities of forces. Sindbad the Sailor, Odysseus, and the Flying Dutchman are forever landing in the estuary while Stephen, like Hamlet, broods about the ghost of the father. The direction of flow in Joycean allusions to past mythological waves and patterns is still predominantly from East to West, while the search for the lost or to-be-restored heritage in his novel involves the symbiosis between raw North and warm South, barbaric vitality and old wisdom. However, Joyce's well-known interest in the cyclic thought of Vico tempers the urgency in the Nietzschean warning about a threatening Western decadence. Joyce reinfuses the handed-down map with a sense of permanent possibility that derives from what he perceives to be its inherent polypolarity. Rebirth is the only cultural and human choice that can fully command his dreaming. With Joyce it is clear that the map has attained a juncture resembling that reached when European writers still used the older Ptolamaic-Platonic spheres as a poetic model, even though they acknowledged the newer Copernican-Galilean cosmos as being the scientific reality.

The New World puts in an appearance in the climax to "Oxen of the Sun," chapter 14 of *Ulysses,* in the spiel of a visiting American preacher whose unrestrainable barbaric yawp parallels the cry of Mrs. Purefoy's newborn son. Though Joyce never visited across the Atlantic, he spun America into his universal picture in the *Wake,* too. In the novel *America,* another nonvisitor, Kafka creates his own version of the younger nation as a field of existential exploration, notably amid the perils of the big city. By 1900, Europe had obtained an elaborate collective alter ego in the immigrant nations that were its former colonies, most importantly the United States. The invention of the "West" inevitably involved consider-

---

11. This subject is treated in chapter eight, "Afterthoughts of Hamlet."

ation of what these offshoots of Europe and their further blendings of European and non-European elements meant in cultural history, and the emergent newer as well as older homelands participated actively in the discourse on this subject.[12] Both European and American authors were keenly aware of the rapid processes of urbanization and of the impact of accruing new technologies in the nineteenth century (telegraph, railroad, steamship, telephone, etc.) that eventually ever more tightly linked continents and transformed the world map in such a manner that great urban centers came to bear analogy to the town centers of the not so remote past, while the rail lines which spread out from them into the continental backcountry resembled streetcar lines going beyond suburban terminals.[13] Wandering away from the safer centers and settled edges of the world was like venturing into the bad districts of one or another megalopolis. Even before yet newer waves of technology further shrank the globe, authors from the sixteenth century onward—for example, the Alsatian Jörg Wickram in the novel *Von guten und bösen Nachbarn* (Of Good and Bad Neighbors, 1556)—were conscious that the elaboration of global networks of commerce and banking was in progress and that an international class of merchant bankers were involved in bringing this about. We encounter the possibility of participating in this new world reality and we learn about its coordinates and its dangerous aspects again in Daniel Defoe's *Robinson Crusoe* (1719). As the detective story and gothic fiction brought to public notice (chapter three has illustrated such cases), dangerous, alien, and/or archaic forces, uncanny kinds of otherness, that lurked out in the hinterlands or colonial outposts, might emerge right in the heart of civilization. In framing his novella *Heart of Darkness* (1902), Joseph Conrad made it clear that proud Europeans on the Thames could unwittingly be endangered by the horror Marlow discovers up the Congo; an unnamed internal listener to Marlow's story thinks back to the time when the imperial Romans, predecessor claimants to the mission of civilization, landed to confront the pagan British. Herman Melville drove home an analogous point with his framing of *The Confidence-Man: His Masquerade* (1857) shortly before the American Civil War. At its start his novel explicitly superimposes the entire story of human development onto the map of contemporary America posited in the

12. See my essay, "Peripheral Echoes: 'Old' and 'New' Worlds as Reciprocal Literary Mirrorings," *Comparative Literature* 58 (2006): 339–59.

13. See my chapter, "Nexus and Connection in the Modern City," in *Echoland: Readings from Humanism to Postmodernism* (Brussels: Presses Interuniversitaires Européennes, 2006), 223–35.

form of a world compass. The Mississippi provides an axis that is both actual and symbolic. The east-west movement of the expanding "young" nation, as it transits through the city of Saint Louis, is transsected by the north-south movement of the ship of fools which sets off down river from the historical traffic midpoint of the continent and, metaphorically, of human affairs, eventually descending out of any real freedom and into spiritual benightment.

The explicit mirroring of Old and New Worlds can be illustrated by Vincente Blasco Ibáñez's novel *Los cuatro jinetes del apocalipsis* (The Four Horsemen of the Apocalypse, original Spanish edition 1916). The sons of an Argentinian family of mixed European background end up fighting on opposite sides in World War I. The conflict is analyzed as a civil war afflicting a greater civilization in which some nations, as members of a larger family, drift into tragic destructive tendencies while others maintain humane decency and reasonable hope for progress. The sickness of Europe threatens the welfare and unity of the host immigrant nation that may possibly fail in its mission as a reasonable version of a terrestial paradise. The Hollywood film version of 1921 was so useful, with Argentinia obviously standing in for the United States, that Hollywood patriotically recycled it in 1961, but in this round applied the story to World War II. Ernest Hemingway's protagonist Jake in *The Sun Also Rises* (1927) maintains his identification as an American in the aftermath of World War I; however, he is a traumatized expatriate who really cannot go home again and feels attracted to a deeper, more authentic past exemplified in aspects of Spanish culture as against a worn-out version of Europe such as France. The hero of *For Whom the Bell Tolls* (1940) escapes the threat of alienation by being willing to sacrifice himself for the Republican cause in the Spanish Civil War, a cause ultimately implicating the larger civilization. Alienation reaches a metaphysical acme in Paul Bowles's *The Sheltering Sky* (1949) when the restless newlyweds, Porter and Kit Moresby, Americans from privileged urban families who arrive in Morocco, are irreversibly attracted into the vastness of the Sahara and an inner desert of the spirit. Once they venture beyond the already dangerous edge held by France as a European colonial power, their immolation as captives to archaic realities (disease and death, sexual exploitation and bondage) is stark.

Another direction for mapping the European and global givens and those of the American heartland appears in the works of Thomas Pynchon and John Barth. It is legitimate to think of their kind of mapping as a postmodern revival of the encyclopedism that flowered in the Renaissance and baroque novel. Pynchon's *V* (1963) exhibits the tendency to subordinate actual global reference points, on several continents, and incidents in history therewith associated, to a cryptic symbolic scheme. One result is to suggest a mysterious convergence of the American and other story lines. An even more grandiose attempt at metahistorical romance is *Gravity's Rainbow* (1973), set in the final days of World War II when the rising imperial powers America and Russia beleaguer the capital and vital rocket grounds of Germany, the crushed would-be European hegemon. Pynchon obsessively draws cartographic coordinates and enhances these with described trajectories of the age's new sky-borne weaponry coursing toward targets. He ransacks every compartment of knowledge, including the natural sciences and mathematics, to impart a dense weave to the narration, a complexity that disempowers its human actors as independent agents and makes paranoid gestures at some recondite logic in world affairs. In contrast, John Barth more openly promotes an interpretation of human evolution in his earlier encyclopedic romance *Giles Goat-Boy; or, the Revised New Curriculum* (1963).[14] *Giles* posits "our" heritage by treating some of its main moments and documents as if they are archaic memories; these developmental traces, so the protagonist is taught, are still cultivated as elements in the curricula of various "campuses" (nations). The book *Giles* is ostensibly a text deliberately written by the library-computer WESCAC, or the collective repository of the brain and experience of Western civilization, in the archaic form known in a remote age as the novel. As we readers recognize, *Giles* spells out the contemporary situation of the world during the cold war, when the entire globe is already spinning under an electronic blanket and the danger of another devastating "campus riot" (world war) looms. Barth both maps and characterizes the cultural contributions of various continents and nations and expresses the hope that the needed balance to survive will be reconstituted. This in the main depends on the capacity of "West Campus" to fulfill its stabilizing mission and maintain its heritage.

The family resemblances between fictions of the late Renaissance, modernism, and postmodernism which constitute labyrinths have been well described in comparative studies.[15] We encounter labyrinths of vary-

14. See my chapter, "Postmodern Mannerism: Context in Text and Text as Pretext," in *Echoland*, 269–81.

15 Manfred Schmeling, *Der labyrinthische Diskurs: Vom Mythos zum Erzählmodell* (Frankfurt: Athenäum, 1987).

ing, sometimes dizzying dimensions. The labyrinthine experience is often conflated with the idea of exploring a library, as in stories by Jorge Luis Borges, in Barth's *Giles*, and in Umberto Eco's novel *Il nome della rosa* (The Name of the Rose, 1980). It may involve wandering about or being disoriented or lost in a city, as in Joyce's *Ulysses*, Michel Butor's *L'emploi du temps* (Passing Time, 1957), and G. W. Sebald's *Austerlitz* (2001).[16] Not infrequently, the imperative of solving a crime is at the heart of the matter, as in Butor's *Passing Time*, or the labyrinth is itself a detective story as in Borges's compact "El jardín de los senderos que se bifurcan" (The Garden of the Forking Paths, 1941) where the act of detection is interlaced with the discovery of a critical connection to the world map and larger history. With increasing frequency as we move into postmodern writing, the detective, an acute instance of the human being as hermeneut, and/or the reader of the work who observes him, fails to solve the mystery or to exit satisfactorily from the labyrinth, as for example in Knut Hamsun's *Mysterier* (Mysteries, 1892), in Alain Robbe-Grillet's *Les gommes* (The Erasers, 1953), or in Butor or Sebald. Joyce's chief male protagonists wander into but also emerge from "Hades" or Nighttown, which serves as the principal dystopic synechdoche for Dublin and the world in *Ulysses;* and it is clearly positive that like Odysseus and Telemachus they make their way to the home. After witnessing Stephen's setting out through the gate, the reader follows Bloom into the dot, the period or egg which the mother Molly embodies in her baffling role as the channel of being. In the *Wake*, the reader remains in the eternity of the human mind, summoned to rebirth by virtue of the symbolic turning of end into beginning. But Joyce's message is decidedly affirmative in contrast to the paranoiac "readings" which hapless directionless protagonists and the reader make of the modern edifice or city in Kafka's *The Trial* and *The Castle* and which we encounter again in the ambiguous world of Pynchon's *Gravity's Rainbow*. The following chapter five will, among other things, examine the importance of dystopic versions of the mythic roots of nations.

16. Regarding psychographic mapping in Sebald, cf. chapter 5, "On Getting Lost," in Eric Bulson, *Novels, Maps, Modernity: The Spatial Imagination* (New York and London: Routledge, 2007).

5 IRONIC REALISM AND THE FOUNDATIONAL ROMANCE

1. *Alienation on the Edge*

Northern Europeans tended to regard Brazil as a boundary zone under-girding the contested Caribbean Basin, a realm where all the races who bordered the Atlantic were being thrown together by the new dynamics of colonization and international trade. In broad outline, Marianna Torgovnick is correct in arguing that Euro-American modernist and post-modernist interest in the so-called primitive world continues earlier fixations like Rousseau's and primarily reflects aspects of European identity.[1] Fernand Braudel is likewise correct in arguing that Europeans in fact only rediscovered the Americas, sub-Saharan Africa, and other areas remoter from their continent, and that Europe's true achievement was to master the Atlantic and thus the "routes of the seven seas."[2] Although it remains moot whether Brenainn of Clonfert, the Irish saint, actually reached the New World some three centuries before Leif Eriksson, and eight centuries before Columbus did, the adventurous sea voyage is at least as old a story form on the Western rim of Europe as the *Navigatio Sancti Brendani* (The Voyages of Saint Brendan), written sometime between the sixth and tenth centuries.

A main and the culminating theme in Homer's *Odyssey* is *nostos*, return home, reintegration in the core. Brendan's Christianized theme, the search for the Earthly Paradise, still figures prominently among the

---

1. Marianna Torgovnick, *Gone Primitive: Savage Intellects, Modern Lives* (Chicago: University of Chicago Press, 1990). I accept (on a "truistic" basis, not necessarily in all the ramifications drawn) the general thesis that a wide variety of motifs in high and popular art, habits of mind in fields like anthropology, and in extensively defective universalizing theories such as Freudian psychology, involve genres of cultural mapping. I have addressed one of the persistent paradigms of European "internal" self-mapping in chapter four, "Prime Coordinates in Modernist Cultural Mappings."

2. Fernand Braudel, *Civilization and Capitalism*, vol. 1: *The Structures of Everyday Life: The Limits of the Possible*, rev. trans. by Siân Reynolds (New York: Harper & Row, 1981), 63. Original French version: *Les structures du quotidien: Le possible et l'impossible* (Paris: Librairie Armand Colin, 1979).

mythic strata in which Camões imbeds the latter-day exploits of the Portuguese. In creating a Renaissance epic, *Os Lusiadas* (The Lusitanians, 1572), to echo those of Homer and Virgil, the poet projects onto earth's farthest reaches the densely overwritten palimpsest. Indirectly, in the pose of a warrior, he asserts the learning that, as he proudly informs us, he has inherited in the line of singers "Of Roman, Greek, or barbarian nation."[3] Camões's depiction of cultural interactions after Da Gama reached Calcutta is a brilliant instance of a noble Renaissance mind attempting, already with some misgivings, to interpret the foreignness of an alternate culture in terms of the heritage of the European homeland. This encounter involves the typical use of cultural intermediaries and it soon necessitates indoctrinating the palpable "other" in European myth—such indoctrination occurs, for example, when Paulo through the Moor Monçaide explicates European paintings to the Cautal: "The one you're seeing now is Lusus because of whose fame our kingdom is called Lusitania."[4] But equally significant in Camões's account is the extent to which the daring Portuguese employ their complex knowledge of the global map to cope with the new geopolitical realities they and other seafaring nations are still in the process of establishing. In celebrating the stages of little Portugal's arrival at vast world empire under the guidance of Providence, Camões caps his epic poem, through Da Gama's famous vision in canto 10, with a grand tour that touches a truly amazing variety of the corners and peoples of our earth, including Brazil (10.63).

One of the first mentions of Columbus's discovery of the New World occurs in Brant's famous *Das Narrenschiff* (The Ship of Fools, 1494). This work also frets over phenomena that today, in retrospect, we recognize as reflecting the Renaissance drive to explore the world, the rise of early capitalism, and the onset of the Protestant revolution. Less well known is that by the mid-sixteenth century, Northern literature had arrived at the explicit formulation of a new perspective for European middle-class entrepreneurs who already operated as a distinct force and class within the international system inaugurated by Renaissance empire builders. Of special interest, because it develops the Portuguese connection, is the novel *Von guten und bösen Nachbarn* (Of Good and Evil Neighbors,

---

3. "Da lácia, grega ou bárbara nação" (*Lusiadas*, 5.97). References by canto and stanza are from Luís de Camões, *Os Lusiadas*, vols. 4 and 5 of *Obras completas*, ed. Hernâni Cidade, 3rd ed. (Lisbon: Sá da Costa, 1968).
4. "Este que vês, é Luso, donde a fama / O nosso Reino 'Lusitânia' chama" (*Lusiadas*, 8.2).

1556) by the Alsatian Protestant Jörg Wickram. Anticipating the broader subject matter that will fascinate authors such as Mann in *Buddenbrooks* (1901) and Galsworthy in *The Forsyte Sage* (1906ff.), Wickram follows the fortunes of a prosperous merchant family over three generations. The sixteenth-century mercantile saga is launched when Robertus moves his family and business from Antwerp to Lisbon in search of a more peaceful environment, and he indeed thrives when he settles among the Portuguese. Through friendships transcending race and religion, a network of families sharing the same middle-class ethic begins to knit together and its members engage in far-reaching business partnerships. Despite all vicissitudes, collectively theirs is a success story. Robertus's daughter marries the Spanish merchant Ricardus whom they have met en route and nursed through illness; the daughter of Ricardus, whom the stranger Lazarus saves and who in turn rescues Lazarus, marries the latter's son; and so forth. From letters and diaries we are instructed in their value system. From accounts of their trading journeys, we learn about the multiplicity of cities and places in old Europe and in the rest of the world where this undaunted new cosmopolitan breed pursues its business ventures. As W. A. Coupe says, Wickram elaborates an idealized picture "contrasting the safe stronghold of orderly bourgeois existence with the dangers and chaos lying in wait for the unwary in the wide and wicked world outside. [. . .] Civil and domestic peace, industry, moderation, practically conditioned respect for the rights of one's fellow men, charity to those less fortunate than oneself, a harmonious family life, and friendship based on mutual respect and mutual advantage: these are the characteristic virtues of Wickram's merchants."[5] The choice of exile in Portugal appears to function as a creative break from constrictive, historically outmoded values based on original identity; this liberation from fixed placement entails acceptance of others, and openness to the racially and territorially foreign, on a new basis of mutual recognition of individual worth.

By the late seventeenth century, the global network of trade and colonization is firmly in place, but European writers increasingly face the perplexing question of how to interpret the violence and oppression so often associated with the gains of a new empire. A classic instance of a self-critical view of newly discovered barbarians as fellow human be-

5. W. A. Coupe, *A Sixteenth-Century German Reader* (Oxford, U.K.: Clarendon Press, 1972), 200–201.

ings is Montaigne's famous essay "Des cannibales" (*Essais,* book 1, chapter 31; 1580). Particularly the backflow of information about the degradation of native peoples and the brutality of the slave trade began to impose on Europeans the task of redefining their own identity in terms of their creation of outposts and their involvement in imperialism as a kind of self-alienation. Aphra Behn's masterpiece *Oroonoko; or, The Royal Slave* (1688), is not just written in the humanistic spirit of Montaigne; her novella draws on her own observations as a young woman growing up in the Surinam area, before the time of her distinguished literary career in England. This work borrows concepts from French classical tragedy and high baroque romance in order to create a hierarchy of values by which to judge character. Using this standard and European concepts of natural law and rights, Behn treats the interplay of African, American Indian, and colonialist modes of life and thought, and breaks through to a complex evaluation of cultural alienation and its implications for European identity. By framing the several story strands as an account assembled by an eyewitness, Behn overcomes the cultural distance between her European readership and the exotic and remote realities of the colonial settlements. In a brilliant stroke of storytelling, she eventually reveals that the high-minded narrator is a young Englishwoman, the daughter of a colonial governor. When the narrator's life becomes closely interwoven with the lives of the chief protagonists later in the novella, and she effectively becomes a character in her own narrative, her proven moral and intellectual authority prevent the reader with any claim to sensibility from evading the hard lessons about the human conflicts that she exposes.

In her prefatory remarks, Behn's narrator—foreshadowing Rousseau's sentiments by some eighty years—pairs two ideas: she evokes the original state of innocence, which she attributes to American Indian culture; and she views the intrusion of European ways as the main precipitating factor in the native peoples' fall from grace. By a reciprocal contamination, the presence of Negro slaves clearly evidences the fallenness of the Europeanized New World. Behn then explores at length the experience of alienation in non-European terms, and thus, implicitly, in universal terms, by shifting the scene to Africa and to the story of Prince Oroonoko and his virtuous beloved Imoinda. Oroonoko, war captain of his nation, is described as possessing a nobility and dignity that make him comparable to the ancient classical heroes. When in battle he takes captives and they are then enslaved, it is not for his personal gain; rather, he acts on behalf of his own people out of a sense of honor. As regrettable as this archaic trait of the culture is, Behn notes that it makes sense within the total framework of values, as it would have for the ancient Greeks and other peoples. The crack in the natural order appears when in lustful dotage Oroonoko's grandfather, the king, cannot forgo choosing Imoinda as one of his wives. The threatened young lovers rebel by consummating their own marriage. There is no question which way Behn's sympathies incline in this contest between natural rights and despotism, the corrupted political state that the king's lapse brings about.

The European connection now comes actively into play. The European captain of a slave ship, who is too weak to live up to his own liberal instincts that gnaw at him, kidnaps the prince by trickery, while the king sells his tarnished bride in order to be rid of the tragic reminder of his own guilt. Thus the noble lovers are destined to remeet as slaves in the New World, where the narrator eventually befriends them and they marry under their slave names as Caesar and Clemene. Expectation of a child introduces the crucial new philosophical and social challenge, the question whether it is morally tolerable to bring a baby into the world in chains.

Behn intensifies the dilemma by having her narrator directly observe Caesar's remarkable adaptation to the tropical zone of the New World. He is formidable in the hunt, as a guide in dangerous jungles, and as an intermediary in visiting the Indians in remote areas—and the narrator's participation in some daring explorations, in turn, enhances her credibility as a special and superior witness. Just as she carefully explains certain facts horrific to the average enlightened person in safe Britain—for example, the practice of ritual self-mutilation among Indian warriors—so she never mitigates her analysis of the moral degeneration into which much of the black population sinks, brutalized by their enslavement. Oroonoko-Caesar, who urges his fellow Africans to risk all to recover their human dignity, emerges as their spokesman for freedom. Through him, Behn indicts the reciprocal European decadence, pointing especially to the criminal component of the white population who are involved in the violent dealings of empire. She directs our attention to the horde—in Oroonoko's words—of "Rogues and Runagades, that have abandoned their own Countries for Rapine, Murders, Thefts and Villanies. Do you not hear every day how they upbraid each other with Infamy of Life, below the wildest Salvages? And shall we render Obedience to such a degenerate Race, who have no one human Vertue left, to distinguish them from the vilest Creatures?" (61).[6] In relating the dynamics of the slave insurrection incited by Oroonoko and its failure, the narrator increasingly emerges as spokeswoman for the moral conscience of the Europeans. She does not withhold her admiration for the inspired heroic leaders of the Africans nor her scorn for the archetypal opportunist politician, "not fit to be mentioned with the worst of the Slaves" (63f.), the deputy governor Byam, who first exacerbates the danger, then deals implacably with the fugitives. The wounded governor, who heads the party of moderation, is unable to do more than contain the carnage when a split develops among the white settlers. The blacks' need for justice precipitates a general breakdown of law and order, and this turn reveals a deep threat of disorder inherent in the European structure itself.

Rather than abandon Imoinda to chains, Oroonoko kills her with Horatian fortitude as a moral duty. Contrastively incarnating the bestial streak in the European population is "Banister, a wild Irish Man, and one of the Council, a Fellow of absolute Barbarity" (76), who takes a special delight in torturing and dismembering the battered, exhausted hero. The narrator, "very apt to fall into Fits of dangerous illness upon any extraordinary Melancholy" (76), is represented at the final grisly scene by her mother and sister who cannot save the prince from the rabble. By the end of this grim novella, Behn has established a complex European typology with correspondences in the mirror African and Indian populations. Without denying the crucial historical gaps in the development of the several societies, she argues the case for the universal presence of important human attributes and insights—for example, Imoinda's shared feminine sentiments—that indicate the possibility of a moral evolution based on natural law. But the colonial tragedy also suggests the frightening possibility that the raw exercise of power can nullify human idealism. Like her hero Oroonoko, Behn is too honest to avoid seeing that this threat is actual, latent in the civilization that prides itself on its own political advancement.[7]

The title figure of Daniel Defoe's novel *Robinson Crusoe* (1719) has in himself such a mixture of good and evil, and one theme of his story is

6. References by pagination are to Aphra Behn, *Oroonoko; or, The Royal Slave*, ed. Lore Metzger (New York: W. W. Norton, 1973).

7. A remarkable, voluminous account of the turbulent history of the Surinam area and the nature of the colonial world there a century after Behn's experiences, also written by an eyewitness (original manuscript, 1790), is John Gabriel Stedman, *Narrative of a Five Years Expedition against the Revolted Negroes of Surinam*, ed. Richard Price and Sally Price (Baltimore: Johns Hopkins University Press, 1988).

the task of recognizing the proper direction for human consciousness that has discovered its own fallenness. With good reason, both professional economists (among them Karl Marx) and literary scholars have made much of the economic teachings that permeate this novel, in the longest stretches of which we observe how a lone person, through self-reliance and accrued technical and agricultural knowledge from his European homeland, adapts himself to the environment of his New World place of exile and there initially builds a one-man colony out of some pieces of wreckage. Very striking in this novel is the appearance of key subgenres within it, most notably the explicit keeping of spiritual as well as material accounts in double-ledger form, and the keeping of a diary that expands into long confessional passages of meditation and self-examination. Defoe links Crusoe's role as a higher representative of the venturing middle class with his intense cultivation of inwardness and interiority. While the spaces in which Crusoe's story unfolds clearly retain a powerful emblematic function from baroque literature, they also have a more precise location within the new global network of commerce, banking, and colonialization by which both the European body and the European mind have expanded their sway—with unforeseen further consequences.[8]

It is clear from the opening sentence that Crusoe incarnates the international bourgeoisie. While the forename "Robinson" comes from the maternal English side, his father is a merchant from Bremen, actually named "Keutznaer." One of Crusoe's important early experiences, ending in a moral failure that will trouble his conscience productively many years after, is to be a slave in Moorish captivity on the Moroccan coast, to manage a daring escape in the company of the devoted Moslem youth Xury, but then to allow Xury to be indentured for ten years to the Portuguese captain who picks them up at sea, whereas Crusoe is privileged to enjoy a generous new start in Brazil, thrives there as a planter, and begins to invest and trade successfully through Anglo-Portuguese channels. Substantial prosperity and good fortune only blind him; not having yet learned his lesson, Crusoe overreaches by going to the coast of Africa for wild profit in slaves who are badly needed by the plantations. Thus he ends up stranded for nearly three decades on his island off the Guin-

8. I have treated the symbolic contextualization at more length in ch. 12, "Erring and Wayfaring in Baroque Fiction: The World as Labyrinth and Garden," of *Garden and Labyrinth of Time: Studies in Renaissance and Baroque Literature* (New York: Peter Lang, 1988), 297–323.

ea coast near the Orinoco River and must learn from scratch again about his basic humanity. His celebrated relationship with the cannibal Friday intervenes only after many years of extreme loneliness that prepare him inwardly to transcend the cultural barriers separating him from the archaic or savage world. This and other steps will eventually alter Crusoe's whole sense of cultural and political identity.

Crusoe initially reacts in horror upon discovering the gory scenes of anthropophagy on his shores and wants to exact a bloody retribution against the savages. But on mature reflection he comes around to the realization that "[t]hey do not know it to be an offence, and then commit it in defiance of divine justice, as we do in almost all the sins we commit" (RC 177), and he reasons that to attack them, except in self-defense, "would justify the conduct of the Spaniards in all their barbarities practiced in America, where they destroyed millions of these people, who, however they were idolators and barbarians, and had several bloody and barbarous rites in their customs, such as sacrificing human bodies to their idols, were yet, as to the Spaniards, very innocent people" (RC 178).[9] Crusoe's yearning for human society attains a peak of grief when he sees the corpse of a young boy in a Spanish wreck and thinks of Xury. When placed in the quandary of hiding for self-protection but thereby letting Friday be killed by an enemy tribe, Crusoe feels "called by Providence to save this poor creature's life" (RC 206). This act begins his new career in building and governing the small island society, one founded on natural law, that gradually grows through the adoption of new refugees. What is remarkable is that Crusoe integrates new citizens on the basis of their willingness to live in harmony and mutual support. Thus a stranded Spanish officer is accepted despite the traditional enmity between Spain and England, while the incorrigible English and Dutch mutineers of a Protestant ship are hanged, and the repentant are advised to remain as law-abiding settlers. What we witness coming into being is the sort of modern migrant nation such as the future Brazil, Canada, and the United States.

When the older and wiser Crusoe at last returns to Brazil, he finds

9. Citations of RC followed by the page number are to Daniel Defoe, *The Life and Adventures of Robinson Crusoe* (= *The Life and Strange Surprixing Adventures of Robinson Crusoe, of York. Mariner: Who lived Eight and Twenty Yars, all alone in an un-inhabited Island on the Coast of America, near the Mouth of the Great River Oroonoque; Having been cast on Shore by Shipwreck, wheren all the Men perished but himself. With An Account how he was last strangely deliver'd by Pyrates. Written by Himself*), ed. Angus Ross (Harmondsworth, U.K.: Penguin Books, 1965).

that, in his absence, his Portuguese friends, the authorities, business trustees, and his old partner have dealt fairly with his multiplying wealth; some of it will continue to "be expended in perpetuity for the benefit of the poor, and for the conversion of the Indians to the Catholic faith" (RC 275). Crusoe finds that the same probity obtains in England where meanwhile his dividends have piled up. In short, already in existence as a sustaining order, is a framework of legal and ethical standards that operates virtually on its own. Crusoe's life is intertwined with a system that in the long run yields results to honest effort and investment: today, in retrospect, we call it capitalism. While old Crusoe feels drawn to England and his Protestant roots, his own life testifies to a capacity to adapt to a variant brand of Christianity and to work with the mixed population of the New World. His grand tour around Europe at the end of the novel underscores the boundary-crossing, restless, reflective mind that, in effect, no longer is really at home in the old homeland but is forever attached now to the role of being an enterprising and caring governor.

In the fictional first-person account of Crusoe, we have an intimation of a principle of alienation that is a necessary precondition for the creation of new composite nation states, if they are to be capable of separation from a dominant founding "old country." By a natural logic, through alienation, not only Europeans and Africans, but also indigenous peoples in the Americas, brought together willingly or unwillingly in a new polity, become de facto aliens with a mutual task of constructing nationhood on some new experimental basis. As in earlier centuries, the shared pathway of merger in a new polity has given birth to various new myths of identity. A puzzling question arises today in view of the intensifying mobility of older and newer population groups in an overcrowded postcolonial world, while self-perceived latecomers such as repressed ethnic groups insist on the devolution of established polities or special status. Can huge newer immigrant nations like Brazil and the United States expect any satisfactory myth of cultural identity to emerge or persist in our times, a sense that transcends the notion of a composite immigrant world? Old Europe is now considering that question; and to conclude on a provocative note, I would say that for many good reasons Europe or India or any other immense civilization with distinct cultural components would be ill-advised to take the large immigrant nations of the Western Hemisphere as a model. That would be a false or distorted mirroring, even though Europe gave the main impetus to the mode of alienation by which the unfinished mixture of peoples occurred in the New World.

2. Renewal of Discourse and Identity: The Example of
John Barth and Alejo Carpentier

In the preceding section, I have discussed novels written from the sixteenth to the early eighteenth centuries by Northern Europeans who felt challenged to redefine their own cultural identity in terms that took into account the global, transoceanic network of colonization and trade spawned by the Renaissance. Notable breakthroughs in fiction at the Enlightenment threshold were, as we have noted, Aphra Behn's novella *Oroonoko* and Daniel Defoe's novel *Robinson Crusoe*. These narratives helped shape a discourse that reflected more deeply on the altered status of Other and Self, a discourse that was consonant with the development of outposts and peripheries into new junctures and potential centers. These works of fiction thus anticipated attitudes fundamental for the emergence of a diverse range of modern immigrant nations like the United States, Argentina, Canada, Mexico, and Brazil. Here I propose to consider the related theme of "renewal" that the Renaissance bequeathed to the major revolutions in the Old and New Worlds as its inheritors, but I shall overleap the intervening colonial centuries to a newer boundary of great importance in twentieth-century literature. Many contemporary Western Hemisphere writers have felt attracted to perceived "originary" moments when key qualitative breaks in discourse occurred, moments that presumably gave rise to New World cultural identities. Once emergent, these perceived new identities gradually invited retrospective celebration and then, in a later reprise, could be critiqued for various omissions and distortions, such as alleged undue neglect of indigenous factors, and so forth.

Among preeminent moments for the self-image of many Western Hemisphere peoples, the Enlightenment redefinition of human liberty and dignity had, by the nineteenth century, acquired a virtual mythic status comparable to that which the Renaissance had accorded to the deeds of glory and the world-altering insights of the ancient Near Eastern and Greco-Roman forebears of modern Europe. Thus we can garner fresh lessons about the complexity of cultural heritages from observing the ways in which insightful novelists such as Alejo Carpentier (1904–1980) and John Barth (1930–) have probed what they perceive to be the inherent strangeness of the inherited "myth" of foundation applicable to their native areas. Carpentier's *El siglo de las luces* (The Enlightenment, 1962; known in English translation as Explosion in a Cathedral) and Barth's *The Sot-Weed Factor* (1960), reconstrue, respectively, the perplexed spiritual story of the Caribbean Basin and of the Chesapeake Bay. Thus, despite all generational, regional, and ideological differences, these novels exhibit the natural kinship among New World authors who re-create the epic of origins by revising an outworn revolutionary legend and by simultaneously admitting and overcoming the linkages of their past to the Old World. The accidents of family background doubtlessly furnished both novelists with a keener sense for investigating the collective, cumulative experience of straddling cultural zones that was basic to colonialism. This shifting of boundaries is still being replicated in countless current instances in mixed families some of whose members are present as immigrants while other members are native-born or of old indigenous stock, but often saturated with awareness of overseas sources of cultural energies in their environment. Carpentier, born in La Habana to a French father and a Russian mother, and Barth, born 1930 in Cambridge, Maryland, to a German-American family, are, in that respect too, eminently suited to bridge the past and present realms of cultural self-imagining of their homelands.

I shall treat Carpentier first, because he belongs to an older generation that was formed by modernism, although he has become better known for helping to invent "magical realism"; and then I shall look at Barth, some of whose writing is thought to pertain to postmodernism. However much Carpentier's narration may be laced with ironies, he strikes a steady serious tone in confronting the decades of the American and French Revolutions, a time noted for high-minded philosophical and social utterances, whereas Barth pursues a comic strategy that befits his irreverent focus on the period antedating the revolutions, the heyday of metaphysical wit, the baroque novel, and Swiftian satire. Yet, in effect, both writers strive to overcome a standard myth whose lasting spell, they imply, has been tantamount to a long bout of cultural amnesia. Carpentier debunks aspects of the revolutions through an omniscient authorial voice as if mentally present to detect the underside of events in the eighteenth century while they are in progress; the narration restores certain powers of baroque perspectival and emblematic vision in order to disclose the geopolitical and human actuality of the Caribbean Sea that is emerging into modern history. Barth anticipatorily debunks the rhetoric of the not-yet-dawned revolutionary episode by revealing the all-too-human secrets underlying it in the more colorful age of the very first European settlements.

Thus one of the themes in common is the imperative to break the an-aesthetic spell of an Enlightenment myth and to tap into the expanding, turbulent world picture evident in baroque literature and art. Concomitantly, both books steer toward a disillusionary awakening that entails recognition of frightening and humbling truths. To a large extent, we move along this general pathway of discovery with Esteban, the chief educational protagonist of *Explosion in a Cathedral,* and with Ebenezer Cooke, his equivalent in *The Sot-Weed Factor.* While moving with them and others, from the Americas to Europe and back again, we rediscover the deeper meaning of origins by encountering clues embedded everywhere in each novel, as if planted by history itself. These occur notably in references to the artistic, philosophical, and scientific heritages available to the figures of the time under examination. Most of the materials and many of the personages alluded to in both books belong to the verifiable historical record; other materials are invented in an effort at sympathetic attunement with qualities of the world as it might have been experienced in the context of the historical givens. To this extent, both Carpentier and Barth create an encyclopedic texture reminiscent of the baroque sense of the immense symbolic "world book."[10] Of course, as I noted in chapter four, "Prime Coordinates in Modernist Cultural Mappings," such blends of documentable and fictive elements in order to characterize an age or its turning point have a more recent lineage in narrative art that we can trace from Flaubert's *Sentimental Education* over Joyce's *Ulysses* and Mann's *The Magic Mountain* in the Old World.

Esteban's function as an educational lead figure is framed by his imaginative relation to a number of artworks that directly exhibit mysterious forces in his world. Perhaps best known—and furnishing the title for the English translation of Carpentier's novel—is the painting titled *Explosión en una catedral* (Explosion in a Cathedral) that fascinates Esteban in subchapter 2 where it is described, from his vantage, as "a huge canvas by an unknown Neapolitan master which confounded all the laws of plastic art by representing the apocalyptic immobilization of a catastrophe" (EC 18).[11] The painting is an actual work by François Nomé and current-

10. Alejo Carpentier, *El siglo de las luces,* intro. by Carlos Fuentes (Caracas: Biblioteca Ayachuco, 1979); henceforth cited by the abbreviation SL and the page number. Carlos Fuentes stresses the baroque vision in his commentary in the Caracas edition of 1979. In a paper entitled "Postmodern Mannerism," given at the 1973 Diacritics Symposium at Cornell, I have discussed both the penchant for baroque literature and a related mannerist ethos in Barth and connected these features to the writing of José Donoso, especially the surreal, neomythic "magical realism" of *El obsceno pájaro de la noche* (1970).

11. English renditions are to Alejo Carpentier, *Explosion in a Cathedral,* trans. John

ly hangs in the Fitzwilliam Museum in Cambridge, England. Likewise, Victor Hugues, the seductive Frenchman who manipulates revolutionary currents for power and wealth in Europe and the Antilles, is based on a real person, although as interpreted by Carpentier he will impress any reader except a specialist in eighteenth-century history as being an archetypal figure bodied forth out of a poet's mind. Among other things, as in chapter 14, the novel *Explosion in a Cathedral* reminds us of the fervent, cultish, and sickly traits of the eighteenth century that standard history ordinarily disentangles from its idealism and rationalism, and of surviving earliest layers of culture such as the Basques. When the invented figures Esteban and his cousin Sofía go forth in the final chapter to die resisting the French in Madrid, while the merchant Carlos will survive as the bourgeois inheritor of the revolutionary drama, they become mysteriously implicated in the symbolism of the exploding cathedral depicted in the painting that they abandon in their house. The structure that once housed authority is shattered, yet it lingers in fragments in our institutions, as well as gothicized in memory, into our moment. One of the repercussions latent in Esteban's and Sofía's decision to resist the abusive exercise of imperial power by the French, who sweep across Europe under the pretext of spreading the blessings of their revolution, is that their human gesture anticipates future acts of opposition to the consolidation of power, a victory with which the emergent dominant bourgeoisie is by and large satisfied.

In addition, the gigantic explosion that is occurring in Europe is, simultaneously, the continuation of a massive implosion of Europe old and new into the Caribbean Basin. This onrolling series of shock waves, overwhelming native resistance and compelling Africans to exist in servitude in exile, represents a titanic clash of mythic energies in perpetual migration: "Two irreconcilable historical periods confronted one another in this struggle where no truce was possible. Totemic Man was op-

---

Sturrock (Boston: Little, Brown, 1963); hereafter cited by the abbreviation EC and the page number. The original Spanish reads: "una gran tela, venida de Napolés, de autor desconocido que, contrariando todas las leyes de la plástica, era la apocalíptica inmovilización de una catástrofe" (SL, 12). Lois Parkinson Zamora, *The Usable Past: The Imagination of History in Recent Fictions of the Americas* (Cambridge, U.K.: Cambridge University Press, 1997), 202–12, discusses a "New World Baroque" that, starting from Carpentier and reaching over Paz, "has become an essential metaphor for the inclusive interactions of cultures and histories in the Americas," and functions in ways parallel to the liberating effect of romanticism in the English, French, and German streams. Though apparently unaware of the extent of Barth's deliberate turn to the European baroque, Zamora sees "neobaroque" manifestation in a number of U.S. authors.

posed to Theological Man" (EC 244).[12] In chapter 24, in what amounts to an epiphanic experience for Esteban, Carpentier draws us into the immensity of the Caribbean Sea as the awesome space of all human venturing and discovery since time immemorial: "Now they were headed for the open sea, and beyond that for the mighty ocean of Odysseys and Anabases" (EC 173).[13] In language reminiscent of Mann, the earliest secrets of nature, its extravagances, "the earliest baroque of Creation" (EC 176),[14] are still open to view in this literal Paradise Lost as the Europeans continue arriving to compete by vaunting their culture. But, ironically, it is no longer possible to separate the strange European forms from the wondrous inventions of nature as inherent elements of the New World: "Going from surprise to surprise, Esteban discovered a plurality of beaches, where the sea, three centuries after the Discovery, was beginning to deposit its first pieces of polished glass—glass invented in Europe and strange to America; glass from bottles, from flasks, from demijohns [. . .]," and so forth (EC 176).[15]

In his comic vein, Barth conveys a similar message, that there is no undoing or pulling apart of the strange new merger of peoples and time layers that have already manifested themselves in the New World. Nowadays most of Barth's readers know that he mixed real historical records of early Virginia and Maryland with brilliant imitations in the styles of that era, but the original effect of his novel has not faded—it leaves us in entertaining uncertainty as to the status of most of the materials that we feel are probably fictional.[16] The same holds for our response to Barth's lead character, the poet Ebenezer Cooke, who in the novel leaves colonial Maryland to be educated in England, there encounters such famous people as Isaac Newton, and returns to his rude birthplace with his head

12. "Dos tiempos históricos inconciliables, se afrontaban en esa lucha sin tregua posible, que oponía el Hombre de los Totems al Hombre de la Teología" (SL, 173).

13. "Ahora se iba hacia el mar, y más allá del mar, hacia el Océano inmenso de las odiseas y anábasis" (SL, 123).

14. "los primeros barroquismos de la Creación" (SL, 125).

15. "De sorpresa en sorpresa descubría Esteban la pluralidad de las playas donde el Mar, tres siglos después del Descubrimiento, comenzaba a depositar sus primeros vidrios pulidos; vidrios inventados en Europa, desconocidos en América; vidrios de botellas, de frascos, de bombonas, . . ." (SL, 125).

16. For a fuller treatment of Barth's baroque orientation, see my essays "Rogues, Fools, and Satyrs: Ironic Ghosts in American Fiction," *Proceedings of the Comparative Literature Symposium* 5 (1972): 89–106, where Melville's importance is also considered at some length, and "Ironic Realism: The Novel as a Mirror of Civilization (Dos Passos and Barth)," *Proceedings of the Seventh Congress of ICLA*, 2 vols. (Stuttgart: Kunst und Wissen-Erich Bieber, 1979), 1.93–102.

swimming with the literature and thought of the age. Through the efforts of scholars, many readers have meanwhile learned that Barth roguishly chose the actual first American-born poet in English for his educational hero, a poet who was indeed educated in England and whose masterwork upon his return to the Chesapeake Bay was actually the sardonic epic named, in the novel, the *Marylandiad*, but already bearing the title *The Sot-Weed Factor*. In this historical work, borrowing from Sebastian Brant's *Das Narrenschiff* (The Ship of Fools, 1494) and Samuel Butler's *Hudibras* (1663–1678), the real Ebenezer Cooke energetically denounced the myth of the New World as an El Dorado or the Earthly Paradise.[17] Even though we are better informed than were the first readers of Barth's *The Sot-Weed Factor*, we can still enjoy these bits of recycled history as if they are clever inventions of a modern storyteller who seeks to re-create the past imaginatively.

The Sot-Weed Factor tells us about the deflowering of the brave New World in the seventeenth century as European man sank roots on the Eastern Seaboard, probed tentatively westward, imported African slaves, transferred Old World technologies, and tied the tobacco plantations and other enterprises into the network of world trade. One of the funniest scenes occurs when three outcasts—the white English-educated, first tidewater poet, an Indian chief, and an African prince—all stare, each from his own hiding place, out of the wilderness at the exotic sight of a small colonial village in a clearing. With its European dwellings, it is as if let down out of the sky. Reciprocally, the observing males represent the three principal, eager genetic strains poised to implode into that transposed vessel and produce the variety of the future. Barth's use of the adventurous prose romance, unified by the metaphor of a world theater, does not gently return us to the enchanting illusions of a receded past as was still feasible for Ariosto in *Orlando Furioso* (1516–1532); rather, this is a naturalistic parody of the times being portrayed and turns the noble conventions on their head. The climactic finish to the main plot of *The Sot-Weed Factor* occurs when the ungainly youth Ebenezer Cooke, virgin

17. In ch. 3 of Armin Paul Frank and Kurt Mueller-Vollmer, *British America and the United States, 1770s–1850s* (Göttingen: Wallstein Verlag, 2000), which is part 2 of vol. 1 of *The Internationality of National Literatures in Either America: Transfer and Transformation*, Armin Paul Frank notes that awareness of Cooke's original *The Sot-Weed Factor* (London, 1708) had faded away before the nineteenth century and Cooke was in effect given new life by "John Barth in his epic expansion of the poem" (116). With its double-edged satire, Cooke's "*The Sot-Weed Factor* is a territorially and culturally—not denominationally—separatist poem that alienates the unknowing British narrator and, above all, his London readers as none of us colonists" (Frank, 118).

and poet laureate, after numerous threats to his chastity, actually consummates marriage with poxy Joan Toast, a strumpet who has followed him from London to the new continent. We learn in no uncertain terms just how the colonies were populated, but Barth forgivingly studies this huge biological romp as a new mode of being in its nativity. This final acceptance of biological reality parallels acceptance, on the readers' part, that the past is all the more interesting when it is debunked.

The Sot-Weed Factor strikingly reinvokes Cervantes's groundplan in *Don Quixote* at the opening of the seventeenth century, with a new twist. Upon reading Cervantes's novel, Ebenezer is spellbound by it just as Quixote was captivated by his own indiscriminately commingled readings of romances of varying levels of sophistication from the popular, late medieval *Amadis de Gaula* to the urbane, Renaissance *Orlando Furioso*. Ebenezer's misprision of Quixote's idealism as a guiding example and his failure to contextualize it within Cervantes's overarching authorial framework thus perpetuates into the eighteenth century the same type of unreasonable innocence as that over which Cervantes invited us to reflect at the start of the seventeenth century. Because Barth's hero undergoes a more timely *desengaño* while still young, he accepts Joan Toast and the future in place of a phantom Dulcinea. Barth modifies the oncoming absurd Rousseauism of the eighteenth century by a Jesuitical reservation with a Cervantine flavor when, at the end, Ebenezer admits: "That is the crime I stand indicted for, the crime of innocence, whereof the Knowledged must bear the burthen. There's the true Original Sin our souls are born in: not that Adam learned, but that he had to learn—in short, that he was innocent" (SWF 788).[18] Through the undeceived poet Ebenezer's story, parody permits history, as a particular and specific mendacious mentality, to survive by speaking of and for itself. The historical period provides through its own events, figures, philosophic questions, and literature all the elements of a dazzling situation. The historical constellation even includes its own saving comic impulse toward disillusionment and thus a redeeming, clarified self-knowledge. Barth has thrown off the shackles of conventional modern naturalism and recognizes—like Laurence Sterne, an intermediary disciple of Cervantes—how interwoven with our existence are the thoughts and writings and utterances of our time.

The underlying affinity to the serious genre cultivated by Carpentier is clear. Barth allows fact and fiction to be so thoroughly and constantly

18. John Barth, *The Sot-Weed Factor* (New York: Grosset & Dunlap, 1966); henceforth cited using the abbreviation SWF.

convoluted in each other, in the spirit of the age portrayed, that we easily grow willing to forget about the difference between fact and fiction when we hear versions of the history of Maryland that Barth directly interpolates into the novel. By this device, accounts of "real" history—in the pseudoscientific sense of the term—serve romanesque functions of narration in the comic vein, such as establishing subplots, recapitulating past events, and so forth. Turbulant struggles with and among Virginians, Pennsylvanians, New Englanders, French Canadians, Indians, Africans, religious factions, royalists, rebels, and pirates widen out the story of Maryland until it touches all neighboring colonies, and finally the general history of the North American continent and the impact of Europe. Simultaneously, the internal efforts of Ebenezer to interpret his own world suggest our own position vis-à-vis the past. In the process of doing research for his *Marylandiad,* he hits upon lost documents that cast an unflattering light on the romance of colonial origins—for example, evidence that the foundational hero Captain John Smith rewrote history, adding the story of noble Pocahontas, to improve both his own image and history. Ambiguously, Barth unmasks Smith through an invented fictional forerunner Burlingame and thereby adds a further dimension of irony by making mythic debunking even more appealing than the supposedly fraudulent original layer of the American myth! Writing in the Maryland way is surely the sovereign confidence game; the honesty of dishonesty in Barth's comic history replaces *la razón de la sinrazón* in Cervantes's comic antiromance. That seems to imply that in human terms we, who are reading Barth's debunking of the colonial foundation in the second half of the twentieth century, have no inherent superiority over the interpreter-experiencers of that time like Ebenezer Cooke.

Explosion in a Cathedral, in its serious mode, and *The Sot-Weed Factor,* in its comic mode, cope with the problem of a proper interaction between the ethos of the truth seeker who rejects the mendacious and that which is rejected, always a significant cluster of persistent human traits. It is symptomatic also that, as writers who arrive on the scene after Joyce, both Carpentier and Barth repeatedly consider the possibility of a cyclic rather than a linear process in human affairs, a winding and coiling of humanity upon itself.[19] Magical realism practices a juxtaposition and

---

19. I have treated Barth's interest in "cycology" in "From 'Baroque' Michael Drayton to 'Enlightened' Ebenezer Cooke: (Re-)Debunking the American Golden Age," in *Erkennen und Deuten: Essays zur Literatur und Literaturtheorie, Edgar Lohner in memoriam* (Berlin: Erich Schmidt, 1983), 326–34.

hence a laying bare of the evolutionary layers that, for all purposes, become copresent in our examination of the past. The comic novel tends to integrate rather than negate when it confronts such disquieting evidence. It obeys a critical discipline rather than a rigid desire to defeat older history in its acts of acknowledgment of the larger patterns of experience. The obverse of its skeptical freedom is Rabelaisian faith in the limitless powers of nature that checks human error and restores balance without regard to our passing limited doctrines or self-images. Barth does not aspire to abolish or disgrace the past, so much as to activate all of it for us as part of an evolutionary repertory, as layers of biological and cultural living that must be superseded but also must inevitably be accepted as elements of the future.

3. Romancing History and Magical Realism

It is a commonplace today to treat the foundational romance as a narrow category, encompassing works about newer nations in the Western Hemisphere; and in the past three decades a considerable contingent of commentators, mostly experts in Ibero-American studies, has sought to narrow the definition of "magical realism" to the geocultural areas of South and Central America and the Caribbean Basin. Because only some foundational romances exhibit magical realism, and because magical realism usually seems to be part of a larger set of traits associated with "postmodern" writing, it is useful to keep in mind that the boundaries of these partially overlapping subsets are arbitrary in many respects. The broadest label, postmodern, which—as Theo D'haen has cogently demonstrated—was originally applied in the main to innovative "white, male U.S. authors," was expanded since the 1980s to cover a very wide variety of authors "in terms of geography, gender and race" around the globe.[20] Once we acknowledge that a series of shifts in point of view has occurred altering our sense of the foundational romance retroactively, we can deal more lucidly with the indeed remarkable tangle of formal and generic attributes that in the real world do not seem to respect ideological strictures.

For the sake of brevity, I will cite just a few preeminent European authors in illustration of the older basis for fictions evoking the historical roots of a culture and society. Walter Scott made the transition from

20. Theo D'haen, "From Fantastic to Magic Realist," in *International Postmodernism: Theory and Literary Practice*, ed. Hans Bertens and Douwe Fokkema (Amsterdam and Philadelphia: John Benjamins, 1997), 283–93.

writing romances in verse to writing historical romances in prose. His repertory as a romantic storyteller was considerably larger, but within it a number of his prose fictions taken together (e.g., *A Legend of Montrose*, 1819; *The Heart of Midlothian*, 1818) can legitimately be regarded as constituting a multipartite foundational story that explains how modern Scotland emerged out of the forces and struggles of the seventeenth and eighteenth centuries. Similarly, Alessandro Manzoni sought to capture the essence of his native world of northern Italy in *I promessi sposi* (The Betrothed, 1825–1827), by depicting its gestation in the seventeenth century. Adalbert Stifter reached back to the twelfth century in the novel *Witiko* (1865) to envision a high ethos underpinning the later polity and culture of East Central Europe. If we jump the Atlantic, we find a contemporary of the above, the romantic James Fenimore Cooper, engaged in writing *The Leatherstocking Tales* (1823–1841), a series of five novels which we can appreciate in their sequence rearranged by historical period and which together exposit the bigger story of the founding days of the young American nation and its gradual westward movement. A full century later, William Faulkner's several novels centering around a fictional heartland, Yokanapatawpha County, and chronicling the decline of older southern families like the Comptons and Satorises, as against the rise of the disreputable Snopeses, together constitute a regional romance with a historical sweep as extensive as that of *The Leatherstocking Tales*. Faulkner's narrative innovations—for example, in his treatment of time—align his work not with naturalistic realism but with a modernist sense of archetypes and myth.

One determinant within the larger framework of a "romance" about cultural formation is the artist's decision on where to peg the key intersection of history that precipitates the founding. Another determinant is the choice of generic form, because as a species of epic, this kind of narrative is still possible—though it appears less frequently after the nineteenth century—in verse. Joyce's prose *Ulysses* (1922), expatiating on Ireland and the world in relation to Ireland, effectively preempted Ezra Pound's ambitious effort in verse in the *Cantos* (1925ff.) at a general interpretation of the modern world, with special attention to the story of America, and also to medieval Europe and China. Stephen Vincent Benét enjoyed considerable success with his epic poem *John Brown's Body* (1928), probably because the American reading public was already disposed to view the Civil War as having given a final stamp to the nation's continent-wide development. Benét projected but never completed a second verse epic, *Western Star* (1943), on the American movement westward. Meanwhile the movie industry was pouring out films on that saga to an insatiable viewership, and today we think of great directors like John Ford as masters of the total epic of westering in North America. Hence Derek Walcott could be and was inspired by both Joyce and Pound, among others, in writing *Omeros* (1990), a verse epic of the coming into being of the many-splendored, highly hybridized Caribbean world of our times, with imaginative excursions to other places such as the American West. The postmodern features in his "novelization" of the verse epic do not erase the ancestral poetic line reaching all the way from antiquity and Homer's sea to the present.[21]

We still need to sort out other confusions entrenched in many current academic treatments in regard to prose fictions about an era when some writer deems that a people acquired its significant lineaments. One is the widespread belief that a work must disown U.S. culture and excoriate Yankee imperialism in order to qualify as a foundational romance; thus, in effect, only anti-American "postcolonial" writing should be considered under this rubric. Sometimes this critical attitude takes the shape of interpreting any display of maladjustments in contemporary life anywhere, or portrayals of the modern city as dystopic, to constitute a critique of the United States and its lackeys at least indirectly. Published close to Barth's *The Sot-Weed Factor* and Carpentier's *El siglo de las Luces*, Gabriel García-Márquez's *Cien años de soledad* (One Hundred Years of Solitude, 1967) followed not too long after the novelist toured the southern area of the United States by Greyhound bus in 1961 because he enormously admired Faulkner and wanted to see with his own eyes the world Faulkner had written about. García-Márquez's Macondo, a composite of the small towns of rural Columbia, is the setting where we witness how, during a recently passed century, largely in obscurity and in a liminal position on the global map, generations have lived, erred, and died; and we can readily understand Macondo's formal function in analogy to Faulkner's fictional composite Yokanapatawpha County. As a novel *One Hundred Years* is ironically self-reflexive and its at times almost ostentatious use of archetypal patterns readily invites comparison with European modernists addicted to myth studies.[22] The fact that García-Márquez is anti-

21. Cf. Line Henriksen, *Ambition and Anxiety: Ezra Pound's "Cantos" and Derek Walcott's "Omeros" as Twentieth-Century Epics* (Amsterdam and New York: Rodopi, 2007).

22. Cf. Michael Palencia-Roth, *Myth and the Modern Novel: García-Márquez, Mann, and Joyce* (New York: Garland, 1987).

American carries no determinative weight when we assess his fiction's mode of fantasy and judge whether it fits well under the label magical realism. The same holds in the case of the perennially anti-American Carlos Fuentes who has spent much of his life resident in the United States. In his breakthrough novel of the sixties, *La muerte de Artemio Cruz* (The Death of Artemio Cruz, 1962), Fuentes was a far more daring experimenter than García-Márquez, for example in using three kinds of narrative voice, in the first, second, and third person. His opposition to the intrusion of American cultural attributes and political power in Central and South America never entailed any rejection of common artistic tradition from Europe on his part—indeed, as an essayist he has often avowed his admiration of writers like Cervantes, Sterne, Joyce, Mann, et al., antecedents whom he often shares with Jorge Luis Borges and various *norteamericanos* like Barth. However, in my judgment, nothing in Fuentes's forays into the fantastic and/or in his skilled bending of the norms of storytelling ever exceeds Barth's brilliant moves in the story collection *Lost in the Funhouse* (1968).[23]

Assessing the actual cultural indebtedness and practice of writers on several continents, the comparatist Charles Scheel concludes that a large contingent of Latin American scholars worldwide has been engaging in self-blinding cultural imperialism, trying to boost their area of interest over others as innovatory and different, against the historical evidence. He deems their view, or cultural animus, to be "reductionist" and "retrograde" and opines that "[t]o *base* a poetic on a notion of postcolonial cultural 'hybridity' exhibits mystification rather than serious comparative analysis."[24] D'haen, in contrast, clings to the idea that a specifically postmodern magic realism must inherently exhibit the rejection of the "West's" ideal of the real, whereas "the primacy of the linguistic realm" was dominant in modernist fantasy of the avant-gardes, roughly up to and inclusive of the work of Borges.[25] Scheel agrees with D'haen that a shift in modes of the fantastic has occurred over the course of the twentieth century; in his list of crucial emphases, probably the most significant trait in the earlier "marvelous-realist" mode is the infiltration of the

23. On Barth's radical experimentation, see "Postmodern Mannerism," in Gerald Gillespie, *Echoland: Readings from Humanism to Postmodernism* (Brussels: Presses Interuniversitaires Européennes, 2006), 272–75.

24. Charles W. Scheel, *Réalisme magique et réalisme merveilleux: Des theories aux poétiques* (Paris: L'Harmattan, 2005). The passage here: "*Baser* une poétique sur une notion 'd'hybridité' culturelle post-coloniale relève de la mystification plutôt que de la littérature générale" (34, emphasis in original).

25. D'haen, "Postmodernisms," 286–87.

narrative discourse by the exaltation of an authorial voice.[26] It is understandable that critics may differ about the constellation of features in particular moments of literature deeply marked by fantasy, but it is hard to justify claims that imaginative works written in one "postcolonial" idiom (e.g., English) are hampered by some hypothetical consciousness of the "West" whereas imaginative works written in another "postcolonial" idiom (e.g., Spanish) enjoy a greater liberty to reach an exuberant and/or liberated level of consciousness, and to implement procedures and insights often associated with "magical realism." Literary history leaves little room for such a proposition except as a willful misprision or actual ignorance of the facts. For example, we can find nothing in Latin American writing that exceeds the Irish author Flann O'Brien's novel *At Swim-Two-Birds* (1939, the year of Joyce's *Wake!*) for astonishing narrative twists, the piling up and interpenetration of strata of cultural mentalities, and sheer metaphysical puzzlement dealt out to the reader. Besides surrealism during the interwar period and its spillover from Europe to the Americas, there is the enormous legacy of complex narrative structures, self-reflexive irony, ludic inventiveness, and dazzling fantasy bequeathed by European romantic writing. As soon as we think of complex novels such as Jan Potocki's *Le manuscrit trouvé à Saragosse* (Manuscript Found at Saragossa, 1805), E. T. A. Hoffmann's *Die Lebensansichten des Katers Murr* (Life and Opinions of Tomcat Murr, 1820–1822), or C. J. L. Almqvist's *Törnrosens bok* (Book of the Wild Rose, 1832–1851), it becomes harder to entertain exaggerations about the structural or thematic achievements of magical realists, as meritorious as many of their fictions may be.[27]

The decades of the sixties and seventies stand out as the stellar period for major novels that anchor the Hispanic American contribution to magical realism. It must suffice here to cite two first-rate works in illustration. The Argentinian novelist Julio Cortázar's *Rayuela* (Hopscotch, 1963), written and set in Paris, starts out with a presumptive chief narrator who is a kind of intellectual *flaneur* (which roughly reminds of O'Brien's opening gambit), but proceeds to switch around among narrative voices, and at times we encounter internal monologue and stream of consciousness. Characters fluctuate in their identity and seem symbolic rather than "real" in any conventional sense, except in terms of being

---

26. Scheel, *Réalisme magique,* 105.

27. On the variety and ingenuity of romantic authors in Europe and the New World, and on their legacy in the twentieth century, consult Gerald Gillespie, Manfred Engel, and Bernard Dieterle, eds., *Romantic Prose Fiction* (Amsterdam and Philadelphia: John Benjamins, 2008).

projections of psychological states and types. The novel offers the reader a variety of ways to read it, including multiple endings. While the well-known metropolis Paris provides a degree of groundedness and stability, we find ourselves experiencing movement around points in it as exploration of a sometimes phantasmagoric labyrinth. Influenced by surrealism, the Chilean writer José Donoso's *El obsceno pájaro de la noche* (The Obscene Bird of Night, 1970) is more radical in evoking both nature and the city as dystopias, indeed mainly as monstrous. The country setting of La Rinconada is a place of grotesque deformations. Our glimpses of the capital city are of a jumble of incongruous juxtaposed strata from various episodes of humanity, including Hollywood's latest products. Attempts to advance the particular story of a society are analogized to the ambiguous processes of narrative doublings and shifts in the self-referential work. Donoso alludes directly to romantic authors, so that we are aware of being entrapped in a kind of nightmarish fairytale. Mobilizing contemporary anthropology and myth studies, he leads us through virtually oneiric metamorphoses of figures and travesties of religious paradigms. A kind of gnostic indignation pervades the interwoven tale of two frightening discoveries. One is the realization that the traditional Western idea of personal identity has collapsed in a plethora of masks (a subject treated more fully in chapter fourteen, "Structures of the Self and Narrative"). Another is the theme of an obscurely necessary rebellion against a father authority who wants to foist his own monstrosity on the world as Eden, but the ritual dismemberment of this god-surrogate leads nowhere.[28]

Literary expressionism and surrealism accompanied and sometimes colored the "classical" modernist novel of the first four decades of the twentieth century. Existentialism and absurdism were similarly coextensive with the later writing of the preeminent modernists Joyce and Mann as the latter were entering and exiting the tumultuous period of World War II. Joyce was clearly the pioneer experimenter far in advance of the waves of his progeny. The heyday of "postmodern mannerism" and "magical realism" stretched from the 1960s to 1990s. Although the dates of works from several streams often overlap and some seem precocious, in general this new postmodern dispensation becomes evident, for example, in an underlying shift from the novels and plays of Albert Camus and Jean-Paul Sartre to those of Samuel Beckett. It can hardly be surprising that what is now called "postmodern" writing by Western Hemisphere authors logically follows in train.

28. On Donoso's novel, see Gillespie, "Postmodern Mannerism," 277–81.

6 CINEMATIC NARRATION IN THE MODERNIST NOVEL

The number of essays and books on cinema of the twentieth century is today oceanic in its vastness, and justifiably so. The "film" medium, born toward the end of the nineteenth century, and related to many arts besides literature, has burgeoned into a universe in its own right and has spawned such progeny as television and computer imaging. The modernist novel shared the historical space not only of silent movies but also of the talkies, and in important respects the era of film with speech, sounds, and music was enabled by the active dialogue between literary and cinematic artists in the decades between World Wars I and II. We can reexperience the rapid transition to the talkies in the pages of a crucial journal like *Close Up* (1927–1933) which reveal to us how filmmaking of the late twenties could build upon an accumulated formal consciousness and the medium's already achieved international standing.[1]

To enumerate all the cross-currents propitious for the rise of cinema exceeds the scope of my concern here with its relationship especially to literary art, but several are worth noting briefly. The drive to create a new mental space of vision in poetry and prose, as described in chapter one ("Cathedral Window Light"), was anything but inhibiting to the impulse to project and manipulate images as a kind of storytelling for the mass market in the industrial age. The symbolist goal of repristinating language, the wish of the imagists to recover a direct poetic idiom that was virtually hieroglyphic, the renascence of interest in the poetic power of Dante, shared across a wide spectrum of modern writers,[2] all contributed, alongside the development of impressionism in painting, to foster a liberated sense of experimentation. The renewed interest in psychology (William James, Henri Bergson, Sigmund Freud, et al.) at the turn of the century was paralleled by the flowering of psychological impressionism

---

1. See ch. 5, "The Moment of *Close Up*," in Laura Marcus, *The Tenth Muse: Writing about Cinema in the Modernist Period* (Oxford, U.K.: Oxford University Press, 2007).

2. See the broad set of studies (but minus consideration of Joyce) in Stuart Y. McDougal, ed., *Dante among the Moderns* (Chapel Hill: University of North Carolina Press, 1985).

in literature. Thus in general movies started out in a period of interplay between the appeals of "realism" and "inner experience" as contending values in the arts. The number of cultural bridges to accommodate both appeals in this age of rapid technological surges is extraordinary. For instance, some symbolists felt fascination for the strange beauty of machinery and instruments, anticipating the futurists and expressionists at least in this regard; it was by no means a monopoly of science fiction. Among its many subjects, early film tried to interpret the role and adventure of science and to reflect the impact of anthropology, the findings of which were being fed back from remote places to audiences in the developed world. Yet, more frequently than not, picture shows about non-European and aboriginal peoples that were thought of as documentary served to unleash waves of neomythologizing fantasy. Similarly, filmic attempts to recover past episodes of history, including the scenes and details of antiquity and biblical times, often exhibit an apparent "realism" in the surface details according to the best information then available, but ultimately amount to "mythic" constructions.

My observations pertain mainly to narrative properties found in literary works that predate movies with sound tracks, but any such retrospection is unavoidably filtered through the many developments in cinematic art and theory since the end of the Roaring Twenties. For example, I am conscious of having been surprised by one of the longest passages in Jüri Lotman's otherwise terse book *Semiotika kino i problemy kinoestetiky* (Semiotics of Cinema, 1973), where the Estonian theoretician expatiates on a film after World War II that I much admired but criticism largely ignored, Roberto Rosselini's *Il Generale della Rovere* (1959), based on an actual incident.[3] In it Vittorio de Sica plays the part of a sordid conman, Bardone, whom the Gestapo chief Mueller presssures into impersonating a Resistance hero, Della Rovere, whom Bardone happens to resemble, so as to feret out another important leader believed to be in prison under disguise. Only the Nazi occupiers know that the general has just been killed during a daring secret mission. Bardone works his way so thoroughly into his role that, heart and soul, he becomes in effect the noble general, inspires his fellow prisoners, and finally the Nazis must execute him too as a hero. What surprised me was not that Lotman detected

3. Yury Lotman, *Semiotika kino i problemy kinoestetiky* (Tallin: University of Tallin, 1973), long passage in ch. 7. English version: *Semiotics of Cinema*, trans. and ed. Mark E. Suino (Ann Arbor: Department of Slavic Languages and Literatures, University of Michigan, 1976).

an "oscillation between two sets of rules" or possible characters that imparted to the audience that convincing "feeling of truth" about Bardone's inner transformation; rather, I was puzzled because he never mentioned that the Italian film boldly adapted a favorite subject of baroque drama, the story of Philemon or Genesius. There are literally hundreds of works in this subgenre of the *actor sui*—the story of a pagan actor who, when assigned by the emperor Diocletian to mock a Christian hero, develops into a genuine Christian and martyr himself and simultaneously realizes the full potential of his art. By citing a specific major play such as Lope de Vega's *Lo fingido verdadero* (The Genuine Feigned, ca. 1607–1608) or Rotrou's *Le véritable Saint-Genest* (The Real St. Genest, 1646), Lotman could have instantly illuminated the narrational complexity borrowed in this case directly from literature. Then a discussion of the film techniques used to tell the story would have more sharply delineated the specific cinematic aspects.

Lotman's abstract reading of a cinematic work that revives a highly marked literary and dramatic tradition reminded me that at its birth the now independent cinema drew upon all the existing arts, much as opera had evolved out of several media around 1600. But except for words shown on screen, oddly enough language was "missing" in the initial film works even though their scenarios and many narrative techniques derived principally from various strata of Europe's huge literary repertory. Prior to World War I a steady stream of books about the new medium of cinema began to appear, often aimed, like industry insider Ernest Dench's *Making the Movies* (1915), at satisfying public curiosity about how the variety of moving pictures were produced technically.[4] A treatise by William James's Harvard colleague, Hugo Münsterberg, *The Photoplay: A Psychological Study* (1916), established an early intellectual high point in analyzing the attributes and artistic potential of cinema.[5] He brought contemporary ideas of perception, memory, imagination, and emotion to bear on the question of how viewers responded to specific devices in filmic art such as depth, motion, close-ups, and flashbacks. Münsterberg drew the conclusion that cinema had rapidly evolved into an art in its own right, attuned to human mental states, but also in the final analysis that film as art was transcendental and autotelic by virtue of positing its object in aesthetic isolation.

Very different in character was the American poet Vachel Lindsay's

4. Alfred Ernest Dench, *Making the Movies*, 2nd ed. (New York: Macmillan, 1919).
5. Hugo Münsterberg, *The Photoplay: A Psychological Study* (New York: Appleton, 1916).

The Art of the Moving Picture (1916). Lindsay was an astute semiotician who sought to grasp the nature of film as a revolution in modern art; his effort contrasts with later treatises such as Siegfried Kracauer's (1925), which are more ideologically driven.[6] Whereas theoreticians of Kracauer's type impose a rigid discursive framework on film from the outside, Lindsay belongs to the special category of hermeneuts who through their deep involvement in the appreciation of the arts were capable of encountering the new medium as a rapidly evolving, authentic gestalt. We can apply to him the distinction later formulated by Suzanne Langer in *Philosophy in a New Key* (1942), who demonstrated the limitations of discursivity in coping with artistic expression.[7] In addition, Lindsay was especially open to folk art and popular culture.

From the start, Lindsay understands the generic range of film by grasping its analogues in literature high and low and names plenty of specific literary works from ancient to contemporary for our guidance. Yet, at the same time, he recognizes the crucial importance of the medium's pictorial power, the "surprising parallelism between Egyptian hieroglyphics and this new silent drama," "picture-writing" that "revives the cave-man point of view on a higher plane" (VL 4, 5).[8] He points to three fundamental filmic impulses: "Action, intimacy, and splendor blend in every kind of reel, but some one of these qualities is dominant in each production" (VL 3). The extant visual arts accordingly are of exceptional importance in his mind as sources of inspiration and understanding for the maker of photoplays. Thus Lindsay never confuses film as being a primarily realistic medium; rather, he accepts that it can express magical wishdreams, religious feeling, ritual experience, social bonding, and much more. Among daring conclusions, he hypothesizes that "Action Pictures are sculpture-in-motion, Intimate Pictures are

6. Testifying to Kracauer's continuing influence are the more recent Suhrkamp editions: Siegfried Kracauer, *Kino: Essays, Studien, Glossen zum Film* (Frankfurt, 1992) and *Theorie des Films* (1996).

7. Suzanne K. Langer, *Philosophy in a New Key: A Study in the Symbolism of Reason, Rite, and Art*, 3rd ed. (Cambridge, Mass.: Harvard University Press, 1963), especially ch. 9: "The Genesis of Artistic Import."

8. Vachel Lindsay, *The Art of the Moving Picture* (New York: Macmillan, 1916); hereafter cited as VL with page number. I am grateful to Dr. Irène Bessière, project chief at the Institut National d'Histoire de l'Art (INHA), Maison des Sciences de l'Homme, Paris, and director of the European/United States cinema program "Les Européens dans le cinéma américain: Emigration et exil," for calling Lindsay's prescient theory to my attention. The revival of interest in Lindsay is underscored by the appearance of a paperback reprint, edited by Martin Scorsese and introduced by Stanley Kaufmann (New York: Random House, 2000).

paintings-in-motion, Splendor Pictures are architecture-in-motion" (VL 4) and urges "painters, sculptors, and architects, preferably those who are in the flush of their first reputation in these crafts" (VL 133) to experiment in cinema.

Lindsay sets the example for a future film criticism by discussing dozens upon dozens of actual films and often relating them to specific works of the literary and visual arts past and contemporary. He also speaks in a prophetic vein that draws upon his penetrating insights into the anthropological dynamics evident in the success of cinema, which already figures as the fourth largest national industry in the United States by 1915, and can be related to "our democratic dream" (VL 263). Lindsay hopes idealistically that "this new weapon of men" (VL 289) will release a powerful river of artistic creativity that, in the hands of "prophet-wizards" (VL 263), "noble magicians" (VL 273) who will exalt the American story as a great saga in human affairs, can be equal in mythic dimensions to anything Europe or Asia possesses. At moments he sounds almost Joycean and Mannian, as when he describes "a nation, America, going for dreams into caves as shadowy as the tomb of Queen Thi" (VL 259), and concludes his chapter on the function of cinema as a communal realm of "enchantment" by saying:

> Because ten million people enter daily into the cave, something akin to Egyptian wizardry, certain national rituals will be born. By studying the matter of being an Egyptian priest for a little while, the author-producer may learn in the end how best to express and satisfy the spirit-hungers that are peculiarly American. And it is sometimes out of the oldest dream that the youngest vision is born. (VL 259–60)

Though of Mann's generation, Lindsay died in 1931 before he could witness how the totalitarian dictators Hitler and Stalin would manipulate the "spirit-hungers" of their peoples through cinema and cinemalike pageantry or how, reciprocally, Roosevelt would grasp the importance of the film industry for the struggle of World War II.

In the second half of the nineteenth century Wagner was concerned to distinguish older drama from opera or "music-drama" as a newer supergenre. Lindsay likewise was convinced that in cinema a higher independent medium, a kind of "advanced experimental drama" which he named among other terms "the super-photoplay" (VL 169), was in the process of establishing itself:

The photoplays of the future will be written from the foundations for the films. The soundest actors, photographers, and producers will be those who emphasize the points wherein the photoplay is unique. What is adapted to complete expression in one art generally secures but half expression in another. The supreme photoplay will give us things that have been but half expressed in all other mediums allied to it. (VL 169)

Lindsay formulated this expectation well before the advent of the "talkie" with its sound track that allowed cinema, in effect, both to incorporate the subject matters and to assimilate the properties (language, music, etc.) of "regular" drama and opera, the most significant predecessor *Gesamtkunstwerk*.

Writers of modernist fiction did not miss the fact that early cinema had rapidly assimilated certain significant powers of narration virtually without wielding fiction's own chief instrument: spoken or written language. The novelists were not slow to turn the tables and start borrowing imaginatively from cinema. Perhaps one of the main reasons why such a reversal could succeed was the extraordinary assimilation of impressionistic techniques in prose narrative as in painting by the end of the nineteenth century. Both the example of symbolist evocation and the widespread adaptation of Richard Wagner's leitmotif principle of musical composition had reinforced this tendency in literary art. Segments or the whole of certain fictions of the 1880s and 1890s—for instance, Joris Karl Huysmans's *A rebours* (Against Nature), Benito Pérez Galdós's *La desheredada* (The Disinherited), or Arthur Schnitzler's *Leutnant Gustl* (Lieutenant Gustl)—evidence kinship with painterly and musical composition, often openly. Psychological and symbolical impressionism in modernist fiction ranges from an older mode of synaesthetic suggestion, as in Joseph Conrad's depiction of moving upstream on the Congo River in *Heart of Darkness* (1902), to the more radical mode of stream of consciousness, as in parts of James Joyce's *Ulysses* (complete version, 1922).

The brilliant polyglot Sergei Eisenstein, an important contributor to *Close Up*, counted among the self-confessed passionate Wagnerites who were attracted to Joyce. While he maintained a lifelong interest in Charles Dickens's and Émile Zola's fictions, Eisenstein came to regard Joyce's *Ulysses* as a model that filmmakers should study because the Irish master's narrative crosscutting between exteriority and interiority bore analogy to montage, and, in a conversation with Joyce in Paris in November 1929, Eisenstein eagerly discussed the possibility of "inner film monologue."[9] In a review slightly earlier, Alfred Döblin, whose own novel *Berlin Alexanderplatz* (1929) was deeply influenced by Joyce, declared that with *Ulysses* cinematic montage and the life of the streets of big cities had penetrated into literature.[10] Döblin's and Eisenstein's responses to Joyce exemplify the natural course of two cultural processes between World Wars I and II. A number of key writers, preeminently Joyce and Kafka, early on were sensitized to the rapidly developing techniques of cinema, to many of its primary subject matters (urban life and settings), and to newer modes of analysis (psychological, anthropological, sociological theorizing) for their usefulness in structuring narration. And reciprocally, many early filmmakers drew inspiration from literature and aspired to a kind of status comparable to that enjoyed by literary authors. Besides the extent of an author's explicit reference to films, above all it often proved crucial whether the life of an author who was responsive to cinema straddled the transition to movies with sound. That largely determined whether his or her writings struck astute critics of the interwar period as possessing filmic qualities, or whether such recognition might be delayed. Kafka's life provides a prime illustration. Because he died in 1924 and his stories reflected cinematic moments only implicitly, a richer awareness of his passion for cinema only gradually followed his posthumous rise to fame from about the middle of the twentieth century onward. Yet today, in a book such as *Kafka Goes to the Movies*, we see unlocked a trove of documentation of how his reception of cinema was an integral part of his response to the modern world.[11]

As in the case of Kafka, we can ascribe the delayed critical and artistic interest in Proust's cinematic qualities in large measure to the timing of his death (in the year of the completion of *Ulysses*) as well as to the relative paucity of direct references to movies in *In Search of Lost Time* (also known in English as *Remembrance of Things Past*). Its culminating volume, the posthumously published *Time Refound* (1927) which explicitly recognized silent film, per force missed any opportunity to reflect the important transition to sound in cinematic art. The integration of voices and music eventually allowed numerous other writers to exploit this even

9. S. M. Eisenstein, "Literature and Cinema," in *Selected Works*, vol. 1: *Writings, 1922–34*, ed. and trans. Richard Taylor (Bloomington: Indiana University Press, 1988), 96.

10. Alfred Döblin, "*Ulysses* by Joyce," in *The Weimar Republic Sourcebook*, ed. Anton Kaes, Martin Jay, and Edward Dimendberg (Berkeley and Los Angeles: University of California Press, 1994).

11. Hanns Zischler, *Kafka Goes to the Movies*, trans. Susan Gillespie (Chicago and London: University of Chicago Press, 2003).

more direct linkage of cinema to literary art. This was of great importance in an era that aspired, as Walter Pater had proclaimed in *Studies in the Renaissance* (1877), to endow language and every art with the deeper logic of musical expression.[12] The tradition of music's special role, reaching from the romantic theoreticians such as E. T. A. Hoffmann and Arthur Schopenhauer over Wagner and Nietzsche, directly flowed into the thought of Proust, Mann, and Joyce.[13] Had Proust lived as long as Joyce and Mann, he most likely would have drawn the lessons linking film as well as music to the flow of the psyche. The historical situation only delayed but could not stop attention to the cinematic potential pent up in *In Search of Lost Time*. A more recent study, *Proust at the Movies* (2004), endeavors to recuperate Proustian fiction as a matrix from which emulating filmmakers and script writers—Luchino Visconti, Harold Pinter, Volker Schlöndorff, Raoul Ruiz, Jean-Luc Godard, and others—have eventually and justifiably drawn inspiration.[14] Scholars such as Robert Richardson in *Literature and Film* and Morris Beja in *Film and Literature* have spelled out the accumulation of factors that fed this sort of retrospective appreciation.[15] To enumerate just a few: the already mentioned intensive use of literature by early filmmakers such as D. W. Griffith (a favorite of Eisenstein's); the naturally evolving relationship of filmic and literary techniques; the growing awareness of specific attributes of literary and filmic languages; and the ever increasing presence of movies in the mental world of twentieth-century fictional characters. All through the twentieth century, directors and scriptwriters avidly "adapted"—that is, appropriated and rewrote—literary works. An extra factor retarding the reception of Proust as an important example for filmmakers was the concerted campaign of the French surrealists to demote him as an artist in the twenties and thirties. We may suspect that behind their efforts was a genuine fear that his method for revealing inner life might be an effective rival to their views and practices. Although Proust grasped the

12. Walter Pater, *Three Major Texts: "The Renaissance: Studies in Art and Poetry"; "Appreciations"; and "Imaginary Portraits"* (New York and London: Oxford University Press, 1986), 214–15.

13. E.g., see Gerald Gillespie, "Schopenhauer's Shadow: Stephen as Philosophic 'Superman,'" in *Bloomsday 100*, ed. Morris Beja and Anne Fogarty (Gainesville: University of Florida Press, 2009).

14. Martine Beugnet and Marion Schmidt, *Proust at the Movies* (Aldershot, Hampshire, U.K., and Burlington, Vt.: Ashgate, 2004).

15. Robert Richardson, *Literature and Film* (Bloomington: Indiana University Press, 1969); Morris Beja, *Film and Literature: An Introduction* (New York, London: Longman, 1979).

significance of the unconscious and depicted the operation of deep impulses streaming from the individual and collective psyches, he also let his readers listen in on his primary internal observer Marcel as he meditated extensively on such phenomena, and such moments of explicit conscious recognition of the interrelatedness of all levels of the mind were anathema to surrealism. To be sure, Proust enjoyed important contemporary recognition for his approach from no less an artist than his fellow novelist Virginia Woolf.[16]

There were many reasons why, with his abundance of thoughts on other artistic media, Proust did not profess a strong interest in cinema, whereas some surrealists as well as expressionists more readily saw the potential of the new medium for their direction in art. The transition from symbolist and impressionist habits to varieties of postimpressionist art was not abrupt at the turn of the century; rather, it was the trauma of the Great War that convinced the newer generation that an epochal rupture had occurred in human affairs and needed to be accompanied by a revolution in art. One can argue that Proust transferred onto the infant medium of cinema in its cruder days some misgivings analogous to Charle Baudelaire's resistance to photography and that Proust had only scant direct experience of actual film showings, at least until cinema took on a more obvious degree of importance for him in World War I.[17] But one can also argue that he already had elaborated his own version of a magical medium of image casting, as exhibited in *Swann's Way* (1913) in the connection between young Marcel's imagination and the magic lantern shows. Proust's reflections on images are so suffused by allusions to works of visual art (painting, sculpture, architecture, scenery, cityscape, etc.) that the act of moving among these points of reference and recollected moments of time within a gallery of accrued experiences produces a related effect at least equal, if not superior, to the most elegant instances of montage in film. Proust has his narrator conduct us through complex synesthetic impressions, for example, the famous pink hawthorn passage in *Swann's Way*, that anticipate the most dazzling visual crosscutting and mood building in yet-to-be-invented technicolor film. In part 2, *Amid a Budding Grove*, the narrator explicitly links his own experience of his world with painting of the later nineteenth century; and in part 5,

16. Florence Godeau, "Peindre l'éphémère: Marcel Proust, Virginia Woolf et l'impressionisme," in *Proust et les images: peinture, photographie, cinema, video*, ed. Jean Cléder et Jean-Pierre Monier (Rennes: Press Universitaires de Rennes, 2003), 39–49.
17. Cf. Beugnet and Schmid, *Proust at the Movies*, 8–13.

The Prisoner, he gratefully acknowledges the Wagnerian musical model to be coordinate with the loadstar for visual experience, his character Elstir, who is a fictional composite of the impressionist painters. Hence it is difficult to pin down with exactness how close Proust's aged narrator is to a feeling influenced by film when, in novel number 7 of the series, *Time Regained,* he watches the strange displays in the skies of Paris during World War I.[18] Is Proust re-creating the effect of actual black-and-white newsreels of searchlights and dogfights, or is this ghostly vision with its measure of expressionistic force a dark abstraction in a purely poetic space, close to the nocturnal dream realm that Joyce will penetrate further in *Finnegans Wake?*

Beugnet and Schmidt have drawn essentially the right conclusion that Proust, despite earlier reservations about the new popular entertainment, "by establishing a link between wartime cinema and its ancestor the magic lantern, and thus, on a symbolic level, by paralleling the Narrator's childhood and evolution with that of the moving image, [. . .] endows the medium with an undeniable magic explicitly expressed in the image of the mysterious twilight in which the projection room is bathed."[19] After the pastiche in *Time Refound* contrasting the realist Goncourt manner to his own in telling the story of his society, Proust analogizes himself to a "surgeon" who probes beneath the surface, "examining them [his contemporaries] with X-rays"; and, a bit like someone assembling slices of observations for a cubist compositon, he comments on how several paintings may in combination better exhibit the "psychological laws" in operation (SLT 6.40).[20] Like the often spectral spaces of then contemporary cinema, wartime Paris at night acquires the aspect of the scene of a communal dream in *Time Refound.* The qualitative irreality of the war makes the aged narrator realize that beneath their surface existences the French people are reenacting the life of humanity in earlier crises over the millennia. The wartime darkness facilitates Dionysian release, both sexual and criminal, and the example of antiquity corrobo-

18. William C. Carter, *The Proustian Quest* (New York: New York University Press, 1992), 13–14, sees a simultaneous analogy to cinema and cubism in many of the flowing constructions in Proust's work.

19. Beugnet and Schmid, *Proust at the Movies,* 17.

20. English citations, indicated by SLT with volume and page number, follow Marcel Proust, *In Search of Lost Time,* trans. by C. K. Scott Moncrieff and Terence Kilmartin, rev. by D. J. Enright (New York: Modern Library, 1998). Citations from the French, indicated by R with volume and page number, follow the Pléiade edition: Marcel Proust, *A la recherche du temps perdu,* ed. Jean-Yves Tadié (Paris: Gallimard, 1987). Here: "comme un chirurgien," "je les radiographiais" (R 4.296f.).

rates that of European modernity. For the narrator the alienation resulting from being in the grip of that master-dream does not cease; he feels
himself like a ghost in the postlude when peace returns, still struggling
to read the hieroglyphs, the "inner book of unknown symbols" (SLT
6.274).[21] Ultimately, to grasp the whole picture contained in the mon-
tagelike surge of memory, he must write a night book ("If I worked, it
would be only at night"; SLT 6.524), a conclusion already implicit as of
the opening page of the overture to *In Search of Lost Time*.[22]

An epigraph from Dante's *Inferno* unmistakably indicates the arrival
of the Joycean tendency in T. S. Eliot's poem "The Love Song of J. Alfred
Prufrock" (1917) in which modern experience at the time of the Great
War is spectrally cinematic, "as if a magic lantern threw the nerves in
patterns on a screen."[23] Eliot's invitation into the urban night, "When
the evening is spread out against the sky / Like a patient etherized upon
a table,"[24] both exploits and interprets the appeal of the fare offered in
the moving picture houses of the early 1900s. These entertainments—
life images and cultural materials cast mysteriously on the screen—directly descend from the magic lantern shows of the nineteenth century.
Besides being a lifelong movie buff, Thomas Mann was an avid reader
of Kafka, sensed a natural rivalry with him, and worried about it. If he
had any inkling of just how deeply the early cinema acted as a stimulus
on Kafka's psyche and art, he would have felt this competition yet more
keenly. In *The Magic Mountain*, Thomas Mann notes not only the ancestry but also the awesome new implications of the movies for modern
mass culture. As hermetic time engulfs ordinary and also narrative time
in his novel, the experience resembles, among other things, "gazing into
one of the optical toys at the sanatorium, the stereoscope, the kaleidoscope, the cinematograph" (MM 84).[25] One of its disquieting parallels

21. "livre intérieur de signes inconnus" (R 4.458).
22. "si je travaillais, ce serait la nuit" (R 4.620).
23. T. S. Eliot, *The Complete Poems and Plays, 1909–1950* (New York: Harcourt, Brace
and World, 1971), 6. On Kafka's obsessive interest in pretalkie film, see Hanns Zischler,
Kafka Goes to the Movies, trans. Susan H. Gillespie (Chicago: University of Chicago Press,
2003).
24. Eliot, *The Complete Poems*, 3.
25. Citations in English are to Thomas Mann, *The Magic Mountain*, trans. H. T. Lowe-
Porter (New York: Modern Library, 1952); hereafter cited by the abbreviation MM and the
page number. Citations in the original German follow the paperback reprint of Mann's
original text: Thomas Mann, *Der Zauberberg* (Frankfurt: Fischer Taschenbuch-Verlag,
1987); hereafter cited by the abbreviation Zb and the page number. The terms appear thus:
"unterhaltende optische Gegenstände [. . .] einen stereoskopischen Guckkasten [. . .] ein
fernröhrförmiges Kaleidoskop [. . .] eine drehende Trommel endlich, in die man kinema-
tograpischen Filmstreifen legte" (Zb, 90).

is the spectral show of the x-ray room. At the carnival party in chapter 5, Hans Castorp, a parodic Werther-Tamino-Faust, will succumb to seduction. Just before that comic fall, Mann takes us into the "Bioscope Theatre," where Hans is guiltily aware that the champion of reason, Settembrini, would disapprove of cinema, like opera, as an antihumanistic medium, one "[c]onstructed [. . .] to cater to the innermost desires of an onlooking international civilization" (MM 317).[26] The Dionysian power channeled by the cinema appears outright as a Carmen figure in the final segment of the picture show, "A young Moroccan woman [. . .] suddenly brought so close to the camera as to be life-sized; one could see the dilated nostrils, the eyes full of animal life, [. . .] her white teeth" (MM 318).[27] The mesmerized audience is caught staring "into the face of a charming apparition. It seemed to see and saw not, it was not moved by the glances bent upon it, its smile and nod were not of the present but of the past, so that the impulse to respond was baffled, and lost in a feeling of impotence. Then the phantom vanished. The screen glared white and empty, with the one word Finis written across it" (MM 318).[28] By this ominous hint, Mann both enacts and reveals the dilemma of the decadent enchantment leading Europe into the Great War.

The historical significance of the name Bioscope Theatre is ironically doubled, for in it now, literally,

> Life flitted across the screen before their smarting eyes; life chopped into small sections, fleeting, accelerated; a restless, jerky fluctuation of appearing and disappearing, performed to a thin accompaniment of music, which set its actual tempo to the phantasmagoria of the past, and with the narrowest means at its command, yet managed to evoke a whole gamut of pomp and solemnity, passion, abandon, and gurgling sensuality. It was a thrilling drama of love and death they saw silently reeled off; the scenes, laid at the court of an oriental despot, galloped past, full of gorgeousness and naked bodies, thirst of power

26. "hergestellt aus sympathetischer Vertrautheit mit den geheimen Wünschen der zuschauenden internationalen Zivilisation" (Zb, 335).

27. "Ein junges marokkanisches Weib [. . .] plötzlich in Lebensgröße angenähert. Ihre Nüstern waren breit, ihre Augen voll tierischen Lebens [. . .] mit weißen Zähnen" (Zb, 335–36).

28. "in das Gesicht des reizvollen Schattens, der zu sehen schien und nicht sah, der von den Blicken gar nicht berührt wurde und dessen Lachen und Winken nicht die Gegenwart meinte, sondern im Dort und Damals zu Hause war, so daß es sinnlos wäre es zu erwidern. Dies mischte, wie gesagt, der Lust ein Gefühl der Ohnmacht bei. Dann verschwand das Phantom. Leere Helligkeit überzog die Tafel, das Wort 'Ende' ward darauf geworfen" (Zb, 336).

and raving religious self-abnegation; full of cruelty, appetite, and deadly lust, and slowing down to give a full view of the muscular development of the executioner's arms. (MM 316–17)[29]

Besides this main feature that rolls together Valentino-like stock movie scripts, the following newsreel and travelogue bring us

> scenes from all parts of the world: the President of the French Republic, in top-hat and cordon, sitting in a landau and replying to a speech of welcome; the Viceroy of India, at the wedding of a rajah; the German Crown Prince in the courtyard of a Potsdam garrison. There was a picture of life in a New Mecklenburg village; a cock-fight in Borneo, naked savages blowing on nose horns, a wild elephant hunt, a ceremony at the court of the King of Siam, a courtesan's street in Japan, with geishas sitting behind wooden lattices; Samoyeds bundled in furs, driving sledges drawn by reindeer through the snowy wastes of Siberia; Russian pilgrims praying at Hebron; a Persian criminal under the knout. (MM 317)[30]

Among the phantoms, then, figure some of the chief European actors who will play out their roles in the onrushing World War; but they coexist here in a new global context of cultural interrelationship, which European expansionism has helped bring about and which is suddenly projected visually as a phantasmagoria that commingles phenomena from all places and times. Qualitatively, film is the contemporaneous analogue for Mann's neoidealist narration that both suspends normative histori-

---

29. "flirrte eine Menge Leben, kleingehackt, kurzweilig und beeilt, in aufspringender, zappelnd verweilender und wegzuckender Unruhe, zu einer kleinen Musik, die ihre gegenwärtige Zeitgliederung auf die Erscheinungsflucht der Vergangenheit anwandte und bei beschränkten Mitteln alle Register der Feierlichkeit und des Pompes, der Leidenschaft, Wildheit und girrender Sinnlichkeit zu ziehen wußte, auf der Leinwand vor ihren schmerzenden Augen vorüber. Es war eine aufgeregte Liebes- und Mordgeschichte, die sie sahen, stumm sich abhaspelnd am Hofe eines orientalischen Despoten, gejagte Vorgänge voll Pracht und Nacktheit, voll Herrscherbrunst und religiöser Wut der Unterwürfigkeit, voll Grausamkeit, Begierde, tödlicher Lust und von verweilender Anschaulichkeit, wenn es die Muskulatur von Henkerarmen zu besichtigen galt" (Zb, 334).
30. "Bilder aus aller Welt: den Präsidenten der Französischen Republik in Zylinder und Großkordon, vom Sitze des Landauers auf eine Begrüßungsansprache erwidernd; den Vizekönig von Indien bei der Hochzeit eines Radschas; den deutschen Kronprinzen auf einem Kasernenhofe zu Potsdam. Man sah das Leben und Treiben in einem Eingeborenendorf von Neumecklenburg, einen Hähnenkampf auf Borneo, nackte Wilde, die auf Nasenflöten bliesen, das Einfangen wilder Elefanten, eine Zeremonie am siamesischen Königshof, eine Bordellstraße in Japan, wo Geischas hinter hölzernen Käfiggittern saßen. Man sah vermummte Samojeden im Rentierschlitten durch eine nordasiatische Schneeöde kutschieren, russische Pilger zu Hebron anbeten, an einem persischen Delinquenten die Bastonade vollziehen" (Zb, 335).

cal time and exhibits all evolutionary time. The sick protagonist Hans explicitly develops by virtue of encyclopedic education into a hermetic medium for containing all these dimensions of time, for discovering the new puzzling modernist context and imaginative capacity, and for exploring the inner realm of human spirituality.

The period of World War I in Europe and the Americas was replete with the necessary materials and suggestions of this new order of the simultaneity of disparate time strata. Teddy Roosevelt's travelogue films of Africa and South America made between 1910 and 1914 were distributed widely to movie theaters. It was filming an encounter with Lawrence of Arabia that started Lowell Thomas's career as a travelogue maker and then, with the addition of a sound track, a global commentator. From 1915 on, the couple Martin and Osa Johnson launched a similarly profitable cinematic vogue with their intrusions into headhunter territory in the South Pacific, glamorously wild East Africa, the forests of the Congo, and so forth. In effect, the newsreels and travelogues of the war period constituted collectively an overwhelming act of crosscutting among stories of various branches of the human family.

To achieve such a convergence was the deliberate aim of the passionate antiwar film *Intolerance* (1913). D. W. Griffith daringly sought to make stages in the historical pathway of European civilization imaginatively copresent for the contemporary audience, who in his view were caught up in an age-old contest between a nurturing, liberating female principle and an aggressive, regimenting masculine principle. *Intolerance* crosscuts with an ever intensifying pace among four stories otherwise widely separate in history: the fall of luxuriant Babylon to the forces of Cyrus, Christ's mission and Crucifixion, the St. Bartholomew Day's massacre in Renaissance France, and labor unrest in the capitalist United States. Griffith mobilizes a vast array of knowledge to reconstruct the actual moments—the best archaeological and anthropological data, the historical record, artworks from or of the times—and obviously expects educated viewers to recognize certain specific uses of operatic staging, actual paintings, historical accounts and romances, contemporary newsreels, and so forth, in the total composition. A quotation from Walt Whitman runs throughout as a binding thread for both the events and the capsule commentary in subtitles. In a magnificent surge, Griffith raised film, yet without a sound track, to the level of a *Gesamtkunstwerk*.

Virginia Woolf was born in 1882 and died in 1941, like Joyce whose *Ulysses* she deprecated, whereas she admired Proust's *In Search of Lost*

Time. Her most famous novels—*Jacob's Room* (1922), *Mrs Dalloway* (1925), *To the Lighthouse* (1927), *Orlando* (1928), and *The Waves* (1931)—were almost all conceived before cinema with sound triumphed. The striking resemblances to filmic technique in them suggest more a spiritual affinity with the evolving medium rather than any single major influence. She was responsive, just as was Proust earlier, to the lively discussion of principles and innovations in the visual arts (painting, architecture, decor, photography).[31] This broad core interest was widely shared in her circle, the Bloomsbury group. As Marcus has explicated in great detail, Woolf's essays on film of the mid-1920s already contain the main ingredients of her rapidly evolving view.[32] Her best known reflection, "The Cinema" (1926), was written while she was working on *To the Lighthouse* and was concerned with questions of representing time and memory and capturing both the rhythm of inner and outer happenings and the simultaneity that big cities suggested—matters she had already experimented with in *Mrs. Dalloway*. *To the Lighthouse* not only implements technically but expounds thematically our experience of modes of perception. The final part of the novel uses both distancing and close-ups analogous to cinema; our sight line shifts now to a larger perspective where we see the surviving family members in the boat far off, and next we are looking with them from the boat and at each other, until in the final memorable image we are cowitnessing the entire scene as it has been unfolding, and sensing its deeper import, gazing out with the painter Lily on shore who is aware of bringing this moment together on her canvas. The middle section of the novel, "Time Passes," daringly sets in without explanation ten years after the death of the principal personage, Mrs. Ramsay, and following the trauma of World War I, as a kind of camera's eye pans about within the vacation house in Scotland that is being reopened. Mrs. Ramsay is both absent and present, an insight we associate with the unavoidable haunting awareness of our own separation from and envisioning of the space and time of the earlier pages of the novel where she was once the animating spirit. The prewar first part presented the fleeting reality the loss of which is poignantly anticipated, felt even before it occurs. The ecphrastic convergence of story strands at the novel's end conjures a powerful sense of ontological mystery that inheres in our witnessing the

31. Consult Diane Gillespie, ed., *The Multiple Muses of Virginia Woolf* (Columbia: University of Missouri Press, 1993).

32. For treatment of all aspects of the relationship, consult Laura Marcus's ch. 2, "The Shadow on the Screen: Virginia Woolf and the Cinema," in *The Tenth Muse*, 99–178.

"presence" of the human beauty of Mrs. Ramsay. Woolf's novel exhibits not only the inroads of cinematic structuring but, as noted in chapter two ("Epiphany"), also the literary achievement of superepiphanic progression. The generic break to the middle section of *To the Lighthouse* broadly resembles that from the "Combray" section to the middle section "Swann in Love" in *Swann's Way* insofar as the reader must adjust to a shift of narrative point of view unexplained until almost the finish of this part when Proust's internal first-person narrator reappears only obliquely. World War I, the major seismic event that reenergized Proust to complete his vision in *Time Refound,* has also already intervened for the younger Woolf and constitutes another felt, though "hidden," reality that informs her departure from older plot formation in *Mrs. Dalloway.*

Perhaps nothing more radically captured the deep horror of the Great War—the sense that European culture had been in the grip of mass psychosis and criminality—than the new expressionist direction exemplified in films like Robert Wiene's *Das Kabinett des Dr. Caligari* (The Cabinet of Dr. Caligari, 1919) which had a considerable impact across Europe. Its phantasmagoric, at times tortured, scenery turned cityscape into dreamscape, in which characters often float ghostlike. When toward the end we perceive that the frame setting is an insane asylum and that the inner narrator may himself be mad, our confidence founders about knowing whether the asylum director is truly an evil, death-dealing manipulator, possibly a modern confidence man who has resurrected the persona and wiles of a medieval magus, or is indeed that very monster who refashions himself over the centuries. The raw contents of *Caligari* were well established in literature; the war acted like a catalyst to bring them back in a startling cinematic form. A long train of tales of terror and identity confusion from E. T. A. Hoffmann and Edgar Allan Poe onward constituted a familiar register. The line from romantic over symbolist drama on into modernism and absurdism was another prominent literary inheritance that often employed such similar vehicles as fairy tales, ghost stories, and mythological allegories.[33] Nineteenth-century naturalists professed the goal of being "scientific," but in their zeal to identify ills and promote reform they also fed the fin-de-siècle obsession with pathologies in people and society; positivistic and naturalist fictions that probed degeneracy and mental illness interfaced with the busy world of

33. On this development, consult *Romantic Drama,* ed. Gerald Gillespie (Amsterdam and Philadelphia: John Benjamins, 1994), 455–64.

medical research. Romantic theorizing about the unconscious, stories about encounters with dangerous alter egos, fear of possession by some alien power, interest in hypnotism, sleepwalking, hallucination, and abnormal states of mind—all found an up-to-date home in cinema. The relationship between the clinical, literary, and cinematic realms at the turn of the century and in pretalkie modernism has deservedly attracted a great deal of attention.[34]

The pervasive fear of being possessed or of being ruled by a secret agency in modernist fiction and expressionist film may have several explanations. It can be understood as a response to widespread gnostic anxiety in complex cultures, the paranoiac dread of being subject to mysterious archons who manage the "system." Sometimes it reflects recognition of ugly archaic levels of human behavior that persist under the veneer of civilization. In many instances it appears to realize cumulative insights, since at least symbolism onward, of the collapse of the "illusion" of individual identity (see chapter fourteen, "Structures of the Self and Narrative"). Gregor Samsa in Kafka's *Metamorphosis* can readily be viewed as reenacting a deeper mythological identity (see chapter fifteen, "Palimpsest, Essay; History, Myth"), whereas the two K.'s, the bank clerk in *The Trial* and the purported surveyor in *The Castle,* seem each to have an archetypal rather than a personal identity, and to deal in ritual discovery of some necessary subservience to a mysterious ruling body. Stephen's deepening grasp in the "Library" chapter of *Ulysses* of his Hamletic role and of the multiplicity of identities which a true artist encompasses is prefaced by his meditative struggle in "Proteus" with an otherness that threatens him in multiple guises, as alien blood, woman, birth, and death, and even as a mysterious father like the Flying Dutchman who "comes, pale vampire, through storm his eyes, his bat sails bloodying the sea, mouth to her mouth's kiss."[35] Some strange power seems to use human beings as a vehicle for its own purposes from time immemorial.

In Proust's *Time Refound,* something primordial has burst its way back to the surface in World War I. In the foreword to *The Magic Mountain,* Thomas Mann stresses the experience of epochal rupture, after which an entire civilization cannot regain its irretrievably lost character, so that he is summoning it as if from the abyss: "The exaggerated past-

---

34. A helpful guide emphasizing the important German expressionist materials is Stefan Andriopoulos, *Possessed: Hypnotic Crimes, Corporate Fiction, and the Invention of Cinema* (Chicago and London: University of Chicago Press, 2008).

35. Joyce, *Ulysses*, 40.

ness of our narrative is due to its taking place before the epoch when a certain crisis shattered its way through life and consciousness and left a deep chasm behind" (MM ix).[36] Robert von Musil opens part 1 of his novel *Der Mann ohne Eigenschaften* (The Man without Qualities, 1930), which is set in the period just before the outbreak of World War I, with a haunting series of images of the streets of the old imperial capital Vienna, conjuring a world that no longer exists and the whole puzzle of how its collective sense of identity vanished and it became a ghost of fiction. The momentary details appear as in a filmic montage in paragraph two, but the feeling they evoke is that of witnessing a phantasm. The fact that an unidentified authorial narrative voice ironizes at the close of paragraph one over the seemingly "old-fashioned" realism of its coldly neutral scientific description of a "beautiful August day in the year 1913" does not subtract from, rather it intensifies, the strangeness of conjuring that vision.[37] It is in films like Michelangelo Antonioni's *L'avventura* (The Disappearance, 1960) and *L'eclisse* (The Eclipse, 1962), that we again experience this kind of tension-laden panning over ordinary corners, streets, and buildings which strangely acquire a ghostly aura.

Fritz Lang's science fiction film set in 2026, *Metropolis* (based on Thea von Harbou's script, written 1924ff., released by UFA in 1927), which expresses postwar anxiety over the viability of society in the capitalist era, radically departs from any pretense to realism. However, its story line transparently reinvokes traditional paradigms and its futuristic vision of a dystopic supercity employs symbolic structures and spaces firmly anchored in European tradition. The audience encounters the archetypal figures of Johann Fredersen who reigns over Metropolis from his lofty penthouse (Zeus, Wotan, the head), of his son Freder (Siegfried, Christ, heir and champion) who develops into the mediator between the ruling class and the workers, of the pure, nurturing Maria (Virgin Mary, power of the heart, beneficent nature) who succeeds in interceding for those who toil and reside in the lower depths, and of Fredersen's rival, the mad scientist Rotwang (Satan, the demiurge, the modern Frankenstein), who creates a seductive robot made to look like Maria in order to sow discord among the elite and mislead the people. Novalis's neomy-

---

36. "[. . .] die hochgradige Verflossenheit unserer Geschichte rührt daher, daß sie *vor* einer gewissen, Leben und Bewußtsein tief zerklüftenden Wende und Grenze spielt . . ." (Zb 5).

37. Robert Musil, *Der Mann ohne Eigenschaften*, vol. 1 of *Gesammelte Werke*, ed. Adolf Frisé (Frankfurt: Rowolt, 1978), 9: "etwas altmodisch"; "ein schöner Augusttag des Jahres 1913."

thological fairytale "Klingsohr's Märchen" (Klingsohr's Fairytale) in the romantic novel *Heinrich von Ofterdingen* (posthumously 1800) is probably the most influential ancestor to Lang's simpler, but importantly updated tale of misdirected human rebellion and the happy resolution of the struggle for the "city's" inner balance and survival. This expressionist film in turn counts as one of the important forerunners of such science fiction classics of the later twentieth century as George Lucas's *Star Wars* series.

The accomplishments of writers like Joyce and filmmakers like Griffith undergird John Dos Passos's trilogy *U.S.A.* (1930–1936), a newer kind of modernist fiction that aspires to narrate a colossal collective story and in so doing employs cinematic concepts from black-and-white film without sound track, as well as literary expressionism. During his lifetime Joyce encouraged critics to elaborate a complex vocabulary to describe the structuring principles of *Ulysses*, the main eighteen parts of which exist both as stylistically separate works in their own right and as interrelated mythological and narrative moments. As is well known, Joyce tried to start a commercial movie house in Dublin in 1909 with Italian partners and, initially doubting *Ulysses* could be translated into another language, he thought of having it translated into a different imaginative medium: film. The "Aeolus" chapter demonstrates just one of the many places where the transfer could readily occur. Joyce interprets the life of a newspaper as an aspect of the life of a city, and explores the metaphors and attributes of the newspaper as institution, such as "circulation" and "headlines," by projecting it visually in a comic imitation of its social rhythms and actual mechanical functioning. An invisible narrative press flows profusely in mock headlines and advertising slogans, which not only carry the historical data and debris marking that day in Dublin, but by underground suggestion advance the book's major themes and romanesque figures. The use of such prominent graphics directly feeds, and is fed by, the newsreel technique of headlines and capsule commentary. Here the headlines are superimposed mainly on segments of language rather than visual shots. But Joyce overtly combines the experience of newspapers and newsreels with a prominent mode of modernist composition: the depersonalized montage. On a higher plane of analysis, it is no exaggeration to see the puzzle-fit of the novel's eighteen chapters as a colossal cubistic assemblage.

One of the interesting lessons of Dos Passos's extensive use of documentary materials is that a partisan approach, as his is, converts the materials into an overtly ideological statement, not a normative, objective historical panorama of the period between 1900 and 1930—no matter how he protests about objectivity. (This does not by necessity detract from the artistic power of Dos Passos's epic narration.) The loosely intertwined strands of his fictional plot treat the several destinies of characters who represent a broad spectrum of American types. Into this virtually impersonal polynarration he interweaves three alternate forms. There are the short impressionistic "Biographies" of eminent Americans in a rhythmic prose; intermittent "Newsreels" composed of bits of speeches, reports, headlines, and popular songs of the times; and sequentially numbered passages under the designation "The Camera's Eye." These last convey an unnamed observer's quasi-autobiographical impressions and thoughts written in a stream-of-consciousness style. The protagonist's mind gradually ages as it moves through the era it beholds. The biography segment "Poor Little Rich Boy," treating the newspaper tycoon William Randolph Hearst, was itself to become the core for an entire film, Orson Welles's renowned *Citizen Kane* (1940).

Despite obvious differences in stylization of the character of the actively interpreting mind behind Dos Passos's "Camera's Eye," nonetheless its gaze is ancestral to that in the French *nouveau roman* of the 1960s and thus constitutes one of many intermediate steps to the reapplication of such a point of view in cinematic art. This gaze structures narration. Dos Passos may seem to integrate the viewing mind in a quasi-documentary reality, but on closer inspection we note the reciprocal possibility that the surrounding context, which is only pseudo-objective, may constitute materials imbedded in an experiencing subject. Alain Robbe-Grillet is among those writers after World War II who have made the broader public aware that literary and filmic technique have become reciprocal in their influence and, for example, in *L'année dernière à Marienbad* (Last Year at Marienbad, 1971), directed by Alain Renais, he has shown that the story-shaping "subject" can be focused outward or inward, and variably, thus combining total subjectivity in narration with technical attributes of hyperrealism. When we look back to the psychedelic shiftings and dream states of the "Nighttown" chapter in *Ulysses*, it is evident that Joyce set a standard of complexity that is avoided by the *nouveau roman* and one that may yet exceed the most evolved cinematic mastery in conveying psychological events and sentient existence. In 1927, Hermann Hesse capped his novel *Steppenwolf* by creating an extended psychedelic experience, titled the "Magic The-

ater," that is meant to convey the drama of a deeper therapeutic questing. A comparison of this section of Hesse's work with the treatment of
images in the contemporary surrealist film by Luis Buñuel and Salva-
dor Dalí, *Un chien andalou* (An Andalusian Dog, 1929), will demonstrate
that in maturing modernism the acceptance of dream structures was
a fundamental factor unifying the narrative approaches of both media:
film and literary fiction. Mann's discovery is echoed when, for example,
Hesse's pacifist quester Harry Haller grasps the powerful immediacy of
the Old Testament through seeing a second-rate film about Moses; in the
half-awake state of a communal viewer, but consciously linking Moses,
the ancient archetype of the order bringer, to figures such as (Wagner's)
Wotan, Haller's mind effectively abolishes time in a modernist montage
of mythological forms.

One of the problems that has surfaced in the twentieth century is that
propagandists have learned all too well from the modernists the latest
literary and cinematic skills for manipulating our psyches. Even if we
discount the cultural biases of postmodern theory in the Western nations, in the aggregate this kind of hermeneutic suspicion and rejection
of our immediate past teaches us an important lesson: that we can no
longer safely believe a priori in the factual status of any so-called documentary or news broadcast, and that it is in our interest to learn the rules
by which persons who want to influence us construct narratives to that
end.[38]

38. See Joel D. Black, *The Reality Effect: Film Culture and the Graphic Imperative* (New
York: Routledge, 2001). Black examines mainly the period since World War II and demonstrates the pervasive presence of filmic imagery affecting and increasingly shaping the
contemporary psyche and examines the cultural ramifications of cinema's vital affiliations
with the nonartistic domains of science and technology.

7 CITY OF WO/MAN

Labyrinth, Wilderness, Garden

From the ancient Greeks and Romans we have the master trope of the *locus amoenus* that pictures both the desired order of nature and poetic ordering in its sustaining fullness. The terrifying wilderness or forest is more a contribution of medieval literature. Renaissance and baroque literature and painting again raise the *locus terribilis* to new heights of symbolic power. Genesis provides the model of the garden whence man and woman, acquiring consciousness, were expelled into temporality and the family romance. That Adam and Eve's first son, Cain, the first murderer, built the first city added complication to the paradox of the fortunate fall. For the city, understood as the sacred capital whose temple is the cosmic center, became a rival image for the home of the restored human community. But the city too, from the tale of its origins and such episodes as the Tower of Babel, acquired a shadow, just as fallen nature devolved from garden into wilderness and desert. Saint Augustine's *Civitas Dei* transposed into Christian thought, as a general metaphor, the yearning for a rebuilt, transfigured Jerusalem. This is what Leopold Bloom still yearns for on 16 June 1904, in the "Circe" chapter of *Ulysses,* when the "gramophone" screeching "Whorusalaminyourhighohhh" drowns out Elijah's naming of the holy city.[1] Joyce counts on our recognition of Dublin as Jerusalem's shadow, as explicitly another Babylon ruled by its own scarlet whore.

Of course, the idealizing projection of nature as garden and the city as a meaningful human order survived down the centuries, despite the literal collapse of the great Western capital: Rome. In the Middles Ages, while a castellated nobility dominated secular high culture and eventually fostered the European love ethic, the monasteries continued the representation of sacred space and cosmic structure, fusing the image of lost

---

1. James Joyce, *Ulysses: The Corrected Text,* ed. Hans Walter Gabler with Wolfhard Steppe and Claus Melchior (New York: Vintage Books, 1986), 414; hereafter cited as U followed by the page number.

paradise with the classical inheritance of villa and garden culture. Monastic establishments absorbed much of the educational function of the ancient academies, before cathedral schools and early modern universities displaced them. Princes in the reemergent cities of the early Renaissance increasingly sought to draw this academic realm into their cultural sphere, while secular writers resurrected the notion of the glory of the city as the heart of civilization. Thus, eventually, the humanist version of the stories of the fall of Troy and the fall of Rome came to rival in importance, in Renaissance minds, that of the expulsion of Adam and Eve.

This blend of Renaissance interests and concerns preformed the conflicted sense that modernist writers would have of the city as the key site of the human drama. Clearly, Saint Thomas More's Christian humanist vision of an ideal city-state in his *Utopia* (1516), in contrast to disordered European society, drew upon Europe's monastic as well as its classical experiences. When More's admirer Rabelais suggested the new secular potential of the Renaissance through the coeducational institution Thélème, a monastery converted into an elegant earthly paradise, he had his age's courtly standards, rather than city life per se, in mind. Nonetheless, city as well as court poets before and after Rabelais, from Guillaume de Lorris to Giambattista Marino, reinvoked the ancient garden of love and stressed the role of sensual experience and feminine sensibility in achieving a modern, cultivated urbanity. The positive sense of nature's vitality found widespread expression in the Renaissance cult of Venus, which we encounter in major humanists like Ficino as well as in the major poets. Many gateways connected the gardens of love, poetry, and philosophy in the Renaissance.

However, any student of early modern culture will remind us that some gardens like the humanist academic precincts in Jörg Wickram's novel *Von guten und bösen Nachbarn* (Of Good and Bad Neighbors, 1554) in the mid-sixteenth century were spiritual and social refuges within cities otherwise extensively perceived as perilous. The Paris Rabelais depicted, more Panurge's than Pantagruel's turf, is exciting, but unreliable, checkered with crime and decadence, and its few ladies resemble the lustier dames of whom Boccaccio already had taken notice by the mid-fourteenth century in the *Decamerone* ([playing on Greek,] Ten Days, 1353), rather than those in his *De claris mulieribus* (On Illustrious Women, 1361–1365). Downright dangerous are the wayward passions and criminal careers of urban women of high and low birth in Fernando de Rojas's *Celestina* (1494) at the close of the fifteenth century. Fernando Delicado's title roguess in *La lozana andaluza* (The Exuberant Andalusian, 1528), the glamorous underworld queen of early sixteenth-century Rome, is among innumerable Spanish ancestresses to figures like the adventuress Moll Flanders whom Defoe shows finally on the down and out in eighteenth-century London. In Henry Fielding's novel *Tom Jones* (1749), the hero has to survive a final challenge posed by London's corrupt ladies of fashion in order to preserve intact the Enlightenment promise of the pursuit of happiness and faith in natural law and morality.

In brief, neither the romantics nor the modernists after them needed to invent the spectacle of the city as a dystopic labyrinth. But two things occurred in nineteenth-century literature that lent a distinctive twist to the symbolic potential of the city. The first was the subsidence of the eighteenth-century master theme of the earthly paradise, which a rival master theme, that of the journey through hell, gradually displaced. The second was the general shift of attention away from nature, away from the beneficent great chain of being, from the ambient nurturing countryside, idyllic Rousseauesque situations, and energy-laden storm-and-stress wildernesses as favorite story locales and topics, and the large-scale transference of the poetic interest in nature onto the city. Already stained by the grotesque episode of the Terror, postrevolutionary Paris became the monstrous organism of deformative drives in Balzac's series, the *Comédie humaine* (1842–1853), the theater of romanticism's self-voiding in Flaubert's *L'éducation sentimentale* (1869), and the admonitory example of pathological hypertrophy in Zola's *Nana* (1880). James Thomson's powerful Dantesque vision of the urban realm of Britain in his poem *The City of Dreadful Night* (published 1874) was begun around the time of Baudelaire's *Les fleurs du mal* (Flowers of Evil, 1857). Baudelaire, one of the most influential reenvisioners of the city and its spaces as the new human topography, a fascinating and perplexing surrogate nature, helped successors from Mallarmé to Rimbaud to Rilke to relate the spaces of postromantic interiority to urban contexts and experience.

It would be advantageous to embark here on an excursus calling to mind how the great realists such as Fontane, Wharton, and Galdós examined women's roles in the new metropolitan societies of Europe and North America at the turn of the century. But it is the related powerful contemporaneous tradition that is my immediate subject here: the symbolic identification of the city with nature, hence also with the body and feminine principles, on the threshold of high modernism. The romantic femme fatale puts in her next appearances for us as the Carmen, Sa-

City of Wo/man: Labyrinth, Wilderness, Garden

lomé, and Venus-in-Furs figures whom writers, artists, and composers of the mid- and later nineteenth century, like Mérimée, Moreau, Bizet, and Sacher-Masoch, use to embody the alluring, but cruel, life force—that power that Schopenhauer termed the "will" in his seminal treatise of 1818 and elsewhere named the "unconscious." This identification was productively ambivalent for modernist writers in the wake of Baudelaire. As Walter Benjamin has noted, "What is unique in Baudelaire's poetry is that the images of woman and death are permeated by a third, that of Paris."[2] I leave it to others to distinguish between sensitive and merely sentimental or sexist portrayals of liberated and/or commercialized female sexuality in the later nineteenth century. I shall merely stipulate what was a completely open theme of the age: the danger that loose women, be they ever so charming, posed to good bourgeois order and public health. Popularizers of the theme of a connection between female sexuality and the physical decay and moral sickness of city life were legion. Works such as Alexandre Dumas fils's play *La dame aux camélias* (The Lady with the Camelias, 1848), Verdi's opera *La traviata* (The Lost Woman, 1853), and Somerset Maugham's novel *Of Human Bondage* (1915) exemplify the higher level of this broad public discourse that sought to define and/or contain the challenge. The banal Lulu figure in several of Frank Wedekind's plays (1895, 1902–1904, 1913), Alban Berg's expressionist opera based on her (1936), and G. W. Pabst's film *Die Büchse der Pandora* (Pandora's Box, 1929) can serve to illustrate how, despite depressing trivialization, such clichés enjoy long afterlives as motifs.

Because it is analogized to the body and woman, the story of the city acquires a deeper evolutionary and existential dimension in the twentieth century. On the one hand, the reification and decrepitude of existence appear in the city as the secret graveyard of all spiritual efforts, or the city as necropolis. On the other hand, within this necropolis, this place of constant dying—as important modernists come to view it—woman is also the source of renewal and survival. The journey through hell in modernist, late modernist, and postmodern fiction does indeed often take the form of a tour of the city as dystopic labyrinth—experiences of Paris in Rilke's *Die Aufzeichnungen des Malte Laurids Brigge*

2. Walter Benjamin, *Reflections: Essays, Aphorisms, Autobiographical Writings*, ed. Peter Demetz and trans. Edmund Jephcott (New York: Schocken Books, 1986), 157.—"Es ist das Einmalige der Dichtung von Baudelaire, daß die Bilder des Weibs und des Todes sich in einem dritten durchdringen, dem von Paris" (Walter Benjamin, *Passagenwerk*, in *Gesammelte Schriften*, ed. Rolf Tiedemann and Hermann Schweppenhäuser [Frankfurt: Suhrkamp, 1972–1979], 5.55).

(The Notebooks of Malte Laurids Brigge, 1910), of "dear, dirty Dublin" in Joyce's *Ulysses*, of gloomy Prague in Kafka's *Der Prozeß* (The Trial),[3] or of grim industrial Bleston in Butor's *L'emploi du temps* (Passing Time, 1958).[4] One of the ambiguities in Mann's *Death in Venice* (1912), as Eros turns into Thanatos in that supreme necropolis where Apollonian palaces repose on Dionysian swamps, is that the suppressed feminine aspect of Aschenbach's existence takes revenge on him. But the city can also be the body as site of the process that love redeems, as in Thomas Wolfe's celebration of New York in *Of Time and the River* (1935), or we can shuttle from behind the scenes in fin-de-siècle Paris into archaic depths, to the park-studded necropolis that is simultaneously the temple of woman's power, as when Mann conducts us to Lisbon in closing *Felix Krull* (1954).

Each of us could name dozens of writers who share the theme of those endless streets we walk with Rilke, Kafka, and Joyce. In *Ulysses* the eternal pattern is:

> Cityful passing away, other cityful coming, passing away too: other coming on, passing on. Houses, lines of houses, streets, miles of pavements, piled-up bricks, stones [. . .] . Piled up in cities, worn away age after age. Pyramids in sand. Built on bread and onions. Slaves Chinese wall. Babylon. Big stones left. Round towers. Rest rubble, sprawling suburbs, jerrybuilt. (U 135)

In his *Notebooks*, Rilke's young poet Malte smells the rotting corpse, the city as a hospital of dying patients and of women giving birth. Its living and dying invades his private space and mind:

> Electric street-cars rage ringing through my room. Automobiles run their way over me. A door slams. Somewhere a window-pane falls clattering; I hear its big splinters laugh; its little ones snicker. Then suddenly a dull, muffled noise from the other side, within the house.[5]

3. Franz Kafka, *Der Prozeß: Roman*, ed. Max Brod (Frankfurt: S. Fischer Verlag, 1953); hereafter cited as P followed by the page number. Franz Kafka, *The Trial*, trans. Willa Muir and Edwin Muir (New York: Schocken Books, 1974); hereafter cited as T followed by the page number.
4. Michel Butor, *L'emploi du temps* (Paris: Les Éditions de Minuit, 1957); hereafter cited as ET followed by page numbers. Michel Butor, *Passing Time*, trans. Jean Stewart (London: Faber & Faber, 1961); hereafter cited as PT followed by the page number.
5. Rainer Maria Rilke, *The Notebooks of Malte Laurids Brigge*, trans. M. D. Herter Norton (New York: W. W. Norton, 1964); hereafter cited as MLB followed by the page number.— "Elektrische Bahnen rasen läutend durch meine Stube. Automobile gehen über mich hin. Eine Tür fällt zu. Irgendwo klingt eine Scheibe herunter, ich höre ihre großen Scherben lachen, die kleinen Splitter kichern. Dann plötzlich dumpfer, eingeschlossener Lärm von der anderen Seite, innen im Hause" (Rainer Maria Rilke, *Die Aufzeichnungen des Malte*

City of Wo/man: Labyrinth, Wilderness, Garden

Malte comes to associate the reality of impoverished street people, the city's human debris, with the spectacle of buildings being ripped down and others replacing them. Viewing the tawdry wrecked interiors, with their shabby walls and exposed pipes, is like peering into torn bodies and lives: "One saw its inner side" (MLB 47).[6] The broken buildings exude the fetid breaths and smells of those who once inhabited these spaces. In existential anguish, like the fleeing figure in De Chirico's streetscapes, Malte runs "as soon as I had recognized that wall. For that is the terrible thing, that I did recognize it. I recognize everything here, and that is why it goes right into me: it is at home in me" (MLB 48).[7] On the streets by night, as in paintings by Ensor or Grosz, Malte is buffeted by carnival crowds, with laughter bubbling "from their mouths like matter from open sores,"[8] crowds wedged together and swaying "as if they copulated standing" (MLB 48–49).[9] One of the most horrible episodes in Rilke's novel is when, on the verge literally of losing his mind and joining the shattered derelicts, Malte almost undergoes electroshock treatments in the public hospital. We must listen with him to the sounds of a system that treats the body as a thing and begins to numb his own humanity: "And I sat and wondered what they were about to do to the stupid girl and whether she too would scream. The machines back there kept up such an agreeable mechanical whirring, there was nothing disturbing about it" (MLB 58).[10] Finally, it is sheer terror over dying that impels Malte to escape from the hospital back into the endless labyrinth of alien signs:

> I cannot recall how I got out through the numerous courtyards. It was evening, and I lost my way in this strange neighborhood and went up boulevards with interminable walls in one direction and, when there was no end to them, returned in the opposite direction until I reached some square or other. Thence I began to walk along a street, and other streets came that I had never seen before, and still other streets.

Laurids Brigge, in *Sämmtliche Werke*, ed. Ernst Zinn [Frankfurt: Insel-Verlag, 1966], 6.710); hereafter cited as A followed by the page number.

6. "Man sah ihre Innenseite" (A, 749).

7. "sobald ich die Mauer erkannt habe. Denn das ist das Schreckliche, daß ich sie erkannt habe. Ich erkenne das alles hier, und darum geht es so ohne weiteres in mich ein: es ist zu Hause in mir" (A, 751).

8. "aus ihren Munden wie Eiter aus offenen Stellen" (A, 752).

9. "als ob sie sich stehend paarten" (A, 752).

10. "Und ich saß und dachte, was sie wohl dem blöden Mädchen tun wollten und ob es auch schreien würde. Die Maschinen dahinten schnurrten so angenehm fabrikmäßig, es hatte gar nichts Beunruhigendes" (A, 763–64).

Electric cars would come racing past, too brilliantly lit and with harsh, beating clang of bells. But on their signboards stood names I did not know. I did not know in what city I was or whether I had a lodging somewhere here or what I must do in order not to have to go on walking. (MLB 59)[11]

We recognize these streets, fifteen years later, in Kafka's *The Trial*, as those the bank official Josef K. navigates looking for the court to which he has been summoned by that intrusive modern device, the telephone:

He had thought that the house would be recognizable even at a distance by some sign which his imagination left unspecified, or by some unusual commotion before the door. But Juliusstrasse, where the house was said to be and at whose end he stopped for a moment, displayed on both sides houses almost exactly alike, high gray tenaments inhabited by poor people.[12]

Kafka's typical scene of a popular quarter on Sunday includes family members gazing from windows, women thronging shops to buy food, disconcerting laughter over K.'s head, and a strident phonograph. K.'s aggressive, maladroit penetration into the private space of Fräulein Bürstner, his attractive fellow lodger, in chapter 1, is now followed in chapter 2 by his entrance through courtyards and his climb up stairways past shabby denizens and roguish children. The tawdriness of ordinary life in the big city is striking:

Most of the flats, too, consisted of one small single-windowed room in which cooking is going on. Many of the women were holding babies on one arm and working over a stove with the arm that was left free. Half-grown girls who seemed to be dressed in nothing but an apron kept busily rushing about. In all the rooms the beds were still occu-

11. "Ich kann mich nicht erinnern, wie ich durch die vielen Höfe hinausgekommen war. Es war Abend, und ich verirrte mich in der fremden Gegend und ging Boulevards mit endlosen Mauern in einer Richtung hinauf und, wenn dann kein Ende da war, in der entgegengesetzten Richtung zurück bis an irgendeinen Platz. Dort begann ich eine Straße zu gehen, und es kamen andere Straßen, die ich nie gesehen hatte, und wieder andere. Elektrische Bahnen rasten manchmal überhell und mit hartem, klopfendem Geläute heran und vorbei. Aber auf ihren Tafeln standen Namen, die ich nicht kannte. Ich wußte nicht, in welcher Stadt ich war und ob ich irgendwo eine Wohnung hatte und was ich tun mußte, um nicht mehr gehen zu müssen" (A, 765).

12. "Er hatte gedacht, das Haus schon von der Ferne an irgendeinem Zeichen, das er sich selbst nicht genau vorgestellt hatte, oder an einer besonderen Bewegung vor dem Eingang schon von weitem zu erkennen. Aber die Juliusstraße, in der es sein sollte und an deren Beginn K. einen Augenblick lang stehenblieb, enthielt auf beiden Seiten fast ganz einförmige Häuser, hohe, graue, von armen Leuten bewohnte Miethäuser" (P, 47).

pied, sick people were lying in them, or men who had not wakened yet, or others who were resting there in their clothes. (T 36)[13]

When K. finally reaches the locale of the court, he is pointed through an open door by "a young woman with sparkling black eyes, who was washing children's clothes in a tub" (T 37).[14] Finding a congregation of people that intimates some kind of community, he aggressively assumes a political role and questions the court's authority in bolder and bolder terms. K.'s lust clearly is redirected toward the proletarian mother who distracts him when she mysteriously becomes involved in a sexual encounter in a corner of the very room where the magistrates and crowd listen to his impassioned speech against official corruption. The atmospherics grow ever more ominous as "the dim light [. . .] made a whitish dazzle of fog" (T 46).[15] Emerging only halfway out of this "fog" (T 46) that characerizes his blindness, K. senses a threat to his freedom and decamps with a burst of defiance. In a later visit to the empty courtroom, where he is again quite captivated by the young mother, K. discovers to his amazement that the literally dirty lawbooks on the judges' table contain "an indecent picture" (T 52)[16] and a pornographic novel. Most striking is the picture's utter banality:

A man and a woman were sitting naked on a sofa, the obscene intention of the draftsman was evident enough, yet his skill was so small that nothing emerged from the picture save the all-too-solid figures of a man and a woman sitting rigidly upright, and because of the bad perspective, apparently finding the utmost difficulty even in turning toward each other. (T 52)[17]

We may sense that this description transcribes, among other things, a subconscious opinion on K.'s part that God as "artist" has botched in real

13. "Es waren in der Regel kleine, einfenstrige Zimmer, in denen auch gekocht wurde. Manche Frauen hielten Säuglinge im Arm und arbeiteten mit der freien Hand auf dem Herd. Halbwüchsige, scheinbar nur mit Schürzen bekleidete Mädchen liefen am fleißigsten hin und her. In allen Zimmern standen die Betten noch in Benützung, es lagen dort Kranke oder noch schlafende oder Leute, die sich dort in Kleidern steckten" (P, 50).
14. "eine junge Frau mit schwarzen, leuchtenden Augen, die gerade in einem Kübel Kinderwäsche wusch" (P, 51).
15. "denn das trübe Tageslicht machte den Dunst weißlich und blendete" (P, 61).
16. "ein unanständiges Bild" (P, 67).
17. "Ein Mann und eine Frau saßen nackt auf einem Kanapee, die gemeine Absicht des Zeichners war deutlich zu erkennen, aber seine Ungeschicklichkeit war so groß gewesen, daß schließlich doch nur ein Mann und eine Frau zu sehen waren, die allzu körperlich aus dem Bild hervorragten, übermäßig aufrecht dasaßen und sich infolge falscher Perspective nur mühsam einander zuwendeten" (P, 67).

nature, which is his art form, this particular subject matter. It would not be going far afield to read this dismissive judgment between the lines also as a statement by the unidentified narrating voice about "the bad perspective" that governs the fate of K. to the very end, as well as specifically his relationship to the feminine. As a modern man who thinks existence is just business and legal conventions, although he punctuates his routine with lurches into lechery, K. doggedly persists in believing he can transfer the categories of his lowly bureaucratic mind to solve his own case:

> These tactics must be pursued unremittingly, everything must be organized and supervised; the Court would encounter for once an accused man who knew how to stick up for his rights. (T 127)[18]

But fog and smoke keep coming through K.'s window. His mind is beclouded, and in his own way he stares as an obtuse clairvoyant into taunting apertures in a surreal opacity as Gregor does in the novella *Die Verwandlung* (The Metamorphosis, 1915). Venus-in-Furs is the worshipped lady in the picture frame in Gregor's room, when on page 1 of the story he awakens transformed into a bug; gradually his view out his window dims away into the blank wall that shuts him out of life. The accused K.'s ever more frenetic explorations are increasingly hellish. For example, where the painter lives (in chapter 7),

> beneath the other wing, in the masonry near the ground, there was a gaping hole of which, just as K. approached, issued a disgusting yellow fluid, steaming hot, from which some rats fled into the adjoining canal. (T 141)[19]

Rilkean and Joycean horror comingle in such repugnant images.

Elsewhere in this volume, in chapter thirteen, "The Haunted Narrator before the Gate," I suggest that K.'s reciprocal blindness toward life and his discovery of the hideousness of its grounding have a direct bearing on the famous parable of the gate in the cathedral episode. K.'s dwarfish stature in relation to the symbolic complexity of the church and his failure to enter into the spirit of the parable constitute a chastening neo-

18. "Von diesen Anstrengungen dürfte man nicht ablassen, alles müßte organisiert und überwacht werden, das Gericht sollte einmal auf einen Angeklagten stoßen, der sein Recht zu wahren verstand" (P, 153).

19. "war unten in der Mauer eine Lücke gebrochen, aus der gerade, als sich K. näherte, eine widerliche, gelbe, rauchende Flüßigkeit herausschoß, vor der sich einige Ratten in den nahen Kanel flüchteten" (P, 169).

mythological moment in European literature. Kafka is a genuine, albeit a negative, cabalist in his treatment of the metaphor of the doorways through which humanity perceives the light of God and attempts to approach God. In the system of the sefiroth, which pictures the emanations of God, the lower aspects of being occur in the feminine vital reality, or Shekinah. Crucial in the erotic cabala is the proper relationship of the male and female creatures whose bodily union, if motivated by genuine love, can provide access to the higher joy that reveals the ultimate joy residing in the recondite godhead of the Creator. Crucial in the theosophical cabala is the cosmic drama of God's own act of self-reflection that is played out in the passionate story of the self-regenerating human species. The human race is construed as love's body; the supreme symbol of affirmation is the incarnation of a child. While God's mystery recedes into higher sefiroth whenever a privileged human creature succeeds in entering the lower earthly doorway from which the light shines forth, the door beckons for a reason. Like Kafka's other system-probing and questioning antiheroes, K. cannot really grasp his own otherness as an aspect of the body of love. But the novel's referentiality comprises and gives us more than his bafflement. We recognize that K.'s ritual execution in the night occurs under a strangely peaceful light that Kafka hints is connected with the nocturnal movement of Fräulein Bürstner who floats through the streets like a tutelary goddess as he goes to his death: "The moon shone down on everything with that simplicity and serenity which no other light possesses" (T 227).[20]

We can contrast K.'s obtuseness as sacrificial victim to Malte's long resistance, as poet and weak vessel, to the power to which all along he has known he will finally surrender. This ineluctable acceptance by Malte as a self-styled prodigal son who must finally come home is expressed in the multipartite coda to the *Notebooks*. This drawing together of the novel's web of themes caps Malte's exploration of the deeper existential resemblances of saints, lovers, and artists, and of the preeminence of women among lovers. Meditating on the complex story of European civilization since antiquity, the unhoused Danish poet Malte who has survived as an exile in Paris moves into the coda with an affectionate address to the "Girls in my native land" (MLB 200).[21] Without having cut off access to the feminine, Malte stands almost as a predictive contrast to

---

20. "Überall lag der Mondschein mit seiner Natürlichkeit und Ruhe, die keinem anderen Licht gegeben ist" (P, 270).
21. "Mädchen in meiner Heimat" (A, 927).

Mann's Aschenbach who will arrive a few years later at the intersection of art's magical space, in Venice. Rilke too evokes this special metropolis as a representatively European construct:

> this Venice, willed in the midst of the void on sunken forests, enforced and in the end so extant, through and through. This hardened body, stripped to necessities. [. . .] This beautiful counterpoise of the world [. . .]. (MLB 204–5)[22]

The natural miracle is that amid the international babble Malte hears the voice of the lost home, a beautiful voice of a woman at a window singing in Danish. This releases the culminating tribute to Abelone, the beloved youthful aunt from whom as a child Malte learned love's virtues. Playing his male role complementary to hers in the androgyne, the artist Malte is reconfirmed in his dedication as the prodigal whose terror before the all-engulfing absoluteness of love has a distinctly mystical flavor.

Whether we should regard Butor's *Passing Time* of 1957 as an early postmodern or a postponed modern novel is a question beyond my present scope. Significant here is that in it we encounter the intensified perception of the city as an entrapping labyrinth that is alive and threatens to swallow the inadequate male hermeneut. Late in the book the narrator even hears the ever-metamorphosing city mock his futile resistance to its power and his utopian desires:

> I endure, I am tenacious; and if some of my houses fall down, don't let that persuade you that I myself am crumbling into ruins, that I'm ready to make way for that other city of your feeble dreams, those dreams that through my power have grown so thin, so obscure, so formless and impotent—maybe you fancied last April that the framework hidden within these walls foreshadowed that dream-city? But my cells reproduce themselves, my wounds heal; I do not change, I do not die, I endure, my permanence swallows up all attempted innovation; this new face of mine is not really new, you can see that, it is not the first sign of my contamination by that imaginary city which my enemies contrast with me, although they can never describe it; no, no, this is the present face of an old, though not an ancient city, a city that some call doomed; look at me [. . .] . (PT 208)[23]

---

22. "das mitten im Nichts auf versenkten Wäldern gewollte, erzwungene und endlich so durch und durch vorhandene Venedig. Der abgehärtete, auf das Nötigste beschränkte Körper [. . .] Das schöne Gegengewicht der Welt [. . .]." (A, 932–33).

23. "[J]e dure, je suis tenace! et si quelques-unes de mes maisons s'écroulent, ne va pas croire pour autant que moi je tombe en ruines et que je suis prête à laisser la place à

Butor's protagonist, the young French sojourner Revel, groping in the labyrinth of the fogbound, rainy British industrial city Bleston, creates his own labyrinth of words as he weaves back and forth among layers of time in his diary, which he begins as a way to cope with his experiences and mistakes after several frustrating months of difficulty in assimilating as an alien. Gradually, he begins to see analogies between Bleston and cities of all ages and climes and the relevance of foundational stories such as that of Cain and Abel. Revel comes to identify himself with the roles of Theseus and Oedipus, but this is insufficient knowledge. His failure to understand the feminine world within, or feminine aspect of, the city, is crucial to his destiny. He eventually loses both Ann Bailey, explicitly his Ariadne, and her sister Rose, clearly a Phaedra figure, who lures him away but then turns to one of the rivals he always perceives too late. Revel's hermeneutic quest is related to the imperative to understand an inner secret of Bleston, a fratricidal murder about which, under a pseudonym, a writer who befriends Revel has published a detective fiction. Revel never understands sufficiently, even in retrospect, how the murder novel relates to the real families associated with the narrated events; nor does he ever anticipate how his interest in the fiction and its shadowy original background will affect the Bailey sisters and the matriarch Mrs. Jenkins, and what their true relationship to the various rival males may be, let alone the motives of the latter. If myth-obsessed Revel in some sense encounters himself depicted everywhere, as in the "eighteen tapestries of the Harvey collection" (PT 141),[24] which cover the story of Theseus from childhood to exile from the city (PT 141–42), he is like an obtuse sleepwalker searching through the evidence of his own dreamscape.

As ambiguously named as the later fictive Bleston, the historically actual Phoenix Park in Dublin is for Joyce the lost Eden as dystopic focal point of masculine failure and transgression. In *Ulysses,* the park prom-

---

cette autre ville de tes faibles rêves, de tes rêves que moi j'ai réussi à rendre si minces, si obscurs, si dispersés, si balbutiants, si impuissants, à cette autre ville dont tu t'imaginais peut-être que cette charpente, si bien enrobée maintenant, annonçait l'approche en avril; mes cellules se reproduisent, mes blessures se cicatrisent; je ne change pas, je ne meurs pas, je dure, j'absorbe toute tentative dans ma permanence; ce nouveau visage que je te montre, tu le vois bien, ce n'est pas vraiment un nouveau visage, ce n'est pas un visage du présent, ce n'est pas le premier symptôme de ma contamination par cette ville fantastique que l'on prétend m'opposer sans être capable de me la décrire, mais c'est le visage présent de cette ville non pas ancienne, mais vieille, que je demeure, de cette ville que certains disent condamnée, regarde [. . .]" (ET, 231).

24. "dix-huit tapisseries Harvey" (ET, 155).

ising resurrection is the place where modern Irish leadership tragically fell; in *Finnegans Wake*, it recurs as the scene of HCE's alleged embarrassing sexual crimes. While tracking the flow of Homer's *Odyssey*, the symbolic progression of Joyce's polytropic fiction *Ulysses* also follows that of Goethe's *Faust* in grand outline. Faust's restless drive as a Renaissance man dominates part 1 of Goethe's cosmic drama, while part 2 expands into the exploration of accrued millennia of archetypes, and the work culminates in acknowledgment of "the eternal feminine,"[25] as the penultimate line states. The beginning focus of the twentieth-century polytropic novel is indeed on Stephen, the Joycean protagonist who stands in conflictual relationship to his world and is dogged by his own Mephisto in such forms as Malachi-Mulligan; but the Telemachus story melts, in *Ulysses*, into the wanderings of the maturer Bloom as he circulates round and about in the complexity of Dublin but finally gets back home to house and garden and wife. The All-Mother's interior monologue, with the famous words "and yes I said yes I will Yes," closes the circle in affirmation of the process in the "Penelope" chapter. A Dantesque aura envelopes the vital mystery at the heart of the labyrinth as the aspects of the father and son, "the centripetal remainer" and "centrifugal departer" (U 577), cross in their relationship of returning to and going forth from the source in the "Ithaca" chapter.

Molly-Penelope, the dot into which Bloom-Odysseus disappears, is the cosmic and zero point, both the ovum and the period set to each life and narration, the gateway in and out of existence of humankind, the creature that goes forever through its own gate. Humanity vampiristically recycles itself as cities rise, blossom, collapse into ruins, and are rebuilt. The symbolism of Ithaca is insistently traditional. The house, the temple in the midst of the labyrinth, is a virtual infinity. This we readers discover in exploring the myriad things and connections the house reveals. It clearly supplants the wilderness of Bella Cohen's bordello, whose false Valhallan light Stephen shatters with his self-liberating gesture as a young Siegfried. Now in Ithaca, in recovering the father, the son is ushered forth through the garden and out the garden gate to be a father himself, a candidate of the human order and reconciled with the nurturing body. In a novel exhibiting the coincidence of opposites, Molly is "denoted by a visible splendid sign, a lamp and is the projected luminous and semiluminous shadow" (U 576–77). We are experiencing the mystery

25. "Das Ewigweibliche" (Goethe, *Die Faustdichtunagen*, ed. Ernst Beutler [Zurich: Artemis-Verlag, 1950], 526).

of the darkness of the Shekinah and the divine light that streams forth through it as the Gate. In the "Nighttown" chapter, the improbable orgiast Stephen senses this coincidence of opposites in such jesting slippages of phrase as "David's that is Circe's or what am I saying Ceres' altar" (U 411).

The "otherness" of the labyrinth-city closes itself and excludes Revel in *Passing Time* as hard as he may try to fathom it by means of his journal. How different an ending is the amazed joy the confidence man (read: artist) Felix feels when the All-Mother Senhora Kuckuck, a Demeter and a Carmen wrapped up in one, takes him to her ample bosom in Mann's *Felix Krull*.

> "Maria!" I cried.
> And: "Holé! Heho! Ahé!" she exclaimed in majestic jubilation. A whirlwind of primordial forces seized and bore me into the realm of ecstasy. And high and stormy, under my ardent caresses, stormier than at the Iberian game of blood, I saw the surging of that queenly bosom.[26]

During Felix's long train ride into the archaic Iberian corner of Europe, he has discovered the story of evolution as whose hero and purpose he duly pictures and appoints himself in a dream on the threshold to this comic reenactment of the Eleusinian rites. Cries of the ancient initiates, of the bullfight, of Wagnerian valkyries commingle in the modernist eternity of mythic identity. Our Hermes-elect, who has enabled our participation, can or will say no more about the sacred mysteries associated with the mother.

This statement of 1955 resonates from nuclei of Mann's work in the period predating World War I. Nothing more aptly illustrates the positive modernist turn in the identification of city, wilderness, and garden than does the coda to Proust's *Swann's Way* in 1913, spun around the fictive narrator's juvenile devotion to glamorous Odette de Crécy, which would impel him to scour the allées of the Bois de Boulogne, hoping to catch sight of her.[27] His Oedipal crush, being an admirer of her husband

---

26. Thomas Mann, *Confessions of Felix Krull, Confidence Man: The Early Years,* trans. Denver Lindley (New York: Vintage Books, 1969), 378.—"'Maria!' rief ich. Und: 'Holé¡ Heho! Ahé!' rief sie mit mächtigem Jubel. Ein Wirbelsturm urtümlicher Kräfte trug mich ins Reich der Wonne. Und hoch, stürmischer als beim iberischen Blutspiel, sah ich unter meinen glühenden Zärtlichkeiten den königlichen Busen wogen" (Thomas Mann, *Bekenntnisse des Hochstaplers Felix Krull: Der Memoiren erster Teil* [Frankfurt: S. Fischer Verlag, 1957], 442).

27. Marcel Proust, *Du côté de chez Swann,* ed. Pierre-Louis Rey and Jo Yoshida, in

Swann, makes him a mildly guilty Hippolyte figure. Whereas it is ominous that the title figure of Zola's novel, the young decadent-elect Renée, who is incestuously attracted to older men, is also addicted to displaying herself to them in the fashionable Bois, Proust allows his remembering narrator in *Swann's Way* to revel in the pleasure of witnessing and worshipping the recently decadent vamp, and now arrived society matron, Odette, that is, Venus in her glory in the North. The approximately seven final pages of *Swann's Way*, a symphonic fusion of the novel's themes and tropes, subsumed in autumnal elegiac recollection, merit being cited in full; but I trust that just a few excerpts will suffice to suggest the flavor of the matured pleasure:

> That sense of the complexity of the Bois de Boulogne which makes it an artificial place and, in the zoological or mythological sense of the word, a Garden, came to me again this year as I crossed it on my way to the Trianon, on one of those mornings in November when, in Paris, if we stay indoors, being so near and yet excluded from the transformation scene of autumn, which is drawing so rapidly to a close without our witnessing it, we feel a veritable fever of yearning for the fallen leaves that can go so far as to keep us awake at night. (SW 456)[28]

Although he has been able to resist the longing to visit the sea (a rival experience of the unconscious and of totality), the Bois, Paris's internalized tamed wilderness, draws him into its complex staging of the drama of her power, nature's and the city's, a staging suited "for the casual exercise of the human figures that would be added to the picture later on" (SW 457),[29] a mise-en-scène containing intimations of spring like the "ampelopsis, a smiling miracle like red hawthorn flowering in winter" (SW 457).[30] The park's "temporary, unfinished, artificial look"

---

vol. 1 of *À la recherche du temps perdu*, under the general editorship of Jean-Yves Tadié (Paris: Gallimard, 1987); hereafter cited as DCCS followed by the page number. Marcel Proust, *Swann's Way*, trans. C. K. Scott Moncrieff and Terence Kilmartin (New York: Random House, 1981); hereafter cited as SW followed by the page number.

28. "Cette complexité du bois de Boulogne qui en fait un lieu factice et, dans le sens zoologique ou mythologique du mot, un Jardin, je l'ai retrouvée cette année comme je le traversais pour aller à Trianon, un des premiers matins de ce mois de novembre où à Paris, dans les maisons, la proximité et la privation du spectacle de l'automne qui s'achève si vite sans qu'on y assiste, donnent une nostalgie, une véritable fièvre des feuilles mortes qui peut aller jusqu'à empêcher de dormir" (DCCS, 414).

29. "pour la promenade épisodique de personnages qui ne seraient ajoutés que plus tard" (DCCS, 414).

30. "ampelopsis merveilleux et souriant comme une épine rose de l'hiver [. . .] enfleur" (DCCS, 414–15).

(SW 457)[31] does not bother Marcel; for this autumnal moment—the equivalent of poetic recollection—is when the Bois, like art, "displays more separate characteristics, assembles more distinct elements in a composite whole than any other" (SW 457).[32] Immersed a while in the almost Joycean "liquid, emerald-green atmosphere" (SW 459)[33] of the groves, "as though beneath the sea," he senses "the life of feminine humanity" and hastens back in his mind to glimpse "masterpieces of feminine elegance" of yesteryear. Nothing contemporary seems any longer to possess the power of Madame Swann "in an otter-skin coat" (SW 461),[34] a blue feather on her hat, against the threat of winter.

In fact, the beautiful women the narrator has known have literally taken flight "through the Virgilian groves" (SW 462)[35]—a fate that ironically always resided in the elegant name of one of the favorite avenues, the Champs Elysées. When feminine beauty is subtracted from the park, nature devolves from garden back into wilderness. The male consciousness, alone in its city, facing mere raw reality, experiences the acute pain of loss. But loss also sets us on the Baudelairean pathway of recollection, "Receuillement," entering the night.

> The sun had gone. Nature was resuming its reign over the Bois, from which had vanished all trace of the idea that it was the Elysian Garden of Woman; above the gincrack windmill the real sky was grey; the wind wrinkled the surface of the Grand Lac in little wavelets, like a real lake; large birds flew over the Bois, as over a real wood, and with shrill cries perched, one after another, on the great oaks which, beneath their Druidical crown, and with Dodonian majesty, seemed to proclaim the unpeopled vacancy of this deconsecrated forest, and helped me to understand how paradoxical it is to seek in reality for the pictures that are stored in one's memory, which must inevitably lose the charm that comes to them from memory itself and not from their being apprehended by the senses. (SW 462)[36]

31. "aspect provisoire et factice" (DCCS, 415). The translation here expands on Proust's term "provisional" ("provisoire") to bring out the total phrase's combination of theatrical and tropic-tropologic nuances with their existential implications.

32. "trahit le plus d'essences diverses et juxtapose le plus de parties distinctes en un assemblage composite" (DCCS, 415).

33. "atmosphère liquide et couleur d'émeraude" (DCCS, 416).

34. "comme sous la mer"; "vivre en commun avec la femme"; "chefs-d'oeuvre d'élégance féminines"; "en paletot de loutre" (DCCS, 418).

35. "cherchant [. . .] dans les bosquets vigiliens" (DCCS, 419).

36. "Le soleil s'était caché. La nature recommençait à régner sur le Bois d'où s'était envolée l'idée qu'il était le Jardin élyséen de la Femme; au-dessus du moulin factice le vrai

Eros and Thanatos. The deconsecrated woods become by allusion the Sainte Baume, the precincts of the Great Mother in her silvan darkness. But Odette, whose clothes, as we observe throughout the novel, instinctively change with the seasons and fashions, always promises to reappear in flower. Ultimately, she is internalized in the tropes of time and season as the sign of the mystery of life. The final symphonic fusion of all tropes occurs in the memory of Odette's triumphant walks in the Bois.

What can happen if it is not a Stephen Dedalus or a Marcel who witnesses, or a Joseph K. who assiduously misreads, the feminine, but the interpreter protagonist is a heroine-artist born to claim her birthright in the city? Dorothy Sayers shows us one possibility in her novel *Gaudy Night* (1936), in which her detective figure Harriet Vane, recently tainted by a tragically ended love affair, returns to Oxford as an alumna in order to assist her women's college where a hate-filled murderer stalks the female scholars.[37] Sayers borrows chapter epigraphs mostly from Renaissance and seventeenth-century authors. The book's epigraph is from John Donne:

> The University is a Paradise, Rivers of Knowledge are there, Arts and Sciences flow from thence. Counsell Tables are Horti conclusi, (as it is said in the Canticles) Gardens that are walled in, and they are Fontes signati, Wells that are sealed up; bottomless depths of unsearchable Counsels there. (GN iii)

As a heterosexual woman and conflicted intellectual, Harriet probes the contrasts between the real world, including the characters and motives of her own classmates who attend their college reunion, and the special life housed in this sanctuary. Portraits she sketches in her own mind, such as of Miss De Vine, her virtual shadow, an intellectual with a "hard mind" (GN 17), cover a range of existential pathways that Harriet might tread because of her fierce independence, painful honesty, and desire for genuine equality with the sort of male she admires: the war veteran Lord Peter Wimsey. She has resisted his marriage proposals out of

---

ciel était gris; le vent ridait le Grand Lac de petites vaguelettes, comme un lac; de gros oiseaux parcouraient rapidement le Bois, comme un bois, et poussant des cris aigus se posaient l'un après l'autre sur les grands chênes qui sous leur coronne druidique et avec une majesté dodonéenne semblaient proclamer le vide inhumain de la forêt désaffectée, et m'aidaient à mieux comprendre la contradiction que c'est de chercher dans la réalité les tableaux de la mémoire, auxquels manquerait toujours le charme qui leur vient de la mémoire même et de n'être pas perçus par le sens" (DCCS, 419).

37. Dorothy Sayers, *Gaudy Night* (New York: Harper & Row, 1964); hereafter cited as GN followed by the page number.

fear he eventually will fail her difficult idealism. Thus, she can respond to the spell of Oxford, and even accept

> that slightly absurd collection of chattering women fused into a corporate unity with one another and with every man and woman to whom integrity of mind meant more than material gain—defenders in the central keep of Man-soul, their personal differences forgotten in face of a common foe. To be true to one's calling, whatever follies one might commit in one's emotional life, that was the way to spiritual peace. How could one feel fettered, being the freeman of so great a city, or humiliated, where all enjoyed equal citizenship? (GN 27)

The murderer turns out to be the establishment's familiar, maternal Annie, an embittered cleaning woman who is revenging herself for the loss of her own spouse, a suicide. She will not accept the truth that he was dismissed at another institution for academic dishonesty, and that he was not victimized by a cabal of heartless academic women, one of whom, Miss De Vine, has joined Harriet's old college. I shall not rehearse in detail Annie's grounds for attacking the female scholars; in essence, Annie voices the widespread lower-class suspicion of liberated women as unnatural for abandoning the care and nurture of the family, and undermining loyal wives and mothers by stealing the livelihoods of husbands and fathers. What is interesting in this novel is that Harriet grasps with imaginative empathy the social and psychological basis for Annie's anger, yet also understands why the college, as a special element of a complicated civilization, must be defended against the irrational forces that have been unleashed. She never condemns her alter ego De Vine for being the unrelenting enforcer of intellectual standards. In *Gaudy Night,* Sayers offers us a meticulous study of the steps in Harriet's thinking that lead her to sense ominous impulses at work in a badly shaken England and Europe after World War I. Her own peril and suffering help her appreciate not only the trauma suffered by fighters like Peter Wimsey in combat, but the quality of their human response then and afterwards. What Harriet comes to share is the complex position of Wimsey as a modern agnostic humanist who has negotiated these epochal shifts mentally and emotionally, has analyzed the structures of contemporary European polity, has embraced the cause of democracy as a cautious conservative, and has a vision of the evolving British tradition as one of the viable channels toward a saner, humane future.

Many commentators claim that, by the 1990s and perhaps continuing into our new century, many of the women scholars and Annie have changed places in some British or at least in some U.S. universities, and that today the irrationalist forces occupy a rather large number of seats in the common room. Then, speaking hypothetically for the academic collective, we might say that our worst Annie-like suspicions about Dorothy Sayers being politically incorrect are richly confirmed in *Gaudy Night*. "Harriet was left to survey the kingdom of the mind, glittering from Merton to Bodley, from Carfax to Magdalen Tower" (GN 455), but when all is said and done her eyes fondly follow her true soulmate. She decides to marry Wimsey and exits definitively from hallowed academic precincts. More shocking yet, it turns out that Sayers has been citing the great Renaissance writers chapter by chapter for a real reason. It is to prepare us for the open admisson as the novel concludes that, deep down, her Harriet Vane has come to identify spiritually with a branch of European civilization that took on such a shape in the English Renaissance as could entrance Orlando-like feminine sensibilities of high modernism. "[S]pire and tower and quadrangle, all Oxford springing underfoot in living leaf and enduring stone, ringed far off by her bulwark of blue hills" (GN 451)—Sayers celebrates her, the City, celebrates all the gardens that fend off the ever-threatening wilderness, and she rejoins and fuses the city of woman and the city of man and of the human spirit as a single city.

PART TWO

METAMORPHOSIS, PLAY, AND THE LAWS OF LIFE

8 AFTERTHOUGHTS OF HAMLET

Goethe's Wilhelm, Joyce's Stephen

We walk through ourselves, meeting robbers, ghosts,

giants, old men, young men, wives, widows, brothers-in-

law. But always meeting ourselves. (U 213)[1]

There is no explicit signal to tell us that this remark by Stephen in the "Library" chapter, with Shakespeare on his mind, paraphrases Baudelaire's sonnet "Correspondances" (lines 3–4), but we may justifiably suspect the echo in a book as polyphonic as *Ulysses*. Of Joyce's novel itself it is fair to say, "Man passes there [in nature's temple] through forests of symbols which observe him with familiar glances."[2] In the "Nestor" chapter, Stephen seems initially a more familiar figure as in a bildungsroman when, troubled by "unsteady symbols" and conflictual "Amor matris: subjective and objective genitive," he cerebrally "proves by algebra that Shakespeare's ghost is Hamlet's grandfather" (U 28). For the reader, however, as Stephen makes a pilgrimage out of the nightmare of history through the shifting signatures of the "Proteus" chapter, he starts dissolving away into the convergence of paradigms as a parodic reminder of the educational protagonist whose task it ever is to discover life's and the world's patterns. By the "Library" chapter, where Stephen's path crosses that of his alter ego, Bloom, sentimental identity persists only as a trace beneath nodular clusters of parody, even though we cling to such identity and it provides romanesque threads to follow from cluster to cluster through labyrinthine Dublin. Yet language, the instrument both of demiurgic narrative control and of the internal discourse

1. James Joyce, *Ulysses* (New York: Vintage Books, 1961). References to *Ulysses* follow this edition and indicate page number, after the abbreviation U if the context is not explicit.
2. "L'homme y passe à travers des forêts de symboles / Qui l'observent avec des regards familiers" (Charles Baudelaire, *Les fleurs du mal*, ed. Jacques Crepet and Georges Blin [Paris: José Corti, 1950], 9).

of psyches within the narration, begins to take over control from the developmental figure, as in his own mind he reconstrues his "self" as a fiction. On the strand Stephen senses language like his own sentient existence emerging from nature's womb: "Rhythms begin, you see. I hear." The inflections of the divine Word appear as a doubling and folding back upon itself, perceived in "the ineluctable modality of the visible" and "the audible" ("Crush, crack, crick, crick. Wild sea money" [37]). This generative power of language will reverberate in comic ghostly echoes in the book's dream-night, as when to the Watch's declension—"Bloom. Of Bloom. For Bloom. Bloom."—the hungry covey of gulls, rising from the Liffey slime with the sacramental "Banbury cakes in their beaks" respond: "Kaw kave kankury kake" (453).

Let us posit, as Saldívar argues, that our artist-elect "seems willing to go one step further than any banal Freudianism. The ego is not simply narcissistic—the idea of the self based on the image of the other can exist only by virtue of the fact that the self is the other." In "searching for the other, [Stephen] thus constitutes himself," but eventually recognizes the "fragmentary quality of his existence."[3] As the mythopoeic structure of Stephen's identity is elaborated in more and more detail, his role as the "son" in search of his "father" in the archetypal "family romance"[4] gradually ceases to be a "personal" matter in the reader's eyes.[5] The shifts and conflicts of narrative voice and perceptual point of view in *Ulysses* undermine the authoritative status of the character even though he remains a center of "interest and consciousness."[6] Stephen's story becomes enmeshed in the novel's "labyrinthine discourse."[7] How, then, should literary history characterize the transmission of literary references in this novel, another more complex order of inflections? The web of allusions seems to expand into an effectively independent universe of signs and in the process virtually swallows the figural "father"-elect Stephen and

3. Ramón Saldívar, *Figural Language in the Novel: The Flowers of Speech from Cervantes to Joyce* (Princeton, N.J.: Princeton University Press, 1984).

4. Christine van Boheemen, *The Novel as Family Romance: Language, Gender, and Authority from Fielding to Joyce* (Ithaca, N.Y.: Cornell University Press, 1987), 161–69.

5. Boheemen asserts that Stephen's idea of "postcreation" nonetheless exhibits a modernist evasion of encounter with the feminine bodily-material "other," because the spiritual principle of imagination, as language or text, is the redemptive Word that "'transcends' the dualistic polarity of masculine-feminine, patriarchy-matriarchy, matter-spirit" (191).

6. Seymour Chatman, *Story and Discourse: Narrative Structure in Fiction and Film* (Ithaca, N.Y.: Cornell University Press, 1978), 154–56.

7. Manfred Schmeling, *Der labyrinthische Diskurs: Vom Mythos zum Erzählmodell* (Frankfurt: Athenäum, 1987), 252–62.

by analogy the "author" as persona. Precisely if and because a Stephen may attain to "epiphanies" that are "Pico della Mirandola like" and become "one with one who once [. . .]" (40), the oceanic realm of signatures will resorb his separate authorial place as a sentimental character in a plot line of history and reception.[8] Joyce prudently furnished many terms and hints via his network of supporters to help criticism start up in an era beyond this point of departure that symbolism had enabled. With time, further patterns have accrued to *Ulysses*, emerging from its internal systems of self-commentary and cross-reference and from their relation to Joyce's earlier works and his later *Finnegans Wake*, until today we can endlessly spin variations upon the textual status of *Ulysses* and its arts and its characters.[9] Our critical preoccupation with the book as a multitext of subtexts is not some latter-day or independent ferment; it reflects and continues the centrality of issues of interpretation within the novel itself.

For example, when we gaze into the antlered mirror with Leopold Bloom and Stephen Dedalus in the epic psychodrama of the "Nighttown" chapter, is the ghostly face there, explicitly called Shakespeare's (567), merely a fleeting intertextual abstraction, or a shared hallucination, or only Bloom's or Stephen's self-misprizing or insight, or an authorial-demiurgic revelation that empowers the reader with or confirms a by-now acquired quasi-divine omniscience? In any case, just how are we readers being implicated in Joyce's voyeuristic time-bending metaphor, as he holds the mirror up to . . . what? This question is complicated by the fact that Hamlet serves us as a kind of inner looking glass and inner face of the mysterious playwright persona Shakespeare and of the principle he incarnates throughout the novel. Joyce knew, of course, that the nineteenth century had been fixated on Hamlet, as he was himself all his life, and he made good use of that widely felt and pondered cultural reality;

8. Fritz Senn (124f.) points out the dizzying historical perspectivism and multiplicity of cultural reference packed into just the title and opening page of *Ulysses*, which stamp the universalizing character of the book well before most readers can take bearings (Fritz Senn, *Joyce's Dislocutions: Essays on Reading as Translation*, ed. John Paul Riquelme [Baltimore: Johns Hopkins University Press, 1984]). Herring sees in the same kind of evidence the breakthrough of a poetics of indeterminacy (Phillip F. Herring, *Joyce's Uncertainty Principle* [Princeton, N.J.: Princeton University Press, 1987]).

9. The appearance of the three-volume critical and synoptic Gabler edition (James Joyce, *Ulysses*, ed. Hans Gabler et al., 3 vols. [New York and London: Garland, 1984]) has rekindled debate both on details and on approaches. The range of current concerns can be gauged from the essays in reaction to that edition gathered in *Assessing the 1984 "Ulysses,"* ed. C. George Sanulescu and Clive Hart [Towata, N.J.: Barnes & Noble, 1986]).

our reading of *Ulysses* thus prolongs the European obsession with Hamlet in some manner.

And nowadays, just mentioning the "Nighttown" or "Circe" chapter, that labyrinthine megachapter, inevitably reminds "competent" readers of a myriad of other thematic clusters, mythological paradigms, generic structures, and linguistic forms that Joyce puts through permutations and combinations there. Hence some readers will instantly think of predecessor literary frameworks of the nineteenth century—for example, the ironic phantasmagoric realms such as Goethe created in *Faust* 1 (1808) and 2 (1832)—which prepared the way for the Joycean conflation of innumerable elements (borrowed, e.g., from Wagnerian neomyth, the work of Sacher-Masoch, surrealist vision, etc.) in a dream-play.[10] Some will enjoy comparing the Joycean combinations of favorite references (e.g., Dantesque, Shakespearean, Goethean) within modern psychologistical plot elements (e.g., Freudian, Jungian) and variant combinations of plot elements in fiction by major contemporaries (e.g., in Mann's *The Magic Mountain*). Grabbing hold of the polysystemic, humoristic-encyclopedic Joycean text is about as simple as encapsulating Rabelais's Gargantuan-Pantagrueline *roman fleuve* in two or three paragraphs. By the nature of the task we tend to pick up only a few pieces at a time as constituents of the ever renewable literary text; and as we sift through the strands and bits Joyce coopted from world literature, we cannot help but recognize our own high and mighty resemblance to the *Wake*'s busy "hen," participating in Joycean consciousness by scratching together readings.[11] Hamlet is so juicy "a worm of consciousness" that we gobble him up quickly, kicking away the lesser detritus.[12]

Granted that Shakespearean motifs constitute one of the most compendious systems, if not the master complex, pervading *Dubliners, Stephen Hero*, the *Portrait, Ulysses*, and the *Wake*, and that Hamlet is a key protagonal figure haunting all these books, who, then, more exactly is this Hamlet as he comes forcefully into our thoughts through Stephen's theorizing about Shakespeare in the "Scylla and Charybdis"

10. Cf. Hayman's speculation (156) that *Faust* may have influenced the structure of *Ulysses* in general; the *Wilhelm Meister* novels, typically, are ignored (David Hayman, *Re-Forming the Narrative: Toward a Mechanics of Modernist Fiction* [Ithaca, N.Y.: Cornell University Press, 1987]).

11. *Finnegans Wake* (New York: Penguin Books, 1976), 10–13.

12. I take the phrase from Chiaromonte's essay of 1962 (Nicola Chiaromonte, *The Worm of Consciousness and Other Essays*, ed. Miriam Chiaromonte, preface by Mary McCarthy [New York: Harcourt Brace Jovanovich, 1976]) discussing the sense of the existential absurdity of sexual intercourse expressed in Alberto Moravia's *La noia*.

chapter? Since the 1960s, relying heavily on Schutte's thorough sorting out of the Shakespearean allusions and of Joyce's use of turn-of-the-century studies of Shakespeare, handbooks such as Thornton's help guide readers line by line through the rich intellectual conversation that takes place in the National Library in Dublin.[13] Cheng has additionally documented the pervasive influence of the Bard and especially his Hamlet in the *Wake*.[14] We need not adopt Schutte's pejorative view of Stephen and Bloom as characterless moderns in order to accept the fundamental outline of what Joyce accomplishes in creating "two images of the dramatist," Stephen's interpretation as against the revered historical figure, "a double standard for judging certain of [the novel's] materials."[15] Stephen's approach in turn is double, since he matches his own and others' readings of the masterpiece *Hamlet* with psychological analysis of the Bard's biography as gleaned from the historical record. It may be a patchwork uttered with mental reservations and fraught with errors, but the attentive reader observes how this doubleness that feeds on itself eventually is folded into a larger compound in which mere oppositions collapse. In spite and because of its polarities, the main exposition on Shakespeare in the "Scylla and Charybdis" chapter not only advances fundamental themes being worked out in the existences of the fictional characters Stephen Dedalus and Leopold Bloom, it also provides an advanced lesson in hermeneutics. This major lesson in our Odyssean training course in reading lifts our participation onto a new plane, because it leads into dream synthesis. Hearing the public interchange of views on Shakespeare in the "Library" chapter, while interloping on the private associative linkages in Stephen's inner thoughts and his hunches about how others think, we learn to distinguish between Stephen's searching obsession with Shakespeare and the ultimate subordination of the motifs associated with that obsession in the larger textuality of the novel. But we also act from moment to moment like a Stephen or a Bloom in relating and synthesizing all materials that come to us and placing them in that textuality, a surrogate for the cosmic textuality we encounter in the signatures of our world.

Thus the return of the intellectual protagonist Stephen to front stage,

13. Weldon Thornton, *Allusions in "Ulysses": An Annotated List* (Chapel Hill: University of North Carolina Press, 1968).

14. Vincent John Cheng, *Shakespeare and Joyce: A Study of "Finnegans Wake"* (University Park: Pennsylvania State University Press, 1984).

15. William H. Schutte, *Joyce and Shakespeare: A Study of the Meaning of "Ulysses"* (New Haven, Conn.: Yale University Press, 1957), 142.

after our main attention has shifted to Bloom for the five chapters from "Calypso" to "Lestrygonians," does have an obvious and important narrative function that is solidly old-fashioned. It parodically sketches and enacts the grand strategy of romanesque plotting, as the pathways of the chief personages of the fiction crisscross symbolically in a world of texts. The less ostentatious parallel consists in the fact that, while Stephen is approaching the invisible boundary of the estate from which the Hamletic character initially appears to be estranged by definition, the novel is busy cross-weaving a more diversely reconstituted Hamletic consciousness, larger than Stephen's, into the texture of "our" fuller knowledge of Shakespeare. Such consciousness too attracts the "ghost"-father principle (Bloom) who passes between the twinned dangers of spiritual estrangement (Stephen) and cynical negation (Mulligan). The turn of talk toward the older Shakespeare and the drift toward the reconciliation theme, reinforced in the references to *Cymbeline* at the end of the chapter, portend a deeper movement in the soul that will transform the son into a father and reconcile him with the mother. Here Joyce, the humorist of affirmation, allows "romance" to subvert "reason" in a foretaste of the *coincidentia oppositorum* that his novel will celebrate in exuberantly histrionic ways—for example, in its self-parody as a black mass when during the nadir or harrowing of hell in "Nighttown" chapter, after her triumphant motherhood in the "Oxen of the Sun" chapter, *"On the altarstone Mrs Mina Purefoy, goddess of unreason, lies naked, fettered, a chalice resting on her swollen belly"* (599). *Ulysses* as a whole critiques Stephen's imbalance as an intellectual, who in asserting spirit lives too exclusively through one organ, the brain, in contrast to the more social and corporeal Bloom, the Christ-like victim of unreasoning love.

As the lesson sinks in that Stephen's personal view as an aspiring artist who identifies with Shakespeare is just one, though certainly a principal, variation on a primary mythos, we are less troubled over other often superficially cited, partial, misprizing, defective views associated with, or tried out by, particular speakers in the "Scylla and Charybdis" chapter and elsewhere. Taken together, all these views seem to resonate as textual variants that emanate from the Hamletic condition of the Western mind. It is this condition with which the apprentice Stephen must grapple. Examined under an impersonal Joycean optic as leitmotifs that convey thematic material, the progression of chief interpretational moments in the "Library" chapter—the start from Goethe, gravitation over to Mallarmé and the symbolists, and arrival at Freud—covers in its broad sweep the "inner" evolution of the nineteenth century in its Hamletized self-understanding. Bailey has chronicled this process of Hamletization in France. [16] The Hamlet problem proves to be independent of Stephen; in fact, it becomes transparent that the dynamic of the conversation in the "Scylla and Charybdis" chapter derives from far more than Stephen's invention; Stephen's own doubts about his interpretation cannot in fact banish the deeper, collective Hamlet experience of Europe.

After the "new" moment achieved by such a recapitulative synthesis in *Ulysses*, the successor critics, who down to the present have been stimulated by the complicated result (the interaction of Stephen and his contemporaries as they relate to Shakespeare), typically have focused on the seeming historical immediacy of innovation at the start of the twentieth century. We tend to look back on "who" Hamlet is in *Ulysses*, as if the "originary" instant of modernity depended principally on supposed terminal authoritative references that actually are merely our retrospective favorites, that is, Mallarmé and Freud (to whose significance I shall return). In an ongoing process of literary parasitism, many dimensions have been and are inevitably neglected that beg for retrieval and that, although they perhaps may never again be brought into the current cultural foreground, continue to pulsate in the text with latent energy. Clearly Joyce forms no exception to the historical rule; the critical weighting of references in his fiction shifts because later recipients of a book like *Ulysses* lose touch with potent earlier readings that lent it a particular tone and authority.

A rather startling illustration of such subtextual fading is the relative neglect of the overt starting point for the "Library" colloquy: the centrality of *Hamlet* in Goethe's *Wilhelm Meisters Lehrjahre* (Wilhelm Meister's Apprenticeship, 1796). The tendency of Joyce's novel certainly should be apparent sooner to readers who recall how Goethe subjects Wilhelm's immature individualism, his proclivity toward abstraction, and his social isolation to an analogous general critique (e.g., WM, book 5, chapter 20).[17] Yet even a specialist like Schutte makes merely passing reference

16. Helen Phelps Bailey, *"Hamlet" in France from Voltaire to Laforgue* (Geneva: Droz, 1964).

17. References to Goethe (after the abbreviation WM whenever the context is not explicit) follow Joyce's main source, Carlyle's translation, in vol. 1 of the reprint (Johann Wolfgang von Goethe, *Wilhelm Meister's Apprenticeship and Travels*, trans. Thomas Carlyle, 2 vols. [New York: Burt, n.d.]). A long interval separated Goethe's *Wilhelm Meisters Lehrjahre* (1796) and *Wilhelm Meisters Wanderjahre* (1829). Although Gelley does not draw any comparison to *Ulysses*, he notes that the *Wanderjahre* (Travels or Journeymanship) "is

to Goethe's view of Hamlet as a dramatic character, ignoring Goethe's interest in the paradigmatic value of the tragedy *Hamlet* within the context of Shakespeare's entire creativity and for grasping the dilemma of his own educational protagonist; and most commentators repeat the same cameo summary and relegate the mention of Goethe to an insignificant status as the individual contribution of Lyster. They overlook the fact that this orientation point has a function independent of its channel, just as do the later mentions of Mallarmé and Freud that have enjoyed extensive commentary. Through the inadequate speaker's voice opening the discussion for us in 1904, there echoes the important suprapersonal fact that the *Apprenticeship* indeed was and remains a statement by "A great poet on a great fellow poet" (U 184). This suggestion of a general parallel between Goethe's authorial reflection on Shakespeare in the *Apprenticeship* and Joyce's in *Ulysses* should alert us to suspect that there are deeper purposes in so setting the terms of the "Library" colloquy. The importance of Goethe's *Faust* at a number of places in *Ulysses*, more readily noted, underscores the suprapersonal connection of references to his work.

The Hamlet problem in fact provided guidance throughout for interpreting what was at stake beneath the surface of events in Goethe's bildungsroman one century earlier. The denouement in the *Apprenticeship* sets in with the long-awaited production of *Hamlet* in book 5, in the course of which the plot mysteries of Shakespeare's play and those of the novel become inextricably entwined. In this regard the parodied "educational" strand in Joyce's *Ulysses* betrays more than a rough resemblance to Goethe's plot. Wilhelm's self-assigned mission is to raise the dismal level of German cultural life by founding a national theater as its shaping in-

---

composed of an assemblage of text forms," not reducible to "a single, authoritative narrative principle," but exemplifying a "dialogic practice: first, in destabilizing genre forms; then, in orienting representational devices toward the instance of reception; and finally, in thematizing the channels of communication as such" (Alexander Gelley, *Narrative Crossings: Theory and Pragmatics of Prose Fiction* [Baltimore: Johns Hopkins University Press, 1987], 124ff.). As Katharina Mommsen's work serves to demonstrate, what is missing in this generic profile by Gelley—and in most Goethean criticism—is the influence of Arabic storytelling (especially the *1001 Nights*) on the structure of the *Wanderjahre* (Katharina Mommsen, *Goethe und die arabische Welt* [Frankfurt: Insel, 1988]). In my view it is reasonable to think of *Ulysses* as evidencing affinity to the *Wanderjahre*, as well as to the *Lehrjahre*, insofar as Joyce connects the plentiful "Semitic" (Sinbad the Sailor, Moses), "Greek" (Odysseus, Aeneas), and both ancient and modern "Japhethic" (Aengus, Flying Dutchman) motifs of wandering in *Ulysses* and relates the ground pattern of the quest or journey to his own Scheherazade-like, authorial shifting among, and exploration of, diverse genres and modes of narration.

strument, while Stephen is driven by the ambition "to forge in the smithy of my soul the uncreated conscience of my race."[18] There is an added resonance in the fascination for Shakespeare insofar as both the German and the Irish author have treated the prehistory of the artistic calling and its Hamletic heritage in an anticipatory version—Goethe's *Wilhelm Meisters theatralische Sendung* (Wilhelm Meister's Theatrical Mission), Joyce's *Stephen Hero* and *Portrait*. Each of their "maturer" books *(Apprenticeship, Ulysses)* conducts not toward the sort of triumph their juvenile aspirants at first fantasize, but reaches an interim solution of the Hamlet problem through ironic transformations. In each book, the key to productive existence is attaining fatherhood. Joyce's psychogram of the inner anguish and struggle of the nineteenth century registers the relevance of Hamletism in three great stages (the versions of Goethe, Mallarmé, and Freud) in the "Scylla and Charybdis" chapter; and it is at the onset of this cumulative stocktaking in *Ulysses* that Goethe's earlier coping with the romantic crisis at large in the *Apprenticeship,* understood in the light of his own earlier storm-and-stress experience, functions as a "model" for epical narratives that self-reflexively incorporate their psychocultural premises. The German romantic critics recognized the *Apprenticeship* as innovative for their era in this respect, and Joyce confirms its status by absorbing it into a modernist rebeginning as a narrative structure worthy of anchoring other key references.

A different order of congruence than imitation springs from the Joycean recognition that the Goethean structure does not have to be replicated in order for it to serve as preformed material, so long as the artist understands how its inner contours fit those of his own work. This too, in fact, is one of the major lessons already evident in Goethe's work. The *Apprenticeship* skillfully brings about an interplay among several fields of action and reference: the unfolding of Wilhelm's destiny, the activity of interpreting and experiencing the play *Hamlet,* the Shakespearean roles associated with persons he encounters, and the threat of the Oedipal tragedy exemplified most pointedly in the story of Mignon and the Harper. The important modernist departure is that Joyce, by such means as Stephen's theorizing, more insistently potentiates the Oedipal theme of "incest" into that of "palimpsest": the inherent paradox that, on the one hand, literature is a narcissistic activity, and on the other hand, a creative

18. James Joyce, *A Portrait of the Artist as a Young Man* (New York: Modern Library, 1944).

affirmation, an affirmation that involves recognition of intertextuality (textuality as nonego). The example of Goethe's use of Shakespeare helps establish the trace beneath the trace of his text, and supports Joyce's view that the power of great texts is manifested in generic and thematic metamorphosis. Moreover, it suits Joyce's purpose that in the *Apprenticeship* the center of gravity shifts almost in subterranean fashion generically from the tragedy to the novel; and that in tandem with this movement a comic, reintegrative, reconciliatory principle asserts itself despite all the hurt of which we learn.

This is the shift signaled in Stephen's thoughts about Shakespeare's late plays and their mature theme of reconciliation—reunion with the mother or through the daughter or granddaughter—as the "Library" chapter ends, well in advance of his symbolic reunion with the "father" in the guise of Bloom. In the framework of books 1–5 in the *Apprenticeship*, Wilhelm's Hamlet experience, causing the ruin of the Countess and Count, forms the first major climax at midpoint (book 3). But in the framework of the whole novel, consisting of books 1–7, his ultimately redemptive encounter with the Amazon and her uncle (book 4) forms the new midpoint. For all their obvious differences, the *Apprenticeship* and *Ulysses* share a larger ground pattern. Both novels move out of tragedy as the threat of thwarted development for the individual and strive toward the social, the plural reality of lives, and acceptance of the universal human. The standard educational story of the artist-elect is resorbed into the miracle and mess of life. Joyce's Stephen, albeit tempered by struggle, remains an artist and Bloom the practical "allround" person is stuck in his own mundane sphere, while it is their symbiosis that exhibits the suprapersonal range of basic roles. In contrast, Goethe arrives at a more radical outcome that shocked Novalis as being a betrayal of spirit and poetry. Able at last to distance himself from his Hamletic experiment, Goethe's Wilhelm decides to abandon art permanently for a more suitable profession. He becomes a useful bourgeois. It is as if he foreshadows the crossing over from being a Stephen to being a Bloom.

As Wilhelm initially attempts to carry out his supposed theatrical mission in books 1–4 of the *Apprenticeship*, the novel exhibits the principle of all narrative as a progressive retardation that allows the tension and movement of desire to be expressed and avoids premature closure. The first major divagation is Wilhelm's escape from his business obligations, hence denial of his bourgeois father, and his involvement with a wandering troupe (players such as a Hamlet would employ!). Amid unsteady circumstances, Wilhelm effectively wanders unhoused and disinherited. He is ancestral to Stephen as the young exile complaining about the spiritual condition of his world and struggling with his own feelings and drives. Wilhelm's early adulation of Racine, the portrayer of regal passions, reveals the implicit cultural humiliation of his own homeland, which as yet boasts no great dramatists, and underscores the fact that his own passionate endowment is without proper outlet. Racine is displaced as his supreme luminary and guide when Wilhelm discovers Shakespeare (book 3, chapter 7). His immediate identification with Hamlet is so overwhelming, however, as to deflect him from the heroic task of founding a national theater; flowing into the most immediate channel that bids, he deviates into an acting career. No reader can miss the ambivalence in the parallel in Shakespeare's tragedy: Hamlet's interest in using plays and playacting for his own personal reasons. On the one hand, Wilhelm's enthusiasm is an elaborate prolongation of his escape, and, on the other hand, his escape is a necessary part of his search for identity. Wilhelm is playing himself as an aspirant interpreter of this greatest of roles in Shakespeare. We will learn with Wilhelm (namesake of William) in due course that in fact truly great performers are distanced and controlled. Thus, in the terms of Goethe's novel, his attainment of "mastery" (a goal announced in his family name Meister) paradoxically will arrive only at the moment when he can abandon being Hamlet.

Early in the novel, as in the case of Stephen in *Ulysses*, the essence of tragedy threatens to assume command over Wilhelm's life. Using Peter Brooks's concept of Freud's "masterplot," David Roberts has shown how Goethe invokes the negative version of the romantic symbolism of incest to hint at the ever-lurking "danger of the short-circuit, of the improper end, of the false choice."[19] While fired up by his probing of the meaning of *Hamlet*, Wilhelm unconsciously acts out aspects of the paradigmatic role of the play's disturbed protagonist, as in his incestuous attraction to the Countess, a surrogate Gertrude (book 3, chapter 12). Goethe does more than ironically transpose single, scattered motifs from Shakespeare's play. In effect, Goethe anticipates all the essentials of the Freudian masterplot, captured in mirrorings of *Hamlet*—an important literary fact not mentioned in Brivic's otherwise thorough treatment of Joyce's

---

19. David Roberts, *The Indirections of Desire: Hamlet in Goethe's "Wilhelm Meister"* (Heidelberg: Carl Winter, 1980), 12.

psychological knowledge.[20] Goethe's Shakespearean allusions possess immense narrative energy and acquire new, specific romanesque functions, shaping a shadow psychological plot. A source of delight for the reader is recognizing the interplay between Wilhelm's conscious searching for Shakespeare via Hamlet and his unconscious quest for his own maturity and fatherhood. Sometimes the relationship appears through ironic travesty. For example, instead of slaying a "Polonius" during a heated encounter with his "mother" as the Countess, Wilhelm himself gives and receives the prick of conscience caused by life's violence. This occurs when through his passionate embrace the Countess is stabbed to her senses by the brooch she wears over her heart containing her husband's picture. Heeding the warning, Wilhelm initially flees the "mother" as Joyce's Stephen will do in leaving Ireland. The parodic wound is repeated more acutely in the *Apprenticeship* during a rehearsal of the duel between "Hamlet" and "Laertes" in the field as the actor caravan pauses. When robbers fall upon them and Wilhelm is stricken down in earnest, he awakens to find himself being tended by a beautiful noblewoman. His earlier aggressive "joke," in wearing the Count's dressing gown, is now balanced through his passive acquisition of the craved paternal mantle when the Amazon bestows her uncle's coat. This symbolic transfer of the father's power to the son can only occur after Wilhelm has begun to experience "love" as a kind of sacrificial death, bodily surrender to and dependence on the feminine.

The by-now more elaborately thematized wounding leads into an acute psychological crisis. The transparent parallel is the intensification and deepening of Wilhelm's relationship to Hamlet. His desire to refind "the beautiful deliverer" (who indeed eventually becomes his wife) overpowers his resolve, which has been inspired by her, to end his "aimless routine of existence" (book 4, chapter 11). Just as his clinging to the "strange society of Mignon and the Harper" (WM 220) symbolizes Wilhelm's confused attachments, so the eventual tragic deaths of these companions will betoken his overcoming of the Oedipal threat to maturation. During this critical transition, Wilhelm not only becomes quite obsessed to explain Hamlet as the key to his own mission and life, but he talks (in Carlyle's rendition) in a way that remarkably foreshadows the basic syntax and manner of Stephen in the "Scylla and Charybdis" chapter.

20. Sheldon Brivic, *Joyce between Freud and Jung* (Port Washington, N.Y.: Kennikat Press, 1980).

We hear this, for example, in Wilhelm's attempt to conjure the figure of Hamlet for the skeptical theater man Serlo (Polonius-Laertes), in the paragraphs beginning "Conceive a prince such as I have painted him, and that his father suddenly dies" (book 5, chapter 13). Laden with imperatives, his remarks suggest stage directions and the active presence of a director instructing performers. Using multiple voices, Joyce ties such projection in with Mallarmé's reflections on *Hamlet*, a topic Best introduces and Stephen quickly picks up (U 187). As Carpenter shows, Stephen is following Mallarmé's lead in associating the murderous impulse in Shakespeare and Hamlet with the artist's guilty need to assert his creativity.[21] But Joyce can draw on the example of specific psychological elements that are already spun by Goethe in the *Apprenticeship*—for example, references to the repeated wounding of Hamlet, the shattering of the mother's image, the ghost as a disturbing revelation—and that tie together the tragedy of Hamlet and Wilhelm's own inner psychodrama. The basic ingredients of Stephen's and also of the Freudian view appear in Wilhelm's emphases in book 4, chapter 13. By chapter 20, in revealing his betrayal of the earlier Ophelia figure Mariana, the would-be German Hamlet provokes a third wounding at the hands of another Ophelia, Serlo's sister, Aurelia, who is half-crazed by Wilhelm's failure to respond to her love and identifies with Mariana's plight.

As book 5 opens, the letter from Werner (Horatio aspect) conveying the surprise news of the death of Wilhelm's father reinforces the figural correspondence between Wilhelm's situation and that of the Danish prince. Stephen's view that Shakespeare "wrote the play [*Hamlet*] in the months that followed his father's death" (U 207) reiterates the reactive pattern that Goethe stresses through Wilhelm's production of *Hamlet* in the aftermath of his own loss. In effect, by marrying Wilhelm's sister and taking her mother into their new household, his friend Werner (Claudius-Laertes aspects) reinstitutes the disinheritance, usurpation, and rivalry faced by Hamlet. Unmistakable in Werner's report (book 5, chapter 2) is the unseemly haste with which people despoil the dead father and disregard his son. This sacrilege was foreshadowed by the loss of the grandfather's "beautiful collection of pictures and statues" (WM 67), sold by Wilhelm's father. Werner's announced business decisions— converting Wilhelm's home and "unprofitable" (256) cultural patrimony

---

21. William Carpenter, "Floating Prologue: Hamlet," in "The Poetic Self in the Work of Art" (unpublished manuscript). I am grateful to Dr. Carpenter for allowing me to read his work in progress.

into capital, and raising further risk capital for commercial investment—breathe the new entrepreneurial spirit of capitalism. This is a surrogate of the military-political drive that makes its reappearance at the conclusion of *Hamlet*. As the wielder of bourgeois money-power who marches on past the person dedicated to "the cultivation of my individual self" (WM 261), Werner thus also is playing Fortinbras to Wilhelm's Hamlet. When Wilhelm plunges deeper into acting under the stress of these developments, Goethe openly draws the comparison with Hamlet who, head in Ophelia's lap, is the unwitting captive spectator of a play within a play, while he weens he is the instigator and controller of a play: "At the moment when our friend was subscribing his assumed designation, by some inexplicable concatenation of ideas, there arose before his mind's eye the image of that green in the forest where he lay wounded in Philina's lap. The lovely Amazon came riding [. . .]" (263). The gentle irony is that Philina plays Gertrude both on stage and vis-à-vis the troupe, and that not only Wilhelm's destined bride rides up to warn him in this reverie, but also the Oedipal victim Mignon "had softly tried to stop him, and pull back his hand" (264) as he signed on as "Hamlet."

As Roberts has analyzed in detail, the "liberating catharsis of his performance of Hamlet" in book 5 clears the way for "the reconciliation with and integration of the father image in the son," when Wilhelm saves the boy Felix and eventually confirms his identity as his own son.[22] Stephen's view of an aging Shakespeare drawn toward reconciliation could readily be applied to describe the pattern completed in the anagnorisis closing book 7 of the *Apprenticeship*. The abandoned Mariana, whom Wilhelm has seen as a spirit who is accompanied by his own father in an earlier dream (WM 376), proves to have been "innocent" and faithful to the "father" after all. Thus the crone Barbara can rebukefully instruct guilty Wilhelm as if he is a character in one of Shakespeare's winter plays: "Take the boy Felix to her grave, and say to him, 'There lies thy mother, whom thy father doomed unheard'" (422). Felix the son has "killed" the mother as the price of his birth, but as his name indicates he is forgiven and enters into the patrimony. As Joyce does later in the "Scylla and Charybdis" chapter, Goethe pulls together the deeper plot line of the educational protagonist's pathway and the question of the "tragedy" of existence raised in *Hamlet*; and like Joyce, Goethe leads us toward an ironic resolution, toward maturation and practical activity

22. Roberts, *The Indirections of Desire*, 128.

for Wilhelm. The formal rite sealing the bond between father and son at the conclusion of the *Apprenticeship* is an integral part of Wilhelm's accepting and endorsing his indenture of apprenticeship as a member of the Tower confraternity. It is not far-fetched to say that in the "Tower Society" ("Turmgesellschaft"), Goethe daringly makes tangible for us our collective production of that realm of shaped and shaping rules and roles that Freud will later call the superego.

Readers who note how intensely Joyce's Stephen feels the power of the Ghost will be intrigued by the importance of that power for Goethe's Wilhelm and its complex associations in the *Apprenticeship*. After the main rehearsal, there is still no cast member available for the part of the Ghost. Nevertheless, Wilhelm feels certitude that somehow the Ghost will appear "at the proper season" (283); and no sooner has he donned his Hamlet costume the night of the performance than the Ghost indeed is suddenly announced (287). On stage, Wilhelm starts "in real terror" at the Ghost's entry; the audience too are as gripped as is the actor by this apparition's voice. The mystery deepens when the Ghost leaves, hidden behind a veil, and is not to be found anywhere. Mignon refers to the Ghost ambiguously as her "uncle" (292). Coming from the cast party, tipsy Wilhelm-Hamlet falls asleep imagining "the image of the harnessed King was hovering there," but the bourgeois actor-prince is "encircled with soft arms" and his mouth "shut with kisses" (293). It is as if Wilhelm's half-conscious fathoming of his own relationship to the Ghost opens the way to complete release, his enjoyment of union with "Gertrude." The juncture of catharsis and danger triggers suspenseful mixed signals. Another warning to flee, the fire set by the Harper, and the peril that almost claims Felix immediately follow the high moment of the visit of the Ghost.

In the opening chapter of book 6, Wilhelm has an involved dream about the threat and resolution of the Oedipal problem. All the characters of his recent adventures play roles. Wilhelm's own father leads his beloved "Mariana by the hand [. . .] into a grove" (376); ultimately Wilhelm, inclined to follow them longingly into the softness of death, is glad to be held back by the Amazon and awake to life (377). Another central theme of his dream is the symbolic death of the tragic substitute child Mignon and the salvation of the destined heir Felix. Using the ambiguous metaphor of drowning-as-baptism (WM 376), which also is prominent in *Ulysses*, Goethe has the mother-elect quench the flames enveloping the boy with her veil and double him magically. The dreaming ex-Hamlet eventually learns from Mignon that she sought Wilhelm during the danger that attended the production in the belief the Ghost instructed her to bring Felix's "father" to his rescue (416). His destined role as a father is confirmed.

The insight gained through Shakespeare that galvanizes Wilhelm into the decision to be a healer is the potentially healing recognition of the larger pattern of the life process that imposes Hamletism upon us as a condition of our earthly passage. Stephen too is caught up in the circular logic (*lege:* hermeneutics) of such discovery. This arrival or return, in Joyce's quite different book, finds a direct application to the artist role, as Bowen notes: "Both Hamlets [king and prince] are a part of and the product of their creator. The dark knowledge of himself emerging as art is part of the substance of consubstantiality shared by father and son."[23] In his study of death and marriage in Joyce and Mallarmé, Carpenter has followed the lead of Henry Miller in seeing how, through Stephen, Joyce works out the orientation of writing to death: "Stephen's story in short, is a poem on his mother's death," while simultaneously he seeks the channel to the mystery of fatherhood.[24] By way of his alienation the Joycean artist figure paradoxically dies, in the best symbolist fashion, merging into the sought "form of forms" (U 26). In Carpenter's view, "The wilder, more relentlessly parodistic chapters of *Ulysses* grow from the tomblike structures of the earlier chapters" (DM 69). Thoth, the tutelary deity of the "Library" chapter, I would add, is both the keeper of the secrets of death and the scribe of the gods. While Stephen develops his own Hamlet persona as part of his necessary rebellion in order to become an artist-creator, his ironic identification with the drowned man and the drowned dog completes "his own dissolution at the end of the 'Telemachiad'" (DM 72). His Shakespeare interpretation in the "Scylla and Charybdis" chapter then allows him to organize his theory of the relation of art to life, the understanding that art, though it be precipitated by the pain of life, is an alternative to fleshly creation, hence "a mystical estate, an apostolic succession, from only begetter to only begotten" (U 207). The paradoxical doubleness of literature is that the past lives through it but is also laid to rest in it. In this respect, Carpenter argues,

---

23. Zack Bowen, *"Ulysses,"* in *A Companion to Joyce Studies,* ed. Zack Bowen and James F. Carens (Westport, Conn.: Greenwood Press, 1984), 479.

24. William Carpenter, *Death and Marriage: Self-Reflective Images of Art in Joyce and Mallarmé* (New York: Garland, 1988); hereafter cited with the abbreviation DM and the page number.

Joyce develops for Stephen and Shakespeare the same relation to their ancestry, to history, as Mallarmé develops for Igitur. In a dialectic of identification and alienation the artist becomes free of his ancestors and of his former self, but only after having absorbed them so thoroughly that he is nothing but they, and "they" more purely than they ever were themselves. (DM 74–75)

I would add that Mann establishes a similar relationship in his "Prelude" to *Die Geschichten Jaakobs* (The Tales of Jacob), when the narrating voice, as Thoth-Hermes, harrows hell and resurrects the "dead" past out of the fathomless source of consciousness.[25] The ultimate verticality of converging paradigms, or modernist "timelessness," has its corollary in the figural mystery of reconciliation between the living and the dead, and this reconciliation also occurs through the copresence of all aspects of being distributed among the avatars of being. Complex composite characters, who appear nominally opposite, a Bloom and a Stephen ultimately partake complementarily in each other's identity and accept the inexhaustible manifoldness of Molly, despite the murderous denial with which the son at first sets forth to define himself on the horizontal axis of contingent existence. Goethe shows us the conflictural throes of such a passage and arrival at reconciliation through Wilhelm's more compact experimentation with being Hamlet. The romantic subjectivist revolution has not shaken Goethe's belief in our individual groundedness in the process of time. Of course, that revolution profoundly permeates and disturbs the sense of selfhood throughout the nineteenth century. Nonetheless, there is no giant leap from Goethe's version to Joyce's understanding that we grow into Hamletic completion when we are transformed into Everyman through the intermediation of art. In accord with the dicta of Mallarmé, Joyce accepts that his book will embrace explicitly or implicitly all the avatars of Hamlet, including Wilhelm.

The artist's search for authority and empowerment that starts as transgression has its parallel in the reader's search that starts with the violation that our curiosity about ourselves entails, but this transgression leads to recognition, to our sense of being part of the story. If borrowing the distinction from Genette we label *Ulysses* as a "hypertext" that takes *Hamlet* up into itself as a "hypotext," the hitch is that still other intermediary "hypertexts"—most notably *Wilhelm Meister*—suddenly are rel-

25. Thomas Mann, *Joseph and His Brothers (The Tales of Jacob)*, trans. H. T. Lowe-Porter (New York: Knopf, 1934).

egated to the status of quasi-hypotexts.[26] This expandable and contrac-
table reality of the ghostly texts in our past Joyce well understood. By the
1920s modernism, through novels like *Ulysses,* had demonstrated (or in
longer range historical perspective, had renewed) awareness that there is
a virtually infinite textual regression. Current narratology certainly helps
us discriminate the tell-tale technical operations, but it can add very little
that is essential to what commonsensical literary history, with attention
to the phenomenological particularity of successive texts, already can say
when it speaks to Hamletized readers about influence, models, cooptation, or—to reinvoke an ancient term—"tradition": our face in the mirroring text.[27]

26. Gérard Genette, *Palimpsestes: La littérature au second degré* (Paris: Editions du Seuil,
1982).
27. The ongoing reception of *Hamlet* and the play's enormous international importance are treated in the special volume *"Hamlet" at Home and Abroad,* ed. Holger Klein
and Christopher Smith (*New Comparison* 2 [Autumn 1986]).

9 EDUCATIONAL EXPERIMENT
IN THOMAS MANN

Tracing the decline of a bourgeois family over several generations in *Buddenbrooks* (1901), his first major success as a novelist, Thomas Mann so skillfully adapted the realist tradition of the nineteenth century that readers could effortlessly assent to crucial features of the book's modernist structure: its use of Nietzschean paradigms and imitation of Wagnerian leitmotifs. Within a couple of years Mann's novella *Tonio Kröger* (1903) registered important steps toward eventual transformation of the older generic features of the bildungsroman too. Through glimpses of its title figure's development from childhood to middle age, *Tonio Kröger* gives a new twist to the romantic theme of the artist as an outsider whose relationship to life as well as to bourgeois normalcy has been profoundly disturbed. This rupture acquires an epochal significance associated with the shift in aesthetics around 1900 in large measure because Mann's story conveys its sociological and metaphysical insights through a more immediately self-evident modernist structure. Right from the opening we cannot avoid thinking of the story as a kind of abstract music developed out of the alienation and identity problem of its overture and bound together by leitmotifs; it amounts essentially to eight thematic variations capped by a coda. The novella's fluctuating temporal perspective, point of view, and narrative voice; its juxtaposed but interpenetrating objective and subjective slices; and its multiple mirrorings also bear analogy to the cubist montage technique in painting. The hero's psychology—the contest of imperatives and values within him—is relativized as a set of data he himself comes to treat as cultural signs. There is no external social or historical resolution; rather, Tonio arrives at a recognition of his artist's destiny as a pattern within the containing system, this moment of truth being recorded in his letter to Lisaweta as conclusion. The ground pattern of a character's growth, which Mann takes over from the older story of apprenticeship *(Lehrjahre)* or education *(Bildung)*, becomes a symbolic outline punctuated by a series of epiphanic moments of heightened consciousness.[1]

Mann converts the late nineteenth-century fictional subgenre about the social and spiritual development of a young person, the actual starting point of *Tonio Kröger,* into a "hermetic" construct.[2] This is the new kind of aesthetic space in which the case of the excessively Apollonian standard-bearer of Western civilization in Mann's novella *Death in Venice* (1912) plays itself out in its final phase, except that, being an unwitting herald of a possible Western collapse, the intellectual protagonist Gustav Aschenbach arrives at a negative epiphany of inward surrender to Dionysus after decades of repressive self-control. Mann could have excerpted and expanded chapter 2 of *Death in Venice*—the foreshortened background story of Aschenbach's development up to his fifties, narrated in historical retrospect by a severely ironic, omniscient voice—as a novel of education. But that would have meant operating in terms of the nineteenth-century genre against his own modernist inclinations.

Thus, these two novellas help us to grasp the new rules that govern Mann's creative reordering of the familiar bildungsroman in his encyclopedic symposium on the fate of the West, *The Magic Mountain* (translated into English in 1927), a work that is avowedly "hermetic." Its protagonist, the bourgeois engineer Hans Castorp, is in his late twenties—approximating the traditional age zone for closure in the educational novel—by the time he exits from the lofty spaces of sickness and enchantment into the turmoil of the Great War.[3] Although in key places we are allowed to identify more closely with the bourgeois quester figure, Mann's authorial irony draws on the complex example of Miguel de Cervantes's stance in *Don Quixote.* We are privileged as readers to observe, both with critical distance and in the amplitude and detail possible in a humoristic-encyclopedic novel,[4] how Castorp too, in his own way, discovers the fundamental powers that, in the flow of Mann's fiction, have

1. On the importance of epiphanic moments in the novel of the early twentieth century, including Mann (illustrated by the "Snow" subchapter of *The Magic Mountain*), consult chapter two, "Epiphany: Applicability of a Modernist Term."
2. On this concept and its various expressions, see chapter eleven, "The Ways of Hermes in the Works of Thomas Mann."
3. A helpful descriptive outline of the succession of Hans's experiences, chapter by chapter, is given in Randolph P. Shaffner, *The Apprenticeship Novel: A Study of the "Bildungsroman" as a Regulative Type in Western Literature with a Focus on Three Classic Representatives by Goethe, Maugham, and Mann* (New York: Peter Lang, 1984), 72–105.
4. Mann's place in the humoristic-encyclopedic tradition is the subject of the final chapter in Herman Meyer, *The Poetics of Quotation in the European Novel,* trans. Theodore Ziolkowski and Yetta Ziolkowski (Princeton, N.J.: Princeton University Press, 1968).

already made their appearance in the artist Kröger's existential anguish and in the intellectual Aschenbach's repressive overweening. The authorial voice even issues Castorp a diploma of maturation near the end of his stay at the sanatorium, certifying that our simple hero, after so many years of hermetic-pedagogic discipline, of ascent from one stage of being to another, has now reached a point where he is conscious of the "significance" of his love and the object of it (MM 642).[5]

If Hans matures "into an intuitive critic" (MM 642) within the novel, the authorial voice gives us advance warning in the brief foreword that the story is also told "for the sake of the story itself" as a revelation about a "certain turning point" yet at work that "has cut deeply through our lives and consciousness" and about the "problematic and uniquely double nature of that mysterious element," time (MM xi).[6] This crisis involves the collapse of the realist epistemology and the concomitant structures of the realist novel as governing principles; they become internalized as subordinate elements alongside other subject matter in a new construct. Mann's problematizing of the time order of fiction and of his own act of imaginative recollection thus touches core issues we find in such great modernist copings with time as Marcel Proust's *In Search of Lost Time* (1913–1927) and James Joyce's *Ulysses* (1922). The modernist author, gazing back in *The Magic Mountain* over a "deep chasm" (MM ix) for European civilization and mankind, a boundary confirmed by the Great War, recapitulates his sense of the mysterious drama of cultural and spiritual forces that have shaped the German nineteenth century and yielded the dilemma of the twentieth, a past first probed in detail in *Buddenbrooks*. There, as mentioned, Mann seemed to practice a relentless pathology in the wake of Gustave Flaubert, but in fact he was using an anthropological dialectics derived from Nietzsche and compositional principles derived from Wagner. Now the already recaptured particular past of the Northern Protestant and capitalist ethos and, tacitly, the stages in Mann's growth as a cultural analyst beyond *Buddenbrooks* and *Death in Venice*—his essays in *Betrachtungen eines Unpolitischen* (Ob-

5. References to the English translation by John E. Woods, henceforth indicated by the abbreviation MM with page number, follow the Vintage International paperback, Thomas Mann, *The Magic Mountain* (New York: Random House, 1995). Occasional references to the original German version, indicated after the abbreviation Zb with the page number, will follow the reprint paperback, Thomas Mann, *Der Zauberberg: Roman* (Frankfurt: S. Fischer, 1967); "Bedeutsamkeit" (Zb, 689).
6. "zu ahnungsvoller Kritik" (Zb, 689); "um der Geschichte willen," "einer gewissen, Leben und Bewußtsein tief zerklüftenden Wende," "die Fragwürdigkeit und eigentümliche Zwienatur dieses geheimnisvollen Elements" (Zb, 5).

servations of an Unpolitical Person, 1918 marking the watershed—are reimbedded in chapter 2 of *The Magic Mountain*. This chapter ostensibly reveals the origins of the youthful protagonist but actually allows us, through mention of Hans's childhood experiences, to deepen our exploration of the network of leitmotifs already operative during his arrival at the sanatorium in chapter 1 and to discover or confirm why these connections are relevant to the larger story of European development, as Hans himself will learn in due course.

Furthermore, in the guise of a romanesque in medias res start to a more traditional omniscient third-person narration, chapter 1 of *The Magic Mountain* establishes the interchangeability of space and time, and their subsumption not only in dream structures but also in the abstract relational framework that obtrusive chromatic and numerological clues hint at. The fair Hans is paired with his darker cousin, Joachim, in chapter 1. Their symbiotic roles are then linked in chapter 2 to the pairings of traits in the familial and cultural heritage that, via the leitmotific network, reaches out over the European geocultural terrain, into the wide world, and back to the roots of European civilization. When in chapter 6 Naphta, exposing the ancient roots of Freemasonry so as to diminish Settembrini's claims, informs Hans that "the primary symbol of alchimistic transmutation was the crypt," Hans instantly thinks of jars of preserves hermetically sealed and sitting on a shelf (MM 501).[7] This image, already present in the coffin holding the grandfather's body in chapter 2—and strikingly similar to such sacramental vessels and sarcophagi in *Ulysses* as "Mrs. Plumtree's Potted Meat"—recurs in important variations. In chapter 7 Hans independently finds solace in the modern "magic" of the gramophone, a "little truncated coffin of fiddle wood," a "temple" (MM 633) that pours forth orchestral pieces, lieder, and operas, "the victorious ideality of music, of art, of human emotion" (MM 636).[8] Clearly, through the half-paraphrasing authorial voice, Mann relates Hans's soaring thoughts, thoughts "enhanced, forced upward by alchemy" by reception of the sacramental content from the "musical coffin," to the highest aspirations of his own book as a hermetic container of spiritual nourishment, capable of releasing "the new word of love and [. . .] the future":

---

7. "Ein Symbol alchimistischer Transmutation war vor allem die Gruft" (Zb, 539).
8. "gestutzten kleinen Sarges aus Geigenholz," "Tempelchens" (Zb, 680); "die siegende Idealität der Musik, der Kunst, des menschlichen Gemüts" (Zb, 683).

One need not be a genius, all one need was a great deal more talent, than the author of this little song about a linden tree to become an enchanter of souls, who would then give the song such vast dimensions that it would subjugate the world. (MM 643)[9]

In chapter 1 Hans's passage through his room, number 34, begins to be connected with movement through the novel's symbolic structure of seven years of enchantment, seven stages of alchemical heightening narrated in seven chapters, and myriad numerological analogues; and chapter 2 confirms for us that Hans has a personal destiny to bring something forth out of the tomb of his cultural past by going through a second educational career, one deeper than he could have known below on the flatlands of normalcy in the bondage to time. Hence the readily analyzable "bob-sled" dream (MM 17) of chapter 1 functions as a seed-crystal precipitating the anguish of an ultimate parting from Joachim, the necessary death of aspects of Hans, while the concretized sociohistorical restatement of this latent theme comes at the opening of chapter 2 through the ecphrasis of the Castorp family's christening basin.[10] Dated 1650 and standing on an austere nineteenth-century base, the basin (like its implicit model, the Buddenbrooks' Bible) records the seven generations of the Castorp family down to the death-imprinted orphan Hans with his telltale teeth "rather soft and subject to damage" (MM 30), whom we have just met in chapter 1 crossing the threshold into the hermetic space of the Swiss sanatorium.[11]

Any competent reader familiar with Mann's earlier works could be presumed to notice the parallel with the structure of *Death in Venice*. Aschenbach is attracted to the spell of Venice, the special European city at a transactional boundary of time and space; by following him there, European—especially German—readers plumb the dangerous ambivalences in their own heritage. Like Thomas Buddenbrook, who, "remembering" too late the teachings of Arthur Schopenhauer, is undone by what they reveal (*Buddenbrooks*, part 10, chapter 5), Aschenbach is inwardly devastated by the seductive horror exposed in Euripides' *Bacchae* and other classics he studied but never faced squarely in his formative years. Now the nov-

9. "alchimistisch gesteigerte Gedanken," "Musiksarge," "das neue Wort der Liebe und der Zukunft"; "Man brauchte nicht mehr Genie, nur viel mehr Talent als der Autor des Lindenbaumliedes, um als Seelenzauberkünstler dem Liede Riesenmaße zu geben und die Welt damit zu unterwerfen" (Zb, 691).

10. "Bobschlitten" (Zb, 22).

11. "die etwas weich waren und mehrfach Schaden erlitten hatten" (Zb, 35).

elist Mann transposes his own Nietzschean critique of the age's spiritual "crippling effect" and "mediocrity" openly onto the "middle-class" world that has shaped Hans (MM 31).[12] Volume 1, consisting of chapters 1 to 5, shows Hans's liberation from the bourgeois work ethic and morality. This entails breaking out of the constrictive order of time inherited from a mechanistic worldview, and entering into the sense of time as an enigma. Volume 2, consisting of the expansive chapters 6 and 7, shows in parallel Hans's probing of the enigma and his growing fascination with life, a scientific curiosity that shatters the narrowness of his earlier vocation as a specialist. In the "Snow" episode of chapter 6 we participate in his encounter with eternity and in his discovery of his own will to affirm and love. Having transcended both Settembrini, the advocate of rational humanism, and Naphta, the voice of irrational mysticism, Hans witnesses the union of all the contradictions of life in Peeperkorn, who embodies personality as a positive value but also the tragic limits of vitalism as an answer.

However, the rules of a modernist "time-novel" (MM 533) differ in an important respect from the ordinary novel of education in conducting the protagonist through all these steps.[13] As the meditative overture to chapter 7 asserts, in following Hans through the various figural, often parodic, dimensions of the "magic mountain"—for example, as a Dantesque harrowing of hell, as Tannhäuser's captivity in the Venusberg, and so on—we are involved in a poetic entry into a kind of "eternity" governed by the "magic during a vacation" (MM 536).[14] Not only the inclusive, integrative principle of the humoristic novel but also a modernist "spirit of a tolerant relativism" (MM 536) hold joint sway in the multiple mirrorings and conflations of literary and mythological references.[15] This same approach governs the nature of the discussants and actors (Behrens, Settembrini, Naphta, Chauchat, Peeperkorn, et al.) who influence or affect Hans as much as it governs the composition of elements in his nature.[16] On one level of the fiction, they are "real" characters with

12. "mittelmäßig," "lähmende Wirkung" (Zb, 37).
13. "Zeitroman" (Zb, 571).
14. "Zauber für Ferienstunden" (Zb, 575).
15. "Im Geiste eines duldsamen Relativismus" (Zb, 575). Perhaps the finest account connecting Mann's post-Nietzschean idealism, his political shift endorsing the new Weimar Republic, and his interest in the Einsteinian world is that in Michael Beddow, *The Fiction of Humanity: Studies in the Bildungsroman from Wieland to Thomas Mann* (Cambridge, U.K.: Cambridge University Press, 1982), 232–43.
16. In *The Way of the World: The Bildungsroman in European Culture* (London: Verso, 1987), Franco Moretti defines the bildungsroman as a "constant elusion of historical turn-

quite particular attachments to the actualities of history and culture at the beginning of the twentieth century; on another level, complexes of forces and memories are transparently bundled together in them in a manner enabling an essaylike analysis of human development over the centuries in Europe. The reader engages in a sweeping act of cultural remembering by means of Hans's restarted "education" because, even when witnessing the higher mystery of personality (MM 583), Hans is no longer the old-fashioned sentimental student like Gottfried Keller's "real" hero in the Swiss bildungsroman par excellence, *Der grüne Heinrich* (Green Henry, 1851–1855), but a hermetic medium in a modernist "experiment." The constituting of Hans resembles the alchemical compounding and transmuting of elements. Mann's treatment of Hans exhibits yet another affinity to some of Joyce's experiments in *Ulysses:* a massive engagement with scientific vocabulary and discourse. *The Magic Mountain* introduces a remarkable wealth of concepts from many different realms of the natural and human sciences. It also maneuvers the protagonist Hans into a kind of stimulative isolation, where his mind can become passionately involved in probing basic questions about the constitution of things, to engage in "Research," as a subchapter of chapter 5 is titled. Although Hans has been trained as an engineer, it is at the sanatorium that he first experiences the fuller importance of science.

The theme of educational experiment emerges in chapter 4 when Ludovico Settembrini, Hans's first important self-appointed mentor, sanctions it in his case, intervening to steer him away from his fascination with sickness, the lure of dark powers:

> "It is characteristic of your years to eschew manly resolve in favor of temporary experimentation with all sorts of standpoints. Placet experiri," he said, pronouncing the c of placet with the soft Italian ch. "A fine maxim. But what disconcerts me is simply that your experiment has taken precisely the direction it has." (MM 98)[17]

The context in which we hear Settembrini's warning rules out our taking him straight simply as an authorial mouthpiece. A provocative

---

ing points and breaks: an elusion of tragedy and hence . . . of the very idea that societies and individuals acquire their full meaning in a 'moment of truth' [and] of whatever may endanger the Ego's equilibrium" (12), but he is silent about *The Magic Mountain*.

17. "'So entspricht es Ihrem Alter, welches männlicher Entschlossenheit noch entraten und vorderhand mit allerlei Standpunkten Versuche anstellen mag. Placet experiri', sagte er, indem er das c von 'placet' weich, nach italienischer Mundart sprach. 'Ein guter Satz. Was mich stutzig macht, ist eben nur die Tatsache, daß Ihr Experiment sich gerade in dieser Richtung bewegt'" (Zb, 104).

underground linkage is knit for the reader when the would-be teacher brings the ambiguous German term "Versuch" (*versuchen,* try, essay, attempt, tempt; *Versuchung,* temptation) and the imported locution "Experiment" together (Zb 104). Settembrini's tic of repeating phrases three times lends a hieratical, suprapersonal suggestion to his conscious literariness in associating his own role vis-à-vis Hans from the start with that of Virgil guiding Dante through hell. Settembrini (in whose name "seven" appears via the Latin root *septem*) proudly identifies himself as a champion of the classics, humanism, the liberal revolution, and progress, a continuer of the Renaissance and the Enlightenment. In this respect his teachings directly exhibit how a worldview under threat overlaps with the ascendant challenge to its stability. In "graphic" speech "free of every trace of dialect" (MM 61), he explains the active critical principle of the West—clearly ancestral to Mann's own narrative irony, even though unbeknownst to Settembrini the newer irony dissolves the older.[18] Consistent with his programmatic "malice" toward debasing, reactionary, and obscurantist phenomena, Settembrini soon warns Hans to flee the luxuriance of disease upon noting his attraction to Clavdia Chauchat (in whose lupine build, cat name, Russian origin, and Asiatic facial traits reside hints of the Dionysian). Settembrini himself as a character may despise paradoxes as a danger to clear thinking, but in the novel's plot one result of his tracing of his libertarian ancestry and praise for the nobility of the beautiful word as the foundation of human dignity is that his teaching also stimulates the emergence of the antithetical elements in the young engineer. Hans now consciously grapples with his own piety toward his authoritarian ancestry, his addiction to music, his retrieved memory of the half-European aspect of his own being in his schoolmate Pribislav Hippe, the irresistible attraction to Clavdia Chauchat, who triggers that memory.

Even though the character Naphta has not yet come into view as Settembrini's dark counterpart, we are predisposed to expect a Naphta after chapters 3 and 4 because Mann prepares the ground by other kinds of suggestive pairing. This figural doubling is as ancient as the contest of a light and dark angel for possession of the soul in a morality play, but now it haunts our thoughts in the form of elusive, indeterminate motifs, refracted in multiple mirrorings. Notable is the duo formed by the sanatorium director Behrens, an ailing physician, and the suspect psychoan-

---

18. "plastisch," "von jeder Mundart freien" (Zb, 68).

alyst (of what retrospectively we deem a Freudian persuasion) from Eastern Europe, Krokowski. In his own right, Behrens acquires ambivalent traits as the possibly failed, melancholic priest-king Sarastro of Mozart's *Magic Flute,* or as the composer Richard Wagner, as the incorruptible judge of the underworld, Rhadamanthus, or as the suffering Radames of Verdi's *Aida.* He is now a gothic scientist of the phantasmagoric in the x-ray room in chapter 5, now a worldly painter, now an image-conjuring Mephisto, now a hoarding Fafnir to Hans's inept parodic roles as Siegfried, Faust-Tamino, and Werther. Krokowski is similarly linked inter alia to nineteenth-century decadent artists, to cabalistic secrets rivaling the appeal of Christianity, and eventually to Martin Luther, thus to regressive religious impulses such as are manifested in a corrupt twentieth-century practice, the spiritualistic séances of chapter 7. In the earlier novella, Tonio Kröger has a German father of nordic type and a darker Southern mother of indeterminate foreign blood; in the novel, inversely, Settembrini claims an Italian grandfather and a German grandmother. Thus while the liberal philosopher preaches against especially "German" weaknesses, his words are both confirmed and undercut by the ambivalences present prior to Naphta's appearance and in Settembrini's own history. A "dialectic" (which Mann models mainly on Nietzsche's critique of cultural decay and his concept of Apollonian and Dionysian bipolarity) is already in action; Hans's mind is already infected by an "Asiatic" antiprinciple that threatens his "European" identity.

Mann's double-edged irony permeates the terms of the European and the human story about which Hans gradually learns. We no longer simply follow a main melodic line of organic development sketched for the protagonist, such as Settembrini wishes for Hans and we might find in the educational genre of Enlightenment persuasions (e.g., in Fielding's *Tom Jones,* 1749). Nor can we rely wholly on the psychological model of romanticism, which modified the older organic pattern of the age of Rousseau and Herder through new techniques for exploration into recesses of the psyche and encounters with possible alter egos. We must think instead of a simultaneity of educational tracks on superimposed levels with many points of intersection. Mann's novel achieves a synchronic and diachronic fullness as an "encyclopedia" because it gathers complexes of factors but also exposes these factors as woven through the whole cultural fabric. In *The Magic Mountain* the educational quester from the Renaissance survives in outline, on the formal plane, as a shadow behind the superseded shadow of the eighteenth-century and nineteenth-century sentimental hero. The authorial voice confirms very early, in case any reader has not yet caught on, that "mediocre" Hans has a "suprapersonal significance," for "[a] human being lives out not only his personal life as an individual, but also, consciously or unconsciously, the lives of his epoch and his contemporaries" (MM 31).[19] Hans thus serves as our "medium" (German *Mittel*), as a vessel to contain or transmit contents, including perceptions of form and the experience of time in all its varieties; and, on the level of hermetic-alchemical symbolism, his progress in achieving new insights exhibits the synthesizing properties of Mann's fiction.

If Settembrini's nature too is composite, why, then, is he, as the first teacher, so closely identified with the building of momentum or motivation in the educational process? His literary "Satanism," quoting Carducci's luciferic hymn, associates his rebellion against crippling and stultifying forces with two major currents flowing from the Renaissance via romanticism: the humanist assertion of man's dignity and self-determination, and Faustian discontent and hubris. Since the concept of *Bildung* has its taproot in the humanistic tradition, the novel establishes a parallel between this important juncture in the larger cultural history of the West and the narrative moment, the juncture in Hans's life, by having a humanist spokesman incite the formal effort of self-shaping.[20] Still tenaciously clinging like a Rousseau to a vision of human goodness, Settembrini claims that man has fallen in history but denies that man is condemned to a fallen state by his very nature as a creature. The intrusion of Settembrini's mission in the novel thus reenacts earlier breaking points in cultural history: the deliberate defection of heroic humanism, the Enlightenment, and nineteenth-century positivism. In the instance of Faust, of course, the rebellion is associated with Lucifer's fall. The "humane" revolutionary-reformist tradition ostensibly has the aim of replacing the authoritarian, obscurantist implications in the religious view of man as fallen. Through Settembrini's essentially Apollonian stance, the novelist lends deeper sense and clearer shape to the release of psycho-

19. I have slightly modified Woods's translation to bring it closer to the original terms: "mittelmäßig," "überpersönliche Bedeutung"; "Der Mensch lebt nicht nur sein persönliches Leben als Einzelwesen, sondern, bewußt oder unbewußt, auch das seiner Epoche und Zeitgenossenschaft" (Zb, 36).

20. Cf. W. H. Bruford, *The German Tradition of Self-Cultivation: "Bildung" from Humboldt to Thomas Mann* (Cambridge, U.K.: Cambridge University Press, 1975), 209ff., on the structural and thematic function of Settembrini as exponent of an earlier master concept of Bildung, and his contest with Clavdia as a major step leading to Naphta.

logical and social factors latent in the characterization of Chauchat and more recessed in the attributes of Joachim, Hans's virtual other self. An important limit is quickly reached by first hearing Settembrini, because his progressive ideology cannot cope with the attack on liberal civilization that Naphta will mount. This theme hauntingly recurs in Mann's novel *Doktor Faustus* (1947) as the tragic exhaustion, failure, and helplessness of Western humanism associated with the figure of the narrator Serenus Zeitbloom, who must witness the horror of nazism and World War II.[21] Naphta appears on the scene just as, in the later nineteenth century, the idealist outlook resurged in new forms to challenge realist ontology and metaphysics.

It is helpful to contrast the tension of possibilities for the educational experience here with "special" cases of the bildungsroman in the nineteenth century. The title hero in Novalis's *Heinrich von Ofterdingen* (1800), a poet-elect of the High Middle Ages, is vouchsafed visionary confirmations of yearned-for reintegration and the ultimate union of contraries. Novalis's romantic utopian aim is to dissolve the boundary between time and eternity through the power of poetry. This intense heroic idealism wanes in the early nineteenth century. By the 1830s, for example, in the novels of Scott, Stendhal, and Balzac, a major theme is the inefficacy, thwarting, and breakdown of romantic aspirations. In Adalbert Stifter's novel *Der Nachsommer* (1857; translated as Indian Summer, 1985), the high-minded young bourgeois Heinrich Drendorf is shielded from the passions, social suffering, and blows of fate and remains protected once he has been attracted into the retreat of his chief educator Risach. Stifter contains the hurt of real history and the dangers of the romantic forces in the human heart—for example, by having Risach (and Heinrich as first-person narrator imitatively) delay his personal revelation of grievous error until Heinrich has been sufficiently imbued with knowledge and values and his maturation is guaranteed—but a hidden threat of sterility seems to lurk within the guarded success of personal cultivation in the afterglow of the greatness of the Goethean age. Flaubert's approach in *Sentimental Education* (1869) is radically inverse, allowing us to follow the symbiotic pair of high and middle bourgeois school friends, Frederic Moreau and Charles Deslauriers, as they commit all the errors representative of the spiritual failure of their age, wit-

---

21. Cf. the treatment of Zeitbloom in Stephen D. Dowden, *Sympathy for the Abyss: A Study in the Novel of German Modernism: Kafka, Broch, Musil, and Thomas Mann* (Tübingen: Niemeyer, 1986), 148ff.

ness the collapse of romantic aspirations, and suffer the loss of squandered vitality. As the passing contents of their world are displayed to the reader through them, these "mediums" are emptied of any meaning except their own terminal anguish and disillusionment. In *A rebours* (1884; translated as Against Nature, 1959) Joris Karl Huysmans thematizes the late nineteenth-century crisis of decadence in the attempt of his radically alienated protagonist Des Esseintes to reconstrue the cultural canon of the entire Western tradition in its time of decline and to create a completely artificial paradise as his personal refuge instead of finding a place in human society.

In reflecting on the romantic, realist, decadent, and other facets of the nineteenth-century heritage, Mann's novel could well be expected to conduct Hans either into a protected utopia or into a dystopia of alienation and disinheritance. The space of education as a hermetic experiment may for a while seem immune from the external pressures of time; indeed, Mann connects such an exemption with the strange hermetic character of modernist works of art that come into being in a different or altered temporal order, this side of the "chasm" separating us from the virtual antiquity of the nineteenth century. However, the protagonist's captivity in the spell of the sanatorium as a pampered, affluent patient certainly affords no protection from the powerful forces of darkness in the modern world that manifest themselves there. By the same token, Hans's ultimate exit from this surrogate "hell" into the actual hell of history upon the eruption of World War I symbolizes, in its Dostoevskian agonies, a profound redemptive change. By the end of the book Hans acquires and recovers but also abandons and loses much. The important point is that he outgrows these layers and attachments without succumbing in his heart to the disintegrative effects of the lessons of alienation and relativity.

The process of separating from the past is itself clearly experimental on several levels. On the level of the protagonist's story, we observe more and more frequently the operations of Hans's own mind as he gradually probes his heritage, reconnecting it to a larger world, and explores the peculiarities of his own heart. Hans learns dialectic from his mentor Settembrini, avidly reads in many fields of the natural and human sciences, expands the terms of the European story by witnessing the ongoing great debate between Settembrini and Naphta, and transcends both of these cardinal figures by achieving his own syntheses out of the materials they cast up and by use of the tools they demonstrate. On another level, Mann engages his readers openly in his ironic management of romanesque figuration and "trains" us to relate this narrative control to the contents brought to our attention in his intermittent moments of public discourse and authorial meditations.[22] We follow Hans as if we are watching the novelist reproduce under laboratory conditions the factors of a mentality (a shadow cast by Mann's own mentality) that was implicated in the war trauma of modernism, yet was significantly altered by it. In this sense, we are looking through the structure of the novel as if through the walls of an alembic at an experiment whose reactants are ingredients of a world that supposedly died when these constituents were transmuted. The fiction, as the epic of those transformed elements, is a hermetic communication from the grave, and as such it also ritually seeks to bury the event, to entomb it, for fear of repetition of the mysterious rupture in human affairs: the horror of World War I.

In tune with its themes of disease and death, the novel is replete with images and metaphors from medicine, and those of inoculation and self-poisoning are prominent for good reason. It is legitimate to say that Mann experimentally reactivates the dangerous combination of elements in the German and European world in order to identify the poison with which to immunize us. One illustration of how such use of metaphor links semantic and paradigmatic levels must suffice here. At the close of chapter 5, Hans—actually drunk in the way traditional for carnival festivities, parodically inebriated by a love philtre in analogy to the potions drunk in opera and romance, and spiritually intoxicated by self-poisoning—is ready to return the "silver pencil" to Madame Chauchat. In chapter 6 the quicksilver bar of the thermometer, another hermetic wand, implicitly confirms his participation in the witches' sabbath, his lovemaking with Chauchat that marks his crossing over into another realm; Hans is deemed to need a shot to dampen his raging fever after Walpurgis Night. We smile when Behrens, to punish Hans for his suspected fever-inducing excesses, plunges the "needle" into his arm. This sharp reminder of the pleasurable pain of Hans's fall replicates comically in miniature the paradoxical deep pleasure-and-pain that the novel as a whole conveys in the "survival" of Hans, with his acquired knowledge and his experience of the "death" of Joachim in his veins.

22. In *The German Bildungsroman from Wieland to Hesse* (Princeton, N.J.: Princeton University Press, 1978), Martin Swales offers one of the most cogent descriptions of the narrative voice and procedure under new challenge in *The Magic Mountain;* facing "the unutterable complexity of life in all its contradictions" and "imprisoned within its own function as reporter of events," the narrative fights its way out of the "constriction" by ironic self-scrutiny (122ff.).

Metamorphosis, Play, and the Laws of Life

The paradox of "life" coming forth out of "death" belongs to the larger cluster of themes in *The Magic Mountain* that have to do with the mystery of time and our relationship to its puzzling varieties, including the strangeness of the internal operations of the mind and of fiction as special orders of time. The famous "Snow" episode in chapter 6 provides a central illustration of how Mann analogizes the reader's recovery or reconsideration of deeply implanted paradigms of myth and the entire "learning" process of the novel. The episode is an open model exhibiting a narrative approximation to vital accomplishments by the subconscious mind in its synthesizing of materials; this creative synthesis in turn recapitulates stages in the age-old development of human awareness as marked in stages of mythological insight known to us from cultural history. The arguments between Settembrini and the "revolutionary of reaction" Naphta (MM 452),[23] advocate of a mystical "nihilism," "obedience," and "terror," have reached a high pitch. In addition, the terms that Hans has been absorbing—as readers of Mann in the 1920s and afterwards instantly recognize—develop further the conflict of forces as treated by the novelist in "Irony and Radicalism," the closing essay of *Observations of an Unpolitical Person* (1918, rev. 1920). There Mann arrived at the psychohistorical view that, in the contemporary situation of Europe,

> Radicalism is nihilism. [. . .] Intellect that loves life is not fanatic, it is ingenious, it is political, it woos, and its wooing is erotic irony. One has a political term for this: it is "conservatism." What is conservatism? The erotic irony of the intellect.[24]

Mann's instinctive conservatism has prompted his shift toward supporting the Weimar Republic as a product of political evolution by the time *The Magic Mountain* was published. Thus, on one level, Hans's carrying the oppositional terms—for example, form, reason, nature versus logos, passion, soul—into the snow resembles an "essay"; but on another level, the metaphor of a journey into the uncanny human core converts the public discourse into mythological testing.

Hans's ski outing becomes a hero's symbolic journey into "hell" to confront danger and retrieve life-enhancing secrets. The pattern of initiation that is at the heart of the "Snow" episode of *The Magic Moun-*

---

23. "ein Revolutionär der Erhaltung" (Zb, 485). Woods overinterprets the original term "Erhaltung" (preservation, conservation) which Naphta uses.

24. Thomas Mann, *Reflections of a Nonpolitical Man*, trans. Walter D. Morris (New York: Ungar, 1987), 419f.

tain is submerged again, like dream life, in the noise of everyday living, even though Hans obviously now carries deep within him a potent seed-crystal around which a new formation can accrete. More important, the reader henceforth bears the seed-crystal. Unmistakable is the parallel between Hans's will to survive and his new capacity to formulate his "dream-poem of humanity," which subsumes all the contradictions and enables him ultimately to resist the lure of "death" ("release, immensity, abandon, desire") and awaken to life, to "goodness and brotherly love" (MM 487).[25]

> Love stands opposed to death—it alone, and not reason, is stronger than death. Only love, and not reason, yields kind thoughts. And form, too, comes only from love and goodness: form and the cultivated manners of man's fair state, of a reasonable, genial community—out of silent regard for the bloody banquet. (MM 487)[26]

By means of the special pattern of an educational restart in the case of Hans, *The Magic Mountain* successfully interweaves three main narrative strands: recognition of the epochal breaking point that the trauma of the Great War confirmed, mythic passage through the figurative and literal hell that is inherent in human development, and participation in the symposium that the ongoing text of the encyclopedic-humoristic tradition promotes.

The choice of genre as organizing principle is crucial to the quite different tone and approach in Mann's entertaining *Bekenntnisse des Hochstaplers Felix Krull: Der Memoiren erster Teil* (Confessions of the Confidence-man Felix Krull: Memoirs, Part 1, 1954). In the sense that the aged writer exploits the conventions of the pseudobiographical picaresque tale to create a special blend—the education of confidence-man Felix, the reader's and the protagonist's gradual initiation into mythological foundations, and an indirect critique of the social and political condition of Europe in the belle époque—his last novel represents a new level of experimentation with the concept of "development" or "formation" (*Bildung*). *Felix Krull* attempts to reconceive and imbed deep contents of the entire Mannian oeuvre in a traditional story form congenial

25. I have slightly modified Woods's translation: "Traumgedicht vom Menschen," "die Güte und Menschenliebe" (Zb, 523).
26. "Die Liebe steht dem Tode entgegen, nur sie, nicht die Vernunft, ist stärker als er. Nur sie, nicht die Vernunft, ist stärker als er. Nur sie, nicht die Vernunft, gibt gütige Gedanken. Auch Form ist nur aus Liebe und Güte: Form und Gesittung verständig-freundlicher Gemeinschaft und schönen Menschenstaats" (Zb, 523).

to the redemptive irony that flows in *The Magic Mountain,* the *Joseph* tetralogy, and other works, and to answer the anguish over the modern artist and World War II in *Doktor Faustus.* The even older ancestral figure of the pícaro subsumes the more proximate ancestral impulses of the twentieth-century artist as a possessor of illicit inner knowledge about us and our world, as a trickster, and as an "enabler." Though born specifically out of the pressures of urban existence in Renaissance Spain and out of humanist and Counter-Reformation questioning of the sinful impulse to survive, to rise out of the underclass or existential fallenness, and to redefine one's lowly origins, the "delinquent" can be understood in retrospect to represent—frequently as its lowest common denominator—the new spirit of individualism in the humanist age. Sentimentalization of the rogue, which set in almost as quickly as the genre caught hold, allowed the conflation of the picaresque tale and a variety of first- or third-person pseudobiographical accounts. This possibility was latent in the character of picaresque tales as parodic shadows of the lives of saints or of creative personalities (e.g., the artists and condottieri of the Renaissance). Daniel Defoe's *Moll Flanders* (1722) and Henry Fielding's *Tom Jones* may serve to remind of the wide range of first-person and third-person variations on the fundamental story of educative error two centuries after the birth of the picaresque.

Mann intuits in the annals of the tradition since *Lazarillo de Tormes* (1554) the basic story of the ordinary person engaged in the pursuit of happiness on the threshold of our century; he links that vitality to the principle of Hermes as bourgeois divinity par excellence; and he presents that drive in a special variety of the artist, the artist as a go-between and shaper of life. Of course, besides being a charming crook, Felix is indeed specifically a writer. An important ingredient of the first-person variety of the picaresque genre inherited from the sixteenth and seventeenth centuries is that the rogue presents his life in its immediacy from childhood on, as if it were happening, but actually tells his story in retrospect with the benefit of experience. The tale involves explicit or implicit arrival at a traumatic juncture: a religious conversion, social desperation, existential anxiety, or the like. In the original Spanish examples, we observe a creature who at first acts and reacts naively, then either cynically or overweeningly, but eventually tastes the bitter cup of disillusionment. Openly or indirectly the narrator comments on the happenings while leading us toward the crisis. Often we get to witness the actual withdrawal from the world or conversion, as in the third-person *La*

Lozana andaluza (The Glamorous Andalusian, 1528), or the first-person *Guzmán de Alfarache* (1599–1604); or we sense spiritual torment in the self-exposure that is broken off, as in *Lazarillo de Tormes*. There are reasons—which cannot be pursued here—to assume that Mann never really intended to add a second part to his *Felix Krull*. In any case, part I ends, in effect, without returning to the realm of history; rather (like *Lazarillo*, which influenced its opening) it breaks off at a high moment of mythic recognition that is only lightly veiled as a biographical incident.[27] The reader, through Felix, moves past the "daughter" (Senhorita Kuckuck) to the "mother" figure (Senhora Kuckuck) in a rite of initiation that parodically conflates the bullfight cry and the Eleusinian cry. The novel leaves us as privileged voyeurs forever peering at this glorious encounter, the onset of a private scene of passionate fulfillment that lends deeper meaning to the delinquent who, among other things, represents the role of the artist.

In resuscitating the pseudoautobiographical tale, *Felix Krull* renews to great advantage the mature mode of picaresque narration that reached its apogee in Germany in the first-person voice of Grimmelshausen's *Simplicissimus* (1668).[28] Mann so nimbly manages the split level of consciousness in the first-person narrator that it accommodates the burden of integrating the "lessons" of life—all those materials that appear expansively in Mann's essays over a lifetime and surface in their 1920s variety in *The Magic Mountain*. The essence is distilled into the uncensored experiences of Felix, whom we follow as he recuperates from his family's fall into penury and disgrace, learns to cope with and outsmart the governing institutions, works his way up from a humble backstairs existence into comfortable bourgeois circumstances, and finally penetrates into the sweet life of aristocratic self-indulgence, even acquiring a surrogate noble ancestry and parents—all these steps tested and savored as roles being tried out. Mann recognizes how the explicit running commentary or implicit roving gaze of the older Spanish genre can permit him effortlessly to bring on board a critique of the abuses and pretenses of the world. *Felix Krull* is indeed remarkable in the way it slices through Europe from North to South in cultural terms and from bottom to top

27. See Oskar Seidlin, "Picaresque Elements in Thomas Mann's Work," *Modern Language Quarterly* 12 (1951): 183–200.
28. On Mann's interest in the hero of *Simplicissimus* as a forerunner of Felix, see "Estebanillo and Simplex: Two Baroque Views of the Role-Playing Rogue in War, Crime, and Art (with an Excursus on Krull's Forebears)," in my *Garden and Labyrinth of Time: Studies in Renaissance and Baroque Literature* (New York: Peter Lang, 1988), 279–95.

in social terms. We notice all the social forces and movements coming into the field of vision of Felix without his needing to analyze them copiously as a sociologist or historian would. The psychological forces and processes too are observed with freshness, as if by the eager learner. But of course these lessons from an unvarnished, at first naive, perspective slowly reveal, as they shape, the wisdom of the retrospective beholder.

Felix, who does not know he represents something archetypal (at least he never is shown by his later narrator persona to act in the possession of such knowledge, as against deep intuition, in part 1), demonstrates his mythological functions; and for us, as readers, one of the greatest pleasures is watching him as a principle in operation: as the modern Hermes. Beyond the rogue's voice, on a different plane of authorial irony in which the character Felix cannot participate, but which he instinctively mimics in writing his own memoirs, elements of Mann's entire writing experience resurface—for example, the fascination for the androgynous doubleness of humanity, felt a half-century earlier vis-à-vis the twins in the story *Wälsungenblut* (Blood of the Volsung) or the fascination for the structures of intersection in the developed West such as the great Parisian hotel, earlier the Swiss sanatorium in *The Magic Mountain*. This novel stops in order to leave education in progress and Mann's art untrammeled by closure. The underground message seems to be the importance of not reaching a fixed or rigid self-awareness, by realizing the eternal quality of development. In this respect, by its resemblance to the final affirmation of Joyce's *Ulysses*, the ending of Mann's *Felix Krull* reconnects with the fundamental modernist overcoming of time and desire for renewal.[29]

29. The analysis of structural principles by Mihály Szegedy-Maszák, "Teleology in Postmodern Fiction," in *Exploring Postmodernism*, ed. Matei Calinescu and Douwe Fokkema (Philadelphia: John Benjamins, 1987), 41–57, should make us cautious about concluding that the implied circularity and repetition in Felix's discovery, the reinstatement of a myth that appears to reveal a continuing palimpsest and to suspend teleology, the novel's "open" ending, and/or part 1 as a hypothetical narrative rupture or discontinuity automatically qualify Mann's final book as "postmodern." More crucial may be how we judge the intent or effect of Felix's possible "misunderstanding" of evolution in his dream after hearing Professor Kuckuck's spontaneous lecture during the train ride from Paris. If "the reaction against evolutionism started by Nietzsche" is a "fundamental" postmodern attitude, as Szegedy-Masák states, should we consider Felix's happy thought that evolution leads to himself to constitute affirmation on the part of Mann?

10 THE MUSIC OF THINGS AND

THE HIEROGLYPHICS OF FAMILY TALK IN

JOYCE'S FICTIONS

It is understandable if many readers may balk at the idea that either *Ulysses* or *Finnegans Wake* contains varieties of language assignable to father, mother, and child.[1] A majority of readers today, as viewers of paintings, accept most post-Renaissance mimetic conventions, even including much of postimpressionism, but many are likely to resist highly analytic cubist or abstract expressionist depictions of a girl or boy as pertinent to their experience of biological real-world examples. Therefore, I should stipulate from the start that I am not concerned here with whether Joyce's choices in his experimentation with language sometimes or never satisfy your own sense of success in "imitating" father, mother, or child talk (according to some cultural model). Rather, my purpose is to characterize some of his approaches to age and gender differences in language and to relate these to his experimental modernism at large.

There are so many linguistic, psychological, aesthetic, mythological, and mystical impulses that motivate Joycean experimentation that even his most ardent fans must disregard important contributing factors in order to focus on any narrower question such as mine. Like Stephen Dedalus, as he experiences "the ineluctable modality of the audible" in the "Proteus" chapter of *Ulysses* (U 31), Joyce's broadly competent readers can neither block out the irreducible music of things nor avoid being entangled with Stephen in the web of impinging symbols that have accrued over millennia—according to the novel. In the "Crush, crack, crick, crick" under Stephen's feet on the beach, we have not only, thematically, "Wild sea money" (U 31), but also, musically, an intimation of Indo-Germanic principal parts, thus of a cosmic order ever bidding to emerge out of primor-

---

1. James Joyce, *Ulysses,* ed. Walter Gabler with Wolfhard Steppe and Claus Melchior (New York: Vintage Books, 1986), hereafter cited as U followed by the page number. James Joyce, *Finnegans Wake* (New York: Penguin Books, 1976), hereafter cited as W followed by the page number.

dial sounds. The heavily replicative sounds, for instance, the Waterfall's "Poulaphouca Poulaphouca Poulaphouca Poulaphouca" (U 446), Black Liz the hen's "Gara. Klook. Klook. Klook" (U 459), and the sex-mad ghostly father Virag's spasmic ejaculations "Hik! Hek! Hak! Hok! Huk! Kok! Kuk!" (U 425) in the psychedelic "Circe" chapter are ascending instances, at a lower level, of what, at a higher level, we encounter in the overtly through-composed "Sirens" chapter: a complex music that is simultaneously concrete, iconic, and verbal. As Samuel Beckett—probably at Joyce's urging—declared, "It is not to be read—or rather it is not only to be read. It is to be looked at and listened to. His writing is not about something; it is that something itself."[2] There is also, virtually inseparable as part of our experience, "the ineluctable modality of the visible" (U 31).

The notes of the real world according to Joyce's fictional account thereof eventually serve as leitmotifs that help sustain the emergent themes of his book. He clearly believes that natural language shares the underpinnings of all the speech and all the thought variations of the human family, even our more elegant cerebrations and music makings. Joyce's interest in sounds in their own right establishes a base for primal orality that is prior to any early articulated stage of human utterance such as those found in children's rhymes or in lullabies—that is, a base antecedent to some supposed starting point of orality on which most theoreticians such as Paul Zumthor ordinarily focus who, in general agreement with Joyce, think that the culture of children provides us with key insights into the preliterate world.[3] Yet Joyce never rests on any single level of sound making or sound use as definitive for the human experience of language. In effect, all simple and complex levels of sounds and their mysterious generic configurations are copresent in the universe of language.

The thematization of the nature of father, mother, and child is a prominent feature of Joyce's works, and thus family paradigms and the structural variations of humankind and of relationships in the basic family romance also occur artistically in the guise of language. In the case of an artist like Joyce, it would be simplistic to regard only instances of the older mimetic approach to constitute a genuine effort at bringing such variations forward; they are today simply more obvious to us. A celebrated

2. Samuel Beckett, "Dante. Bruno. Vico. Joyce," in Samuel Beckett et al., *Our Exagmination Round His Factifications for Incamination of Work in Progress* (London: Faber & Faber, 1972), 14.

3. Paul Zumthor, *Oral Poetry: An Introduction*, trans. Kathryn Murphy-Judy (Minneapolis: University of Minnesota Press, 1990); original French edition, *Introduction à la poésie orale* (Paris: Editions du Seuil, 1983).

example of the older mode is the opening page of *A Portrait of the Artist as a Young Man*, the first sentence of which reads: "Once upon a time and a very good time it was there was a moocow coming down along the road and this moocow that was coming down along the road met a nicens little boy named baby tuckoo. . . ."[4] In a sudden leap that implicitly telescopes ontological, psychological, and narrative time and draws in the developmental line that ultimately links the baby boy to the later father role, yet also swiftly reasserts the childish and fairy-tale-like perspective that unfolds, sentence 2 continues: "His father told him that story: his father looked at him through a glass: he had a hairy face." From such baby talk in the brief opening segment, clearly of a male slant, the chapter and novel *Portrait* swiftly move into pubescent and juvenile modes both of narrated feelings and of memories; schoolboy and youthful utterance rules and soon the galaxies of highly structured language intrude with its full power and complexity as a growing aspect of the fictional character's own mind, through and alongside the accumulating pieces of recollected adult conversations. By this layering technique Joyce rapidly and economically suggests the life pathway and an acquirable repertory that exhibits enormous potential—elements that we are quite used to in the genre of the bildungsroman.

Although Joyce never elaborated a female parallel to *Portrait* in comparable detail, he scattered telling elements of a potential female bildungsroman throughout his polyphonic, polytropic later fictions. The opening words of the "Lestrygonian" chapter of *Ulysses*, "Pineapple rock, lemon platt, butter scotch" (U 124), pick up the "lemon platt" motif that appears in the first six dozen words of *Portrait,* but we now follow Bloom's stream of consciousness, which includes daring but affectionate fatherly thoughts about his teenage daughter Milly's budding sexuality. Such virtually incestuous glimpses prepare us for the expansive portrait of the teenage emotions and romantic fantasies of the teenagers Cissy Caffrey and Gerty MacDowell whom Bloom, our Ulysses laid bare to us readers, encounters in the "Nausicaa" chapter. Cissy's preternatural cuddling of her little brothers includes dripping "golden syrup" on their bread (U 284). Joyce weaves vocabulary from an extraordinary range—from childhood games, religious associations, books for girl readers, private girlish fetishes, the mental drama of early sexual attraction—into the strands of Cissy's and Gerty's musings. Bloom's interior

4. James Joyce, *A Portrait of the Artist as a Young Man,* ed. Hans Walter Gabler with Walter Hettche (New York: Vintage Books, 1993).

analysis of Gerty's coy gestures and mooning look, as this is spun into his own musings on other women in his existence, recontextualizes the delicious boundary moment between girlhood innocence and womanly involvement in the procreative chain. The ribald touch is that pious, mature Bloom experiences in the achievement of an actual orgasm what the virgins experience as an image of promise when they witness the thrilling fireworks that burst over Dublin at evening on Coronation Day.

One of the most moving passages in *Finnegans Wake* is its famous closing that reconnects to the novel's opening words as the eternal return occurs. On one level of reference, the tired, polluted River Liffey, representing the ever circulating feminine life and time stream, is completing the theological and cosmic mystery of reentry into the unfathomable creative source; the mother and father principles are about to rejoin in the pristine wholeness of "riverrun, past Eve and Adam's" of the opening page (W 3). The father principle is present in hundreds of mythological, historical, and symbolic guises—and appears, on an everyday level, as A. L. P.'s (Anna Livia Plurabelle's) husband H. C. E. (H. C. Earwicker), a Dublin tavernkeeper. The aged river more than six hundred pages later in the larger process senses: "Yes, you're changing, sonhusband, and you're turning, I can feel you, for a daughterwife from the hills again. Imlamaya. Swimming in my hindmoist. Diveltaking on me tail. Just a whisk brisk sly spry spink spank sprint of a thing theresomere, saultering" (W 627). The feminine falls as the rain from God's heaven to replenish life, flows onward, and passes out into the oceanic strangeness, the mysteriousness of the immeasurable source, to return again from the clouds: "sad and weary I go back to you, my cold father, my cold mad father, my cold mad feary father, till the near sight of the mere size of him, the moyles and moyles of it, moananoaning, makes me seasilt saltsick and I rush, my only into your arms" (W 628). In her mind the Liffey becomes the totally trusting loved child again: "So soft this morning, ours. Yes. Carry me along, taddy, like you done through the toy fair! If I seen him bearing down on me now under whitespread wings like he'd come from Arkangels, I sink I'd die down over his feet, humbly dumbly, only to washup" (W 628). The mother, A. L. P. or the Liffey, has gone through it all, but she falls eternally through her girlhood back into it. Joyce manages to link the simplest childhood elements of her story as the eternal repristination of our human origins to the dream language of his nightbook. (Among other subjects, chapter fifteen, "Palimpsest, Essay; History, Myth," will take up the special achievement of the coda of the *Wake* as a reinstatement of mystical insight.)

It is a cardinal proposition that any sequentiality, as from mother to daughter or the reverse, such as unfolds in the *Wake*'s Viconian cyclic masterframe, never suspends the governing contextual eternity of dream. That is why the unstoppable feminine principle can reclaim her innocent incestuous attraction to the father, a relationship reciprocated by him in various guises, and yet be the all-mother, concerned for her sons and daughters. And that is why, in what Thomas Mann dubbed the age of psychology and myth, we can simultaneously, with the Joycean dreamer-author, playfully enjoy A. L. P.'s story as "incestuish salacities among gerontophils" and function professorlike as "grisly old Sykos who have done our unsmiling bit on 'alices, when they were yung and easily freudened" (W 115). As this wry bit reminds us, Joyce felt more than coequal to Carl Gustav Jung and Sigmund Freud, and if he had lived longer, he perhaps would have spun in for fun some of the psychoanalytic theorists of later date who built upon them. Since Joyce sprinkled an extraordinary range of psychological insights throughout his texts, scholars such as Sheldon Brivic can readily both categorize the historical resemblances to Freud and Jung and detect anticipations of Jacques Lacan in Joyce's games with psychic identity and multiplicity.[5]

Because Joyce believed there was a kind of language inherent to the feminine, but obscured by the passage to masculine language, he wanted to tap into that neglected source and allow it voice in its own right. Hence, instead of unfolding a manifesto, Joyce reveals her, the mother Anna Livia Plurabella's "Mamafesta" in book 1, chapter 5 (104–25) of the *Wake*. It opens with an oddly familiar ring, a portmanteau of parody:

> In the name of Annah the Allmaziful, the Everliving, the Bringer of Plurabilities, haloed be her eve, her singtime sung, her rill be run, unhemmed as it is uneven.
>
> Her untitled mamafesta memorializing the Mosthighest has gone by many names at disjointed times. Thus we hear of, [. . .].

And there follows a fulsome Rabelaisian catalogue, replete with literary allusions and exhibiting the secret thematic underground of a world scriptural tradition that flows out of and extends nature's own telling of the story of God, on one plane that of A. L. P.'s husband H. C. E. We move into her "letter" proper to and about husband and family, but it is a

5. Sheldon Brivic, *Joyce between Freud and Jung* (Port Washington, N.Y.: Kennikat Press, 1980), and Sheldon Brivic, *The Veil of Signs* (Urbana: University of Illinois Press, 1991).

tangled "polyhedron of scripture" (W 107) over which a professorial consciousness broods, not certain as to its actual origins or authorship. On
one level, as Tindall has argued, Joyce extensively models the "feminine"
style here—as in the "Penelope" chapter of *Ulysses*—on his own wife No-
ra's semiliterate letters that "flow in a redundant stream, unimpeded by
punctuation or capitals,"[6] a flow that fascinated the novelist and seemed
to him to be still remarkably close to the origins of language before the
masculine mind regimented it. But on another level, we hear the associative Molly-like frankness about the dark as well as light features of the
family romance in A. L. P.'s "mamafesta" and "letter" through the palimpsestial texture of the dream being recorded in the dreamer, a cumulative collective consciousness. The very flow of this river generates the
question, Who wrote the letter?, a riddled "chaosmos" (W 117), which is
swathed in digressions and to which fragments of all letters of all times
seem to adhere, "a multiplicity of personalities inflicted on the documents or document" (W 107)? One comico-mythic possibility is that the
Isis-like little hen, Biddy, has pulled it out of the world's midden heap, or
from a globe of dung, reconstituting the cosmic egg with that mysteriously mindless courage in an act of recycling that is eternal affirmation.
The curlicues and arabesques of the mother still are visible on the latter-
day historical surface in the lineaments of works like the *Book of Kells,* as
the scriptural and scribal aspect eventually makes its appearance in her
onflowing letter. This emergence is signaled by mention of A. L. P.'s son
Shem the Penman, whose name closes this section of the novel (W 125).

It is a necessary paradox that we readers, especially professorlike
interpreters who try to make sense out of the scraps of documents in
the midden heap, belong on the side of Shaun, the brother who usurps
the divine word, and assumes the job of delivering it. The pure inspiration flows through the poet Shem who often appears to be ridiculous
and disorderly. The accusatory, political brother and the uncensoring, at
times seemingly crazy, brother are sides of a single coin. In a chapter
entitled "The Comic Gospel of Shem," Robert Polhemus has captured
the essence of Joyce's self-mockery and serious jesting in the principal
Shem section of *Finnegans Wake* (book 1, section 7, pp. 169–95).[7] Joyce

6. William York Tindall, *A Reader's Guide to "Finnegans Wake"* (New York: Farrar,
Strauss & Giroux, 1969).

7. Robert Polhemus, *Comic Faith: The Great Tradition from Austen to Joyce* (Chicago:
University of Chicago Press, 1980), ch. 9: "Joyce's *Finnegans Wake* (1924–39): The Comic Gospel of 'Shem,'" 294–337—henceforth cited as P followed by the page number. Polhemus does not draw explicit connections between Joyce and Rabelais, but is clearly

overcomes repression by regrounding existence in its lowliest aspects, and his own irrepressible Shem-like, authorial arabesques, seen in the *Wake*'s metamorphosing language, resemble a titanic confessional act on behalf of humanity. Out of the patterns of life, the sounds of the world, the fiction-spinning power of the psyche, and the virtually infinite malleability of language over the ages, we glimpse "a hieroglyphic effect and function" (P 305). As Polhemus points out, Shem's ludicrous utterance "Quoi-quoiquoiquoiquoiquoiquoiq!"—when he raises his magical "life-wand" as Mercius "and the dumb speak" (W 195)—leads directly into our perceiving the vital flow of the mother Anna Livia, the unfathomable reality of life and love. Polhemus reminds us that "interpretation is a clownish process for a faithful foolish few" and Joyce hoped his ideal readers would "take on the best traits of the twins" (P 332–33); his "comic gospel moves to baptize and confirm us into a faith of the living word" (335). We can supplement Polhemus by recalling a well-known strand of literary tradition. This new attitude that Joyce aspires to mobilize reinstantiates with amazing verve the "mysterious" Pantagrueline doctrine that Rabelais directed to the poxicratical humanists: the divine folly of an unreasoning joy upheld in the face of all adversity and even absurdity. Rabelais was the early modern "classical" author who demonstrated the will to create a representative total inventory of life and language in all its ranges and to release the power of the Word again to transmute and levitate our material world. The ecstasy the child Gargantua experiences playing music on the tableware, while he adds body noises such as farting, is one of the hints early on in Rabelais's great humoristic novel *Gargantua and Pantagruel* (book 1, chapter 7) that the whole gamut of human nature will be shown to be in mysterious correspondence with the music of the spheres. Joyce's ambition as a liberator is no less astonishing.

We can regard the "Oxen of the Sun" chapter in *Ulysses* as a precedent for this more than double orchestration in the *Wake* that, on the one hand, reveals or celebrates a moment of human language, and, on the other hand, envelopes it in the multireferential, evolving text into which the speech-using human race is ever being reborn. "Oxen of the Sun" is so often cited that I can limit mention here to the barest outline for our immediate purposes. In a sequence of nine major sections, the chapter presents the gestation of a baby over nine months and the effective miracle of renewal, its birth. Starting from Anglo-Saxon times, month by

---

conscious of this relationship as shown in his introductory remarks on Erasmus, Rabelais, Cervantes, Swift, Fielding, and Sterne (13–16).

month, each section in the chapter reenacts the evolution of English over nine centuries until it becomes the language with the potential Joyce aspires to unlock. In a tour de force, parodying a quite astonishing range of the structures, styles, vocabularies, and authors from the time of Alfred into his own day, the novelist both creates a delightful chrestomathy and through it advances the development of his book's main themes. His supercatalogue outdoing Rabelais leads by a kind of imitative magic to the divine moment of the reincarnation of language; and in tandem the bawling of Mrs. Mina Purefoy's (i.e., love, the true faith's) baby in the maternity hospital expresses the creative energy reaffirmed.

The curious parallel for the noisome event, as drunken students pour out of the hospital at chapter's close, is the parodied vulgar ranting of the actual historical American evangelist Alexander Dowdie, who had come to proselytize in Dublin in 1904, the time of the action. The disconcerting moment of primal utterance, the appearance of the divine child, the baby's statement startles us in the guise of the barbaric yawp of the New World:

> Christicle, who's this excrement yellow gospeller on the Merrion hall? Elijah is coming! Washed in the blood of the Lamb. Come on you winefizzling, ginsizzling, boozeguzzling existences! Come on, dog-gone, bullnecked, beetlebrowed, hog-jowled, peanutbrained, weasleyed fourflushers, false alarms and excess baggage! Come on, you triple extract of infamy. Alexander J Christ Dowdie, that's my name, that's yanked to glory most half this planet from Frisco beach to Vladivostok. The Deity aint no nickel dime bumshow. I put it to you that He's on the square and a corking fine business proposition. He's the grandest thing yet and don't you forget it. Shout salvation in King Jesus. You'll need to rise precious early, you sinner there, if you want to diddle the Almighty God. Pflaaaap! Not half. He's got a coughmixture with a punch in it for you, my friend, in his back pocket. Just you try it on. (U 349)

If inter alia the novel *Ulysses* is enacting the central stories of the family, this kind of baby squawk confirms that—in his own way—Joyce shares the Mallarméan attitude that reborn language occurs as a magical act, rather than represents. David Hayman pointed to this basic relationship in his seminal book *Joyce et Mallarmé* and referenced such important evidence as Joyce's citing of Mallarmé's essay "Crise de vers."[8]

---

8. David Hayman, *Joyce et Mallarmé*, 2 vols., Vol. 1: *Stylistique de la suggestion;* Vol. 2: *Les éléments mallarméens dans l'oeuvre de Joyce* (Paris: Les Lettres Modernes, 1956), 1.31.

Clearly, Joyce was searching for ways that would meaningfully allow the elocutionary disappearance of the artist into the magical substance of the words of the work of art. The early compendium *The Books at the Wake* is instructive because an assiduous tracer of mythological and metaphysical materials of all sizes in it still encounters a riotous surplus of forms and traditions out of which, hypothetically, multiple syncretic patterns can be assembled. Essentially there is always some cultural residue dragged in willy-nilly by Joyce, an irritating reminder we're operating inside of a cultural repertory built into our dream spaces. Even when Joyce screws himself up from time to time to assert the hubristic idea that he can create a new kind of human speech, appropriate to a new approach to the world, it is practically impossible to assert its qualities in the midst of the debris of past human forms. Except for some special mystical insights that float into view (and belong to quite a different order of experience) Joyce has to play the magus role as the poet in charge of the night. The care is not to let our cultural awareness drag us from the level of symbolist linguistic purity.[9]

And so, accordingly, just as *Ulysses* follows in the episodic shadow of Homer's *Odyssey* and of other literary corpora, we have to treat the loose analogies with Viconian ages in the *Wake* as occurring in a simultaneity of repristinations that suggest the eternally recurrent pattern as it manifests its energies through sounds and signs. The governing grand analogy in the *Wake* is of the divine age to the Book of the Parents, the heroic age to the Book of the Children, the demotic age to the Book of the People, and the ricorso to the *Wake*'s recirculative coda. But nothing in realist narration prepares us for listening to "All Lilivia's daughtersons" (W 215) in the night condition we have already entered, for listening to their childish and youthful sounds through the filter of all human experience and history high and low. The *Wake* is characterized by an incredible variety of games and phrases of children at play, albeit their play is as often as not a tussle or contest. Yet we hear these voices and the comic moments of family life definitely as integral to "a farced epistol to the hibruws" (W 228), one of Joyce's many self-deprecatory labels for his book.

Jean-Michel Rabaté has argued that, both in his notebooks for the *Wake* and in letters to friends, Joyce toys through his famous dozen or so basic sigla with intimations of the earliest ideogrammatic scripts that

---

9. James S. Atherton, *The Books at the Wake: A Study of Literary Allusion in James Joyce's "Finnegans Wake"* (New York: Viking Press, 1960).

the human mind probably devised before letters.[10] The basic sigla, which include the Ur-father and Ur-mother, theirs sons, the snake, St. Patrick, Tristan and Isolde, the four old men (or four masters), and the Book, yield variations for things, places, processes, and even concepts, and the manipulation of the sigla tends toward producing recognizable letters. Joyce at times attains a referential density that it seems will never again be exceeded in literature, as when he invites us readers into the Book as the supreme mystery: "(Stoop) if you are abecedminded, to this claybook, what curios of signs (please stoop), in this allephbed" (W 18). This could be a sexual or psychological act of engaging the biblical clay body of humankind as a living text. It could be a descent into the human past, to scrutinize the first hieroglyphics and all successive records. Or it could be a plunge into the generative power of language itself, language being generated out of the All Father's primal vowel in the allephbed (which is also nature); or an entrance into the dream that flows as language thought or uttered, a voyage into its eternity. In the final analysis, even the unfolding of the high and sacred mystery of the sefiroth in and into the Nightletter (W 308)—lined up at one point on the page like a line of annotated hopscotch—bubbles in the *Wake* with a ludic bounciness that only the humblest child's play captures. To this extent, child talk is foundational to Joysprik.

10. Jean-Michel Rabaté, "'Alphybettyformed Verbage': The Shape of Sounds and Letters in *Finnegans Wake*," *Word and Image* 2 (1986): 237–43.

II THE WAYS OF HERMES IN THE WORKS
OF THOMAS MANN

Any examination of the more familiar Hermes principle in Thomas Mann's writings after World War I will always lead us back to one of the stellar epiphanies in twentieth-century literature: Aschenbach's rediscovery of Dionysos in *Death in Venice* (1912). This moment in the novella represents Mann's arrival at the insight that it is consonant with the very nature of Hermes for us to notice him after the fact of his agency in the affairs at hand. Whereas considerable attention has been devoted to Mann's Nietzschean interest in the relationship of Apollo and Dionysos,[1] only a few scholars such as Moeller and Berger have underscored the presence of Hermes as early as in *Death in Venice*.[2] Criticism has instead largely followed Dierks's view, downplaying the solidity of Mann's "knowledge" of Hermes as a constitutive element around 1910.[3] Such a purist approach, too oriented toward classical learning, undervalues the novelist's modernist response, in subsequent works, to the cultural logic latent in the Hermes reference of *Death in Venice*. When Mann later associates his own ironic authorial technique with "Hermetic" procedures, he realizes a deep organic imperative in himself while simultaneously, through artistic practice, finding his own natural place at one of the innumerable intersections of two great traditions descended from the Re-

1. Postwar attention to the Nietzschean dimensions has been strong at least since the monograph by Roger A. Nicholls, *Nietzsche in the Early Work of Thomas Mann* (Berkeley and Los Angeles: University of California Press, 1955), 77–91. The excellent book by John Burt Foster Jr., *Heirs to Dionysus: A Nietzschean Current in Literary Modernism* (Princeton, N.J.: Princeton University Press, 1981), has placed this relationship in a comparative European framework.

2. Hans-Bernhard Moeller, "Thomas Manns venezianische Götterkunde, Plastik und Zeitlosigkeit," *Deutsche Vierteljahrsschrift für Literaturwissenschaft und Geistesgeschichte* 40 (1966): 184–205; Willy R. Berger, *Die mythologischen Motive in Thomas Manns Roman "Joseph und seine Brüder"* (Cologne and Vienna: Böhlau, 1971), 4–6. A study from a Jungian perspective is Heidi M. Rockwood and Robert J. R. Rockwood, "The Psychological Reality of Myth in *Der Tod in Venedig*," *Germanic Review* 59 (1984): 137–41.

3. Manfred Dierks, *Studien zu Mythos und Psychologie bei Thomas Mann: An seinem Nachlaß orientierte Untersuchung zum "Tod in Venedig," zum "Zauberberg" und zur "Joseph"-Tetralogie* (Bern and Munich: Francke, 1972), 13–59.

naissance: syncretic Hermetism and literary humorism, both eminently compatible with his psychological bent.[4]

In *Death in Venice,* most critics repeatedly remind us, Apollonian vision gives way to bewitching foreign sound, Tadzio's voice and name, as Dionysian "music." And with the word "plague" (the overly explicit standard translation of the more ambiguous German "das Übel," actually cognate with English "ill," "evil"), we are introduced in section 5 to the connection between Aschenbach's dark "disorder and affliction" and the "wicked secret" of the city. An all-pervasive sickness is still the chief subject matter of *The Magic Mountain* in which the Hermetic principle is, however, now richly thematized and overtly serves to mediate knowledge in the dream suspension of a humoristic-encyclopedic symposium. In *The Magic Mountain* we move forward in history, on a horizontal plane of narration, toward the outbreak of World War I; yet, whether in epic, essaylike, or oneiric passages, we also weave back and forth vertically through time layers stratified in the book's literary and mythological allusions. This double register of procedures helps enormously to amplify the narrative technique, as well as the thematics, of *Death in Venice.* But the novelist's enhanced interest in Hermes is also reflected in his treatment of the protagonist. The reader is gradually induced to regard Hans Castorp as an internal explorer of the symposium. This middleman, in assimilating materials, arrives in due course at a conscious appreciation of the strange new compounds engendered through his own Hermetic-alchemical education. Since the authorial narrator encourages the reader to analyze the literary and mythical paradigms informing the story, in parallel to Castorp's own efforts to grasp them, the power of irony becomes internalized in the book as an attribute in some measure attainable by ordinary experiencers of our actual world. On the one hand, in minutely scrutinizing a nonheroic figure (here his deviance takes the form of "sickness," suspect curiosity, flight from duty in the normal bourgeois world), the novelist reinvokes a timeworn strategy that we can trace back to the sentimentalization of the picaresque protagonist in the seven-

---

4. The thesis that modern culture has been permeated with varieties of Hermeticism via romanticism is upheld, e.g., by Ernest Lee Tuveson, in *The Avatars of Thrice Great Hermes: An Approach to Romanticism* (Lewisburg, Pa.: Bucknell University Press, 1982). Mann's place in the humoristic-encyclopedic continuum from Rabelais and Cervantes over Sterne, has been treated by Herman Meyer, *Das Zitat in der Erzählkunst: Zur Geschichte des europäischen Romans* (Stuttgart: J. B. Metzler, 1961). Already seven decades ago, the spiritual affinities with Sterne (as against the lessons garnered from Cervantes) were pointed out by Oskar Seidlin, "Laurence Sterne's Tristam Shandy and Thomas Mann's Joseph the Provider," *Modern Language Quarterly* 8 (1947): 101–18.

teenth and eighteenth centuries. On the other hand, the novelist creates in Castorp a transactional mind as "medium," a person who is an intellectual go-between. To this extent, Mann characterizes the Western type as inherently Hermetic (rather than Apollonian or Dionysian) in our era.

For this reason, we cannot escape the jocoserious game of mythological identities as "our" game. Only subliterate readers will fail to recognize the rules when, for example, playing Lilith rather than Gretchen in the "Walpurgis Night" episode, Madame Chauchat teases Castorp, as a quite confused latter-day Faust, about his taint and infection, which is so charmingly inappropriate in a good bourgeois engineer. Like Proust's fur-clad Odette de Crécy, the queen of the Champs-Élysées and the Bois de Boulogne in the famous coda of *Swann's Way* (1913), Clawdia Chauchat wears the official regalia of the powerful Slavic woman popularized by Leopold von Sacher-Masoch's *Venus im Pelz* (Venus in Furs, 1867). However, the Great Mother attributes appear in Marusja, while Clawdia initially suggests lupine Dionysian foreignness. In the later case of Adrian Leverkühn in *Doktor Faustus*, the European disease will transparently be associated with a notorious presumed instance, Nietzsche's syphilitic progress into insanity, through Leverkühn's visit to the piano-equipped brothel of Esmeralda Hetaera where, rapt in music, the composer contracts the infection that ravages his nervous system. In *The Magic Mountain*, the femme fatale Clawdia hands Hans the silver pencil that links her with his boyhood companion, the "Asiatic" Pribislav Hippe—a hermaphroditic connection Hans himself grasps in dreaming. Simultaneously a writing instrument and a phallic token, simultaneously pointing to mediation through art, to Dionysos, and to the feminine, the pencil functions as the perfect Hermetic wand.

In the celebrated "Snow" episode, Mann presses beyond the ending of *Death in Venice* to probe the paradoxical similitude between the dynamics of dream structure and its incorporation in art. In Hans's vision of Apollonian civilization, a comely, solemn youth—with traits as much like those of John the Baptist in Renaissance iconography as those of Hermes, and reminiscent of Tadzio—points Hans into the pre-Christian temple that contains the horror at the heart of achieved order. Just as Hans passes by the archetypal image of the (unnamed) Madonna with Child, so he penetrates past the (unnamed) forms of Demeter and Persephone—that is, past prior advanced embodiments of the myth of the life process—to glimpse through an iron door the witches who dismember and eat the child. Over and beyond this archaic perception of a mindless life cycle, humanity has willed to erect culture and society. Unlike Aschenbach, Hans survives with such crucial retrieved knowledge, asserting the value of the "dream" too as structure:

> We dream anonymously and communally, though each in his own way. The great soul, of which we are just a little piece, dreams through us so to speak, dreams in our many different ways its own eternal, secret dream—about its youth, its joy, its peace, and the bloody feast. Here I lie against my column, with real remnants of my dream still inside my body—both the icy horror of the bloody feast and the previous boundless joy, my joy in the happiness and gentle manners of that fair humanity. (MM 485–86)[5]

Because love transcends both death and reason, Hans can conceive his synthesizing "dream-poem of humanity,"[6] and in the novel this is a representative act of anamnesis, recollection as the shaping of human identity. Mann affirms the parallel between the power to love and the power of poetry which connects signs. Because words liberate our experience from materiality and entombment, art can incorporate meaning.

After opening chapter 7 with the great meditation on inner and outer time, biological and historical time, time narrated and time of narration, Mann clearly indicates Castorp's participation in a question all artists must ask through a startling metaphor reminiscent of James Joyce:

> Are hermetically sealed preserves on the shelf outside of time? That is a question for the professional philosopher—and it was only out of youthful presumption that Hans Castorp had got himself mixed up in the topic. (MM 534)[7]

---

5. English versions of the novella, indicated by the abbreviation DV and pagination, follow the translation by David Luke, *"Death in Venice" and Other Stories by Thomas Mann* (New York: Bantam Books, 1988). References to *Der Tod in Venedig* and other works of fiction in the original German are indicated by volume and page number after the abbreviation GW in the edition (often cited as the Frankfuter Ausgabe) under the care of Peter de Mendelssohn: Thomas Mann, *Gesammelte Werke in Einzelbänden* (Frankfurt: Fischer Verlag, 1980). English versions of *Der Zauberberg*, drawn from *The Magic Mountain*, trans. John E. Woods (New York: Vintage International, 1996), are indicated by page number after the abbreviation MM. The German citation here is: "Die große Seele, von der du nur ein Teilchen, träumt wohl mal durch dich, auf deine Art, von Dingen, die sie heimlich immer träumt,—von ihrer Jugend, ihrer Hoffnung, ihrem Glück und Frieden [. . .] und ihrem Blutmahl. Da liege ich an meiner Säule und habe im Leibe noch die wirklichen Reste meines Traums, das eisige Grauen vor dem Blutmahl und auch die Herzensfreude noch von vorher, die Freude an dem Glück und an der frommen Gesittung der weißen Menschheit" (GW, 5.692).

6. "Traumgedicht vom Menschen" (GW, 5.694).

7. "Es ist eine Frage für Berufsdenker—und nur aus jugendlicher Anmaßung hatte

The Ways of Hermes in the Works of Thomas Mann

Unmistakable is the analogy Mann draws between the narrational space of the novel and the fictive experiment "out of time" at the sanatorium; both are Hermetic processes and enclosures. We again encounter this metaphor of the "preserved" message in the later section, "Fullness of Harmony," when Hans sits before his "magic box" (MM 631), "small [. . .] temple" (633), or "musical coffin" (643), borne toward "thoughts enhanced, forced upward by alchemy" (643) as he listens to "favorite recordings" (643) before the shot at Sarajewo in the final chapter awakens him from "the hermetic magic" (MM 699).[8] Out of the banally flat, rotating opera records, the Hermetic needle elicits the powerful utterance of *Carmen, Aida, Faust*, and so on. Out of the circularity of the laws of life, we "hear" (read) both permanent truths and the insistent march of forces that impel the direction of contemporary history.

In the *Joseph* tetralogy—*Die Geschichten Jaakobs* (The Tales of Jacob, 1933), *Der junge Joseph* (The Young Joseph, 1934), *Joseph in Ägypten* (Joseph in Egypt, 1936), *Joseph der Ernährer* (Joseph the Provider, 1943)—Mann next examines the development of historical consciousness and ego out of a mythical permanence and the collective from the days of Abraham onward. The storyteller's entrance into the buried past, his search for the "double sense of the word 'once,'" is a manifestly Hermetic act, a "feast of death, descent into hell" (JB 33).[9] (Chapter twelve, "Harrowing Hell with Proust, Joyce, and Mann," will treat the theme of journeying through hell more broadly in modernism.) In this post-Goethean "Prelude" ("Vorspiel") to the *Joseph* tetralogy, Mann harrows hell to refind poetically the "original man" and the "original document" (JB 10), the remote primal sense "from the days of Set" (JB 11) and the "original home of articulate man" (JB 16), the "art of writing [. . .] 'from the days of Thoth'" or the Egyptian scribal avatar of Hermes. (JB 15); and we expect to witness how "myth" turned into a "mystery" (JB 18) and attained sacramental embodiment, in which by tacit analogy art participates: "But the holiday garment of the mystery is the feast, the recurrent feast which bestrides the tenses and makes the has-been and the to-be present to the popular sense" (JB 33).[10]

---

also Hans Castorp sich einmal damit eingelassen—, ob die hermetische Konserve auf ihrem Wandbort außer der Zeit ist" (GW, 5.762).

8. "Fülle des Wohllauts" "Zauberkasten," "Tempelchen," "Musiksarge"; "alchimistisch gesteigerte Gedanken"; "Vorzugsplatten" (GW, 5.893–918); "diesem hermetischen Zauber" (GW, 5.996).

9. "Doppelsinn des 'Einst'" (GW, 9.32); "Todesfest, Höllenfahrt" (GW, 9.52).—English versions drawn from Thomas Mann, *Joseph and His Brothers*, trans. H. T. Lowe-Porter (New York: Alfred A. Knopf, 1974), are indicated by page number after the abbreviation JB.

10. "Ur-Mann" and "Ur-Kunde" (GW, 9.17), "aus den Tagen des Set" (19) and "Ur-

Metamorphosis, Play, and the Laws of Life

This elaborately staged "doctrine and romance of the soul" (JB 25) also becomes, secondarily, the romance of "spirit" whose mission unfolds out of the soul's situation.[11] Under examination is the potential interactive bonding that "the soul involved with nature and the spirit detached from the world, the principle of the past and the principle of the future" (JB 29) are destined to establish.[12] Mann understands this evolution in Schopenhauerian and Freudian terms as the emergence of the conscious out of the unconscious, and as a transcendence prefigured in the primal seed. Roles and experiences that advance the story of mankind and portend release from the older Egyptian world are bodied forth out of Joseph's dreams. Joseph tries out in various ways the roles of Tammuz, Adonis, and Osiris, before he achieves identification with the higher manifestation of Thoth in Hermes. Mann writes to Kerényi in 1934:

> It is certainly true that my Joseph furthers his own career by means of a dazzlingly crafty adaptation of the Tammuz-Osiris pattern, which allows him, along with the beauty of his "appearance," to induce men to take him partly, yet rather more than less, for a god, for the god. The idea that this deception has a higher justification because of a fundamentally real mythical identity is something I have taken from the novel of antiquity—without knowing it.[13]

The hero's intellectual achievements are as formidable as his storytelling prowess. As Joseph draws closer to God as a kind of divine supernarrator, his self becomes artistic, breaks forth into the affairs of outside reality, becomes a mediator, enabler, provider. The power of the word to move and link things, ultimately producing consciousness and history, earns the god of science, rhetoric, and writing a high position in the

Heimat des sprechenden Menschen" (26), "die Schreibkunst [. . .] aus den Tagen des Thot" (25); "Mysterium" (30); "[. . .] aber des Geheimnisses Feierkleid ist das Fest, das wiederkehrende, das die Zeitfälle überspannt und das Gewesene und Zukünftige seiend macht für die Sinne des Volks" (52).

11. "Lehre und Roman der Seele"; "Geist" (GW, 9.40).

12. "die naturverflochtene Seele und der außerweltliche Geist, das Prinzip der Vergangenheit und das der Zukunft" (GW, 9.46).

13. "Tatsächlich hilft mein Joseph selbst seiner Laufbahn besonders durch eine blendende und verschmitzt hochstaplerische Anpassung an das Tammuz-Osiris-Schema nach, wodurch er, im Verein mit der Schönheit seiner 'Erscheinung', die Menschen bestimmt, ihn halb und halb, für einen Gott, für den Gott zu halten. Die höhere Rechtfertigung des Betruges durch die weitgehend wirkliche mythische Identität ist ein Motiv, das ich aus dem antiken Roman übernommen habe,—ohne ihn zu kennen" (Thomas Mann and Karl Kerényi, *Gespräch in Briefen* [Zurich: Rheim-Verlag, 1960], 50; translated into English *as Mythology and Humanism: The Correspondence of Thomas Mann and Karl Kerényi*, trans. Alexander Gelley [Ithaca, N.Y.: Cornell University Press, 1975], 47).

moral hierarchy of the novel. Joseph moves through a discovery of language to the humanistic worldview as he moves beyond his identification with Tammuz-Osiris (nature, harvest) and toward that with Thoth-Hermes (script, numbers, learning, wisdom, magic).

During World War II, Mann sidelines the happier positive association with the Hermetic for an anguished reassessment of Nietzschean problematics in *Doktor Faustus* (1945). The philosopher is absorbed into the artist figure Leverkühn, the climax of whose musical career coincides with the zenith of modernism in the twenties. Through Mann's typical montage technique, the internal narrator Zeitblom, a Catholic humanist filled with the bourgeois-liberal spirit, and Leverkühn, evidencing an abstract modernist bent, not only divide between them aspects of an Apollonian-Dionysian dichotomy, but also exhibit the involution and evolution of factors in German and European culture since the waning of the Middle Ages. Leverkühn fulfills a longer range Faustian destiny too. As witnessed by Zeitblom, the history of a decadent Germany going toward and through damnation in World War II constitutes a painful admission of how their tradition went wrong after Goethe and Beethoven. On the one hand, Mann indicates that, persisting in underground channels, the forces that are undermining a recent golden age of humanism are religious in origin, in a primitive rather than a higher way. Yet, on the other hand, the novel depicts—in John B. Foster's words—how the "philosopher's mythic self-dramatization" as Antichrist, envisioning the end of Christianity, yields to a "reassertion of Christianity's power to enforce some sense of absolute values."[14] The appearance of the devil in several forms underscores the complex reversals and interchanges by which the Dionysian is revalued in terms of the demonic in the West; and correspondingly, Zeitblom's rival image of man as Homo Dei makes its countervailing claim on our allegiances.

Mann accomplishes his ultimate reconciliation with Hermes in the picaresque novel begun in 1911 and taken up again some four decades later. So-called "Part 1" of *Confessions of Felix Krull Confidence-Man*, finished in 1954, gives the impression of thematic completion though technically it remains a "fragment." In purely formal terms of narrative amplitude, it hovers between the deliberately interrupted prototypical *Lazarillo de Tormes* and the fulsome *Guzmán de Alfarache*. If some readers perhaps miss the literary pointers in the opening of *Felix Krull*,

14. Foster, *Heirs to Dionysus*, 366.

the deeper identity of the antihero soon is made explicit. Diane Philibert is ecstatic that Felix, who has the youthful beauty of the suave god of thieves and can be induced to humiliate her by stealing from her, has never before heard of Hermes. Mann discretely ends his search, both veiling and revealing identifications in a heady humor, at a ticklish moment that also seems to be a self-quotation, matching the finale of chapter 5 of *The Magic Mountain* (1924). The "open" closure of *Felix Krull* can be read, on yet another level, as a reenactment of ancient mysteries. The Mercurial or Hermetic mediator Felix, now an accomplished con man, passes from the daughter (Proserpina) to the mother (Demeter), and—as Donald Nelson interprets—"the union with the Great Mother symbolizes Krull's attainment of psychic wholeness through a union of the conscious and the unconscious."[15] I would add that Felix's cry of recognition and Senhora Kuckuck's countercry fuse the ancient Mediterranean and Christian-European allusions in the novel in its very final words, worth repeating here:

"Maria!" I cried.
　　And: "Holé! Heho! Ahé!" she exclaimed in majestic jubilation. A whirl-wind of primordial forces seized and bore me into the realm of ecstasy. And high and stormy, under my ardent caresses, stormier than at the Iberian game of blood, I saw the surging of that queenly bosom.[16]

Characteristically, Mann seems to be echoing here not just the Eleusian cry and Brünnhilde's shout at the opening of act 2 of Wagner's *Die Walküre*, but also Lazarillo's "olé, olé" at the end of the first Tratado, when the rogue obtains his revenge on the blind man by getting him, as if in a bullfight, to butt his head against a post. Oskar Seidlin pointed out immediately after its publication that the opening of *Felix Krull* recapitulates that of *Lazarillo de Tormes*.[17] I have argued elsewhere that Mann furthermore understood there was an identification of the pícaro Felix with his distinctly Hermetic predecessor Simplicius, the thief, trick-

15. Donald F. Nelson, *Portrait of the Artist as Hermes: A Study of Myth and Psychology in Thomas Mann's "Felix Krull"* (Chapel Hill: University of North Carolina Press, 1971), 96.
16. Thomas Mann, *Confessions of Felix Krull, Confidence Man: The Early Years*, trans. Denver Lindley (New York: Vintage Books, 1969), 378.—The original German reads: "'Maria!' rief ich. Und: 'Holé, Heho, Ahé!' rief sie mit mächtigem Jubel. Ein Wirbelsturm urtümlicher Kräfte trug mich ins Reich der Wonne. Und hoch, stürmischer als beim iberischen Blutspiel, sah ich unter meinen glühenden Zärtlichkeiten den königlichen Busen wogen."
17. Oskar Seidlin, "Picaresque Elements in Thomas Mann's Works," *Modern Language Quarterly* 12 (1951): 183–200; German version: "Pikareske Züge im Werke Thomas Manns," *Germanishe-Romanische Monatshefte* 36 (1955): 22–40.

ster, dabbler in alchemy, rhetorician, clown, actor, and scribe, in Grimmelshausen's great baroque novel. Among his artistic triumphs, which Mann could not fail to savor, Simplicius writes a Joseph novel and as "Beau Aleman" plays Orpheus on the Paris opera stage![18]

Like the aged novelist who suspects or knows too much, the transactional intermediary Felix is ever operating not just on the scene but behind the stage props. Moving about as only a Hermes can, yesterday's sin-burdened rogue now reappears as the humanized enabler and discoverer. The inevitable—the pain and trauma of discovery that will impel the pícaro to become a writer, to tell his story—is left eternally in suspense amid laughter. As in the picaresque genre, the criminal socialized speaks as the artist, a knower of the secrets. Thus indeed a great distance separates Felix from the abandoner of art, Gustav Aschenbach, who finally undergoes inward desocialization while appearing to represent his world, after having for so many years championed an increasingly arid social heroism.

The novella *Death in Venice* was published in 1912. With veiled irony, its opening sentence gave ominous hints about the long walk undertaken by aging Aschenbach: "On a spring afternoon in 19—, the year in which for months on end so grave a threat seemed to hang over the peace of Europe" (DV 195).[19] Finally, with the open irony of cold neutrality, the closing sentence related: "And later that same day the world was respectfully shocked to receive the news of his death" (DV 263).[20] On one level, then, the narrating voice seemed to situate the demise of a great intellectual firmly, with unrelenting naturalistic scrutiny. The novella furnished in contemporary life an admonitory tale about the twinned dangers of repression and decadence—central themes that haunted European literature as Europe was drifting toward the Great War. But unmistakable on another level, in the inner experience of Aschenbach, was a turning away from the imperative of action in time to the "truly godlike beauty" discovered in Tadzio, "an incomparable seductiveness," timeless "mystery."[21] Even today we are provoked by the inferential anal-

18. Gerald Gillespie, "Estebanillo and Simplex: Two Baroque Views of the Role-Playing Rogue in War, Crime, and Art (with an Excursus on Krull's Forebears)," *Canadian Review of Comparative Literature* 9 (1982): 157–71.

19. "an einem Frühlingsnachmittag des Jahres 19.., das unserem Kontinent monatelang eine so gefahrdrohende Miene zeigte." (GW, 4.559).

20. "Und noch desselben Tages empfing eine respektvoll erschütterte Welt die Nachricht von seinem Tode." (GW, 4.641).

21. "wahrhaft gottähnliche Schönheit" (GW, 4.589).

ogy between the story's references to biographical and cultural history and the achievements of time-obsessed Aschenbach, who has served as historian of major heroes and deeds, as dedicated preserver of German and European identity.

What complicates any analysis of the representative value of Aschenbach's experience is the fact that Mann not only has Nietzsche in mind, but is working out his own Wagner crisis through this figure. The little essay Aschenbach pens in Venice, while listening to Tadzio's voice and using his body as the model, alludes to Mann's own "Über die Kunst Richard Wagners" (On the Art of Richard Wagner, 1911), actually written on the Lido. It is indeed important to recognize the haunting presence of Wagner in the novella. After all, Wagner's death in Venice was the actual famous death there that the whole world heard reported, and Mann expected his readers to think of that event. But it is inaccurate to conclude, as James Northcote-Bade does, that this veiled connection reveals a straightforward turning away from Wagner, anticipated in the 1909 essay *Geist und Kunst* (Spirit and Art), and an affirmation of Goethe and classicism.[22] Rather, the episode is drenched with ironic ambivalence. On the one hand, the essay has "limpid nobility and vibrant controlled passion" that will soon excite admiration; on the other hand, "It is as well that the world knows only a fine piece of work and not also its origins, the conditions under which it came into being" (DV 236).[23] The sexual overtones of the German are unmistakable: "How strangely exhausting that labor! How mysterious this act of intercourse and begetting between a mind and a body!" (DV 236).[24] Aschenbach leaves the beach "worn out, even broken, and his conscience seemed to be reproaching him as if after some kind of debauch" (DV 236).[25]

We can hardly say that Mann reaches a firm conviction in the value of classicism in this instance. Mann explores the ambivalent task of the modern artist and intellectual through the case of Aschenbach who for

22. James Northcote-Bade, *Die Wagner-Mythen im Frühwerk Thomas Manns* (Bonn: Bouvier, 1975), 86. The survival of parodistic echoes of Wagner to the very end of Mann's artistic endeavors is clear, e.g., as noted in the article by L. J. Rather, "The Masked Man(n): Felix Krull Is Siegfried," *Opera Quarterly* 2 (1984): 67–75.

23. "Lauterkeit, Adel und schwingende Gefühlsspannung"; "Es ist sicher gut, daß die Welt nur das schöne Werk, nicht auch seine Ursprünge, seine Entstehungsbedingungen kennt" (GW, 4.608).

24. "Sonderbar entnervende Mühe! Seltsam zeugender Verkehr des Geistes mit einem Körper!" (GW, 4.628).

25. "erschöpft, ja zerrüttet, als ob sein Gewissen wie nach einer Ausschweifung Klage führe" (GW, 4.609f.)

decades has "willed [himself] to be classical" but surrenders will-less, re-invoking in his own mind the contest between the masculine warrior principle and the unmanning love principle celebrated in the ancient classics. Aschenbach's dedication to form, because it ultimately masks a "heroism of weakness" (DV 203), entails a dubious martyrdom associated with the patient nobility of the "figure of Saint Sebastian" (DV 203). Idealized in a "boyish manly virtue" (DV 202), the intellectual sufferer is a decadent avatar of that earlier incarnation of human dignity whom Mann later describes in the "Prelude" to the *Joseph* novels as "a youthful being made out of pure light" (JB 23).[26] Even Aschenbach's initiation into the vision of eternal beauty amounts ambiguously to the eventual retrieval of sublime and terrifying memories which, long and patiently ignored, sweetly revenge themselves. In the course of admitting his sympathy with the abyss, Aschenbach indulges expansively in reliving the classics as a fated act of recollection, making the paradox of his failure as a protagonist of Western virtues all the more acute. *Death in Venice* thus engages us, through him, in defeat by an authority that we vainly seek to deny through our forgetful toil. In a letter written seven years later to Carl Maria von Weber regarding *Death in Venice*, Mann expressly refers to its Nietzschean and Schopenhauerian paradigm, the distinction and interplay "between the Dionysian spirit of an irresponsibly individualistic lyrical outpouring and the Apollonian spirit of objectively framed epic which is socially and morally responsible."[27] But we have to do here not with a simple matter of affirming a Nietzschean sense of the standard or model established in the Greek experience. Rather, beyond the reenacted Platonic discourse in Aschenbach's thoughts and the terrifying Euripidean insights half-glimpsed in the historian's dreams, there is a third realm of reference. In his homosexual adoration of the Polish boy Tadzio, Aschenbach reencounters in a series of twinned shiftings not one but three youthful gods: the divinity of Eros, of Dionysos, and of Hermes.

As Terence Reed has shown, Aschenbach is at first enacting his own artistic ideal of a reconciliation between beauty and men's spiritual and

---

26. "Heroismus [. . .] der Schwäche" (GW, 4.509); "Sebastian-Gestalt"; "jünglinghaften Männlichkeit" (GW, 4.568); "ein Jünglingswesen aus reinem Licht" (GW, 9.i, 37).

27. "zwischen dem dionysischen Geist unverantwortlich-individualistisch sich ausströmender Lyrik und dem apollonischen objektiv gebundener, sittlichgesellschaftlich verantwortlicher Epik" (Letter of July 4, 1920, reproduced in *Dichter über ihre Dichtungen*, vol. 14, part I: *Thomas Mann, Teil 1: 1889–1917*, ed. Hans Wysling [Munich: Ernst Heimeran, 1975], 414). Mann also reiterates here as in many other places that the novella grew out of an original plan to write a story about Goethe's Marienbad experience.

intellectual life.[28] The text of *Death in Venice* is rich in phrases, images, and ideas from Plato's *Symposium* and *Phaedrus* and from Plutarch's later essentially Platonic dialogue, *Erotikos*. The fascination for Tadzio begins, on the conscious level, as an aesthetic appreciation couched in painterly and sculptural terms that echo the concerns of German modernism; the precedent classical enthusiasm of the German eighteenth century in Winckelmann, Goethe, and Schiller; and the ancient Greeks themselves. Tadzio becomes linked with Aschenbach's literary aspirations to free "from the marble mass of language that slender form which he beheld in the spirit, and which he was presenting to mankind as a model and mirror of intellectual beauty" (DV 234).[29] Section 4 opens with a hymnic evocation of a world bathed in the splendor of Apollonian light, paralleling the unprecedented joy in the contemplation of Tadzio whose individual charm conducts Aschenbach up the ladder of forms to wonder at the glory of all nature—or so at first he imagines. Inwardly the savant addresses the boy as Eros and Phaedrus and casts himself in the role of Socrates. As the southern day progresses and is "strangely exalted and mythically transformed" (DV 239),[30] his mind is flooded with images as if we are glimpsing the cardinal moments of myth in a passing repertory of the greatest Renaissance painting and poetry inspired by antiquity.

But as this Apollonian vision crests, Aschenbach is not restored to "wholesome disenchantment" and is "no longer disposed to self-criticism" (DV 237). Bewitched by the foreign sound and smitten by the mysterious smile, he is drawn by desire toward the lips of "Narcissus" (DV 241).[31] This moment, ending section 4, brings about the simultaneous penetration beneath the Apollonian mask and loss of self through reflection when attraction to otherness devolves into attraction to the abyss. Increasingly, Venice assumes the symbolic role as the strange construct of European man perched on top of swamps, as a borderline between the North and the West as against the South and the East, as the edge where form is suspended in formlessness; and the labyrinth of this "city" embodies the conspiracy of disease and greed, Western corruption.

---

28. Terence J. Reed, *Thomas Mann: The Uses of Tradition* (Oxford, U.K.: Oxford University Press, 1974).

29. "aus der Marmormasse der Sprache die schlanke Form [. . .], die er im Geiste geschaut und die er als Standbild und Spiegel geistiger Schönheit den Menschen darstellte" (GW, 4.606).

30. "seltsam gehoben und mythisch verwandelt" (GW, 4.611).

31. "heilsame Ernüchterung"; "zur Selbstkritik nicht mehr aufgelegt" (GW, 4.609); "Narciß" (614).

Another thing we have long suspected—that Aschenbach's curious walk in Munich, his journeying to the sea's rim, and his boat rides were all symbolic crossings toward the realm of the unconscious and of death—grows ever clearer. The would-be Socrates, who will, instead of hemlock, eat tainted strawberries in Venice, has already actually met Dionysos in section 1 at sunset by the North Cemetery, while gazing at a neoromantic monument to death, "the mortuary chapel with its Byzantine styling" (DV 196):[32]

> Its facade, adorned with Greek crosses and brightly painted hieratic motifs, is also inscribed with symmetrically arranged texts in gilt lettering, selected scriptural passages about the life to come, such as: "They shall go in unto the dwelling-place of the Lord" or "May light perpetual shine upon them." (DV 196)[33]

As if out of the bronze doors, there comes into view a strange herald figure, snub-nosed, red-haired, with fresh milky complexion, obviously not Bavarian, having, rather, "an exotic air, as of someone who had come from distant parts," and in his bearing "an air of imperious survey, something bold or even wild about his posture" (DV 196). Aschenbach will encounter other such avatars of Dionysos—the unlicensed gondolier of "brutal appearance," who was "not of Italian origin," and the jester, "half pimp, half actor, brutal and bold-faced, dangerous and entertaining" (DV 212, 213, 249),[34] not Venetian, who panders to the lowest instincts of his audience and lies to Aschenbach regarding the pestilence, as the smell of carbolic acid and rot hovers over the canals.

The unsettling exotic element in the stranger's appearance in section 1 not only awakens Aschenbach's yearning to travel, but provokes the primordial dream of "a tropical swampland [. . .] a kind of primeval wilderness" (DV 197)[35] in which, among other strange forms, crouches the tiger, the fearsome Oriental beast of prey associated with Dionysos. By the middle of the final act in section 5, the raging cholera plague has mean-

---

32. "das byzantinische Bauwerk der Aussegnungshalle" (GW, 4.560).

33. "Ihre Stirnseite, mit griechischen Kreuzen und hieratischen Schildereien in lichten Farben geschmückt, weist überdies symmetrisch angeordnete Inschriften in Goldlettern auf, ausgewählte, das jenseitige Leben betreffende Schriftworte, wie etwa: 'Sie gehen ein in die Wohnung Gottes' oder: 'Das ewige Licht leuchte ihnen' [. . .]" (GW, 4.560).

34. "ein Gepräge des Fremdländischen und Weiterkommenden"; "etwas herrisch Überschauendes, Kühnes oder selbst Wildes" (GW, 4.560f.); "[von] brutaler Physiognomie"; "nicht italienischen Schlages" (580); "halb Zuhälter, halb Komödiant, brutal und verwegen, gefährlich und unterhaltend" (623).

35. "ein tropisches Sumpfgebiet [. . .], eine Art Urweltwildnis" (GW, 4.562).

while marched from the swamps of the Ganges delta, "that wilderness of rank, useless luxuriance, that primitive island jungle shunned by man, where tigers crouch in the bamboo thickets" (DV 252f.)[36] by the chief caravan and sea routes to Europe—a recapitulation of the triumphant progress of Dionysos, arriving from the East to claim the allegiance of his mortal kinsmen in Thebes. Hearing the infernal din of the vaporetto and the flutelike u-sound of its whistle, Aschenbach at last dreams vividly of "the stranger-god!" (DV 256).[37] On mountains like those about his own summerhouse, he witnesses the approach of the frenzied bacchantes, the erection of their "obscene symbol" (DV 256), and their orgiastic rites, and then submits to joining the worship, his soul tasting "the lascivious delirium of annihilation" (DV 257).[38] What complicates the passage is that Aschenbach's mountain home directly resembles Nietzsche's, so that Nietzsche too, despite his own conscious indictment of Western decadence and Wagnerism, is implicated in the humiliating surrender to the Dionysian principle. An ironic comic parallel is the result of the wrestling match seen by Aschenbach, when stocky Jaschu topples the beauty Tadzio, "the less muscular beauty" (DV 263).[39] In the collapse of Aschenbach, Mann brings together the problematics posed by Euripides' *Bacchae* and completes the Nietzschean pattern that dominates the tripartite structure of the tale. In Euripides' tragedy, the youthful Dionysos, doubly born son of Zeus and the Theban princess Semele, returns disguised from Asia to Hellas with his divine attributes as leader of his own cult. But his half-brother Pentheus, in the role of ruler, fears the impulses in his converts, who already include their royal grandfather Cadmus, the aged seer Teiresias, and Pentheus's mother Agave, and he vainly seeks to curb the seductive power of the mysterious foreigner. Eventually Pentheus is tempted to spy on the ecstatic revels and, inwardly surrendering to Dionysos's promptings, goes to his death on the mountain Cithaeron where his own mother and countrywomen tear him to pieces in their frenzy as an impious interloper. Pentheus expiates his crime of denying the god, even as he serves as a high victim for the god, and the Thebans are cursed for not having recognized Dionysos.

Foster suggests that Mann deliberately "reverses the pattern that Nietzsche found in Greek culture, which moved from an influx of the Dio-

36. "jener üppig-untauglichen, von Menschen vermiedenen Urwelt- und Inselwildnis, in deren Bambusdickichten der Tiger kauert" (GW, 4.628).
37. "Der fremde Gott!" (GW, 4.632).
38. "obszöne Symbol"; "Unzucht und Raserei des Unterganges" (GW, 4.633).
39. "de[n] schwächeren Schönen" (GW, 4.639).

nysian through the tragic age to the establishment of theory," that is, toward Apollonian form giving and philosophy.[40] The opening of *Death in Venice* introduces us to a hero who has suppressed his passionate, spontaneous self; then, as he rediscovers submerged parts of his character, he begins to experience a new joyous fullness; but, in the last stage, he surrenders compulsively and nihilistically to the savage god. While Aschenbach's activity as a creative writer is a "less extreme form of Apollonian one-sidedness [. . .] its relationship to the Dionysian is one of stubborn resistance; it recalls the situation of Doric art in *The Birth of Tragedy*." Section 2 of the novella depicts the deeper conflict in Aschenbach's career, when earlier he almost slipped into a theoretical denial of art, but decisively altered course with his short story "A Study in Abjection" (DV 204; in German "Ein Elender," a sufferer). His admission of the validity of his art drive is nevertheless ambivalent, because "he resists the instinctual realm this decision apparently justifies" and turns instead to the classicistic worship of pure forms. The narrator's direct commentary about the duplicity of form is unambiguously severe in its misgivings:

> And yet: moral resoluteness at the far side of knowledge, achieved in despite of all corrosive and inhibiting insight—does this not in its turn signify a simplification, a morally simplistic view of the world and of human psychology, and thus also a resurgence of energies that are evil, forbidden, morally impossible? (DV 204–5)[41]

Aschenbach's struggle to "uphold an Apollonian artistry that can ignore the Dionysian" is reflected in his hierarchical social consciousness and stress on dignity, discipline, and duty—right up to the moment when he dolls himself up at the barber's, hypnotically lingers with the vulgar mob in the piazza, and connives in the official cover-up. Dionysos revenges himself on repressive culture through the sudden barbarian upwelling, social demoralization, and class hatred instead of an awakened communal sense.

But if the tale solely illustrates the bipolar relation of Apollo and Dionysos, why, then, does the expiring Aschenbach, looking for the last time into Tadzio's "twilight-gray eyes," feel

---

40. Foster, *Heirs of Dionysus*, ch. 4: "From Nietzsche to the Savage God."
41. "Aber moralische Entschlossenheit jenseits des Wissens, der auflösenden und hemmenden Erkenntnis,—bedeutet sie nicht wiederum eine Vereinfachung, eine sittliche Vereinfältigung der Welt und der Seele und also auch ein Erstarken zum Bösen, Verbotenen, zum sittlich Unmöglichen?" (GW, 4.570).

as if the pale and lovely soul-summoner out there were smiling to him, beckoning to him; as if he loosed his hand from his hip and pointed outward, hovering ahead and onward, into an immensity rich with unutterable expectation. (DV 263)[42]

The word "Psychagog" in the original German reiterates the notion of love as educator and bears some faint coloration of Aschenbach's self-assigned role as Socrates. But it also now more openly lends retrospective confirmation to the Hermes character of the heralds who conduct Aschenbach in a death-boat bound for the underworld. The early intimation of this revelation comes to Aschenbach in section 4 under its Apollonian aspect as transport to the Elysian Fields.[43] The attributes of the figures at the North Cemetery in Munich ambiguously suit both Dionysos and Hermes. His cane with a crook,[44] while subtly picking up the Christian motifs of the cross and crook (crosier), suggests either Dionysos's thyrsus, a staff surmounted by a pinecone and entwined with ivy and vine branches, or Hermes' caduceus, a wand of wood or gold, twined with snakes and surmounted by wings. The broad-brimmed hat,[45] however, is more reminiscent of Hermes. To the relationship of Apollo and Dionysos, exemplified in their union in the temple on Delos, Mann may here tentatively be adding the relationship of Hermes to both Dionysos and Apollo. In Christian and humanist tradition, both Dionysos and Apollo had long been interpreted as foreshadowings and aspects of Christ, and great romantics such as Friedrich Hölderlin had reexplored a deeper identity between Dionysos and Christ.

In a letter of 1941, acknowledging Kerényi's just published book, *Das göttliche Kind* (The Divine Child) Mann states:

> I could not help being pleased to note that the psychopompos is characterized as essentially a child divinity: I thought of Tadzio in *Death in Venice*. And the absence of a "unity of the individual" in primitive thought of which Jung speaks is something that I have treated quite on my own as a humoristic element in *The Tales of Jacob* (Eliezer).[46]

42. "dämmergraue Blick"; "als ob der bleiche und liebliche Psychagog dort draußen ihm lächle, ihm winke: als ob er die Hand aus der Hüfte lösend, hinausdeute, voranschwebe ins Verheißungsvoll-Ungeheure" (GW, 4.641).

43. "als sei er entrückt ins elysische Land" (GW, 4.603).

44. "Stock [. . .] auf dessen Krücke" (GW, 4.561).

45. "der breit und gerade gerandete Basthut" (GW, 4.561).

46. "Den Psychopompos als wesentlich kindliche Gottheit gekennzeichnet zu sehen, mußte mich freuen: er erinnerte mich an Tadzio im Tod in Venedig. Und den primitiven Mangel an 'Einheit der Person', von dem Jung spricht, habe ich in den Geschichten

The Ways of Hermes in the Works of Thomas Mann

The bridge to and from Christ as a divine child was anything but a recondite way for modernist writers. Like Dionysos, Hermes was traditionally depicted by the Greeks in the prime of youth, as beautiful, persuasive, and sweet-toned. Many inventions were ascribed to him, including the lyre and flute, the instruments associated with Apollo and Dionysos. While these gods were credited as sponsors of the arts and civilization, Hermes similarly was a patron of mathematics, astronomy, industry, and commerce, as well as a guardian of travel and boundaries. Yet, at the same time, he was patron of gamblers, tricksters, and thieves. Nor is that the only ambivalence attaching to him. The substitution of Tadzio as Platonic love partner for a Western poet in place of a feminine beloved fits the pattern of Aschenbach's reveries from which Aphrodite is nominally and conspicuously absent, but as mother and sister is implicitly latent in the references to Eros and the imaginative summoning of Apollonian glory. In the later *Felix Krull*, the Hermes figure will quite straightforwardly discover his own androgynous nature and delight in it as in other secrets beneath the world's appearances. In *Death in Venice*, Tadzio's delicate looks already suggest the higher aestheticized androgynous moment beyond the grotesque perception of the hermaphroditic state, the archaic link of Hermes and Aphrodite, or primordial sexual unity. The missing Venus principle is represented by the novel *Maya* coming, as section 2 relates, between Aschenbach's Apollonian "massive epic unfolding of Frederic's life" and "the famous short story 'A Study in Abjection'" (DV 202, 204).[47] Maya was the mother of Hermes, but equally relevant is that Schopenhauer's usage of the Indian term *maya* for the veil of illusions cast by the life force was more firmly imprinted on the German literary mind by the early twentieth century.

In *Death in Venice* Mann's search for keys to mythic patterns in any age is well underway, and not surprisingly—as Haskell Block has shown—his search, like that of many great modernists, rotates around the unavoidable, useful Renaissance-romantic myth of the artist.[48] Although the twinned Apollonian and Dionysian impulses are configured

---

Jaakobs ganz auf eigene Hand als humoristische Tatsache behandelt" (Thomas Mann and Karl Kerényi, *Gespräch in Briefen*, 98).

47. "mächtigen Prosa-Epopöe vom Leben Friedrichs von Preußen"; "jener starken Erzählung, die Ein Elender überschrieben ist" (GW, 4.563, 565).

48. Haskell M. Block, "The Myth of the Artist," *Yearbook of Comparative Criticism* 9 (1980): 3–24. Also on the related question of the modernist urge to reconstitute a literary "system," see in the same volume Sam Dresden, "Thomas Mann and Marcel Proust: On Myth and Anti-Myth," 25–50.

in this story mainly in reaction to Nietzsche, Mann's personal exploration of the relationships between love and death, creativity and sickness, life and spirit makes him hyperconscious of the drastic absence of
the feminine in the deeper being of Nietzsche, whose mountain home
he connects with Cithaeron. The epiphany of section 5, when Aschenbach salutes the strange god, is accordingly more than a statement
of the necessary revenge of Dionysos on us if we realize too late like
Pentheus-Nietzsche that our own culture is self-undermined through
denial of the life force. This epiphany is also the appearance of Hermes,
the "soul-guide."[49] Through Aschenbach's gazing at the Byzantine cross
in the early twentieth century, the realm of Death, so large for Christian
thought, visibly obtrudes into his representative Apollonian presumption. But this unmitigated gazing also releases a surprising insight that
will burgeon in significance throughout Mann's further writings. The
oblique reference to the supreme soul guide and divine child reveals that
underground, beneath the distracting manifestation named Dionysos,
are being effected the transactions to which Hermes carries the key.

49. In Luke's translation, "soul-summoner" (DV, 263); in the German, literally, "Psychagog" (GW 4:641), from the Greek.

12 HARROWING HELL WITH PROUST, JOYCE, AND MANN

The hero who penetrates to the netherworld and returns is a familiar figure in the ancient classical and biblical traditions. There were two main types of champions in antiquity capable of crossing the boundary between the realms of life and death: the Orphic and the Odyssean strains. The story of ancient Orpheus, the human poet who attains divine status through the magic of his art and whose mission embodies ennobling human aspiration and reveals the power of love to transcend the limits of mortality, thrilled the Renaissance and the Enlightenment in turn. The Orphic theme was popularized through the new medium of opera, starting from works such as Jacopo Peri's *Euridice* and Claudio Monteverdi's *Orfeo* in the early 1600s down to Christoph Willibald Gluck's *Orfeo ed Euridice* in the later 1700s. The jocoserious uses of the myth of the poet-lover after the Renaissance can be illustrated almost as frequently. Examples stretch at least from the symbolic moment in book 4 of Johann J. C. von Grimmelshausen's baroque novel *Simplicissimus,* when the hermetic protagonist plays this operatic role on the Parisian stage, down to Jacques Offenbach's *Orphée aux enfers* (Orpheus in the Underworld) of the mid-nineteenth century. Walter Strauss has sketched the renewed fascination for the Orphic dimensions of poetry, its power of transformation, from romanticism to modernism on the part of Novalis, Nerval, Mallarmé, Rilke, Yeats, Valéry, Cocteau, Broch, and others.[1] While the Orphic strain is very important to high modernism because of its direct relevance for art, it remains a special case of the general interest in penetrating what is hidden from ordinary human vision.

The harrowing of hell too is just one among many forms of the hero quest, as Joseph Campbell and other students of myth have noted.[2] When the Greco-Roman and Judeo-Christian mythologem of a journey

1. Walter Strauss, *Descent and Return: The Orphic Theme in Modern Literature* (Cambridge, Mass.: Harvard University Press, 1971).
2. Joseph Campbell, *The Hero with a Thousand Faces,* 2nd ed. (Princeton, N.J.: Princeton University Press, 1978).

into the depths recurs in high modernism, it often quite deliberately shadows the composite plot line and increasingly self-reflective narrative awareness of what Northrop Frye has called the scriptural "Great Code."[3] In book 11 of the *Odyssey*, the wanderer of many turns exits from Circe's domain with the knowledge of where to find the entrance to the underworld. Odysseus's initial encounter with recently dead Elpenor provides us with the crucial assurance at the start of his venture into this realm beyond human ken that the quester who is privileged to hear or witness key figures of Greek myth and to gain insights into his own story will return to the world of striving and carry these discoveries with him. In book 6 of the *Aeneid*, the hero gains knowledge of how to enter the netherworld from the Sibyl of Cumae; and—in a crucial positive sign to readers—minions of his protectress Venus guide him in pursuing the key, gaining control of the Golden Bough. Virgil reveals his own authorial presence (e.g., lines 350–55) in this complex, multipartite vision that includes the witnessing of Elysium and is sprinkled with hints of Aeneas's return to the plane of history and to his foundational mission.

Thus, the medieval protagonist seeker, Dante, understandably is very eager to meet Virgil in canto 4 of the *Inferno* because he believes that the beloved pagan poet, dead more than a millennium, can corroborate the doctrine of Christ's triumphant descent into hell after the Crucifixion. For Christians, the Savior's liberating visit to the netherworld reinforces, among other things, the theme of God's miraculous intervention in history. By the time of *La divina commedia*, the nonpunitive outer precincts of hell harbor a host of distinguished poets and philosophers active before and after Virgil, from Homer and Plato to Seneca and Avicenna. Well before Renaissance writers set about integrating recovered materials such as the Egyptian realm of death into Europe's polyhistorical register, several literary hells are already copresent as foundational layers in this Dantesque involution.

Seekers in late Renaissance literature often reenact the journey to the underworld, but many major writers treat the pattern with increasing figural looseness and ambiguity. This is strikingly evident if we consider the cases of four early modern protagonists, all conceived in about a score of years, who over the intervening centuries down to our times have gained an entrenched place as archetypal manifestations.[4] Marlowe allows his

3. Northrop Frye, *The Great Code: The Bible and Literature* (New York: Harcourt Brace Jovanovich, 1982).

4. Gerald Gillespie, "Domesticating Don Juan," *Dedalus* 6 (1996): 207–20.

magus to explore hell in the *Tragical History of Dr. Faustus* (produced 1588), among other grand tours, but retains from the chapbook the theme that this is a delusionary voyage—even though quite possibly the playwright's covert intent is to convert Faustus into a seductive overreacher and thus undercut the pious source. Tirso de Molina lets us peer into the horrors of a gaping hell to which wayward Don Juan finally is committed in *El burlador de Sevilla* (The Trickster of Seville, ca. 1616), but he does not let us exceed our own earthly limits imaginatively by plunging with him. Realizing the potential of that temptation is reserved for such later writers as Molière (1605) and Da Ponte (1787, premier of Mozart's opera). Shakespeare's title hero Hamlet, a young humanist, in communication with his father, now a ghost from the other world, searches for certainty through the confusing tenebrae of an earthly reality that has metamorphosed into a virtual hell of realpolitik, the passions, and the mind. He emerges finally with "readiness" in the theater of the world only to face the immense mystery of the "rest" which, for perplexed earthlings, is "silence." In one of several paradigmatic episodes that function as internalized models for his ambiguous baroque antiromance, Cervantes allows errant Quixote to be lowered into and extracted from the Cave of Montesinos in the heart of La Mancha (*Don Quixote,* part 2, chapter 22), there to enjoy a vision of the chivalric absolute that is fraught with curious details which even a Sancho must question, let alone the reader.

The Renaissance was devoted to the Orphic theme because this enabled a positive expression of confidence in the survival of the deepest human values despite mortality. Baroque problematization of the Orpheus role can be illustrated by the above-mentioned episode at the start of book 4 of Grimmelshausen's *Simplicissimus* when the adventurer-fool literally performs it as an idolized opera star in corrupt Paris and is drawn into the innermost recess of the metropolitan labyrinth to serve a masked high lady, avatar of the hidden goddess Venus, rather than a rescued Eurydice. In *Die Bekenntnisse des Hochstaplers Felix Krull* (Confessions of Felix Krull, the Confidence Man), Mann's title figure enacts a parallel initiation rite when he discovers Senhora Kuckuck, that is, the imperious Great Mother, in the exuberant ending of the never continued part 1 of his picaresque adventures. That is a positive revaluation of the rediscovery of the primordial basis of life by means of a trip into the interior of the mind and of human evolution. But as such it parallels in grand outline the symbolic journey on which, for instance, Conrad takes us in *Heart of Darkness,* invoking actual terrains and waters of the almost fully mapped globe. This favorite journey of twentieth-century literature is frequently admonitory, if not the vehicle of an outright tragic vision.

At the time of *Simplicissimus*, that is, two-thirds of the way through the seventeenth century, Satan and hell reestablished their high credentials in Joost van den Vondel's play *Lucifer*, the awesome baroque drama of the fall of a cosmic superprince, and in Milton's biblical epic *Paradise Lost*, which by so frequently focusing on the business and pretensions of the underworld and its ruler, God's antagonist, made them again central to our imaginative engagement with the bigger human story. It is largely from Milton that the European romantics drew their dark antiheroic look and stance. There was a concurrent tendency of considerable importance. The dislocations and disorders of the French Revolution helped bring about a gradual shift from a general literary addiction to the notion of an earthly paradise, after its apogee in the Enlightenment. Despite the transformative hopes of romanticism, the paradigm of the journey through hell became prominent by the turn of the eighteenth and lasted throughout the nineteenth century. Innumerable French romantic writers descibe their anguish over entrapment in their own passions, their dream life, and social reality as a descent into the infernal. When Baudelaire links the sense of being cursed, the experience of the city as an ambivalent realm that has usurped nature, and his "Luciferic" desire for the creative act in *Les fleurs du mal* (Flowers of Evil, 1857), he prepares the ground for Rimbaud's dazzling prose-poem *Une saison en enfer* (A Season in Hell, 1872).

The historical passage through revolutionary upheaval and the fascination for the growth of the city as a sometimes dystopian labyrinth occurred in tandem with the flowering of European subjectivism. Romantic reshaping of mythic exploration of the depths or uncanny realms includes innumerable metaphoric transcriptions of descent into the mind, into the horrors of death and annihilation, and into the abyss of meaninglessness when values collapse. In the internal narration of Klingsohr's "Märchen" (fairy tale) in the medievalizing quester novel *Heinrich von Ofterdingen* (1800), Novalis dares to let Fabel (poetic fancy) penetrate to the sinister dungeon, witness the horrors of humankind's primordial drives, but emerge undefeated and proclaim the triumph of love and wisdom. Not all romantic visions could end so positively. In the visionary "Rede des toten Christus" (Dead Christ's Speech) appended to his novel *Siebenkäs* (1804), Jean Paul allows the disillusioned Savior to survey the terrifying vastness of the universe as a pulsating hell and proclaim its meaninglessness and the death of God. In the drama *Cain* (1821), Byron permits Satan to reveal to our ancestor, the first murderer in Genesis, the horrific extent of death also in the monstrous proportions of evolutionary supersession in actual nature. All these possibilities for poetic excursions out of the fictional plane of a hypothetical "real" arena of human endeavors and into hidden or forgotten realms were established means of narration by the second decade of the nineteenth century. Goethe's use of phantasmagorias and dreamscapes in *Faust* 1 (1808) and 2 (1832) in order to guide us as poetic anthropologists through evolutionary stages subsumed in human culture and in the psyche represents the culmination of this new capacity in the early nineteenth century.[5]

How well these lessons had been absorbed by the time of high modernism is readily seen in director Fritz Lang's and scenarist Thea von Harbou's popular, dreamlike film *Metropolis* (1926), which combines attributes from older and newer big cities (notably London, Paris, and New York) and freely borrows motifs from older literature (notably romanticism) and religion (notably Catholicism). The film organizes both hierarchical social relationships in the contemporary industrial age and psychological and evolutionary principles along a vertical axis. The interactions among characters that occur at various architectural levels in this fantasy cityscape work out an elaborate allegory of interdependency and crisis. What the film "means" depends on the broad public's intuiting, and the educated viewers' reading, the symbolic properties of the mighty City. Its life-sustaining machinery and its toiling masses are located in the lower depths, close to the dark, rooted origins of humanity, while management of the total construct is now in the hands of a new technocratic (and capitalist) elite who enjoy the air, light, and privileges high above in their skyscraper. The brain of the City is its Zeus-like refounder John Federsen; its destined mediator or heart is his son, Feder, clearly a Christ figure; while Mary, who preaches in the catacombs to the suffering workers, embodies its feminine nourishing foundation. The major plot line posits the necessary marriage of heaven (masculine principle) and hell (feminine principle) in order to restore the human world that is threatened by destabilization as a result of its own transformation in modern times—a theme that D. W. Griffith had already broached in his film *Intolerance* in 1913, and which was familiar to many in the au-

5. Gerald Gillespie, "Classic Vision in the Romantic Age: Goethe's Reconstitution of European Drama in *Faust* II," in *Romantic Drama*, ed. Gerald Gillespie (Philadelphia: John Benjamins, 1994), 379–98.

dience from Wagner's opera cycle *Der Ring des Nibelungen* (1854–1874). In Lang's treatment, first, in a reversal or upwelling, heaven is suddenly harrowed when Maria penetrates to the penthouse pleasure gardens with suffering children and stirs Feder's conscience. Then, reciprocally, Feder figures out how to descend into the lower depths and learn about, and thus contribute to redeeming, the denizens of this social and metaphoric hell. A key subplot involves the attempt of the sinister scientist Rotwang, a figure like the "Scribe" in the fairytale in Novalis's *Heinrich von Ofterdingen* and Hoffmann's evil artificers, to overpower the system by inventing a mechanical false Maria.

There is no disrespect for their unique gifts in approaching Proust, Joyce, and Mann via this highly foreshortened preface as modern novelists who understand how and why "readers" should harrow hell. All three writers explicitly accept being creatures of an unfathomable preface already written by the world and interpreters of an immediate particular literary history. They thematize—with a sweep this chapter can only sketch suggestively—that the relation of any present to the depths of our experience of time and consciousness is a surface we must break through for more adequate understanding. Proust exploits three master paradigms of the journey through hell in his grand narrative, the seven novels of *In Search of Lost Time*.[6] The overture to the "Combray" section of Swann's Way, the first novel, introduces to us evolutionary time and relates this discovery of the virtually infinite grounding of our psyche to inner time as it manifests itself in the unnamed experiencing subject, in his fluctuating descents into and ascents from sleep. Later in the same novel, the episode of the evening at Sainte Euverte's conveys the felt reality of the wounded psyche confronting life as if it is traversing hell. In the seventh and final novel, *Time Refound,*[7] the horror of World War I is experienced often as a transmutation of reality into dreamscape, and the Elysian Fields furnish a shadow identity for a Paris so proud of its grand boulevard bearing that appellation. And, in general, the pressures of an underground manifest themselves throughout *In Search of Lost Time* in surface phenomena ranging from linguistic oddities to rever-

6. Marcel Proust, *À la recherche du temps perdu*, ed. Jean-Yves Tadié et al., 4 vols. (Paris: Gallimard, 1987–1989); vol. 1 hereafter cited as R followed by page number. Marcel Proust, *In Search of Lost Time*, trans. C. K. Scott Montcrieff and Terence Kilmartin, rev. D. J. Enright, 6 vols. (New York: Modern Library, 1998–1999); vol. 1 hereafter cited as MKE followed by the page number.

7. *Time Regained,* trans. Andreas Mayor, rev. D. J. Enright (New York: Modern Library, 1992–1993; paperback, 1998–1999).

ies to gestures and more. Clearly, Proust was aware of the unconscious.[8]

The episode of some thirty pages depicting Swann's inner torment during the musical evening at the residence of the Marquise de Saint-Euverte appears in the part of volume I entitled "Un amour de Swann" (Swann in Love), narrated until close to its finish almost exclusively in the third person. "Swann in Love" suddenly follows the first-person "Combray" part. Without explanation, we move into a virtually independent work in the Flaubertian tradition, the sort of work that implicitly a matured artistic consciousness, such as that budding in the earlier disclosed narrator persona, might eventually be capable of writing. Thus, many crucial thematic clusters have already been established in the first-person overture and "Combray" sections that recur in the third-person, omniscient treatment of Swann and allow it to be woven together with the surrounding parts of the novel. In this sense, the particular human story of Swann, who is being diverted from his own more refined level of existence and from his pursuit of an ideal vision as he succumbs to the will of the socially ambitious Odette, is just a fuller case study in the ample typology that Proust elaborates over many volumes. At the same time, the central episode of Swann's anguished insight into Odette's perfidy and his own captivity is an intensely focused recapitulation of the overture; it illustrates the necessity of journeying through hell as a precondition of attaining any higher consciousness and of liberating one's being from annihilation by time. The example of Swann's extensive alienation from his earlier self during his subsequent role as Odette's husband is an emblematic instance of a lost world troubling us and crying out for recovery. When we observe the later, sick Swann, our knowledge of his existential pain on the verge of his surrender functions, in the Baudelairean-Mallarméan words of the first-person narrator on page 1 of the entire *In Search of Lost Time*, "as the thoughts of a previous existence must be after reincarnation" (MKE 1).[9] The recovery of the otherwise lost earlier Swann from beneath the encumbering debris of his "failure" counts among the miracles of art performed in the novel.

Also emblematic of his special role as a tragic shadow amidst the fig-

8. Doing for Proust what Brivic does for Joyce, Malcolm Bowie in *Freud, Proust and Lacan: Theory as Fiction* (Cambridge, U.K.: Cambridge University Press, 1987) asserts the novelist's high stature as a subtle pathologist of human motivation and error. Robin MacKenzie, *The Unconscious in Proust's "A la recherche du temps perdu"* (Oxford, U.K.: Peter Lang, 2000), traces Proust's sources in romantic thought (e.g., Schelling, Schopenhauer) and illustrates a host of devices and moments in the novel when dreaming, traits of language, mannerisms, structures in art, and so forth reveal unconscious impulses.

9. "comme après la métempsychose les pensées d'une existence antérieure" (R, 3).

ures who populate the narrator's mind is Swann's ingrained habit, parallel to the narrator's, of interpreting things largely in terms of art.[10] This important linkage begins to be spun from the moment the narrating voice utters the famous analogy in the complex second sentence of the novel: "it seemed to me that I was myself the immediate subject of my book: a church, a quartet, the rivalry between François I and Charles V" (MKE 1).[11] Arriving at Saint-Euverte's in a disturbed state of mind, Swann is predisposed to see the grooms as figures from Balzac and "to look for analogies between living people and the portraits in galleries"; social life, from which he now is detached, presents itself to him "as a series of pictures" (MKE 459).[12] Rapidly, actual persons and created figures in the sumptuous, art-laden town palace assume gigantic, grotesque, tormented, and lurid features. Swann's mind runs through a gamut of horrors, martyrdoms, and Last Judgments associated with works from Giotto to Goya. In itself impressive as an accrued repertory of appreciated art, this exploration by way of painting and sculpture applies the truths present in art to perceived deformities of the high society in which Swann circulates as a harrower of hell. Yet, despite being filled with "melancholy irony" (MKE 466),[13] amidst the strains of Gluck's *Orfeo* and Liszt's "Saint Francis Preaching to the Birds," or rather because of his condition, Swann witnesses like a clairvoyant and attains to a new capacity to hear music. Its deepest messages flood into his ken, and he becomes receptive, at an ultimate level of his own special capacity, to the revelation embodied in "the little phrase from Vinteuil's sonata" (MKE 490),[14] recognizes its virtually supernatural status, and is thrilled by the audacious experimental genius it exhibits, equal to that of scientists like Lavoisier and Ampère, "discovering the secret laws that govern an unknown force" (MKE 499).[15] Swann rises to a new plane in recognizing his brotherhood with Vinteuil. He becomes momentarily the Schopenauerian "pure

---

10. There have been numerous useful studies of Proust's interest in art. Jonathan Paul Murphy, *Proust's Art: Painting, Sculpture and Writing in "A la recherche du temps perdu"* (Oxford, U.K.: Peter Lange, 2001), meticulously examines the interaction of thought processes—especially the narrator's—and the web of the novel's mythological and psychological constructs. Murphy invokes Lacanian paradigms to link to Proust's sense of language.

11. "il me semblait que j'étais moi-même ce dont parlait l'ouvrage: une église, un quattuor, la rivalité de François Ier et de Charles Quint" (R, 3).

12. "chercher des analogies entre les êtres vivants et les portraits des musées"; "comme une suite de tableaux" (R, 317).

13. "mélancolique ironie" (R, 322).

14. "la petite phrase de la Sonate de Vinteuil" (R, 399).

15. "decouvrant les lois sécrètes d'une force inconnue" (R, 345).

subject" experiencing the suffering of creatures afflicted by love. Out of these torments of the soul emerges the compensatory epiphany that makes Swann's story also precious to us readers as a drama of struggle toward insight. We are privileged by the narrator to be "coreaders" of a specific case of a general paradigm: that of human beings aspiring to rise above the base of existence. The life stories of less evolved persons such as Bloch implicitly belong to the generic superclass that Swann was on the verge of transcending.

It is no accident that the dimensions of all human evolution informing the framework of the descent into and emergence from the netherworld of dream in the famous overture also yield the primary metaphors. The overture is very much in the spirit of the opening of Novalis's *Heinrich von Ofterdingen* and *Hymnen an die Nacht* (Hymns to the Night) in the way Proust interweaves erotic arousal and awakening, on the one hand, and the sensuous surrender to dark origins and the desire to go home, either through the flesh to the mother or through death to God, on the other. The struggling consciousness circling between sleep and wakefulness, as between life and death, is a "traveler" but happy at the prospect of "being home again" (MKE 1.3–4).[16] In dream the narrator returns to the primordial oneness of the androgyne, whereupon Adam and Eve separate repeatedly (3); he loses his sense of the coordinates of time and space that fix his existence in the world as made manifest to reason, then regains them from the remotest "depths of an animal's consciousness" below that of the "cave-dweller" (4).[17] All levels of time from time immemorial are implicated in the act of self-location, such that the succession of moments organized as memory resembles both a succession of "rooms" and of sensations and feelings (5). Thus, the "body" of memory—whether as the sentient organism involved in the world or as the encompassing world—suggests the mysterious vehicular "envelope" of being that so frequently appears in some guise or other in Proust's pages. In the "Combray" part, the narrator speaks of "our friend's corporeal envelope" with regard to Swann; and it is clear that time is inverted by a return through the time-space flow, "as though one's life were a picture gallery in which all the portraits of any one period had a marked family likeness, a similar tonality" (24).[18] The musical analogy is that Swann, or

16. "voyageur"; "la douceur prochaine du retour" (R, 4).
17. "le sentiment de l'existence comme il peut frémir au fonds d'un animal"; "l'homme des cavernes" (R, 5).
18. "L'enveloppe corporelle de notre ami"; "comme s'il en était de notre vie ainsi que

indeed any other Proustian character or "envelope," exists as variations on a theme. To release that full music, finally symphonic, the mind must return to its own origins and recapture the rhythm of its own journey lightwards, a way once punctuated by something as simple as the (Wagnerian) "note of a bird in the forest" (2),[19] eventually by the irreducible human equivalent of art as in Vinteuil's phrase.

The vertigo unleashed by the aged narrator's realization of his position in time at the close of *Time Refound,* of his being like a church steeple soaring out of and over the abyss of human evolution and groundedness, reaffirms the earliest childhood experiences. Marking the coordinates, witnessing the steeples of Martinville in their perspectival dance as a teenager, which the as yet unnamed narrator Marcel does in *Swann's Way,* is prelude to his becoming such a steeple, a pinnacle of consciousness. William C. Carter argues that the ground pattern of the entire sequence of novels, as well as that presented in the first two, which remained closer to Proust's heart, was that of the fall from the quasi-paradise of childhood into the toils of error, vice, society, vanity, loss, and self-betrayal. The fall meant the necessary struggle upward in response to suffering, and against the threat of spiritual, therefore tragic, failure. In the case of the narrator, this struggle is heroic; he emerges from the exploration of human hell, and counters the obliterating assaults of time with moral vision. Because of suffering, Marcel is inspired to affirm the primary values of life and love such as he knew in the beginning, when half innocent.[20]

Richard E. Goodkin has explored several relatively neglected complexes of motifs in Proust involving vertical as against horizontal dimensions both in life and in storytelling. As he traces it in chapter 2 ("Proust and Home[r]: An Avuncular Intertext"),[21] the manifestations of the Odyssean principle in *In Search of Lost Time* are connected with digression, deferment, and lying (fiction), although eventually this horizontal, "avuncular" axis must reintersect with the vertical, "parental" axis of life-furtherance in the condition of time and the deep emotions that the realities of life and death impose. In Goodkin's elaborate argument about

d'un musée où tous les même portraits d'un même temps ont un air de famille, une même tonalité" (R, 19).

19. "le chant d'un oiseau dans une forêt" (R, 3). This reference to Wagner's Siegfried was probably clear to most of Proust's contemporaries.

20. See William C. Carter, *The Proustian Quest* (New York: New York University Press, 1992), especially ch. 5: "The Prison."

21. Richard E. Goodkin, *Around Proust* (Princeton, N.J.: Princeton University Press, 1991).

the doubleness of Odysseus as protagonist and storyteller in the Homeric original to which Proust openly alludes, one senses the persistence of a discovery Goodkin does not cite in a foundational novel about similar axes: Tristram's realization in book 1, chapter 22, of Laurence Sterne's *Tristram Shandy*, that "my work is digressive, and it is progressive too—and at the same time" and that his business is to provide "intersections" without causing the "whole machine" of his narration to founder, while at the same time Tristram recognizes, as in book 5, chapter 6, "our family was certainly a simple machine."[22]

In my view, Sterne is ancestral to each of our three chief artists, Proust, Mann, and Joyce, in multiple and specific regards. What Goodkin describes as Proust's "avuncularization" of the "parental" Homeric text, "the ultimate collapse of the parental axis" (Goodkin 36–37) seems to fit even better the story of the bachelor orphan Hans Castorp in *The Magic Mountain*, who is surrounded mainly by adoptive tutor-uncles, is a mourning melancholic, and achieves his most intense epiphanies via the vertical polarity of music, rather than on the safer horizontal plane of history, progress, and classical prose that Settembrini extols. Although the reintegrative Homeric metaphor of marriage triumphs at the end of *Ulysses*, the crisis in Joyce's novel involves Stephen's alienation from his natural family and reciprocally Bloom's loss of his son and bafflement at the crazed sexuality of his own father.[23]

But the intersections do occur, and, in larger outline, Proust's sevenfold novel grapples with a mystery that can only be glimpsed at moments in its sacramental wholeness. Much like Joyce's *Ulysses*, *In Search of Lost Time* is replete with sacramental symbols, especially with surrogates for the Eucharist such as drinking lime-tea with madeleines. But Joyce's treatment of the harrowing of hell in the "Circe" or "Nighttown" chapter stands closer to the Dantesque and Goethean models as modes of poetic vision.[24] The analogy to Odysseus's visit to the underworld in Homer is quite loose in the latter-day *Ulysses*; Joyce blends the Homeric infernal

22. Laurence Sterne, *The Life and Opinions of Tristram Shandy, Gentleman* (New York: Modern Library, n.d.), 73–74, 372.

23. James Joyce, *Ulysses: The Corrected Text*, ed. Hans Walter Gabler, with Wolfhard Steppe and Claus Melchior (New York: Vintage Books, 1986); see esp. the "Nighttown" chapter.

24. Why such modern analogues for harrowing hell as retrieving lost time, plumbing the unconscious, reinstantiating faded myth, and so forth, fit within the broader Dantesque framework is clear from an overview of the broader comic tradition by Haskell Block, "Theory of Comedy from Dante to Joyce," in *Comparative Literary Dimensions: Essays in Honor of Melvin J. Friedman*, ed. Jay L. Halio and Ben Siegel (Cranbury, N.J.: Associated University Presses, 2000), 19–30.

journey with the preceding episode at Circe's island, which ends when ancient Odysseus breaks her spell and gains valuable directions from her how to find hell's entrance. The analogous moment of liberation from abasement and of remobilization occurs as a double highpoint or symbolic marker in the respective careers of the parodic Virgil-Odysseus and Dante-Telemachus wandering through Dublin's bordello district. "Father" Bloom demands his "moly" back from the whore Zoe after grotesque humiliations and is reenergized to guide "son" Stephen to safety and home. In the later "Ithaca" chapter, out in the garden, we will get a glimpse of the ending of the *Paradiso* in the radiant light from Molly's window and from the stars overhead. In the "Nighttown" bordello, Stephen gets wound up to the point where, acting like a Siegfried, he raises his ashplant cane as his Nothung and smashes the false light of Bella's chandelier. Although it is more opera buffa when the young hero also falls on his face and must be helped by a solicitous non-Wotan, nonetheless the artist-elect Stephen reasserts his creative rebellion. With his usual deft touch, Joyce undercuts the grandiosity of Stephen's gesture of aspiration and simultaneously reinstates the theme of artistic mission.

Similarly, in a psychedelic insight vouchsafed to the reader rather than to the characters, Telemachus-Hamlet and Odysseus-Hamlet Senior fuse with the many identities of Shakespeare in the antlered looking-glass of "Nighttown." That is, as in Goethe's *Faust* 1 and 2, a larger framework encompasses the phantasmagorias. Far more is involved than a main psychodrama attributable to a chief protagonist (and comically explainable as a result of inebriation on a realistic plane). The reader experiences far more than merely advancing to an outcome for one privileged character or elaborating his fuller psychomachia. Actually, it is Bloom's idealized vision of his dead son Rudy as a teenager at the close, rather than Stephen's witty, alcoholic utterances, which we may justifiably consider the major culminating epiphany among several notable epiphanies of the "Circe" chapter. Neither Stephen's nor Bloom's psyche is the central motivator of the phantasmic moments; rather, the supreme narrator's demiurgic consciousness playfully spins togeher into a more comprehensive artifice a variety of fantasy constructs that could be plausibly attributed to them individually on the basis of earlier chapters. That is clear from a myriad of specific details such as the litany that the Daughters of Erin intone to a Christlike Bloom ("marked I.H.S."): "Kidney of Bloom, pray for us / Flower of the Bath, pray for us" and so forth for twelve lines (U 407). This series with its liturgical structure, imaginatively capped by a "choir of sixhundred voices" singing the Alleluia chorus "from Handel's *Messiah*" to the sound of an organ, serves the narrative function of recapitulating the many roles in which we have seen the All Father in prior chapters. It is something shared between author and reader. Here in this parody of sacred text Joyce shows himself once again to be a worthy heir to Rabelais for inventiveness in mobilizing story motifs as musical-linguistic elements.

As odd as the combination may seem, to understand the overarching format of a drama that contains wild Rabelaisian patches, it is worthwhile recalling the Goethean model. In its completed form, *Faust* not only comes wrapped in multiple layers of prologue and is posited as a vision in the tradition of baroque world theater, but it constantly reminds us of itself as a fiction. In the "Walpurgis Night" section of part 1, Mephisto assumes the role of a theater master at a very high level, staging illusions appropiate for dominating Faust. But at an even higher level, an authorial mind directs the composite fantasy that includes even Mephisto's function. Moreover, we are given unmistakable pointers as to the complexity of the series of events during an ostensible witches' sabbath by allusions to Shakespeare's multilayered *Midsummer Night's Dream*, to ancient myths, and to contemporary culture. Goethe's wildly anachronistic referentiality emerges ever more powerfully in part 2, as the play expands to reflect on "our" (i.e., the nineteenth-century reader's) present as the current product of a story of several millennia. When Joyce, in his turn, brings all time into the tropic space of a single day in Dublin, the many facets of Bloom and Stephen seem to float in the principal phantasmagoria of "Nighttown" as surfacing human moments that a deeper matrix spawns. Any closer inspection soon reveals that a controlling demiurgic irony is the arranger. We may argue, if our convictions so incline us, that this ironic voice takes its cues from an ultimately ungraspable source such as a Bergsonian, or Freudian, or Jungian unconscious. That does not change much in the observable authorial conduct of the "Circe" chapter or its rich literary referentiality.

Certainly, there is no presumptive "actual" hell behind the metaphoricity of hell or the hellish surface phenomena of a "life-force" in Joyce's *Ulysses*. In the "Wandering Rocks" chapter, the antagonist Buck Mulligan opines to Haines that "[t]hey drove his [Stephen's] wits astray [. . .] by visions of hell," thus incapacitating him for poetic creativity (U 204). But Haines, in turn, in disapproving tone, reports of Stephen, who in this instance is a fairly reliable gauge of authorial opinion, that "he can find no trace of hell in ancient Irish myth" (U 205). We have to assume that Stephen's insight conveyed to Haines was not fraught with double-edged, cultural self-doubt, because in the "Library" chapter he links his own struggle with the "nightmare" of time and his thesis of Shakespeare's struggle for reconciliation and atonement:

> If you want to know what are the events which cast their shadow over the hell of time of King Lear, Othello, Hamlet, Troilus and Cressida, look to see when and how the shadow lifts. What softens the heart of a man, shipwrecked in storms dire, Tried, like another Ulysses, Pericles, prince of Tyre? (U 160)

When the demiurgic narrator recasts Mulligan's voice in the gothic tale Mulligan utters in the "Oxen of the Sun" chapter, mocking Stephen's obsessions and playacting him as a guilt-obsessed, dark hero who is haunted by a vampiristic pursuer, Mulligan actually reinforces the thematic linkages with the hell of time and history in the reported speech: "My hell, and Ireland's, is in this life" (U 336–37). There are other more authoritative confirmations of these linkages as in the "Eumaeus" chapter when the "tired" old sailor, an avatar of Odysseus, talks about the necessity to venture on the ocean and "fly in the face of providence though it merely went to show how people usually contrived to load that sort of onus on to the other fellow like the hell idea and the lottery and insurance" (U 515).

Stephen also obviously possesses an imagination that presages the most extravagant demiurgic potential, although the survivor everyman, Bloom, like the archetypal sailor, shares something of Stephen's convention-piercing vision in his observations of his world as an insider-outsider. Stephen qualifies early on in the novel as the model for the future artist, just as clearly as does Proust's Marcel in *Swann's Way*. There is an important parallel between the way *Ulysses* makes us stare at the horror of life straight on, as in the bone-crunching mastication of the "Lestrygonians" chapter, but moves to a final affirmation, and the way Stephen's own initially "luciferic" understanding never buckles under the weight of the terrifying aspects of life and, reciprocally, Bloom prefers masochistic martyrdom to any negating struggle against life's terrible power. In the long run, Stephen will not permit himself to convert the hell of the mind into a "real" hell; that for him would be metaphysical capitulation, and in the "Circe" chapter he withstands the traditional "fire of hell" (U 474) and cries out "Non serviam" (U 474), when his mother as a ghoulish "green crab with malignant red eyes sticks deep its grinning claws in Stephen's

Harrowing Hell with Proust, Joyce, and Mann

heart" (U 475). Despite this peak of anguish, Stephen's destiny is to understand the father and mother and the primary creative act of engendering life and the affirmation to which art is related. His pathway bears broad analogy to that of Thomas Mann's tormented artist figure Tonio Kröger, who in the so-named novella of 1903 ends by affirming his love of the healthy and beautiful and ordinary. But there is a final twist in the conclusion of *Tonio Kröger:* it is only, and ironically, through its articulation in art that this passion for life can find enduring expression.

When Joyce lets his drunks roam through Nighttown in a Dionysiac frenzy, we sense deep down that we readers, following their story with ironic distance, are on the road to a new kind of paradise that supersedes Dante's. The goal is restated in modern, but not in essential, terms. We readily think of the quester figure Faust who explicitly has not reached the goal at the close of *Faust 2,* although Goethe's play tells us movingly what light guides us onward in the quest. This wonderful light floods forth into the garden of the "Ithaca" chapter after the searchers in *Ulysses* have been through hell. We cannot speak of an epiphany that is primarily experienced by a lead protagonist when the glow of Molly's lamp or the light of nature shines forth. Rather, the epiphany manifests an inner truth of the chapter itself, a chapter dense with the prolific and banal details of ordinary existence in an ordinary household, so dense that it suggests the infinite and, upon actually opening to macrocosmic distances, amounts to an incantatory buildup to the comic giganticism of the couple Bloom-Molly who serve as universal androgyne, and to the mysterious generative singsong of the divine alphabet. This incantation, which is not in the minds of the characters, but rather of the author and reader as sharer, finally returns the just intimated infinity into the dot, that is, into the end of a sentence, the cosmic center, the ovum, the zero point, and gateway of God. The key figures of this priviliged moment in the novel bear a relationship of coincidence that is magical in character as Gose argues generally for *Ulysses.* Gose corrects Goldman's

> thesis that Joyce adopts many styles in order to show the impossibility of any objective or finally authoritative view. As far as it goes, this approach is helpful in placing Joyce as a "complete artist," definitely above his creation. But it gives insufficient emphasis to that other side of Joyce, the artist within his work.[25]

25. Elliott B. Gose Jr., *The Transformation Process in Joyce's "Ulysses"* (Toronto: University of Toronto Press, 1980), 72.

Metamorphosis, Play, and the Laws of Life

In a first step, we may perceive that Stephen struggles initially to assert the position "above" creation, while Bloom muddles accommodatingly as an allround man within the world as created. However, Stephen gradually learns the necessity of merging with all the phenomena of life, is attracted toward his reciprocal other, and both he and Bloom recede into the huge mystery of Molly, who contains their mystery and exhibits attraction to them generically as their reciprocal other.

The closing "Penelope" chapter, with its startling linkages of the affective-poetic with the trivial, functions as the "other" that the novel flows into and is mirrored by. But the internal textual evidence of *Ulysses* permits no convincing case to be made that either the novel as a whole or the final chapter as a *pars pro toto* enacts symbolically a permanent entry into hellish captivity to life. Some critics like Kenner have sought to construe this culmination as a reinforcement of an ultimately religious insight into the horror of humanity's fallenness.[26] However, the love Molly still feels for Bloom reemerges from all her nitty-gritty musings as a turning point that leads toward the famous "yes" and this occurs in a manner that structurally reciprocates the recovery and affirmation in "Ithaca." Wachtel pushes to an opposite extreme a view of Stephen that counterbalances any overwrought interpretation such as Kenner's that Joyce is not truly affirming life through Molly. In effect, Stephen is not just a Telemachus, but also an Orestes who in his own mind has indeed committed the crime of killing his mother and who resists the emotional realities she represented—in an evasion and rejection of something fundamental in himself.[27] Gose formulates more moderately and convincingly, on the basis of the "Oxen of the Sun" chapter, the general conformity between Joyce's unsentimental approach to nature, frequently perceived as grotesque, and the work as a whole with its bewildering plethora of elements and styles:

> [. . .] the embryo itself in its organic metamorphoses is also constantly distorted, any stage appearing ugly and unrecognizable by our standards of humanness. Yet each stage is essential to the next and to the creature we finally call human. [. . .] One of Joyce's purposes [. . .] was to make us face the grotesque history of our evolutionary growth. (Gose 84)

---

26. Hugh Kenner, *Ulysses*, rev. ed. (Baltimore: Johns Hopkins University Press, 1987).
27. Albert Wachtel, *The Cracked Looking Glass: James Joyce and the Nightmare of History* (Selinsgrove, Pa.: Susquehanna University Press, 1992), ch. 7.

Ultimately, by going through the poetic hell of observing the bizarre details of which life is compounded, we learn there is no actual hell. While Stephen as intellectual may reenact discovery of the gonopsychical connection expounded by Sterne, and while Bloom as practical allround man may wallow in the flesh, their high and low are reciprocal as heaven is to hell or, as Joyce notes with a touch of Rabelaisian reminiscence in the *Wake*, "The tasks above are as the flasks below, saith the emerald canticle of Hermes."[28] The miracle of *Ulysses* is that Joyce goes beyond any gnostic rebellion when he subsumes the "no" (of the spirit which negates) and the "yes" (of life or the flesh which affirms) in a Cusanan coincidence of opposites.

In chapter thirteen, I shall discuss the conjunction of zero and infinity in the cabalistic metaphor of the gate. In chapter ten, I have considered ways in which language participates in the same mystery, when Joyce demonstrates how meaning emerges even at the seemingly lowest levels of natural sounds, how words exhibit evolutionary traces from their primordial origins, and how utterance in speech and writing embodies psychodynamic factors that spring from the family romance. On first reading, *Ulysses* appears chaotic and incomprehensible for long stretches. In a chapter section entitled "Determinism Is Not Enough," Rice has astutely noted that behind this initial perception more is at work bringing forth order than just the patterns Joyce embeds that "represent the immanent design of the novel, the deterministic structures of the creator, the lawgiver"; for there is also the "emergent structure" comprising random features that "gradually combine into a community of behavior as the novel takes on a mind and life of its own."[29] The meaning of this living complex system eludes its participants much as the meaning of our world eludes us. Rice argues that, whereas Stephen resists acceptance of his own limitation by reason of existential involvement, in contrast Bloom's acceptance is radical, and this direction, not merely Stephen's still unripe sonhood, should guide critics in grasping also the deeper sense of *Finnegans Wake*. Once again, Gose is more temperate in describing how Joyce may be training the reader to cope with the grotesque that assaults us in the Circean psychodrama in which Bloom "reverts to the animal in order to gain more of the human" and the "imperfect world is a chal-

28. James Joyce, *Finnegans Wake* (New York: Penguin Books, 1976), 263.21–22, hereafter cited as W followed by page and line number.
29. Thomas Jackson Rice, *Joyce, Chaos, and Complexity* (Urbana and Chicago: University of Illinois Press, 1997), 107.

lenge to the artist who has a better chance to create a better world, not by reducing the natural one to a static condition of pleasant unreality, but by reproducing the vitality which social convention tries to hide, by restoring the terrible mystery that materialism tries to assuage" (Gose 165).

Proust certainly pays attention to physical tics and oddities, to family, class, and racial traits; especially in the latter five novels of *In Search of Lost Time,* he devotes inordinate space to obsessions, perversions, and decadence. In *Time Refound,* he is a profound psychohistorian in analyzing the strangeness of the conditions of wartime and individual and collective motivations and responses in a suspension of "daytime" rules as this occurred in real history. And in these respects he resembles Mann rather than Joyce. In Proust, generally the focus remains meditatively on the psychological laws of development and on existential suffering, although evocation of joy in fleeting privileged moments offsets everything demeaning, so that Proust affirms a vision of sacramental wholeness in a fashion clearer on a traditional basis. What poses difficult choices for interpreters of Joyce becomes more obvious when he takes us permanently into the night in his nightbook *Finnegans Wake.* Does the continuity of the powerful organicist tradition of the West break down under the burden of the grotesque, the fragmentary, and the weird in Joyce, despite all the reassuring cabalistic, alchemical, and mystical hints; does haunting awareness of the sacred founder in the atomistic bric-a-brac, the myriad of puzzles, a "mirrorminded curiositease" (W 576), when the text is exposed as a machine recycling detritus? Treip argues that awakening is problematic in the *Wake* because "a questionable recollection or reinscription of effects of the unconscious within the lawbound subject, then, doubles up through the ricorso structure as a questioning of the laws of history, too."[30] That is, the repression inherent in patriarchal authority is confronted in the unending story of the course of language and the family romance. However, we must always keep in mind that the telling of this eternal story is an enactment of a mystery that subsumes the coincidence of opposites and involves a transaction between the realms of life and death. Understanding the relationship between coming into being and the permanence of the ungraspable origin requires hermetic knowledge.

Hugh Kenner, one of Joyce's most insightful readers, has concluded that Einstein, Gödel, Picasso, and Joyce, each in his own way, "and oth-

30. Andrew Treip, "'As per Periodicity': Vico, Freud and the Serial Awakening of Book III, Chapter 4," in *"Finnegans Wake": "teems of times,"* ed. Andrew Treip (Atlanta: Rodopi, 1994), 22.

ers, terminate the dualism between the art or science and its materials," that the existence of Joyce's characters is "wholly conferred by systems of words," and that "*Ulysses* is the first book to be a kind of hologram of language, creating a three-dimensional illusion out of the controlled interference between our experience of language and its arrangement of language" (Kenner, 154, 155, 157). Thus, the book may attract a plethora of linguistic materials associated with myths and religions, but Joyce strikes us as being a reenactor of mythologems and archetypes primarily because he recognized these as excellent materials for composing a work of art, without the work necessarily being a medium of advocacy or rescue of particular beliefs or mentalities. Such a view places Joyce more squarely on one side of a divide with Mann on the other side, as John J. White has formulated the distinction between two strains in the modern novel: "Whereas the role of mythological motifs is analogical, describing the modern world in the light of a readily available set of models, works that are mythical do not offer myths as analogies, but make them their principal subject-matter or structural principle."[31] If we were to reverse Kenner's proposition, we might wonder whether the subordination of various motif clusters to the disparate stylistic demands of chapters actually overwhelms any deep attachments on Joyce's part to specific mythologems or only occultates and protects the reenactment of sacred patterns. In Mann's case, there can be no doubt about his keen interest in the older concept of prefiguration. His remarks about the difference between the ancient and modern understandings of self in his essay "Freud und die Zukunft" (Freud and the Future, 1936) demonstrated this at the time he was beginning his *Joseph* project.

There is a striking affinity between Joyce and Mann as novelists who see the hermetic principle in artistic creation as a transaction with death, because the artist literally crosses the boundary that separates the past from the present and any present, in turn, from its future. One of the most powerful expressions of this insight into the artist's role of mediating between life and death is the subchapter "Fullness of Harmony" ("Fülle des Wohllauts") in *The Magic Mountain* (1927) when Hans Castorp maintains his sanity in the sloughs of saturnine despair by playing that curious new device, the electrical gramophone.[32] The needle, an-

31. John J. White, *Mythology in the Modern Novel: A Study of Prefigurative Techniques* (Princeton, N.J.: Princeton University Press, 1971), 7.

32. Thomas Mann, *The Magic Mountain*, trans. John E. Woods (New York: Vintage Books, 1995); hereafter cited as MM followed by the page number.

other among many manifestations of the hermetic wand in this novel, elicits an incredible variety of instrumental and vocal music from seemingly identical dead records in a simultaneously undulating, circular and straight flow. The inexorability of onmoving time is as unmistakably visible as is the permanence of the crypt. The gramophone is "[t]he German soul, up-to-date"; and the records, a new form of "library" (MM 628).[33] As Hans sits before "this truncated coffin of fiddlewood" (MM 633),[34] he faces the puzzling lure of death in music as in life, "this enchantment of the soul with dark consequences," but his thoughts are "enhanced, forced upward by alchemy" (MM 643).[35] By triumphing over himself and discovering "love," Hans embodies, in the fullness of his sentiments, as the representative "middle" and our "medium," a nobly human attitude in harmony with the sublime message of his favorite opera *Aida*.

Jason Apuzzo has argued that the tetralogy *Joseph und seine Brüder* (Joseph and His Brothers, 1933–1944)[36] completes the movement from an older, essentially romantic orientation to the Dionysian, which the assumption of a modernist, essentially hermetic vision displaces.[37] Mann's conscious turning away from the "bourgeois" to the "mythic" as subject matter was a way of coping with the actuality of the crisis that *The Magic Mountain* instinctively feared could recur in a more virulent form. As Apuzzo shows in a careful contextualization of Mann's work on the biblical story, the author never abandoned his advocacy of humanistic and political democracry after World War I or his special orientation to Goethe as the world-historical representative of bourgeois civilization. This lasting mature commitment may in part explain why Mann employs a serial variety of mythic condensation in the *Joseph* tetralogy, finally linking the ancient chapters of the romance of the soul with the contemporary world (from Tammuz-Adonis to Roosevelt!), rather than merging mythological motifs in a mosaic of repetitive fragments—the primary Joycean habit, in White's view (chapter 5).

33. "Die deutsche Seele up to date. Da haben Sie die Literatur" (Thomas Mann, *Der Zauberberg: Roman* [Frankfurt: Fischer Taschenbuch Verlag, 1987], 774; hereafter cited as Zb followed by the page number).

34. "dieses gestutzten Sarges aus Geigenholz" (Zb, 680).

35. "dieses Seelenzaubers mit finsteren Konsequenzen"; "alchimistisch gesteigerten Gedanken" (Zb, 691).

36. Thomas Mann, *Joseph und seine Brüder*, 4 vols. (Frankfurt: Fischer Taschenbuch Verlag, 1991), vol. 1, *Die Geschichten Jaakobs*; hereafter cited as GJ. Thomas Mann, *Joseph and His Brothers*, trans. H. T. Lowe-Porter, introduction by Thomas Mann (New York: Alfred A. Knopf, 1974); hereafter cited as JHB followed by the page number.

37. Jason Alexander Apuzzo, "The End of the Millennium: Thomas Mann and the Last Romantic Generation" (Ph.D. diss., Stanford University, 1998).

Harrowing Hell with Proust, Joyce, and Mann

There are, of course, earlier highpoints in Mann's fiction when descent into an abyss or into lost or repressed knowledge of the past and the psyche provoke a manifestation of a hermetic principle. The more explicit emergence of Hermes, following the initial sequence of avatars who intimate Dionysus in *Death in Venice,* imparts a final heightening complexity to the reference to Venice as a necropolis and Aschenbach's final entry into death on the beach at the Lido.[38] Mann openly analogizes the enchantment on the Swiss "magic mountain" to a Dantesque entry into and traversing of hell. Mann's humoristic-encyclopedic dissertation on the educational pathway restates the requirement that the spiritually enervated Western protagonist "fall" so as to regain the road to his humanity. One of the most important internal synedochic models for the entire passage is the archetypal dream in the "Snow" subchapter. Hans is lured into the heartless indifference of the mountain heights, and in parallel he regresses into the forgotten horrors of a mindless nature, drawn back toward a primordial origin, before human culture and with it the romance of the soul emerged. But Hans penetrates only to a provisional depth; going the whole unimaginable distance would mean annihilation as a human creature. Clinging to the ski hut, surrogate of home and temple, and borne by the magical power of music in his mind, he arrives in the precincts of the ancient Mediterranean and witnesses the archaic moment when humanity has already, recently (the temporal measure is relative), attained form and dignity. Instinctively responding to the direction pointed by a youth who combines attributes of Hermes and St. John the Baptist, Hans walks backwards in evolutionary time from the harbinger of Christianity, a lovely mother with child; passes the statutes of unnamed Demeter and Persephone; and discovers in a secret chamber behind the temple altar witches who are dismembering and devouring a child. The shock of this plunge into the remoter depths of the past from his provisional arrival point precipitates Hans's inner avowal of loyalty to a humane vision and solidifies his resistance to the abyss. As our protagonist of the democratic-bourgeois era, Hans discovers that "in the middle is where the homo Dei's state is" (MM 486);[39] of course, on the level of the reader's relationship to the novel, Hans has "dreamed a poem of humankind" and succeeded in dreaming "it to its end, to its goal" (MM 487)[40] because the author has invested

38. See chapter eleven, "The Ways of Hermes in the Works of Thomas Mann."
39. "in der Mitte ist des Homo Dei Stand" (Zb, 522).
40. "einen Reim gemacht, ein Traumgedicht vom Menschen"; "zu Ende geträumt und recht zum Ziele" (Zb, 523).

him with hermetic character as our "medium" and in so doing identifies the task of the modern artist and age as hermetic.

Mann's *Joseph* tetralogy begins in the reconstructive hermetic mode. The narrative voice who speaks in the overture to *Die Geschichten Jaakobs* (The Tales of Jacob), the opening volume, envisions untold eons with a demiurgic distance worthy of Joyce, yet recalls them within the framework of a meditative wisdom that reminds us of Proust during the prelude to the invocation of Combray in springtime. One difference from Proust is that we do not work our way through explicit existential attachments of a perceiving subject whose own particular story is striving to be born. Rather, in Mann's "Vorspiel" (Prelude), subtitled "Höllenfahrt" (Descent into Hell), the narrating voice as "we" engages us readers as "you" collectively in the virtually magical act of transporting ourselves imaginatively to the "reality" of the "mild spring freshness of a summer-starry night" (JHB 34)[41] in the ancient Near East. Only after the protagonist Joseph is brought into focus does the narrator slip back into the traditional singular as "I." The guiding voice that harrows hell swiftly synthesizes insights that are based on "our" accrued historical and literary lore; Mann's narrator summons accrued anthropological knowledge in order to evoke and enter the distinct ancestral mentality of a key family cited in Genesis (the book about origins) through whom the Jewish people imparted a special shape to religious development and to the "romance of the soul" (JHB 25).[42] Like Proust and Joyce, Mann conveys the modernist realization that all evolutionary time is copresent in the immediate act of coming to consciousness.

The starting proposition and question on page 1 of the *Joseph* novels boldly implicate our present being in a "mystery" that recedes deeper and deeper from one provisional origin to another:

Very deep is the well of the past. Should we not call it bottomless?

Bottomless indeed, if—and perhaps only if—the past we mean is the past merely of the life of mankind, that riddling essence of which our own normally unsatisfied and quite abnormally wretched existences form a part; whose mystery, of course, includes our own and is the alpha and omega of all our questions, lending burning immediacy to all we say, and significance to all our striving. For the deeper we sound, the further down into the lower world of the past we probe

41. "die milde Frische der sommerlich ausgestirnten Frühlingsnacht" (GJ, 39).
42. "der Roman der Seele" (GJ, 30).

and press, the more do we find that the earliest foundations of humanity, its history and culture, reveal themselves unfathomable. (JHB 3)[43]

Instead of landing at some proximate surface, nearer a comforting
provisional origin of our twentieth-century world such as the Middle
Ages, we come to rest at a remoter juncture amidst the names of gods,
people, and places that formed the context for Joseph's sense of a beginning, for his rootedness in the tradition of being descended from a
brooding unquiet ancestor from Ur. Serendipitously, "Ur" is the German syllable that suggests the originary, foundational, and archetypal. In rehearsing the sometimes murky, variant strands of the ancestral
story, and introducing mythic awareness on Joseph's part, the narrating voice acknowledges the trace of a pathway that led to Joseph and also
the qualitative differences in the sense of Time governing at that "morning" threshold (implicit in the German term "Morgenland" for Orient),
in contrast to what the passage of centuries comes to mean later "in our
western history" (JHB 7),[44] a history that eventually is conscious of its
"evening" status ("western" actually is "abendlich" in Mann's original
German). Nonetheless, Joseph's brain reels when peering into Time's
abyss just as ours does because he is already human like us, "almost contemporary," and "just as remote as we, mathematically speaking, from
the beginnings of humanity" (JHB 9).[45] As harrower of hell, the novelist lifts back into the light of a poetic Today the mythological lore of the
Near East and Egypt, and reinstates that Yesterday's feeling of pastness
and origins, of a boundary between things pertaining to life in the here-
and-now and things "'from the days of Set'" (JHB 12).[46] This conjuration
of the days of Joseph has the effect of making him seem more present for
his being on his own side of a boundary beyond the days of Set, much as
we ordinarily sense ourselves to be in our own existences vis-à-vis the

43. "Tief ist der Brunnen der Vergangenheit. Sollte man ihn nicht unergründlich nennen? Dies nämlich dann sogar und vielleicht eben dann, wenn nur und allein das Men-
schenwesen es ist, dessen Vergangenheit in Rede und Frage steht: dies Rätselwesen, das
unser eigenes natürlich-lusthaftes und übernatürlich-elendes Dasein in sich schließt und
dessen Geheimnis sehr begreiflicherweise das A und O all unseres Redens und Fragens
bildet, allem Reden Bedrängtheit und Feuer, allem Fragen seine Inständigkeit verleiht.
Da denn nun gerade geschieht es, daß, je tiefer man schürft, je weiter hinab in die Unter-
welt des Vergangenen man dringt und tastet, die Anfangsgründe des Menschlichen, seiner Geschichte, seiner Gesittung, sich als gänzlich unerlotbar erweisen . . ." (GJ, 5).
44. "in unserer abendlichen Geschichte" (GJ, 10).
45. "fühlen wir uns ihm nahe und zeitgenössisch"; "von den Anfangsgründen der
Menschheit . . . mathematisch genommen ebenso weit entfernt wie wir" (GJ, 12).
46. "'Aus den Tagen des Seth'" (GJ, 15).

past. But the narrating voice by no means simply allows that evoked ancient context to swallow us. Instead, Mann zestfully cites anthropological theories about the evolutionary steps in human culture: the earliest domestication of animals, the expansion of agriculture, the invention of writing and other arts, the accretion of myths and emergence of religious systems, the attempts by earlier thinkers to explain phenomena and beliefs, and so forth. He counterpoises theories of the geological and environmental processes that have affected human life over the ages to relatively newer cultural traces. Situated against this distinctly modern repertory of interpretation, Joseph the biblical figure assumes a position much closer to us.

In a very fine chapter on the *Joseph* overture, Clayton Koelb has paid particular attention to the balance between the unfathomability of the past and the effective permanance of things human, and to the precision of Mann's rhetoric in relating the search for origins to the nature of storytelling.[47] Koelb also notes the paradoxical relationship between life and death (56), the necrophilia in history (62), and the interplay of linear and circular motion (64)—aspects of Mannian narration where, in my view, Hermes became as necessary for Mann as he was for Joyce. Koelb justifiably notes in passing as a special form of the Eros-Thanatos tension the Mannian narrator's homoerotic bond with Joseph as ephebe. George Bridges has argued that this relationship is part of an elaborate revisionist interpretation of the Old Testament reaching throughout the tetralogy.[48] In Bridges's reading, Mann detects a phallic theology in the development of the highly patriarchal Jewish religion wherein love of a Father God displaces the bonding between the generations and subsumes the feminine.

This possible twist to a late moment in the family romance which Genesis sets forth is not the only direction in which our minds are tasked to move. Quite explicitly our "deluded pilgrimage" and "onward luring hoax" in search of the origins yields nightmarish intimations as we penetrate beyond and before such traditions as the Garden of Eden and the Fall, beyond the oldest "time-coulisse" to the larval state of humanity, until Eden appears to metamorphose into hell (JHB 23).[49] But at the end

---

47. Clayton Koelb, *Legendary Figures: Ancient History in Modern Novels* (Lincoln: University of Nebraska Press, 1998).

48. George Bridges, Thomas Mann's *"Joseph und seine Brüder" and the Phallic Theology of the Old Testament* (New York: Peter Lang, 1995).

49. "Blendwerk und hinlockende Fopperei einer Wanderschaft!"; "kulissenhaft scheinbares Wegesziel" (GJ, 27).

of section 7, the "Prelude" indeed takes a remarkable metaphysical turn out of time by asserting that "the history of man is older than the material world, which is the work of his will, older than life, which rests upon his will" (JHB 23).[50] As a more secure anchor point, we take hold of "a very ancient tradition [. . .] incorporated into the succession of religions, prophesies and doctrines of the East," the idea of "a youthful being made out of pure light, formed before the beginning of the world as prototype and abstract of humanity [. . .]" who was "God's chosen champion in the struggle against that evil which penetrated into the new creation," yet "fell into bondage to lower nature"—which explains "man's double self" (JHB 23–24).[51] In the narrator's overview of the myth or romance, which is heavily influenced by Novalis, God eventually sends spirit, drawn out of the divine substance, "to awaken the soul, in its self-forgetful involvement with form and death, to the memory of its higher origins" (JHB 25–26).[52] Mann's supplement to the tradition ("obviously the tradition requires filling out on this point" [JHB 25])[53] consists in his positing that spirit too was prone to alienation from its duties because it could not wholly enjoy its "reputation as the principle of death and the destroyer of form" (JHB 26)[54] and became virtually traitorous out of sympathy for the soul's passional involvement in form and life. A related dialectic springs from the fact that the spirit is "essentially the principle of the future," whereas "the goodness of the form-bound soul has reference to the past

50. "die Geschichte des Menschen ist älter als die materielle Welt, die seines Willens Werk ist, älter als das Leben, das auf seinem Willen steht" (GJ, 27).

51. "Eine lange [. . . [Denküberlieferung] . . .] als Erbgut eingegangen in die Religionen, Prophetien und einander ablösenden Erkenntnislehren des Ostens [. . .]"; "zu fassen als ein Jünglingswesen aus reinem Licht, geschaffen vor Weltbeginn als Urbild und Inbegriff der Menschheit"; "der erkorene Streiter Gottes im Kampfe gegen das in die junge Schöpfung eingedrungene Böse gewesen"; "sei in die Bande der niederen Natur geraten"; "die Doppelnatur des Menschen" (GJ, 27–8). Mann adroitly suggests the "East" as a general locus of religious heritage, and avoids privileging an Indic or Persian or any other specific homeland. He gestures backwards toward Zoroastrian, Gnostic, Alexandrian, and other sources, and forwards toward Christianity with its redeemer figure, while his main drama is set in the Holy Land and Egypt. It is interesting to consider Mann's Joseph tetralogy in the light of an evolving cultural debate over "identity" from the Renaissance onward in which Europeans could feel attracted to the "authority" of various origins. Especially relevant for the terms pertinent to an analysis of Mann's options and choices is Dorothy M. Figueira, *Aryans, Jews, and Brahmins: Theorizing Authority through Myths of Identity* (Albany: State University of New York Press, 2002), which explains the thematics from the eighteenth century to the Nazi debacle.

52. "der selbstvergessenen, in Form und Tod verstrickten Seele das Gedächtnis ihrer höheren Herkunft zu wecken" (GJ, 30).

53. "nach dieser Richtung deutlich der Ergänzung bedarf" (GJ, 30).

54. "seinen Ruf, das tödliche und auf Zerstörung der Formen ausgehende Prinzip zu sein" (GJ, 31).

and the holy," but "the mystery, and the unexpressed hope of God, lie in their union, in the genuine penetration of the spirit into the world of the soul, in the inter-penetration of both principles, in a hallowing of the one through the other" (JHB 29).[55]

What concerns Mann is "not calculable time. Rather it is time's abrogation and dissolution in the alternation of tradition and prophecy"— when various aspects of "the myth [. . .] became a mysterium, and there was no distinction left between being and meaning" (JHB 18).[56] Thus, as he descends "into the unsounded depths of the past" (JHB 27),[57] into an eternal present as timeless as death, the narrator feels a kinship with the restless wanderers, Jacob and his family, whose world he conjures. Mann spells out his favorite analogy between the work of art as mythic embodiment, thus a lawful feast exempt from ordinary time, which we know already from the "Foreword" ("Vorsatz") to *The Magic Mountain*. The reformulation in the Joseph overture is striking:

> For the essence of life is presentness, and only in a mythical sense does its mystery appear in the time-forms of past and future. [. . .] For it is, always is, however much we may say It was. Thus speaks the myth, which is only the garment of the mystery. But the holiday garment of the mystery is the feast, the recurrent feast which bestrides the tenses and makes the has-been and the to-be present to the popular sense. (JHB 33)[58]

And as in *The Magic Mountain*, there is a sacramental feasting on death and the depths when the artist creates an epic, but the restless smitten spirit infuses the celebration with its blessing from above. As Mann fluctuates to and fro among anthropological speculation, med-

55. "ganz wesentlich das Prinzip der Zukunft"; "die Frömmigkeit der formverbundenen Seele dem Vergangenen gilt und dem heiligen" (GJ, 34); "Das Gedächtnis aber und die stille Hoffnung Gottes liegt vielleicht in ihrer Vereinigung, nämlich in dem echten Eingehen des Geistes in die Welt der Seele, in der wechselseitigen Durchdringung der beiden Prinzipien und der Heiligung des einen durch das andere" (GJ, 34–35).

56. "ist nicht die bezifferbare Zeit. Es ist vielmehr ihre Aufhebung im Geheimnis der Vertauschung von Überlieferung und Prophezeiung"; "der Mythus wurde [. . .] ein Mysterium, und zwischen Sein und Bedeuten fehlte es an jedem Unterscheidungsraum" (GJ, 22).

57. "hinab in den nie erloteten Brunnenschlund der Vergangenheit" (GJ, 38).

58. "[Vorsatz]: Denn das Wesen des Lebens ist Gegenwart, und nur in mythischer Weise stellt sein Geheimnis sich in den Zeitformen der Vergangenheit und der Zukunft dar"; "Denn es ist, ist immer, möge des Volkes Redeweise auch lauten: Es war. So spricht der Mythus, der nur das Kleid des Geheimnisses ist; aber des Geheimnisses Feierkleid ist das Fest, das wiederkehrende, das die Zeitfälle überspannt und das Gewesene und Zukünftige seiend macht für die Sinne des Volkes" (GJ, 38–39).

itation on the nature of time and on the romance linking soul, spirit, and matter, and evocation of a youthful Holy Land on a moon-lit spring night, the encantatory rhythms transport us much as the prelude to the "Snow" subchapter in *The Magic Mountain* carries us to the eternal ancient Mediterranean and as Proust's overture summons Combray in springtime. The archmodernist and hermeticist Mann abrogates time in order to celebrate life lived in the condition of time and to redeem humanity's lost past as a spiritual romance ever relevant to the fulfillment of the human.

13 THE HAUNTED NARRATOR BEFORE THE GATE (JOYCE, KAFKA, HESSE, BUTOR)

Go through, go through the gates. (Isaiah 62:10)[1]

Yes. Gate. Safe! (Ulysses 183)[2]

This seemed to me to be worth looking into and I went in at this door. (Steppenwolf 217)[3]

The master narrative is the account of our expulsion from the Garden of Eden, the start of the human family in the condition of time and the flesh, and the foundation of the first city (Genesis 3, 4). The gates of life and death as entrance and exit still demarcate our passage through this condition, although a higher City has meanwhile superseded the lost Garden as the refuge beckoning to the pilgrims who journey homeward as a consequence of the fortunate fall. Hence the Psalmist speaks of "This gate of the Lord, into which the righteous shall enter" (118:20), while the Evangelist advises "Enter ye at the strait gate" (Matthew 7:13–14).

By the twentieth century, James Joyce's demiurgic eye gazes unflinchingly at more recent wanderers in life's labyrinth. The crisscrossing paths of Stephen Dedalus and Leopold Bloom—among so many other things in a representative lower city, "dear, dirty Dublin" (U 145)—enact the perplexity that the mind experiences before the fundamental story. Stephen searches in heroic anguish, dispossession, and exile as Telemachus-Hamlet for the creative source. The all-too-human father figure Bloom yearns for a son and heir and disappears back into the mys-

---

1. Scriptural references in this chapter are based on the King James version.
2. Citations of this work, henceforth indicated by the abbreviation U, are drawn from James Joyce, *Ulysses* (New York: Vintage Books, 1961).
3. Citations of this work, henceforth indicated by the abbreviation S, are drawn from Hermann Hesse, *Steppenwolf,* trans. Basil Creighton, rev. Joseph Mileck (New York: Bantam Books, 1969).

terious, inexhaustible totality of the All Mother, his wife Molly. The sign closing the "Ithaca" chapter and thus standing as our gate to Molly's famous monologue of the "Penelope" chapter is a printed dot. It is the ovum, the virtual zero point of entrance and exit, qualitative infinity at the core, the gateway between waking and dreaming, and the final period rounding out every life sentence. Surrender through faith reaches its comic extreme in Bloom's masochistic dedication to the "yes," while Stephen's filial cerebrations gradually reveal the promise of his own maturation and fatherhood as a creative artist.

The novel *Ulysses* (1922) seems to function as a gate of convergence through which all the past emerges reconstituted in an infinite present. From the "Oxen of the Sun" chapter onward, Joyce ever more closely interweaves Bloom's and Stephen's roles. The obsession with *Hamlet* as one of the great "ghost-stories" in the "Nestor" chapter and with Shakespeare as the supreme model of the haunted artist in the "Proteus" chapter attains a major turning point in the "Scylla and Charybdis" chapter.[4] Joyce once again links the Judeo-Christian Adamic and Logos myths and the theme of the haunted condition of modern narration through Stephen's theory of "postcreation" in the "Oxen of the Sun" chapter—the idea that "In woman's womb word is made flesh but in the spirit of the maker all flesh that passes becomes the word that shall not pass away" (U 391). In the psychedelic "Circe" chapter, father and son become consubstantial for us when we cowitness their images merging with the face of cuckolded Shakespeare in the tarnished mirror held up to nature (U 567). In the "Ithaca" chapter, the father and son repeat this act of "each contemplating the other in both mirrors of the reciprocal flesh of theirhisnothis fellowfaces" while the mystery of an "invisible person," the wife-mother, is "denoted by a visible splendid sign, the lamp," the light of nature (U 702). Stephen sets forth through the garden gate from the father's house by the glow of the feminine principle without which creation cannot occur.

Only a few years later, in Franz Kafka's *The Trial* (1925), the bank functionary Joseph K. awakens under arrest in the muted light of Prague, another labyrinth, and is condemned to go forever knocking at portals, searching in rooms and halls, for a way to define his condition and justify himself. There is something he ought to know that eludes him right

4. The thematics of Hamletism are treated at greater length in chapter eight, "Afterthoughts of Hamlet."

up to the moonlit moment when, still without an answer, he is sacrificed in a mysterious rite (which may parodically modify the biblical story of Isaac). Among the many synecdochic parts that can stand on their own and also serve as complete models of the novel, the culminating chapter "In the Cathedral" provides unmistakable equivalences for the modern experience of being lost in one's own "city." It contains, in turn, its own synecdochic core, the parable of the gate to the Law, to which Joseph K. is drawn and summoned. When he enters the cathedral—as if into a forgotten interiority, a lost cultural universe, and a haunting enigma—the impaired condition of his soul is apparent from his reliance on a dictionary and a tourist album.

K. is the lonely, obtuse modern person reduced to cultural tourism within the monumental construct left as a ghostlike provocation in the heart of the city. He gropes in its complexity with the puny aid of his pocket torch, but, symptomatically, when he is attracted into yet more interior space, a side chapel, he has difficulty recognizing the key scene in its altarpiece as a coherent totality: "a portrayal of Christ being laid in the tomb, conventional in style and a fairly recent painting" (T 205).[5] Observing this revelation of the sacrifice of a son through K.'s eyes piecemeal, the reader discovers that a witness of the key scene in antiquity is still present in a puzzling way. He appears as a figure in the painting, a recent interpretation that echoes those forming the tradition over the intervening ages. This atavistic figure conveys the urge to draw near and witness the mystery, and soon the verger acts overtly as a herald directing K.'s attention toward the high altar, sanctuary lamp, and pulpit, to which a preacher ascends. Figures gradually emerge out of the "deep caverns of darkness" of the "empty" church as in the drawings of Odilon Redon. In the night condition of K.'s mind, which Kafka conveys by indirect speech, thoughts well up in a way similar to the emergence of such personae in his environs. One of K.'s notions signals his need for the missing feminine ("But somewhere there was an old woman before an image of the Madonna; she ought to be there too"; T 207).[6]

5. Citations of this work, henceforth indicated by the abbreviation T, are drawn from Franz Kafka, *The Trial*, trans. Willa Muir and Edwin Muir, rev. E. M. Butler (New York: Schocken Books, 1984). German citations, indicated by the abbreviation P, are drawn from Franz Kafka, *Der Prozeß: Roman*, ed. Max Brod (New York: Schocken Books, 1953). The original here reads: "eine Grablegung Christi in gewöhnlicher Auffassung, es war übrigens ein neueres Bild" (P, 246).

6. "Übrigens gab es ja noch irgendwo vor einem Marienbild ein altes Weib, das auch hätte kommen sollen" (P, 49).

The Haunted Narrator before the Gate

At last "the size of the Cathedral strikes K. as bordering on the limit of what human beings could bear" (T 208f.),[7] but the reader's apprehension leaps because of K.'s persisting desire to evade the spirit of the priest's message. In a futile repetition of his resistance to the Court, K. still tries to insist on his innocence and attributes his troubles to a lack of women supporters who could influence "this Court, which consists almost entirely of petticoat-hunters" (T 211).[8] There is no meaningful retreat back through the church "doorway" (T 209)[9] into the day-world we have left permanently behind; Kafka underscores that with a macabre touch of gothic humor:

> There was no longer even a murky daylight; black night had set in. All the stained glass in the great window could not illumine the darkness of the wall with one solitary glimmer of light. And at this very moment the verger began to put out the candles on the high altar. "Are you angry with me?" asked K. of the priest. (T 211)[10]

The priest gives K. a small lamp to carry and, pacing up and down with him in the darkness as if in a Jewish ceremony (cf. Bloom and Stephen in the "Ithaca" chapter), imparts the parable of the open "door leading into the Law as always," but guarded by a powerful "doorkeeper," beyond whom stand yet more powerful guards at further doors (T 213).[11] In the priest's tale, an entire lifetime of arguments, importunities, and bribes by a seeker eager to enter are to no avail, and finally the world darkens around him. "But in the darkness he can now perceive a radiance that streams inextinguishably from the door of the Law" (T 214).[12] The seeker's lifetime condenses into the single question, "why no one

7. "auch schien ihm die Größe des Doms gerade an der Grenze des für Menschen noch erträglichen zu liegen" (P, 250).

8. "diesem Gericht, das fast nur aus Frauenjägern besteht" (P, 253).

9. "dem Ausgang" [literally, "way out"] (P, 250).

10. "Das war kein trüber Tag mehr, das war schon tiefe Nacht. Keine Glasmalerei der großen Fenster war imstande, die dunkle Wand auch nur mit einem Schimmer zu durchbrechen. Und gerade jetzt begann der Kirchendiener, die Kerzen auf dem Hauptaltar, eine nach der anderen, auszulöschen. 'Bist du mir böse?' fragte K. den Geistlichen" (P, 254). It is the priest who initiates the intimate second-person form of address (employed by family members and good friends) when he firmly identifies the protagonist, declaring: "Du bist Josef K."; and this elicits K.'s rare, pain-laden "Ja" (P, 252). "Du" imbues the priest's severe admonishments to K. with a paternal tone, and makes K. sound like a son. Because believers speak to God as "du," this form has a biblical directness and intensifies the sense of inescapability from one's identity.

11. "das Tor zum Gesetz offensteht wie immer"; "Torhüter" (P, 256).

12. "Wohl aber erkennt er jetzt im Dunkel einen Glanz der unverlöschlich aus der Türe des Gesetzes bricht" (P, 257).

else has come seeking admittance but me?"[13]—to which the doorkeeper replies that the door, now about to be shut, was intended solely for the
seeker. The priest engages in meticulous exegesis to correct K.'s evasive
conclusion that "the doorkeeper deceived the man" (T 215),[14] which disre-
gards the scriptural word. However, as the priest begins citing commentators on fine points, this midrashic expansion spun around the parable
as our primary text introduces anew the dilemma that is like a shadow
cast by the parable itself. This probing into the nature of the doorkeeper,
which ostensibly K.'s misprision initiates—or, so we may infer, any minute analysis of understanding or interpretative capacity as an internal
factor in a text—uncovers a situation that itself calls for and is subject to
interpretation. As the priest concedes: "'The commentators note in this
connection: The right perception of any matter and a misunderstanding
of the same matter do not wholly exclude each other'" (T 216).[15]

The reader appears initially to occupy the position both of K. and of
the seeker in the parable, vis-à-vis an "official" authorial voice who, like
the doorkeeper, "'allows himself the jest of inviting the man to enter in
spite of the strictly maintained veto against entry'" (T 216).[16] Analogous-
ly, with K., we are drawn into an ever-deepening darkness, and into extreme recesses of interiority and interpretation, to glimpse a haunting
radiance from a yet more recondite source. It does not seem to matter
whether we share or reject K.'s prevarications or reservations. This interi-
or of the text, of existence, and of the world suggests the encounter with
something as unfathomable as the En-Sof of the cabala, the hidden godhead that manifests itself through the emanation of the sefiroth, "a process which" (as Scholem summarizes) "takes place in God and which at
the same time enables man to perceive God."[17] Gradually, through midrashic searching, our "door" (the text) evolves into a labyrinth, an interior that seems simultaneously to shut the reader-interpreter "in" and
"out" as a failed Theseus. The door invites but blocks access to the glory of union with the absolute. The "official" voice of that labyrinth, implicitly the priest's, who represents at a high level the internalized storyteller's voice, is our Dedalian mirror. Although Stephen Dowden is skep-

13. "wie kommt es, daß niemand außer mir Einlaß verlangt hat?" (P, 257).
14. "Der Türhüter hat also den Mann getäuscht" (P, 257).
15. "Die Erklärer sagen hiezu: 'Richtiges Auffassen einer Sache und Mißverstehen der
gleichen Sache schließen einander nicht aus'" (P, 259).
16. "macht er den Spaß, daß er den Mann trotz dem ausdrücklich aufrechterhaltenen
Verbot zum Eintritt einlädt" (P, 260).
17. Gershom G. Scholem, *Major Trends in Jewish Mysticism* (New York: Schocken
Books, 1961), 209.

tical with respect to any concerted use of Jewish literary paradigms by the urban, secular modernist Kafka, he proposes an interpretation of Kafka's "light imagery" in *The Trial* that, in my view, is not incompatible with a poetic appropriation of cabalistic metaphor:

> Just before he dies, at a time when his eyesight is failing (the waning of the bodily senses points toward a waxing of the spiritual one), a radiance (Glanz) breaks forth inextinguishably (unverlöschlich) through the door of the law. It is the sublime epiphany of the unnameable, indestructible happiness that awaited the man. . . . that the light is inextinguishable is of central importance, pointing toward the undiscovered radiance that was simultaneously within the man (a finite being) but also transcends him as a common property, the "law" of human nature. While the man's life can be extinguished, the light in us cannot.[18]

Accused and chaplain, seeker and guard, reader and author ultimately converge in the aperture called the door. As the priest notes:

> "The scriptures are unalterable and the comments often express the commentators' despair. In this case there even exists an interpretation which claims that the deluded person is really the doorkeeper. [. . .] The argument is that he does not know the Law from inside, he knows only the way that leads to it, where he patrols up and down. His ideas of the interior are assumed to be childish [. . .]." (T 217)[19]

By raising the possible identity and reciprocal bondage of the seeker and the doorkeeper, and the question why the guard has his back to the radiance and refuses or fears or is unable to know the interior from which it glows, even though appointed by it (T 219), Kafka reconstitutes important mystical insights that Nicholas of Cusa (Kues) formulated in the mid-1440s in such treatises as *De docta ignorantia* (On Learned Ignorance) and *De possest* (On Actualized Potentiality): the metaphors of the "coincidence of opposites" and of God as a city through whose gate we cannot enter because our reason guards it. Constantly corrected,

18. Stephen Dowden, *Kafka's "Castle" and the Critical Imagination* (Columbia, S.C.: Camden House, 1995), 132.

19. "Die Schrift ist unveränderlich und die Meinungen sind oft nur ein Ausdruck der Verzweiflung darüber. In diesem Falle gibt es sogar die Meinung, nach welcher gerade der Türhüter der Getäuschte ist. [. . .] Man sagt, daß er das Innere des Gesetzes nicht kennt, sondern nur den Weg, den er vor dem Eingang immer wieder abgehen muß. Die Vorstellungen, die er von dem Innern hat, werden für kindlich gehalten" (P, 260–61). The translators have overinterpreted the German word *kindlich* (childlike, naive), pushing it toward German *kindisch* (childish).

K. modifies his first rationalizations to impugn the doorkeeper as a deceived or simpleminded informant. But the priest refutes this presumption too, by noting, "Many aver that the story confers no right on anyone to pass judgment on the doorkeeper" who "as a servant of the Law [. . .] is beyond human judgment" so that "to doubt his dignity is to doubt the Law itself"; he even adds the specific qualification that "it is not necessary to accept everything as true, one must only accept it as necessary" (T 220).[20]

The inveterate nay-sayer, K. replies, though with inner reservations, that this "melancholy conclusion [. . .] turns lying into a universal principle" (T 220).[21] His stubborn reversion to the indirect statement of this existential and/or gnostic position in the novel's opening line ("Someone must have been telling lies about Joseph K., for without having done anything wrong he was arrested one fine morning") has eventually caused the "simple story" to lose "its clear outline"; and his lamp—in parallel to the ungrasped sense of the parable—has been extinguished (T 221).[22] The seeker K., wrapping himself in his paltry secular identity as chief bank clerk, and the doorkeeper-priest part, without K. having truly entered into the important door, the parable. This negative proof by virtue of K.'s failure leaves the reader, in turn, facing the text that one cannot question but must accept in spirit, must enter into. In Joyce's novel, the chain of generations is the earthly reality that explains why a "centripetal remainer" (Bloom, in his fathering role) can "afford egress to the centrifugal departer" (Stephen, the heir); the sexual rite of unlocking the garden door reveals that it is "an aperture for free egress and free ingress," the gateway where death and life and all times meet (U 703).

In contrast, in *The Trial*, going through the (feminine) door into the text or into life is experienced as estrangement. K.'s fear of universal mendacity bears a strange resemblance to a long tradition of extreme philosophical positions opposing art as illusion (e.g., Plato). In the early seventeenth century, the suspicions raised against the fictions of art were extended to the snares of language itself, and various "methods" (e.g., Baconian empiricism, Cartesian metaphysical rationalism) were proposed to assert programmatic control over language as an instrument

20. "Manche sagen nämlich, daß die Geschichte niemandem ein Recht gibt, über den Türhüter zu urteilen"; "ein Diener des Gesetzes [. . .] also dem menschlichen Urteil entrückt"; "an seiner Würdigkeit zu zweifeln, hieße am Gesetz zu zweifeln"; "man muß nicht alles für wahr halten, man muß es nur für notwendig halten" (P, 264).
21. "Trübselige Meinung [. . .] Die Lüge wird zur Weltordnung gemacht" (P, 264).
22. "Die einfache Geschichte war unförmlich geworden" (P, 264).

for building moral and scientific certainty. The collapse of confidence in interpretive capacity, as reflected in K.'s blunders and paranoia, signals the possibility that the connective web of language and Scripture that once held an interpretive community together has meanwhile disintegrated beyond repair.

However, the paradox (inherited from symbolism) is that we learn about a lost meaning through the narrating voice that is impelled to speak upon its realization of being haunted by the trace of what is lost. Stanley Corngold points out that Kafka engages in rare but deliberate authorial "breaks" in the narrative by which we can espy a framework for the construction of meaning.[23] For this reason, "It is misleading to talk of the absence or refusal of overt meaning as a necessarily meaningless oversight" (Corngold, 173), unless, following an improbable French deconstructivist line of undecidability, we are ready to allow "the appropriation of the author Kafka in an impersonal linguistic exchange" (175). This aspect of Corngold's analysis does not necessarily clash with the implication of some deeper authorial level of truth claim. But Corngold goes on to suggest that, in order to appreciate such a level, we may not be able to rely simply on discerning a surrogate authorial presence through the narrator's voice:

> The narrator has to be brought in from behind the scenes, and once in a play within the fiction, even as a disembodied mind, he is as much subject to inauthenticity and blindness as any character. At such moments the naive, unconscious, but errant hero possesses an ironical superiority over the narrator. His blundering self-love is really no falser than the diabolical asceticism of the self-effacing narrator. (Corngold 177)

If Corngold is correct, this possibility complicates our attempts to appreciate instances when Kafka seems to engage in some more direct, self-critical internal marking of the text by insertion of surrogates for the authorial mind.

The possibility of an understanding that eludes K. simultaneously suggests the large family of modernist supramoral categories such as expressed in Nietzsche's formula "beyond good and evil." Behind and through K.'s moral obtuseness, his existential nightmare, his spiritual numbness in the cathedral may still reverberate an order of distinct-

---

23. Stanley Corngold, *The Fate of the Self: German Writers and French Theory* (New York: Columbia University Press, 1986).

ly moral insights ancestral to Nietzsche's and Freud's psychologies, and to fin-de-siècle obsessions with the cruelty and glory of life. These Schopenhauer formulated most forcefully in his treatise *The World as Will and Representation* (1818, rev. ed. 1844).[24] Book 4, dealing, as its subtitle states, "With the Attainment of Self-Knowledge, Affirmation and Denial of the Will-to-Live," seems especially pertinent, by anticipation, to the case of K. *ante portas*. Through "representation," the "will obtains knowledge of its own willing," and "the phenomenal world" we experience is "the mirror, the objectivity of the will." Ultimately, "neither the will, the thing-in-itself in all phenomena, nor the subject of knowing, the spectator of all phenomena, is in any way affected by birth and death" (W 275), even though these are the portals for the myriad individual expressions of the eternal Will in the present tense of existence (W 278). We may individually resist and obscure the evidence of our human condition "by our limited view," but that does not alter the fact that "the will and the pure subject of knowing lie outside time" (W 282). The permanent truth about being is corroborated when (book 3) a sublime artist pierces the veil of illusion and witnesses our human condition, or when (book 4) a blossoming of character occurs so that a person acquires self-knowledge and in a special moment of "elective decision" rises above enthrallment to life (W 301). Of the many variations discussed by Schopenhauer (375ff.)—for example, "disinterested affection," concern for the "welfare of all mankind," "asceticism," "renunciation," "denial of the will-to-live," saintly conduct, meditation, mysticism, and more—K. at the end appears, though far from being "a beautiful soul," at least, on a low rung, "quiet" (385).[25] K.'s acquiescence at the gateway of death, tinged by a strange new subdued curiosity so well fitting the surreal moment, may enact a modernist "mortification" of the unknowable will.

In addition, Kafka structures our experience of K.'s series of probes or discoveries as a surreal theater of the mind.[26] The apparent linearity of the separate scenes proves, in the final analysis, to be a circular exploration—much as the separate dreamscapes by Dali in the 1930s prove to be a cluster of intertextually linked acts of dreaming by an ironic beholder

24. References, henceforth indicated by the abbreviation W, are to vol. 1 of Arthur Schopenhauer, *The World as Will and Representation*, trans. E. F. J. Payne, 2 vols. (New York: Dover Books, 1969).

25. The argument that Schopenhauerian categories appear in *The Castle* has been made by John Zilcosky, "Kafka Approaches Schopenhauer's Castle," *German Life and Letters* 44 (1990–1991): 353–69.

26. This structural principle is the subject of James Rolleston, *Kafka's Narrative Theater* (University Park: Pennsylvania State University Press, 1974).

who sometimes focuses on emblematic details of a single master dream, and sometimes exposes the depths in these details. In every instance, the dreaming always yields further layers of interiority and exegetical puzzles. Collectively, these dreamscapes convey not a progression, but a haunted eternity of the mind. A comparable modernist eternity inheres in K.'s nightmare; its collective burden is dramatically underscored in the permanent existential trauma that the Court's dismissal of K. inflicts: "It receives you when you come and it dismisses you when you go" (T 222).[27] This epiphanic caesura is the clicking shut of the door. Ritual fulfillment of the sentence follows in a timeless setting that blends the urban wasteland and ancient myth. K. contests a power he cannot fathom. The sequentiality of K.'s struggle against the verdict collapses into the permanent legendary state of a parable when the delusionary character of his "defense" is confirmed in the uncanny moment of his execution. K., the failed reasoner and functionary, becomes the sacrificial victim in the postfiguration of prerational rite. Everything that is hidden from K. and seems mysteriously inaccessible returns to haunt us when he dies like a dog in oblivion.

This drastic moment calls to mind Stephen's thoughts about the rotting dog's body (= God's body) on the beach in the "Proteus" chapter. Here Kafka may seek to grasp the mystical paradox that, by facing the void, we encounter absolute being and its creative transformational potential. As Scholem notes (217), "Nothing can change without coming into contact with this region of pure absolute Being which the mystics call Nothing." However, what is tormenting for the informed reader (one conversant with the basics of Jewish mystical ideas) is the question of whether K.'s failure to believe in the scriptural teaching is part of this glimpse into the abyss, a complete mortification through despair, or whether his shame signals a tragic truncation of the living word. In this regard, consider Scholem's comments on Hassidic theosophy that emphasizes Revelation:

[. . .] God, who remains infinite and unknown also in the role of Creator, has produced the glory as "a created light, the first of all creations." This Kavod is the great radiance called "Shekhinah" and it is also identical with the ruah ha-kodesh, the "holy spirit," out of whom there speaks the voice and word of God. This primeval light of divine glory is later revealed to the prophets and mystics in various forms and modifications. [. . .] It serves as a guarantee of the authentic char-

27. "Es nimmt dich auf, wenn du kommst, und es entläßt dich, wenn du gehst" (P, 265).

acter of the words heard by the prophet and excludes any doubt as to their divine origin. (Scholem, III)

It is not necessary to conclude that Kafka is in some deeper spiritual sense beholden to Hassidic tradition, as Scholem would like to believe, in order to understand how he might respond to long-entrenched Jewish literary motifs (even if by probatory negation thereof).[28] By the same token, the fact that in his fictions Kafka makes no overt reference to such motifs does not exclude their exercising a covert power or of their being combined in a seamlessly woven montage with motifs from the dominant surrounding Christian tradition.

Kafka's prose offers us a stellar example of a widespread turning away from reality into other realms—into the psyche, into the imaginary, into language—in the early twentieth century. The antirealist principle of narrating a series of surreal experiences recurs in another guise in the cinematic-psychedelic passages of the "Magic Theater" section of *Steppenwolf* (1927). Through the first-person narrator of the frame story and through comments in the partly biographical, partly imaginative text by Harry Haller, which the editor-narrator conveys as a document, Hesse internalizes explicit authorial self-reference to the larger narrative process underway throughout the book. The novel's antirealist critical discourse intensifies as Harry plunges into the Dionysian realm that thrives in the modern city and the masses, and is revealed through new media, such as the cinema and jazz, which are characteristic of the modernist period. We witness Harry, our guide in his own internalized first-person account, being conducted through the multiplicity of potential selves, even though he self-critically depicts right to the novel's close his deep inner resistance to the implications of his discoveries. The result on the level of the plot "action" at the very end is that Mozart, one of the certified Immortals, laughs at this spectacle of human folly. No matter how many "doors" Harry tries, he cannot get through for an explicit reason: his clinging to the illusion of a distinct identity, a limit that Joyce's Stephen too is learning to surmount in *Ulysses*.[29] The psychegogue Pablo informs Harry: "This little theater of mine has as many doors into as many boxes as you please, and behind each door exactly what you seek awaits

28. Ritchie Robertson, *Kafka: Judaism, Politics and Literature* (Oxford, U.K.: Clarendon Press, 1985), is one of the strongest advocates of a Jewish foundation to Kafka's works. Dowden has critiqued the weaknesses of such a position in *Kafka's "Castle,"* 98–111.

29. The modernist theme of the death of the self is discussed at more length in chapter fourteen, "Structures of the Self and Narrative."

you"; however, "it would be quite useless for you to go through it as you are," that is, "blinded at every turn by what you are pleased to call your personality" (S 201).[30]

By rejecting the symbol of the androgyne in the section entitled "Harry's Execution" (in a remarkable echo of the ending of Kafka's book?), Hesse's Steppenwolf fails the test as he traverses "the hell of my inner being" (S 248).[31] K., who lusts after Miss Bürstner and other women in Kafka's book, is impelled by a "desire to assure himself that the inside of this legal system was just as loathsome as its external aspect" (T 66–67);[32] and when he looks into the literally filthy lawbooks on the judges' table, he finds that one contains the banal pornographic picture of a human couple, a man and woman, "sitting naked on a sofa" and another is "a novel entitled: How Grete Was Plagued by Her Husband Hans" (T 52).[33] Kafka's dry humor—K. is sitting with an attractive wife who is plagued by her husband and others, and perhaps is inclined to be plagued by him—here exploits a subject matter familiar in Joyce: the encounter with the absolute, baffling banality of life. Joyce takes us into the tackiest nooks and crannies, into the absurd and horrible aspects of existence, into the terrors of dream; he hides nothing about sexuality and animal needs; but like Hesse's Immortals, he laughs and he accepts.

The romantic discovery that dream structures provide a model for narrative processes is widespread in modernist fiction. Both Kafka and Joyce at moments, moreover, gravitate toward the cabalistic metaphor of the story (including now the modernist dream story) as life, a textuality "beyond good and evil." The incentive to treat this double aspect of narration—the mystery of the text (life), as against the banality of the text (life)—gives rise to a strand of hermeneutic obsessiveness in works that belong to the "postmodernist" phase of modernism. A notable example is Butor's novel L'emploi du temps (Passing Time, 1956). This fiction, supposedly a diary kept by Revel, a lonesome young Frenchman in Bleston, a dreary English industrial city, exhibits the first-person narrator's post-Proustian investigation into time, the mystery of which fits into the zero

30. "Mein Theaterchen hat so viele Logentüren, als ihr wollt [. . .], und hinter jeder Tür erwartet euch das, was ihr gerade sucht"; "aber es würde Ihnen nichts nützen, es so zu durchlaufen, wie Sie sind"; "durch das gehemmt und geblendet [. . .], was Sie gewöhnt sind, Ihre Persönlichkeit zu nennen" (HH, 192).

31. "die Hölle meines Innern" (HH, 237).

32. "aus dem Verlangen, festzustellen, daß das Innere dieses Gerichtswesens ebenso widerlich war wie sein Äußeres" (P, 84–85).

33. "saßen nackt auf einem Kanapee"; "ein Roman mit dem Titel: 'Die Plagen, welche Grete von ihrem Manne Hans zu erleiden hatte" (P, 67).

space between the opening and closing moments when the minute hand of the clock at the railway station stands precisely at twelve. Like K., Revel seems to be a consciousness summoned in order to be dismissed. The virtual infinity gathered into the doubleness of his arrival/departure constitutes, paradoxically, a disappearance of the "real" content of the city into some vanishing point that the narrating voice accedes to, even though the admission of this vanishing comes after bitter struggle that conjures the vision of the recessed, lost content. Moreover, Revel's story is a detective novel at the core of which lodges an internal detective novel, entitled *The Bleston Murder,* a book that provides one of Revel's original guides to the urban labyrinth and its secrets.

The temporal order by which modern industrial society organizes things appears in the successive headings of each diary entry. However, in its five large monthly installments, the diary actually deals with a full year of experiences colored by a timeless tropology of the seasons. Revel has begun his diary on May 1, examining October in retrospect, in an attempt to obtain some grip on reality, because he is shaken by his own anger over the elusiveness of Bleston, a bafflement that has caused him, among other things, to burn his valuable map of the city impetuously. In seeking to understand the deep changes in himself, he begins to reconstruct and recapture his life from the moment of his arrival in the labyrinth. In parallel to Revel's inner explorations, gradually his sentences lengthen and their syntax grows ever more complex and is punctuated with cumulative climaxes. Not only does he continue analyzing his past existence in Bleston month by month, but as of the June section he also starts recording the contemporary layer of observations from June onward. Then, beginning as of the diary's current July, in a third layer of recollection, he goes backwards month by month from the May when the diary was initiated, to the preceding April and next to March. In the current August, additionally, he picks up again the forward direction from the recent May to June. Thus in the September entry, at the conclusion of which the diary breaks off, five entire months (February, September, March, July, and August) are stratified, telescoped, and interwoven in a new hermeneutic order. Chronological time seems engulfed in the emerging network of multiple references—except for a nagging gap, the never disclosed happenings of 29 February, the strange intercalated spot in time. (29 February, be it noted, is the spot of time when Hans Castorp succumbs to Clavdia Chauchat in *The Magic Mountain.*) This potent blank bears a mysterious resemblance to the zero point on the station clock, as it completes its circle and dominates the arrival and departure of Revel who, though losing his way, his nominal identity, and his mental stability, could not resign himself to the dehumanizing secret of Bleston.

A narrative order emerges that seems to abrogate ordinary temporality, although it affirms the hermeneutic dimensions of involvement with experienced time, including the perception of a temporal order that is expiring in juxtaposition with one that is being born. The multidimensional narrative order is constituted by the enduring power of patterns that we glimpse through Revel's references to myths of all times and places; like Joyce's Stephen and Proust's Marcel, he is an authorial agent constantly resuscitating and recomposing complex models of mythic reimbodiment. Revel comes to identify himself with Cain through his own betrayal of the inner detective-author Burton's identity, with Oedipus because of his own struggle against the curse of the city which results in guilt and exile, and with Theseus in his quest for release from the labyrinth. In his search, he is aided by the map-seller Ann as an Ariadne whom he abandons, in vain, for her younger sister Rose, his Persephone and Phaedra. As an internal guiding text, the detective novel we readers cannot actually read, *The Bleston Murder,* is as ambivalent as the labyrinth city it is named after. It conducts us, through and with our reader-narrator Revel, toward the meaning that appears to reside in the opposition between the venerable Old Cathedral (Roman Catholic) and the bold New Cathedral (Protestant). The latter, which initially inspires a sense of hope in Revel, is derided by Burton, and in due course it is overshadowed by a crass ten-story department store (postfiguring the Tower of Babel), still under construction as Revel first reaches Bleston.

In the tapestries and windows of the Old Cathedral, built on the ruins of a Roman temple of war, Revel rediscovers the mythological avatars and the stories of biblical and ancient cities haunting modernity. Though these places have fallen with once flourishing civilizations, he finds them again in the newsreels at the movie house when he views contemporary examples of strife and destruction. The mythological montage, which Revel himself constructs through his brooding over the human heritage, suggests more than an evolutionary model for the cultural strata in our world. As Revel reviews his own earlier diary entries and deepens his awareness of his own earlier failures of judgment, he progressively reinterprets the inner novel by Burton and thus assumes the detective's mantle of this spiritual father whose teachings on and through crime fiction (reported in the very center of the diary) constitute the central scriptural text, and incite Revel to interpret. Revel's diary is thus a kind of midrash spun around the irreducible text that is ever being rewoven. It is through his obsession to unearth the key clues that Revel starts digging down into his own being and discovers the malignancy of the city in himself. Through resentment of the writer-detective Burton, Revel is identified both with the drive to interpret and with the crime it entails, with Cain's jealousy over his brother's election and with Cain's invention of the arts and the city. Revel also consciously assumes the mantle of the detective as Oedipus, a "son" who owes his existence to the criminal aspect of humanity as "father."

The age-old story, whether shining as images from stained glass windows or a movie projector, infests Revel to the extent that he parts from Bleston as the violator of its secrets who reciprocally is wounded by them, as a complicitous survivor:

> And so I thank you, Bleston, for taking such cruel and blatant revenge on me; I shall be gone [. . .], but I shall still be prince over you since, by acknowledging my defeat, I have managed to survive (as secretly you wished me to) the fate you had in store for me, I have not been engulfed; and now, having endured the ordeal of your fury, I have become invulnerable, like a ghost; I have won from you this offer of a pact, which I accept. (PT 234)[34]

However, in effect, Revel sees the future as permanent personal "doom" (PT 238).[35] Being a flawed Theseus, he cannot contemplate his failure "without that sense of frozen isolation which ghosts must experience" (PT 237).[36] The narrator-interpreter survives in a living death, associated forever in the mind of the reader with the dim glow out of the text he has sought to interpret. The authorial persona will still be troubling

34. Citations of this work, henceforth abbreviated as PT followed by the page number, are drawn from Michel Butor, *Passing Time*, trans. Jean Stewart (London: Faber & Faber, 1961). French citations, indicated by the abbreviation ET and followed by the page number, are drawn from Michel Butor, *L'emploi du temps* (Paris: Editions de Minuit, 1957). The original reads here: "C'est pourquoi je te remercie de t'être si cruellement, si évidemment vengé de moi, ville de Bleston que je vais quitter [. . .] mais dont je demeurerai l'un des princes puisque j'ai réussi, en reconnaissant ma défaite, à exaucer ton désir secret de me voir survivre à cet engloutissement, à cette sort de mort que tu m'avais réservée, puisque je suis devenu maintenant, par ce baptême de ta fureur, invulnérable à la manière des fantômes, puisque j'ai obtenu de toi cette proposition de pacte que j'accepte" (ET, 261).
35. "condamnation" (ET, 265).
36. "sans ce sentiment de gel et d'isolement que doivent éprouver les fantômes" (ET, 265).

"us" as a revenant after his passage through a gate when, as in the final words of the novel, "my departure closes this last sentence" (PT 267).[37]

Are we caught in the labyrinth of his text, or, from another perspective, do we feel shut out permanently by the act of apparent closure—a parallel for which is the period placed after the ultimate or death sentence? The self-assigned ghostly character of this narrator has a double aspect that aligns it with an important tradition, and it is our recognition of the connection that binds us into the textual web. Revel's defeat or negation is the restatement of something he and "we"—a multitude of readers under threat of disinheritance, or already unchurched exiles— no longer easily accept but also cannot forget. In his celebrated poem "L'azur" (1864), Mallarmé summed up the dilemma of modern knowledge after the collapse of belief. The martyred and disinherited mind, burdened by all that it has cumulatively experienced, no longer knows how to take refuge from the wounding power of the infinite manifested in the world, from the divine that seems impervious to the mind's own story, its rebellion and desolation. Before the concluding fourfold cry "l'Azur!" which chastises the speaker's impotence and cowardice, the insight in answer to the question, "Where to flee in the unavailing depraved rebellion?" appears dramatically in Mallarmé's poem in axiomatic recognition, "I am haunted!"[38] This tormenting sense of loss clearly is a suffering that affirms.[39]

The fact that Kafka first published the parable section of the later cathedral chapter in its own right under the title "Before the Law" in the Jewish weekly *Selbstwehr* (Self-Defense) in 1915 ought to caution us against misreading K.'s failure as the author's statement of pure negation.[40] The need to treat K.'s interaction with the priest and its mise en abyme, the parable within the cathedral experience, as a legend, and to subject the legend to exegesis in a Jewish scriptural context, holds true even if the novel also reflects Kafka's own inner struggles—for exam-

37. "mon départ termine cette dernière phrase" (ET, 299).
38. "Où fuir dans la révolte inutile et perverse?"; "*Je suis hanté*"—Mallarmé's emphasis.
39. On the lineaments underlying Mallarmé's and Joyce's shared sense that "History does not grow, it leaps; the artist comes from the past, but across an abyss," and that "the eternal cannot be hauled out from the religion and poetry of the past, but must be reborn in the matrix of the nonexistent present" (35), consult William Carpenter, *Death and Marriage: Structural Metaphors for the Work of Art in Joyce and Mallarmé* (New York: Garland, 1988).
40. On the contextual reasons for such caution, see Hartmut Binder, *Kafka-Kommentar zu den Romanen, Rezensionen, Aphorismen und zum Brief an den Vater* (Munich: Winkler, 1976), 241–48.

ple, balancing his professional work and artistic vocation, or his paternal "country-folk" side with his maternal "priestly" heritage, and so forth. Among possible contributing traditions two deserve special mention. One is the heroicization of the Moses figure who cannot enter the Holy Land toward which he conducts his people. Another is the gnostic drama of the soul's difficult journey toward the highest heaven, a passage blocked by doorkeepers, in Jewish mysticism. In Joyce's novel, father and son, as Bloom and Stephen, engage in consubstantial union and—by way of the birth canal—they move "from obscurity by a passage from the rere of the house into the penumbra of the garden," to be greeted in the night of the flesh by a reassuring "spectacle" that combines the ending of Dante's *Divine Comedy* and the notion of all humanity as the fruit dangling forever from the All Mother's womb: "The heaventree of stars hung with humid nightblue fruit" (U 698). In the eery final episode of K.'s execution, Fräulein Bürstner, resembling a De Chirico herald, appears in a Diana-like aspect, as if secretly guiding or accompanying K. at a distance, but then drops out of sight.[41] This archetypal feminine light reappears, however, in the natural radiance that envelops the sacrifice: "The moon shone down on everything with that simplicity and serenity which no other light possesses" (T 227).[42] Is K.'s avoidance of plunging the knife into his own breast (T 228), then, a last gesture whereby he seeks to identify Isaac with Abraham, the father whose hand was stayed from sacrificing his son? As the son who yearns for that loving father, K. is baffled by the tremendous mystery that radiates through the gate of being into the darkened space of the human mind, and through the Shekinah. In his own fashion, K. combines aspects of the roles of Stephen and Bloom.[43]

Whether or not Kafka consciously made a crucial decision not to ex-

41. Peter Salm, "The Reflected Text: Kafka's Modern Inferno," in *Countercurrents: On the Primacy of Texts in Literary Criticism*, ed. Raymond Adolph Prier (Albany: State University of New York Press, 1992), 214–16, astutely attributes a "Dantesque aura" to Fräulein Bürstner in her appearance as a momentary manifestation of the Beatrice-like guidance by the feminine, but like the "feeble light" of the candle in the cathedral, this may serve "only to intensify the darkness."

42. "Überall lag der Mondschein mit seiner Natürlichkeit und Ruhe, die keinem anderen Licht gegeben ist" (P, 270).

43. For an elaborate presentation of Bloom's and Stephen's roles in the cabalistic context, consult ch. 4, "*Ulysses:* Joyce's Kabbalah," of Jackson I. Cope's *Joyce's Cities: Archaeologies of the Soul* (Baltimore: John Hopkins University Press, 1981), 62–102. On K.'s role as a failed seeker for entrance into the light of the Torah, consult ch. 2, "*Der Prozeß* und die Torhütertradition in der Kabbala," of Karl Erich Grözinger's *Kafka und die Kabbala: Das Jüdische in Werk und Denken von Franz Kafka* (Frankfurt: Eichborn Verlag, 1992), 2–45.

plore the father principle in relation to the mother principle, because he sensed that the father could not be "humanized" without sacrilege, we encounter more than strong hints of that cabalistic relationship when the unnamed narrating voice tells us, in an ironic matter-of-fact way, about such moments as when obtuse K. finds the pornographic lawbooks. The pressure to capitulate to this earthly expression of the Law and the intermittent surrenders to it by K. shape a comic drama of resistance to "life" on the part of a most unlikely, yet thematically most appropriate, protagonist, a punctilious bank official. Tirelessly, K. tries to apply his metonymic rulebook to draw apart the metaphoric veils that cloak divinity. As odd as it may seem—because, of course, in the longer pull we cannot help responding to the awesome drift of the nightmare—Kafka expects us to laugh at the futility of K.'s rebellion, just as Joyce expects us to critique immature Stephen's pretensions, while we admire his tenacious drive to read the "signatures of all things" (U 37), and as Hesse wants us to hear and be haunted by the peal of Mozart's laughter over Harry Haller's bafflement.

1. Preludial Selves (Humanism, Enlightenment, Romanticism, Symbolism)

This two-part chapter is intended as a meditation on the many-stranded modernist heritage rather than as an argument privileging any one mode of modernism or the modern novel. I hope my excessively monothematic, scattered references to works that merit a far more detailed scrutiny will stimulate discussion about the complex tasks of diachronic literary comparison. When a critic recites one of our favorite metanarratives, his or her tendency is to choose an *in medias res* point of departure much as in ordinary storytelling. And so, the question easily arises: Should I rehearse some instances of the well-known contribution of Christianity to shaping the European concept of individual identity? I could, for example, start in the High Middle Ages with St. Thomas Aquinas's vision of the human being as a creature grounded in nature but endowed with reason and will, a creature appearing in individuals who bear responsibility concomitant with identity. While the mystical insights of Meister Eckart two generations later may diverge from this normative picture, especially insofar as societal and institutional involvement is concerned, Eckart's mysticism in fact exalts the single soul as the true core of identity to an even more majestic position. And humanism, as promulgated in the early modern period from Pico to Rabelais, teaches that if human beings reclaim their conformity with a splendid cosmos they can participate creatively as individuals in a high destiny.

The humanist age drew less on retrieved narrative models of classical antiquity than on Europe's own recent Latin and vernacular writers and the wealth of story forms inherited from the Middle Ages. Humanism also refurbished the late medieval essentialist view that the self, at its pinnacle an *ens rationalis,* was capable of discovering its place in the hierarchical aggregate of selves, or mankind, and in the scheme of a meaningful creation. Complex neomythological allegories such as Edmund Spenser's verse romance *The Faerie Queene* (1589–1596) represented the bigger picture of human development through protagonists who were archetypal rather than "realistic." François Rabelais made humanist criticism into a structuring principle of narrative itself by using humor to organize his five-part saga of *Gargantua and Pantagruel* (1532–1562) for an encyclopedic examination of competing medieval and Renaissance values. Rabelais's thematizing of the search for elusive answers in a universe qualitatively altered by the Renaissance also helped shape a humoristic approach to the issue of the reliability of human consciousness and humanity's accrued knowledge, which radical philosophers such as Henricus Cornelius Agrippa of Nettesheim broached in *De incertitudine et vanitate scientiarum* (On the Uncertainty and Vanity of Knowledge, 1530). Michel Eyquem de Montaigne's interiorization of the question of reliability in a minute examination of his own mind over time in his *Essais* (1580–1588) marks the boundary with the baroque age. We may regard the painter Rembrandt van Rijn's lifelong series of self-portraits as a related venture in observing oneself in the condition of time.

In the early seventeenth century, both empirical (Francis Bacon) and metaphysical (René Descartes) rationalism shared the aim of overcoming the mind's suspected proclivity to delusion and of sorting out the muddled human heritage by devising a method to construct and expand certain knowledge. Ostensibly a satire to curb the power of brain-addling romances, Miguel de Cervantes Saavedra's two-part novel *Don Quixote* (1605, 1615) probed the contest between reality and imagination as foundational in human affairs, but in the process it reaffirmed the attractive ties linking idealism, the arts, and creative fantasy. Moreover, Cervantes's teasing game with the structures of fiction, which matched William Shakespeare's sometimes accutely self-reflective drama as in *Hamlet,* internalized critical irony as a principle in the modern stream of the novel. In the full-fledged baroque generation, the post-Machiavellian prudentialist Baltasar Gracián asserted that human beings were in fact theatrical creatures under moral obligation to invent their own proper roles in the fiction called history. He illustrated the quest for personhood through the form of the educational novel in *El criticón* (The Faultfinder, 1619).

The disillusionistic naturalism of Cervantes and Gracián is part of the general Renaissance experience of the possibility and problematics of individual self-creation. In Italy, in a collection of their *Lives* (*Vite*, 1550), Giorgio Vasari's glorification of artists as virtually self-divinizing creators sets the new tone. Benvenuto Cellini's autobiography as a fiercely independent self-made artist (*Vita,* 1562), however, has a strongly picaresque flavor, probably unintended, that at moments bears resemblance

to the harsh, first-person Spanish fictions about underdog criminal striv-
ers, artists of life, in the urban realm. The ironic authorial voice commenting on the action in picaresque pseudo-autobiographies such as the
anonymous *Lazarillo de Tormes* (1554) or Francisco de Quevedo's *El Bus-
cón* (The Sharper, ca. 1606) makes manifest the split consciousness that
recurs in a complex high baroque form in Cervantes. We can readily distinguish Cervantes's ironic reflection on the struggle of a self for status
from the standard bourgeois stories of education and social success in
the sixteenth century such as Jörg Wickram's *Der jungen Knaben Spiegel* (Mirror for Young Boys, 1554) and *Der Goldfaden* (The Gold Thread,
1557). An allied type of educational novel occurring between the Renaissance and the late Enlightenment—from John Lyly's *Euphues* (1578–
1580), through Gracián's *Criticón* (Criticaster, 1619) and François de la
Mothe-Fénelon's *Télémaque* (Telemachus, ca. 1695)—transposes the contemporary challenge of education and a survey of the social philosophies
and institutions of the author's times onto antiquity.[1]

I should perhaps also visit important exponents of empirical and metaphysical rationalism in the late Renaissance such as Bacon and Descartes,
who agree on the hierarchical role of reason in human self-fulfillment.
And even in a grossly foreshortened account, I might well add the juxtaposed idealist and sensationalist approaches of the philosophers Berkeley
and Locke at the end of the seventeenth century, who from their separate
perspectives maintained a distinction between reason, on the one hand,
and the effects of sensation and experience, on the other, in the formation
of our knowledge, including our consciousness of self. The contest between sensationalist-materialist and idealist-essentialist views persisted
throughout the eighteenth century. In the year 1744, Swedenborg experienced his major illumination that turned him away from his passion for
the physical sciences to ecstatic mystical visions. In the same year, 1744,
no less than the enlightened despot Frederick II of Prussia contributed
a glowing foreword to La Mettrie's treatise *L'homme machine* (Man a Machine). This latter book expresses the extreme sensationalist-materialist
doctrine that all nature, including human nature and individuals, springs
from mechanical processes and combinations that science will eventually
succeed in analyzing. Occupying the opposite pole around the mid-

---

1. On narrative genres in the Renaissance, cf. Gerald Gillespie, "The Incorporation of
History as Content and Form: Anticipations of the Romantic and Modern Novel," in *Proceedings of the 9th Congress of the International Comparative Literature Association* (Innsbruck: Innsbrucker Gesellschaft zur Pflege der Geisteswissenschaften, 1982), 4.29–34.

eighteenth century and onward are the teachings of Hamann and Herder that individuals, cultures, and humanity at large express living, organic development, and that natural law and morality, both deriving from a divine creative origin, underpin our organic integrity as sensoria and persons.

In yet another direction quite distinct from La Mettrie's materialism, his contemporary Hume regards one of the standard oppositions in European philosophy, both Berkeley's concept of spiritual substance and Locke's of material substance, to be illusory. Instead, he proposes that it is in the imagination, in great measure under the influence of custom, that we connect things and ideas. It is worth citing a bit from Hume's *Treatise of Human Nature* (1739–1740),[2] because his line of thought will ultimately have disturbing repercussions in romanticism and modernism:

> The mind is a kind of theater, where several perceptions successively make their appearance; pass, repass, glide away, and mingle in an infinite variety of postures and situations. There is properly no simplicity in it at one time, nor identity in different [moments]; whatever natural propension we may have to imagine simplicity and identity. (Hume 246)

Observing that the imagination constructs the relationships among successions, and the faculty of memory induces us to form the notion of causation, Hume draws the conclusion that "all the disputes concerning the identity of connected objects are merely verbal, except so far as the relation of parts gives rise to some fiction or imaginary principle of union" (Hume 253). Only Hume's impeccable British manners and *savoir vivre* save him from an unseemly subjectivist crisis in the face of the corollary that we "are but a bundle or collection of different perceptions" (253), which our imagination mistakenly construes as a coherent identity, a single permanent self.

Important cross-fertilizations of narrative conventions and insights about the mind and identity appear in the early eighteenth century, with a revolution in the novel as one result in its final decades. For example, Daniel Defoe's *Robinson Crusoe* (1719) is narrated in a pseudopicaresque voice, but as the protagonist starts keeping a diary the novel becomes

---

2. David Hume, *A Treatise of Human Nature*, in *The Age of Enlightenment: The Eighteenth Century Philosophers*, ed. Isaiah Berlin (New York: New America Library, 1956), 164–260.

a confessional probing of interiority. Simultaneously it treats a subject matter already found in Wickram's *Von guten und bösen Nachbarn* (Of Good and Bad Neighbors, 1556): the new global drama and text of colonization and capitalism being directed by the self-examining European mind. Another example of adaptation is Henry Fielding's new way of wielding Cervantine irony in *Joseph Andrews* (1742) and *Tom Jones* (1749). As a man of the Enlightenment, he debunks superstitions and prejudices out of a full confidence in natural morality in order to encourage his fellow citizens to accept a beneficent view of their own potential for the pursuit of happiness. Explicitly grateful to Fielding, Christoph Martin Wieland eagerly builds these Enlightenment hopes into his equally Cervantine *Agathon* (1766–1767, 1794), but he is troubled by the counterpointed spiritual claims of the mind and the crisis of sentiment as well, themes that preoccupy authors such as Jean-Jacques Rousseau in *La nouvelle Héloïse* (The New Heloise, 1761). In *Joseph Andrews,* in contrast to Wieland, Fielding answers the sentimental extremism of Samuel Richardson's *Pamela* (1740–1741) and *Clarissa* (1747–1748). Donatien Alphonse-François de Sade travesties such noble pretensions in his paired novels *La nouvelle Justine ou les malheurs de la vertu* (The New Justine; or, The Misfortunes of Virtue) and *L'histoire de Juliette, sa soeur, ou les prospérités du vice* (The Story of Juliette, Her Sister; or, the Good Fortunes of Vice) in the name of an equally extreme doctrine of the absolute liberation of the self from artificial social texts (1799–1801). In the political sphere, the American and French Revolutions eventually are less demanding and must strike a compromise between the individual and society.

Richardson's middle-class books trace their lineage in part to the great psychological novels of the seventeenth century, such as Marie Madeleine de LaFayette's *La Princesse de Clèves* (1677), treating the ineluctable tragedy of self-delusion and self-discovery. The important developments in narrative of the eighteenth century flow from experiments with modes of privileged communication connected with intimate selfhood, mainly the diary and letters, so as to suggest the complex realm of intersubjectivity in which individual selves are enmeshed. The case of Crusoe, as caught in his diary, exudes the loneliness of singular being in an expanding pluralistic world. Henry Mackenzie's *The Man of Feeling* (1771) investigates the crisis of sentiment in the face of life's cruelty by reconstructing an individual tragedy partly from tattered remains of a diary and traces of community memory. Johann Wolfgang von Goethe presents the felt horror of a dead end for sentimental refinement, when creative vitality or social preferment is absent, through letters like diary entries written by his desperate title hero in *Die Leiden des jungen Werther* (The Sorrows of Young Werther, 1774). The "editor" figures who frame these two stories both make the explicit point that readers of sensibility, by their sympathetic understanding of human breakdown, will be reaffirming intersubjective community. In Pierre Choderlos de Laclos's epistolary novel *Les liaisons dangereuses* (Dangerous Relations, 1782), power-seeking manipulation of language, the key instrument of human expression, poses a more dire threat yet to the sentimental ideal of genuine sharing.

The status of the individual was a central matter for the sentimental-enlightened mainstream of the revolutionary age leading to the romantic threshold. Kant's essay of 1783, answering the question "Was ist Aufklärung?" ("What Is Enlightenment?"), is one of many statements that advanced the Renaissance definition of human identity to a new stage by insisting that individual responsibility must replace dependence on authority, as the basis both of self-fulfillment and of social justice. The American Declaration of Independence of 1776 had already enshrined this august view of selfhood by claiming that all human beings "are endowed by their Creator with certain unalienable Rights" and "that among these are Life, Liberty, and the pursuit of Happiness." The representatives of the third estate in France gathered in 1789 for more effusion over human emancipation through reason and for the purpose of happiness. But romantic subjectivism soon began to spawn threats to the Enlightenment hope that the plurality of selves in their organic condition could be liberated for realization of their potential under natural law in reasonable social collaboration. As noted above, worrisome questions about the liabilities of human sentience and selfhood were raised in such seminal novels of the second half of the eighteenth century as Rousseau's *La nouvelle Héloïse*, Mackenzie's *The Man of Feeling*, and Goethe's *Werther*. In the 1760s and 1770s, protoromantic puzzles about subjective existence and intersubjectivity appeared in Sterne's *Tristram Shandy* and again in Diderot's *Jacques le fataliste et son maître* (Jacques the Fatalist and His Master). These burgeoned into a full romantic exploration of perilous aspects of an identity with hidden compartments in many early nineteenth-century authors, for example, in E. T. A. Hoffmann's tale "Der Sandmann" (The Sandman) and novel *Die Elixiere des Teufels* (The Devil's Elixers).

Metamorphosis, Play, and the Laws of Life

The import of David Hume's thesis in *A Treatise of Human Nature* (1739–1740) that the mind is a "theater" of successive perceptions and that "all the disputes concerning the identity of connected objects are merely verbal, except so far as the relation of parts gives rise to some fiction or imaginary principle of union" was to reach a broader public through Laurence Sterne's radical experimentation with narrative in the novel *Tristram Shandy* (1760–1767). By amalgamating the pseudopicaresque voice, Rabelaisian humoristic encyclopedism, and Cervantine irony, Sterne re-creates the confrontation between selfhood and imposed social texts and reengages the problematics of imagination and creativity, but resolutely from a subjectivist vantage. In a startling innovation, his first-person narrator, Tristram, an eccentric, battered sensorium, makes the motions of his own mind into the determinant structuring principle of his narration, while he continuously dismantles and exhibits the conventions of literature before the eyes of the reader as a fellow "subject" and repeatedly analyzes the biological-psychological grounding of selfhood. Teleological linearity gives way to circularity, the mind revolving around and in and out of itself in the act of reflection. Denis Diderot's *Jacques* (written ca. 1771–1778) takes the lead in drawing daring lessons from Sterne's so-styled "gonopsychic anthropology" and metafiction—for example, that humanity is engaged in the coproduction of psychohistory. Exploration of the strange new infinity of the mind and its rules eventually is staple fare in romantic fiction. Going beyond romantic irony, E. T. A. Hoffmann dares to implement psychotic states as narrative paradigms and to release demonic and terrifying forces in the stories gathered in his *Nachtstücke* (Night-Pieces, 1817). In his novel *The Devil's Elixirs* (1815–1816), the self splinters into a proliferation of doppelgängers to the extent that it disappears as a stable, knowable entity.[3]

Since the Western poet has long functioned as the lead figure especially charged with the affairs of selfhood, we can legitimately view more recent stages in the debate about the fate of the self as natural elements in an ongoing devolution of an older romantic subject who comprehended all creaturely and spiritual aspects of being in his own being. This access for singular existence to a vision of universal connection Brentano interprets at the start of the nineteenth century in the poem "Swansong"

---

3. Cf. Gerald Gillespie, "Disembodied Voice, Disinherited Mind: 'Development' in Pre-Romantic and Romantic Fiction," in *Proceedings of the 7th Congress of the International Comparative Literature Association* (Stuttgart: Kunst und Wissen-Erich Bieber, 1980), 1.479–86.

("Schwanenlied") as the poet's tragic destiny. All the scenes of life's passion flash in the mind of the swan or poet as winter claims him; his once torrid wings now immured in ice, the creature's final thoughts simultaneously embrace life and death. The last four lines of this densely emblematic poem read, here rendered in crude prose:

> All sufferings are joy, all hurts jest,
> And the whole of life sings from my heart:
> Sweet death, sweet death
> Between morning's and evening's glow.[4]

Brentano's act of fusing the personal and the universal story in one text as the swansong fits Friedrich Schlegel's dictum that

> Artists make mankind an individual by connecting the past with the future in the present. Artists are the higher organ of the soul where the vital spirits of all external humanity join together, and where inner humanity has its primary sphere of action.[5]

The experience of Brentano's swan is our preface to the symbolist agony of Mallarmé's swan, in the sonnet "Le vierge, le vivace et le bel aujourd'hui" (published 1885), whose dazzling plumage is "taken from" the "sun" and who knows the challenge of "sterile winter."[6] As Robert Cohn has cautioned, Mallarmé's "purification of means" results in "a richer, tighter, sweeter art, anything but a bloodlessly 'ideal' or 'pure' one."[7] Thus even though he has become a "phantom," the poet still retains, beyond any metaphoric "suicide" through which literature is purified, the trace of his human experience and connectedness. In the foreword to *The Magic Mountain* (1924), Thomas Mann speaks of the great divide that separates modernism from the nineteenth century. Looking

---

4. In the original: "Alle Leiden sind Freuden, / alle Schmerzen scherzen, / Und das ganze Leben singt aus meinem Herzen! / Süßer Tod, süßer Tod / Zwischen dem Morgen- und Abendrot!" (Clemens Brentano, *Werke*, ed. Wolfgang Frühwald et al. [Darmstadt: Wissenschaftliche Buchgesellschaft, 1968], 1.246).

5. English version from *Friedrich Schlegel's "Lucinde" and the Fragments*, trans. Peter Firchow (Minneapolis: University of Minnesota Press, 1971), 247. The original wording of "Idea 46" is: "Durch die Künstler wird die Menschheit ein Individuum, indem sie Vorwelt und Nachwelt in der Gegenwart verknüpfen. Sie sind das höhere Seelenorgan, wo die Lebensgeister der ganzen äußern Menschheit zusammentreffen und in welchem die innere zunächst wirkt" (Friedrich Schlegel, *Kritische Schriften*, ed. Wolfdietrich Rasch [Munich: Carl Hanser, 1964], 96).

6. Original text available in the Pléiade edition, *Oeuvres complètes*, ed. Henri Mondor and G. Jean-Aubry (Paris: Editions Gallimard, 1945).

7. Robert G. Cohn, *The Writer's Way in France* (Philadelphia: University of Pennsylvania Press, 1960), 225.

back across from his side of the the rim in 1903, the artist-protagonist of Mann's novella *Tonio Kröger* recapitulates the whole process that has led to the Mallarmean vocabulary: "But what of all these years he had spent in becoming what he now was? Paralysis; barrenness; ice; and intellect! and art!"[8] Mann subtly underscores the altered relationship by narrating Tonio's artistic rededication to "life" in the midst of his own existential anguish, not through any traditional medium such as the bildungsroman, but by means of a cubistic montage that abolishes ordinary time and organicism and subordinates older literary patterns as pieces of an abstract composition.[9] Mann writes in the neoidealist climate that prevails once Nietzsche, Bergson, and Freud, in their respective manners, promote the notion that identity is a fiction.

This juncture occurs long after the romantic fascination for the productive interplay between "self" and "otherness" has been displaced as the central innovation. Of course, the problem of identity has risen out of acute earlier formulations such as those—cited above—by the well-tempered atheist philosopher Hume. Nerves will, however, eventually fray. The varieties of radical subjectivity at the start of the nineteenth century which Hegel and Schelling examine in their *Kritisches Journal der Philosophie* (Critical Journal of Philosophy, 1801ff.) exhibit the enormous potential for fictionalizing the self after the Kantian turning. By 1850 European literature abounds in major writers such as Hoffmann and Nerval who pursue the subject's "doubleness," probe the unconscious, recognize the fictionality of existence, and unleash the proliferation of selves as an older unitary self collapses.

The romantic atheist Schopenhauer attempts to imbed the project of "knowing" ourselves firmly in the biological actuality of the species, with its variety of individuals who objectify the "idea of man" in its phenomenal guises. Schopenhauer's seminal work, *Die Welt als Wille und Vorstellung* (The World as Will and Idea, 1819), emphasizes that human life is driven by the same inexorable law that governs all aspects of the nearer and remoter universe. This unknowable law or "will" manifests itself in our psychological and corporeal experience as a total organism. In the famous passage in book 3, he defines tragedy—notably the great

8. "Was aber war gewesen während all der Zeit, in der er das geworden, was er nun war?—Erstarrung; Öde; Eis; und Geist! und Kunst!" *Tonio Kröger* (Frankfurt: S. Fischer Verlag, 1956), 78; English translation by David Luke, *"Death in Venice" and Other Stories by Thomas Mann* (New York: Bantam Books, 1988), 188.

9. Cf. my characterization of this novella in chapter nine, "Educational Experiment in Thomas Mann."

symbolic dramas of Shakespeare and Calderón—as the highest literary genre because the true tragedian achieves momentary insights into the deceptive appearances of identity:

> [. . .] finally, this knowing, purified and elevated through life itself, reaches the point where appearance, the veil of Maya, no longer deceives it, the form of appearance, the principium individuationis, is seen through by it, so that the egoism based thereon dies, with the result that henceforth the previously so powerful motives lose their force, and in their stead the complete knowledge of the essence of the world, working as a sedative on the will, induces resignation, the giving up, not just of life, but of the entire will to life itself.[10]

The demiurgic status of the tragedian is purchased by a kind of dying of any illusory individual self, a transcending of the principle of individuation that masks the generic. Still recognizable in this view is the function of the romantic artist comprehending all being in or through his own. Schopenhauer rejects, however, any "theoretical egoism" that holds "all phenomena outside one's own individual self to be phantoms"; to his way of thinking, such a sophism "as a serious conviction [. . .] could only be found in the madhouse."[11]

The crucial departure from romantic idealist comprehension to programmatic destruction of otherness, including all pretenses of transcendence and indeed any traces of otherness clinging to the self, appears in the philosophy of the anarchic nihilist Stirner. His main work, *Der Einzige und sein Eigentum* (The Ego and His Own, 1844), carries atheism to a logical extreme intolerable to either Marx or the positivists. Stirner deals a body blow to romanticism by negating one of its unifying principles:

---

10. I follow the text of *Die Welt als Wille und Vorststellung*, in Arthur Schopenhauer, *Sämtliche Werke*, Bd. 1, ed. Paul Deussen (Munich: Carl Hanser, n.d.); hereafter abbreviated as WWV. The original German reads: "bis endlich, im Einzelnen, diese Erkenntnis, geläutert und gesteigert durch das Leben selbst, den Punkt erreicht, wo die Erscheinung, der Schleier der Maja, sie nicht mehr täuscht, die Form der Erscheinung, das principium individuationis, von ihr durchschaut wird, der auf diesem beruhende Egoismus eben damit erstirbt, wodurch nunmehr die vorhin so gewaltigen Motive ihre Macht verlieren, und statt ihrer die vollkommene Erkenntnis des Wesens der Welt, als Quietiv des Willens wirkend, die Resignation herbeiführt, das Aufgeben, nicht bloß des Lebens, sondern des ganzen Willens zum Leben selbst" (WWV, 299).
11. "theoretischen Egoismus"; "alle Erscheinungen, außer seinem eigenen Individuum, für Phantome hält"; "Als ernstliche Überzeugung hingegen könnte er allein im Tollhause gefunden werden" (WWV, 124).

If at first I said I love the world, then I now just as well add: I don't love it, because I'm annihilating it as I annihilate myself: I'm dissolving it.[12]

Foreshadowing Nietzsche, Stirner attacks the "holy" or "sacred" in any form, including any attempt to reapply the supposed beneficial message of a demythologized Christianity to the overall process of social evolution. Like the Hegelians, he views his times as a boundary period at the end of Christianity but resolutely rejects as mere substitutes for God such principles as Absolute Spirit, Humanity, History, and the like. The only reality after the death of God is not "Man," but a plural collection of "Us."[13] Stirner's practical atheism desacralizes the world to the extent of asserting that the ego belongs only to itself as its own fiction. He daringly posits his own existence, his "cause" on a void:

In the unique one the owner returns into his creative nothing out of which he is born. [. . .] If I ground my cause on Me, the unique one, then it rests on the transitory, the mortal creator of himself, who himself consumes himself, and I may say: I've posited my cause on nothing.[14]

Whereas later atheist existentialists assume the pose of feeling condemned to create a personal world in the absence of God, Stirner's "unique one" does not elaborate a role as intellectual martyr who suffers dread, anguish, or other tribulations. The total atheist is without remorse or excuse, a person who rejects anything like Fichtean "absolute ego" and just speaks of "Me, the transitory ego" (E 199), an identity in a constant state of flux and dissolution, but also seeking full possession, enjoyment of its real world. Not only would any binding commitment

12. I follow the original text of Max Stirner, *Der Einzige und sein Eigentum*, ed. Ahlrich Meyer (Stuttgart: Reclam, 1972); hereafter abbreviated as E followed by page number. This passage in the original reads: "Sagte Ich erst, Ich liebe die Welt, so setze Ich jetzt ebenso hinzu: Ich liebe sie nicht, denn Ich vernichte sie, wie Ich Mich vernichte: Ich löse sie auf" (E, 330).

13. The complete eradication of transcendence through the demolition of Man, and the emergence of a plural "me" in its place, is proposed in such formulations as this: "Das Jenseits außer Uns ist allerdings weggefegt, und das große Unternehmen der Aufklärer vollbracht; allein das Jenseits in Uns—ist ein neuer Himmel geworden und ruft uns zu erneutem Himmelstürmen auf: der Gott hat Platz machen müssen, aber nicht Uns, sondern—dem Menschen" (E, 170).

14. "Im Einzigen kehrt selbst der Eigner in sein schöpferisches Nichts zurück. [. . .] Stell' Ich auf Mich, den Einzigen, meine Sache, dann steht sie auf dem Vergänglichen, dem sterblichen Schöpfer seiner, der sich selbst verzehrt, und Ich darf sagen: Ich habe' mein' Sach' auf Nichts gestellt" (E, 412).

amount to alienation of self; the "unique one" insists on a world that mirrors his own constant disintegration and reconstitution, thus striking a devastating blow to the rationalist and realist doctrine of integrity of character. The self becomes a self-writing text that can go where it will. By the same token, Stirner views the unique self as a statement that says nothing, a thought without content, as a permanently "manifest" or "open phrase."

> With the unique one the realm of absolute thoughts is closed, that is, of thoughts which have a content of their own, just as concept and the conceptual world expire with the contentless name: the name is the contentless word which can be given a content only through opinion. [. . .] The unique one is the frank, incontrovertible, open—phrase; it is the keystone of our world of phrases, the world in whose "beginning was the word."[15]

The act of "possessing" or "using" language leads nowhere, establishes no new convention, except perhaps the absence of norms and a dehumanization. Stirner reiterates in one startling formulation after another the incommunicability of self, a proposition that follows logically from the dismantling of language as a source of values, as a collective product or human ordinance, and thus no more immune from liquidation than other representative institutions. Language emerges as a mere surface phenomenon, borrowed tatters concealing a more profound reality—the hidden recesses of the self. The human means of language are strangely alien insofar as they are human and not personal. This conclusion carries to its extreme the eighteenth-century pessimism over language that had its most brilliant moment in Sterne's *Tristram Shandy*.

These foreshortened notes on Stirner must suffice to demonstrate by midcentury the possibility of the convergence of a denial of transcendence, a rejection of secular communitarian idealism, the unprivileging of language as a web of conventions, and the radical redefinition of the self as a fictional construct. The purpose is not to arrive at the point when we can record the epigonal reverberations of nihilistic deconstruc-

---

15. "Mit dem Einzigen ist das Reich der absoluten Gedanken, d.h der Gedanken, welche einen eigenen Gedankeninhalt haben, abgeschlossen, wie mit dem inhaltsleeren Namen der Begriff und die Begriffswelt ausgeht: der Name ist das inhaltsleere Wort, dem ein Inhalt nur durch die Meinung gegeben werden kann . . . Der Einzige ist die aufrichtige, unleugbare, offenbare—Phrase; er ist der Schlusstein unserer Phrasenwelt, der Welt, in deren 'Anfang das Wort war'" (*Max Stirners kleinere Schriften* [. . .], ed. John Henry Mackay [Berlin: Schuster & Loeffler, 1898], 115).

tion in such contemporary philosophers as Derrida. Rather, it is to provide a backdrop against which to appreciate the artistic cooptation of the notion of the dissolution of self in modernism.

Romanticism meant and brought many positive changes in European and New World cultures. But the fragmentation and dissolution of a coherent, stable self, which was an unintended consequence of romantic idealism and psychology, must count as one of the important developments stretching from late romanticism over symbolism into modernism, an outcome coextant and frequently intermixed with alternate realist views and/or with varieties of older humanism, alongside traditional religious understandings. The cumulative effect of encountering innumerable doppelgänger in works ranging from Hoffmann's and DeQuincey's down to Stevenson's *The Strange Case of Dr. Jekyll and Mr. Hyde* (1886) and Conrad's "The Secret Sharer" (1909) was to carry over into modernism, in conjunction with the spread of a new literary mentality, a pervasive deconstructive irony that emerged from waning romanticism. As it aged and turned upon the subject wherefrom it allegedly derived, romantic irony ultimately fought the tendency in mainstream narratives to treat the self as an observable biological-social entity in a conceptually stable reality.

In this subchapter of our metanarrative, a few markers must stand for the hundreds of texts contributing to the ironical dissection of consciousness and organicism that countered nineteenth-century confidence in science and progress. In 1804, Jean Paul appends to his novel *Siebenkäs* a vision in which a disillusioned Christ envisions the universe, including all cosmogony and evolution, as an infinite nightmare of the perceiving subject and proclaims the death of God. This vision had a profound impact on such French romantics as Vigny and Nerval. In 1835, Büchner's title figure in *Dantons Tod* (Danton's Death) anguishes over what the pernicious dark force is that works its will in him and in history through the French Revolution, a monster that eats its own children. In 1871, in closing his *Studies in the Renaissance,* Pater posits the isolation of every self in the prison of its own perception and feeling. In 1901, in Strindberg's *Ett Drömspel* (A Dream-Play), "the characters split, double, dissolve, condense, float apart, coalesce" under the authority only of "the mind of the dreamer" who, implicitly, hopes to awaken from the painful vision by dying.[16] In 1897, in *Mysterier* (Mysteries), Hamsun creates an absurdist an-

16. "Personerna klyvas, fördubblas, dunsta av, förtätas, flytas ut, samlas"; "drömmarens sinne" (August Strindberg, *Samlade Skrifter* [Stockholm: Albert Bonniers, 1916], 36.215).

tidetective novel in which the detective cannot solve the crime, if indeed there is a crime, and everything ultimately eludes the reader's grasp, including the basis of personal identity—not to speak of the possiblity of happiness. In 1902, the title figure in Gide's *L'immoraliste* (The Immoralist, 1902) experiences the eruption of the Dionysian power of the lifeforce that shatters confidence in the Apollonian surface of European order and the traditional basis of identity, although Gide still embeds his Nietzschean themes in a conventional confessional framework.

Our metanarrative is now hovering around the prior turn of the century as a new axial moment. The time has arrived when modern pyschological theorists such as Bergson and Freud build on the foundations of romantic psychology, its interest in internal as against external time, in the unconconscious, in the complexity of the self, in the psychological structures of myth, and so forth. The late romantic notion that identity might be a constructed fiction had profound consequences. The most radical form of the absolutism of selfhood as a kind of willed fiction appears—as mentioned above—in the philosophy of the anarchic nihilist Max Stirner. Foreshadowing Nietzsche, Stirner attacked any attempt to reapply the messages of a demythologized Christianity to the overall process of social evolution, to substitute Love, Spirit, Humanity, History, and the like for God. He desacralized the world to the extent of asserting that the ego or self belongs only to itself as its own fiction and daringly posited his own absolute, though finite and transient, existence on a void.

Kierkegaard, of course, was simultaneously repositing a quite different radical answer: Christian existentialism. But the romantic discovery of the power of the unconscious and of the nature of the ego as a selfconstructing fiction had ineluctable consequences in the modern period. Many authors who first distinguish themselves as naturalist analysts of social ills drift toward fascination for the mysterious allure of dreaming (e.g., Benito Pérez Galdós). To omniscient selection of "facts" or notes on the psychological events in characters' lives, the realist novel adds psychological impressionism as one of its alternative modes, and in due course novelists (e.g., Galdós, Edouard Dujarin, Arthur Schnitzler) hit on the idea of substituting over extended passages or composing exclusively an interior flow of the mind. Symbolist writing brings yet another appropriation with a significant twist. On the one hand, the structuring grammar of dream is accepted; on the other, the older sentimental view of the self, lingering on in the exaggerations of romantic individualism, is rejected. But the symbolist "death of the self" acknowledges the historical loss of an earlier dramatic selfhood as a trace that carries its own ontological mystery. We can regard the modernist project of dismantling the self as one of the inevitable repercussions of romanticism, mediated via symbolism and fin-de-siècle psychological theory (Bergson, Freud, Jung). Once the self was recognized to be a "fiction," even if only by the way of metaphor, it too was subject to metafictional scrutiny.

2. Selfhood in the Modernist Novel

Nineteenth-century positivistic literature, by converting the threatening and perplexing aspects of the mind into a clinical science, will attempt to contain as pathology the psychological universe opened by the intrepid romantics after Sterne.

Already in 1887, Galdós lets the title figure of El amigo Manso (Our Friend Manso), a professor of philosophy, open this fictional autobiography with the startling existentialist declaration: "I do not exist."[17] When Manso tosses the personae of his own life story into the closet as empty puppets at the end, we have a bitter modern reenactment of the grand baroque gesture of closing the world theater. The novel Niebla (Mist) of 1914 by an actual, that is, the historically attested philosopher-poet, Miguel de Unamuno, defines itself internally as a "nivola," an invented term fusing the Spanish term novela, or novel, with the fog or dream state. Spinning the tale at first through an intermediary narrator persona but then appearing as a first-person supernarrator under his own name, Unamuno relates the strange experience of being challenged by an invented character, Augusto Pérez, who rebels against Unamuno's control as author, even challenges his ontological status, and takes on a mysterious aura of selfhood as a person in the process. This complicated questioning of the basis of selfhood in Unamuno's works exudes postromantic perplexities.

But it also explicitly builds from the far older ancestral interrogation of the status of our identity in relation to human subjectivity and imagination, and their centrality in literature, which Cervantes undertook in his masterpiece Don Quixote. Unamuno correctly and unavoidably relates Cervantes's work to the "dream" problematics of baroque drama, a thematic complex we also encounter in Shakespeare and Calderón. Hemingway is notoriously resistant to the open entertainment of philosophy in his own fiction, but his technique of so-called underwriting in his powerful story "A Clean, Well-lighted Place" depends on readers' fa-

---

17. "Yo no existo" (Benito Pérez Galdós, El amigo Manso [Madrid: Perlado, Paez y ca., 1910]).

miliarity with the general terms of existential anguish developed by a host of his immediate predecessors like Unamuno. When we hear the thoughts of Hemingway's insomniac older waiter, the internal observer, in the justly praised *nada* passage of this tale, his quiet desperation is framed in a humanistic context of fellow suffering and the task Hemingway sets for us is to recognize this human condition as not alien to ourselves. Let me dip into the passage briefly as a reminder:

> It was a nothing that he knew too well. It was all a nothing and a man was nothing too. It was only that and light was all it needed and a certain cleanness and order. Some lived in it and never felt it but he knew it all was nada y pues nada y nada y pues nada.[18]

The problem of nihilism overhanging the fin-de-siècle certainly permeates both Unamuno and Hemingway, but their works rescue a humanistic sense of the authenticity of the other and thereby of the self too. But in my view their modernist versions make no substantial advance beyond the metaphysical dilemmas that we find in the great early and high romantic disciples of Cervantes, notably, in the 1760s, in the already mentioned eight volumes of *Tristram Shandy* by Cervantes's avowed follower Sterne, and in the 1790s, in the fantastic comedies of Tieck, translator of both Cervantes and Shakespeare and grandfather of absurdist drama. The crucial thing that certain authors brought about in the late eighteenth and early nineteenth century that would eventually lend vitality to the modernist novel was to resituate the propositions of the several branches of European rationalism and of Erasmian-Cervantine humanism within the newer framework of the radically subjectivist approaches of European idealism and romantic psychology.

James Joyce's *Ulysses* is the monumental achievement in narrative experiment after Sterne's *Tristram*. It works out the altered modernist appreciation of the self as an intertextual juncture, and of all possible selves as variations on themes in a palimpsestial, ultimately circular supertext. Although on one level, intermittently, we still encounter the symbols in the mental spaces of dominant or interactive experiencers, they blend into a polyphonic context that suggests a virtual infinity. The fictional plurality of lives and the complex historical situation merge as variations on timeless "ghost-stories"—for which humanity has haunting models such as Shakespeare's *Hamlet*—and the artist figure Stephen must transcend his

18. Ernest Hemingway, *The Short Stories of Ernest Hemingway* (New York: Charles Scribner, 1953), 379.

own incarnation and recognize he is the channel for eternity. In *The Magic Mountain* (1924), Thomas Mann, like Joyce, resurrects the humoristic-encyclopedic tradition as a means to encompass the entire ontology of his world up to the crisis for civilization in World War I. Like Joyce, acting as a demiurge, Mann conducts his Hans, the educational protagonist who taps into death mysteries, but also into the redemptive "dream poem of humanity" in the "Snow" subchapter, through stages of an alchemical-hermetic experiment. Hermann Hesse's *Steppenwolf* (1927) climaxes in an extended psychodrama, as the main protagonist Harry is guided through the Magic Theater with its myriad doors and pictures, that is, various possible selves, and the Christian-Western idea of a single, eternal identity is debunked. The Dionysian mystagogue Pablo teaches him to re-create with pieces of the soul in a game that suggests the free play of postmodern writing, but Harry fails to break through the illusion of selfhood and prompts Mozart's divine laughter over his all-too-human folly.

In *L'emploi de temps* (Passing Time, 1956), Michel Butor has his baffled narrator Revel search through the "foreign" labyrinth of the age-old, now industrial city Bleston for comprehension of it. We follow this metaphysical detective story through his diary entries, which by their own time layering and symbolic mirrorings suggest his entrapment in a circularity out of time, a labyrinth that is also selfhood. Jacob in John Barth's *The End of the Road* (1958) must finally face the inherent fragility of any particular fiction of the self, in a world that now offers only "mythotherapy" to those who find their life is dissolving into meaninglessness. This anxiety is hardly surprising in characters who, hypothetically, read the kind of narrative patterned by dream logic that arrives with World War I—for example, Franz Kafka's portrayal of existential nightmare as actuality, in parallel to surrealist art, as in "Die Verwandlung" (The Metamorphosis, 1915). This development is exactly what we should expect after Mann and Hesse who, in the novels mentioned above of the 1920s, take note that the modern medium of film, experienced in a movie house, constitutes a new phantasmagoric communal dream space.

Let me now turn to high modernism, prevailing more or less from the prelude to World War I until about the outbreak of World War II. Mann's 1936 essay on Freud describes fiction of this period as under the twin stars of psychology and myth. Clearly, while they use new anthropological understandings of psychology and myth, British humanists such as Huxley, Forster, Sayer, and Orwell uphold a staunchly libertarian view of the importance of individual identity and of involvement in history. Many key

American contemporaries, such as James, Hemingway, and Dos Passos, though also affected by symbolism and expressionism, stand close to this revived humanism in many respects—an example would be Hemingway's *For Whom the Bell Tolls* (1940) in contrast to Sartre's pessimistic existentialism in *La nausée* (Nausea, 1938). In addition, the first years of the twentieth century yielded a cluster of brilliant works in which individuals function extensively as vehicles whereby deeper psychohistorical and archetypal patterns manifest themselves, rather than as "free" agents involved in self-fulfillment—examples would include Mr. Kurtz in Conrad's *Heart of Darkness* of 1902 and Aschenbach in Mann's *Death in Venice* of 1912. Despite the fact that Rilke's protagonist poet Malte undergoes dangerous self-dismantlement as a consequence of his plumbing his own consciousness and being, Rilke reinstates the promise of the symbolist novel. His *The Notebooks of Malte Laurids Brigge* of 1910 both retools the sentimental-confessional modes and affirms spiritual attainment as the goal of selfhood. We follow the developmental story of the self as truancy, but the result is that the personal and universal stories knit together in a way that still fits Schlegel's romantic dictum.

Mann, Proust, and Joyce, and many another of their contemporaries link representative artist figures to a universal vision, but often in conjunction with other modes of encounter that the reader is encouraged to enjoy—for example, with the self as exploration of a labyrinth, as a trying out of roles, as hermetic experiment, and as interior illumination of a psychodrama. A locus classicus for the altered modernist sense of self are Stephen Dedalus's thoughts in the "Library" chapter of Joyce's *Ulysses*.[19] This oft-cited part of the novel has served too as a convenient marker for the hazy boundary between modernism and postmodernism because it links such older metaphors as life as a journey of discovery and the world as theater to new-fashioned puzzles inherent in acts of narration, symbolization, and self-conception. These acts unfold on another level for the reader of *Ulysses* not just in the mental space of a dominant experiencer or through the intersubjective exchange among experiencers, but in a polyphonic context that suggests a virtual eternity, a labyrinth of textual registers, regressions, and interconnectivity. As Diane Gillespie has documented, Woolf as an author shared in the experience Stephen artic-

19. James Joyce, *"Ulysses": The Corrected Text*, ed. Hans Walter Gabler, with Wolfhard Steppe and Claus Melchior (New York: Vintage Books, 1986), ch. 9; hereafter cited as U followed by the page number.

ulates, feeling that her own identity was not limited to a single sentimental life but linked with entire sets of characters she invented.[20] In *Orlando* (1928), this new kind of identity acquires a breathtaking evolutionary sweep whereby the metamorphosing protagonist ties together the formative breakthrough of the Renaissance and its historical successors down to modernism as a deeper pattern in which "she" is implicated.

The sense of being somehow connected with others and her world at large is highly developed in Clarissa Dalloway, the title figure of *Mrs. Dalloway* (1925), whose particular art is giving fashionable parties. Woolf portrays her as both shrewdly analytic and instinctively empathetic— for example, able to appreciate the unknown suicide Septimus and to despise the heartless psychiatrist Lord Bradshaw. This empathetic trait persists from her youth when "[. . .] sitting on the bus going up Shaftesbury Avenue, she felt herself everywhere; not 'here, here, here'; and she tapped the back of the seat; but everywhere. She waved her hand, going up Shaftesbury Avenue. She was all that."[21] The narrating voice that encompasses all the shifting focal points of consciousness in the novel seems closest to the mind of Clarissa in a rare moment when a fissure occurs in the surface of both narrative and historical time. Peter Walsh hears the strange murmurings of a female derelict, but it is the narrator who is conscious that the sound emitted by the woman is the flowing of an eternal source:

> Through all ages—when the pavement was grass, when it was swamp, through the age of tusk and mammoth, through the age of silent sunrise [. . .] singing of love—love which has lasted a million years, she sang, love which prevails, and millions of years ago, her lover, who had been dead these centuries, had walked, she crooned, with her in May [. . .]. As the ancient song bubbled up opposite Regent's Park Tube station still the earth seemed green and flower; still though it issued from so rude a mouth, a mere hole in the earth [. . .] the old bubbling burbling song [. . .].[22]

The tension in the opening chapters of *Ulysses* between Stephen's struggle to preserve his own inner identity as a subject and the pull of his creative vision toward the otherness discovered in the world's pat-

20. Diane Gillespie, "Through Woolf's 'I's': Donne and *The Waves*," in *Virginia Woolf: Reading the Renaissance*, ed. Sally Greene (Athens: Ohio University Press, 1999), 211–44.

21. Virginia Woolf, *Mrs. Dalloway* (1925; reprint, New York: Harcourt Brace Jovanovich, 1953), 231.

22. *Mrs. Dalloway*, 122–23.

terns prove to be by far not the sole motivating proposition of this novel. Joyce's work metamorphoses continuously for the reader, and quite significantly once Bloom comes into view. Stephen's attraction toward the loss of an older type of personal self resurfaces rhetorically in his use of the alienated authorial "we," which reenacts mysteries already present in the world-historical case of Shakespeare—a topic I have treated in chapter eight and therefore here mention in extreme abbreviation. Stephen senses being the shadow of a shadow, telling ghost stories; he wonders why a vital, spiritual power possesses him vampiristically. The celebrated conflation of Bloom's and Stephen's images with Shakespeare's in the antlered mirror in the labyrinthine "Nighttown" chapter entangles the threads of all orders of stories: the world-book of signatures, the fictional plurality of lives being lived in Dublin, the universes of Shakespeare and Homer, and so forth. Such a dissolving of distinct selves also subsumes even the dichotomy between Stephen's metaphoric and Bloom's metonymic habits of mind, basic polarities of our century—polarities that David Lodge finds exemplary of a "double tendency" in the language of modern fiction at large.[23]

In chapter ten, looking mainly at *Finnegans Wake,* I examined the phenomena of family talk—Joyce's experiments with the language of father, mother, sons, and daughters—as a dispersal of voice into voices in a larger dream process and ontology. At times Stephen is closer to the demiurgic-authorial narrative mind that unconcernedly hears language emerging from the sound of things in nature; at other times Stephen agonizes over his unfulfilled personal existence as a single human being and artist-elect. Not infrequently, he is allowed to look petulant and ridiculous. Readers sense a powerful, productive tension between "identity" (or the establishing of an authentic particularity) and "otherness" (or the threat of absorption of particularity into larger patterns). This results from Joyce's attempt in *Ulysses* to capture the identity of an exact world, of Dublin on Coronation Day, 16 June 1904, and simultaneously to retell an eternal story, a story first adequately revealed by Homer, a story that activity in Dublin shadows. The primary artist figure Stephen is caught up in one of the most ostentatious forms of this conflict between identity and otherness, because he is aware enough to witness himself making his own Hamletic pilgrimage out of the protagonist-centered genre

23. David Lodge, "The Language of Modernist Fiction: Metaphor and Metonymy," in *Modernism,* ed. Malcolm Bradbury and James McFarlane (Harmondsworth, U.K.: Penguin Books, 1976), 484f.

of the Goethean bildungsroman and beyond the Mallarméan symbolist dissolution of the self.

In short, Stephen is a lead figure drawing us readers permanently out of the nineteenth century into the newest unknown, into the modern condition and also into a condition which, so many feminist critics argue, is no longer sustainably patriarchal. I shall concentrate here on only one of the many themes that greatly complicate this literary migration: Joyce's fascination for the drama of the "androgynic angel," that is, the drama of the hypothetical complete human being, neither feminine nor masculine alone, who from antiquity to modernity is ever seeking to be reborn. Like Stephen, we move into and away from Stephen's special role. Switching attention back and forth among main and secondary figures of the novel is one of the many ways *Ulysses* plays focused narrative consciousness against an elusive totality that finally must envelop all narration on the epic scale. Joyce openly thematizes how particular individual and cultural experience is pitted against the whole known human record and cosmological vastness. It is the manner of resolving this major dramatic conflict that determines whether the supernally grotesque novel *Ulysses* remains gripped in tragedy or turns into a human and divine comedy. The many parallels in *Ulysses* to such a juxtaposition of identity and otherness or sublime unity and horror include the hurtful separateness of sexual roles as against the miracle of incarnation, of stages in individuation as against privileged moments of wholeness, and of particular conditioning milieux as against remembered archetypes and their metaphysical implications.

All of these considerations seem to converge in the thoughts of a rather touchy and bitter Stephen in the banter of the "Library" or "Scylla and Charybdis" chapter where he is determined, as a latter-day Aristotle, to "hold to the now, the here, through which all future plunges into the past" and muses, grimly and admiringly, on the life and works of Shakespeare and on the significance of Shakespeare's alter ego and spiritual son Hamlet. Something of the potential demiurge is present in Stephen's statements and inner thoughts that relate the artist's creative action, the chain of being in nature, and the reality of spiritual succession as things that are both process and outcome. For example:

> As we, or mother Dana, weave and unweave our bodies, Stephen said, from day to day, their molecules shuttled to and fro, so does the artist weave and unweave his image. [. . .] so through the ghost of the unquiet father the image of the unliving son looks forth. In the intense

instant of imagination, when the mind, Shelley says, is a fading coal, that which I was is that which I am and that which in possibility I may come to be. (U 159–60)

Joyce, who dared to think more variations on the foundational family romance and sexuality than Freud's imagination was capable of, uses Stephen among other vehicles in order to weave into *Ulysses* a myriad of variations on ugly and disturbing relationships that the romance engenders. Thus, we must be careful not to overidentify any one limited aspect of Joyce's larger message about identity and otherness as the supposed governing core of authorial belief.

On the one hand, Stephen is working out in his own mind a dichotomy that separates two chains of ontology. On the other hand, he is working his way out of immaturity and toward a more generous synthesizing capacity, which will cause the dichotomy to vanish, at least in the hypothetical miracle of a future work of art.

In accord with his need for analysis or involvement in the mode of separation, there are two distinct mythological or theological patterns that Stephen frames in quite traditional Trinitarian terms in the "Library" chapter. These appear as rival propositions in great compactness in the following excerpt from his tendentious, but intricately spun, argument about the meaning of the father in Shakespeare:

> Fatherhood, in the sense of conscious begetting, is unknown to man. It is a mystical estate, an apostolic succession, from only begetter to only begotten. On that mystery and not on the madonna which the cunning Italian intellect flung to the mob of Europe the church is founded and founded irremovably because founded, like the world, macro and microcosm, upon the void. (U 170)

One pattern in the above quotation is the mystical and organistic metaphor of godhead perceived in action and as reflected through its creation. As the word is uttered, it is the glorious marriage of heaven and earth exhibited in the great chain of being. In this pattern, the world process is inherently bisexual, and the mother is indispensable to its dynamics, since she is the channel for birth and rebirth of the divine child, heir to the father. The other pattern—which Stephen privileges here— is the mystery of spiritual heritage and authority expressed in the male Trinitarian dynamic of father, son, and holy ghost. In this pattern the miraculous power of the creator is awe-inspiring; his creative act is superior to the creation he brings forth.

Metamorphosis, Play, and the Laws of Life

The extent of Stephen's confusion and existential pain is apparent from another passage in his audacious speculations in the "Library" chapter. In a few sentences he tangles together a remarkable insight into the dissolving of rigid identity and an angry slur against the divine power as embodied or operating through the life-force:

> We walk through ourselves, meeting robbers, ghosts, giants, old men, young men, wives, widows, brothers-in-love, but always meeting ourselves. The playwright who wrote the folio of the world and wrote it badly (He gave us light first and the sun two days later), the lord of things as they are whom the most Roman of catholics call dio boia, the hangman god, is doubtless all in all in all of us, ostler and butcher, and would be bawd and cuckold too but that in the economy of heaven, foretold by Hamlet, there are no more marriages, glorified man, an androgynous angel, being a wife unto himself. (U 175)

It is clear that the first sentiment—the journey through ourselves—reflects the symbolist understanding that the self must disappear in order to release a more comprehensive, deeper vision of human life; and that especially the artist is capable of discovering in himself the multiplicity of selves that the human race bodies forth. The second sentiment, accusing the divine author of a botched work, just as clearly resonates with gnostic anguish, paranoia, and rebellion. If God is no better than Shakespeare, who began life in Stratford as a butcher's son, we are facing nightmarish entrapment in a fallen creation, unworthy of mankind's noble birthright. As the Gnostics feared, we are separated from the radiant power of our true progenitor because we are caught in a false universe. Seen from a certain angle, then, the existential victim Shakespeare is indeed a terrifying model of the supreme artist as demiurge.

The reference to the "androgynous angel," the third major complex in the above-cited passage, sounds drenched in sarcasm. The utter deadness, in earthly terms, of the finally wiser, sacrificed prince of Denmark in Shakespeare's tragedy indeed resolves the horror of the family romance he has explored. But in a dialogic turn rather typical of *Ulysses*, Joyce never permits Stephen to continue in his train of thought at this crucial moment when he might lead us readers overtly into the avenue of a powerful tradition of androgynous imagery that is inseparable from the mysteries of being and language—the Cabala. As often occurs in Joyce's novel, psychological and thematic development dives underground like a disappearing river. The intense antagonistic response on the part of Buck Mulligan, Stephen's detractor, who deflects the discussion into a mocking satyr play he invents on the spot, signals the importance of the surfacing idea of the androgyne.

The resolution of the chapter immediately after Buck's derisive intervention is a vintage example of how Joyce manages leitmotifs in order to build thematic bridges, without obtrusive surface events of plot or character development. Among the telltale materials is Mulligan's own deprecatory identification of Stephen as "wandering Aengus of the birds" (U 176). Aengus the bird-man, who in Irish mythology flutters crazed in the tree tops, serves well to suggest ironically the desperate would-be artist as an ineffectual outsider: this is the kind of demotion that Judas-like Buck would like to see. But Aengus also happens to be the Irish male god of love, one of the strangest love gods in Europe to be sure, and in Stephen's' thoughts as the chapter closes the same bird-man motif reappears with positive hints. Because we are allowed to eavesdrop on his stream of consciousness, we know that Stephen is desirous of innocence and reconciliation vis-à-vis the daughters of Erin and is troubled by the tension between the polar roles of "Socrates" and "Judas" (U 178). This bubbles to the narration's surface exactly at the moment he senses the presence of another person, as the ruling narrator informs us: "About to pass through the doorway, feeling one behind, he stood aside" (U 197–98). The "doorway" reannounces the important motif of the gate, the gate of life and death and every significant passage, which recurs throughout the novel.[24] This gate will figure prominently in the "Ithaca" chapter when Stephen passes out of the father's house and garden, and conversely the father returns to the womb.

Exactly as the emblematic father figure Bloom-Odysseus passes between Stephen and Buck, the menacing Scylla and Charybdis polarities, Stephen undergoes an inner transformation. He is able to draw together his own sense of relationship to the Dedalian hawk, accept the oddness of Aengus, and reaffirm the mystery of election for deeper discovery. Stephen's inner thoughts also establish intertextual linkage to his original venturing forth for wider discovery in the ending of *A Portrait of the Artist:* "Here I watched the birds for augury. Aengus of the birds. They go, they come. Last night I flew. Easily flew. Men wondered. Street of harlots after. A creamfruit melon he held to me. In. You will see" (U 179). Stephen is attracted to the fruits of the promised land that the father Bloom-Moses offers. The latent power of the androgyne, or unity between male

---

24. For a more detailed treatment, consult preceding chapter thirteen, "The Haunted Narrator before the Gate."

and female, is foreshadowed in an underground moment of inclination to self-forgiveness, toward reconciliation. Buck futilely whispers "with clown's awe" (U 179) into Stephen's ear—analogous to the poison poured into King Hamlet's ear—in an attempt to thwart the union of father and son, and of father and mother. But the famous, virtually magical, last sentences of the "Library" chapter convert dirty Dublin into a smoking altar pleasing to the gods. The wisdom and peace of Shakespeare's *Cymbeline* permeates Stephen's mind and the narration for a fleeting instant.

The nearness of Bloom, who in the psychedelic dream play of the "Circe" or "Nighttown" chapter will be hailed as the "new womanly man" (U 403), conveys the symbolic promise of closeness to the father. All our observations of Bloom in earlier chapters prepare us for the realization that the pathway to fatherhood is via motherhood, as in the androgynous primal scene of the Ithacan bed where Bloom and Molly form a cosmic unity. I shall not examine the inherently androgynous character of father Bloom on whom feminist critics such as Suzette A. Henke and Ginette Verstraete—to name just a sample—understandably lavish rapt attention.[25] It is no exaggeration to say one of Joyce's major breakthroughs is outbrooding Freud and Jung in staring the horror of real life and human evolution straight on, with Rabelaisian encyclopedic obsession. His meditations on the dialectic between identity and otherness also constitute a monstrous hermetic act of thievery or boundary crossing insofar as by his comments on the weird realities of life and psychosexual fantasy he steals everything and more than feminist theoreticians could otherwise have hoped to discover in the wake of modernist psychoanalytic labors. If Joyce was Bloom and Molly, he was also the self-identified Hermes-Thoth or Stephen who had to cry out loud in amazement when he contemplated the horror and mystery of the androgyne. That hermetic mentality includes witnessing the grotesque phenomena of evolution and the therewith linked astonishing nuances of human transformation about which so many astute critics such as Gose have written.[26]

Joyce is far from alone in his ironic use of psychodrama in the "Nighttown" episode to make the reader more critically aware of relationships between the singular and plural aspects of identity. The number of books that employ dream structure and psychoanalytical process as ar-

25. Suzette A. Henke, *James Joyce and the Politics of Desire* (New York: Routledge, 1990); Ginette Verstraete, *Fragments of the Feminine Sublime in Friedrich Schlegel and James Joyce* (Albany: State University of New York Press, 1998).
26. Elliott B. Gose Jr., *The Transformation Process in Joyce's "Ulysses"* (Toronto: University of Toronto Press, 1980).

tistic means to question the older sense of an organically coherent self is legion by the 1920s. In Hesse's *Steppenwolf*, upon conducting Harry into the Magic Theater with its myriad doors and pictures, or various possible selves, Pablo observes:

> "You have no doubt guessed long since that the conquest of time and the escape from reality, or however else it may be that you choose to describe your longing, means simply the wish to be relieved of your so-called personality. That is the prison where you lie." (Sw 201)[27]

Harry's self dissolves into manifold images in the mirror, and he hears this direct challenge to the Christian-Western idea of a single, eternal identity:

> "The mistaken and unhappy notion that a man is an enduring unity is known to you. It is also known to you that man consists of a multitude of souls, of numerous selves. The separation of the unity of the personality into these numerous pieces passes for madness. Science has invented the name schizomania for it." (Sw 218)[28]

Pablo proceeds to demonstrate how to play with pieces of the soul as in a game, a game that will recur in an extreme form in the metonymic assemblages and free play of postmodern writing:

> "As the playwright shapes a drama from a handful of characters, so do we from the pieces of the disintegrated self build up ever new groups, with ever new interplay and suspense, and new situations that are eternally inexhaustible." (Sw 219)[29]

Like Joyce, Hesse nonetheless appears to rescue the polarity of the singular self that is capable of witnessing the manifoldness of identity.

27. References to Hermann Hesse's *Steppenwolf*, indicated in parentheses by Sw followed by page number, are drawn from the translation by Basil Creighton, revised by Joseph Mileck (New York: Bantam Books, 1969). The original German reads: "Ohne Zweifel haben Sie ja längst erraten, daß die Überwindung der Zeit, die Erlösung von der Wirklichkeit, und was immer für Namen Sie Ihrer Sehnsucht geben mögen, nichts andres bedeuten als den Wunsch, Ihrer sogenannten Persönlichkeit ledig zu werden. Das ist das Gefängnis, in dem Sie sitzen" (Hermann Hesse, *Der Steppenwolf*, in *Gesammelte Dichtungen* [Berlin: Suhrkamp, 1958], 4:370); henceforth abbreviated as HH followed by the page number.
28. "Die fehlerhafte und Unglück bringende Auffassung, als sei ein Mensch eine dauernde Einheit, ist Ihnen bekannt. Es ist Ihnen auch bekannt, daß der Mensch aus einer Menge von Seelen, aus sehr vielen Ichs besteht. Die scheinbare Einheit der Person in diese vielen Figuren auseinanderzuspalten gilt für verrückt, die Wissenschaft hat dafür den Namen Schizophrenie erfunden" (HH, 387).
29. "Wie der Dichter aus einer Handvoll Figuren ein Drama schafft, so bauen wir aus den Figuren unsres zerlegten Ichs immerzu neue Gruppen, mit neuen Spielen und Spannungen, mit ewig neuen Situationen" (HH, 388).

Metamorphosis, Play, and the Laws of Life

In spite or because of his failures, Harry, like Stephen, aspires toward a maturer comprehension after his initiation into the fictionality of the self; the trace of the older educational protagonist is not wholly extinguished in either of these figures. Yet the fundamental drive is to spatialize consciousness, to control the biological and historical vector of time by subordinating it to the circularity of themes and symbolism in the narration. Like *Ulysses*, *Steppenwolf* projects—through its own labyrinthine mirrorings—psychic, cosmic, and dialectic patterns greater than the now extensively discredited single ego. Something even more mysterious occurs in literature long before Hesse's "magic theater." The renowned polyglot lyricist and essayist Fernando Pessoa, a Portuguese contemporary of Unamuno, starts implementing "schizomania" as a high modernist program through his numerous "heteronyms," fictional poets invented by Pessoa with their own temperaments, ideologies, and styles, who at times even comment about one another or even about Pessoa in his works issued under his own legal name and various pennames.

Henceforth many an at first seemingly traditional protagonist of the twentieth century, such as the narrator Jacob Horner in John Barth's *The End of the Road* (1958), must face the inherent fragility of such reconstructions of the self. This ordinary English teacher discovers in dream that, without change, "except in a meaningless metabolic sense," he has "ceased to exist," and that change only means "that my successive and discontinuous selves were linked to one another by the two unstable threads of body and memory" (ER 33).[30] To remedy his "cosmopsis" crisis, the Doctor prescribes a Hesse-like "Mythotherapy":

> "[. . .] a man's integrity consists in being faithful to the script he's written for himself. [. . .] It's extremely important that you learn to assume these masks wholeheartedly. Don't think there's anything behind them: there isn't. Ego means I, and I means ego, and the ego by definition is a mask. Where there's no ego—this is you on the bench—there's no I. If you sometimes have the feeling your mask is insincere—impossible word!—it's only because one of your masks is incompatible with another. You mustn't put on two at a time [. . .]." (ER 84f.)

A decade later, in Barth's story cycle *Lost in the Funhouse* (1968), historical and biographical data, including those of the hypothetical author-protagonist, a Joyce-like artificer ("secret operator" [LF 94]), dis-

---

30. References are to John Barth, *The End of the Road* (Garden City, N.Y.: Doubleday, 1967); henceforth abbreviated as ER followed by the page number.

solve into sheer myth, while myth, that is, any order of story, reflects all other "codes."[31] These include the patterns of biological reality, our cultural heritage, and the deep structures of language, all such codes being carried by identities who are "both vessel and contents" (LF 3). The "triply schizoid," Beckett-like authorial voice of the interior monologue entitled "Title" bemoans the inner logic of an unwinding of the once reassuring organic metaphor, that "Love affairs, literary genres, third item in exemplary series, fourth—everything blossoms and decays, does it not, from the primitive and classical through the mannered and baroque to the abstract, stylized, dehumanized, unintelligible, blank" (LF 105). Because consciousness is mirrored in itself, what used to be termed "factual" existence now appears to be "fictional," but in turn the paradox supervenes that such "fictionality" must be false because it is based on a "fiction." The blank, or empty center, actually puts in an appearance. The narrating voice—reduplicating the I-You polarity of consciousness on the first page of the story "Menelaid" with the question, "Anyone there? Anyone here?"—is human mentality itself, splendidly vibrant in isolation as an ongoing, self-writing fiction. Since this voice incorporates all as itself, it responds to itself: "No matter; this isn't the voice of Menelaus; this voice is Menelaus, all there is of him" (LF 127). The story contains six further layers of narration set in quotation marks within quotation marks, but all these internal utterances are subsumed as folds and strata in the master telling, the channel of which is not distinctly identified though it engages in the imposture of speaking for Menelaus. A qualitative simultaneity results, and we no longer find it easy, or even possible, to separate whose ear is hearing or whose cited voice is telling which things. When we reach the brace of seven versus seven encapsulated quotation marks bracketing the ever open possible utterance (" ‘ " ‘ " ‘ " ’ " ’ " ’ " ”), we—like pseudo-Menelaus—feel "Epic perplexity" (LF 153). Following the implications of the Möbiusband of "Frame-Tale," the "middle" of the story "Menelaus" is actually the rebeginning of a mirroring. Seven parts numbered 1 to 7 wind toward this middle, and seven numbered in reverse 7 to 1 wind back to the "beginning" that occurs at the "end." By midpoint, then, the empty space between the seried quotation marks contains the eternal potential tale that no longer "belongs" to any single name, but is the "Heritage." Being a species of writing that is spawned of and spawns quotation, Menelaus cannot be deemed either the object or the subject of fiction, but is both at the same time. In effect, in the wake of Joyce, Kaf-

31. References are to John Barth, *Lost in the Funhouse* (New York: Bantam Books, 1969).

ka, and Borges, Barth reconfirms the status of our identity as something we apprehend through constructs of language. Caught in the web of language, the self as a rewritable fiction resembles an overly edited palimpsest and not a unified, distinct, stable manuscript.

In the "Preface" to *Les mots et les choses* (The Order of Things, 1966) Foucault claims to take his cue as to the ordering power of codes built by language from Borges's fantastic imagination that links the incongruous and establishes chimerical heterotopias, but he goes on to rehearse great epistemological shifts in Western culture and to critique the human subject, humanism, and "'anthropology' understood as a universal reflection on man" with a glumness that hardly is Borgesian.[32] It is hard to take Foucault's recognition of the Kantian turn or his announcement of the end of man very seriously, when it comes 120 years after Stirner's.[33] The imaginary universe of Tlön found in a recondite encyclopedia in Borges's ironic narrative "Tlön, Uqbar, Orbis Tertius" suggests the shadow or mirror relationship between our natural "real" world, as a baffling, seemingly disorderly labyrinth, and man-made constructs, such as languages and works of art; the story provokes us to investigate the ordering rules, but never allows a decisive answer as to which (dis-)order is illusory. Ion T. Agheana suspects that Borges's fascination for haunting symmetries and the duplication and multiplication effects of mirroring reverts to Kant's finding of the actual incongruity in the reflected image:

> What can be more like my hand or my ear, and more equal in all points, than its image in the mirror? And yet I cannot put such a hand as is seen in the mirror in the place of the original: for if the original was a right hand, the hand in the mirror is a left hand, and the image of the right ear is a left ear, which could never seem as a substitute for the other.[34]

Self-deception may thus be attributable to misunderstanding of this paradox inherent in acts of reflection. In postmodern terms, reflection can be seen—as in Derrida's philosophy—as a parasitical reproduction of what already constitutes a fiction; reflection spawns another version,

32. Michel Foucault, *The Order of Things: An Archaeology of the Human Sciences* (New York: Pantheon Books, 1970), xxiii.

33. It is interesting that Stirner anticipates fully the deconstruction specifically of forms of the humanist "imagination," a move that current commentators routinely ascribe to Foucault, Barthes, et al.—e.g., Richard Kearney, *The Wake of Imagination* (London: Hutchinson, 1988), ch. 7: "The Parodic Imagination."

34. Kant is cited in Ion T. Agheana, *The Prose of Jorge Luis Borges: Existentialism and the Dynamics of Surprise* (New York: Peter Lang, 1984), 245.

difference. Mankind strives, in the multitude of individual creatures who constitute the species, for expression in biological succession and in cultural building, and has envisioned and envisions its own origin or creative godhead in a multitude of ways; but the endless multiplications produce only a similar, not an identical, image. The ambiguity of the mirror applies, in Borges fiction, to all of its analogues—for example, the "library" or "memory" as projections of identity into a hypothetical eternity. Borges, however, appears to nurture the hope that, although that eternity may be illusory, so long as the human entity can cling to being even a shadow it endures.[35] In this sense, he bridges the realms opened by Proust through the principle of anamnesis and by Joyce through that of the infinity of the moment, be that moment a dream. When we speak of the textualization of the self in such writers, we touch on a profound mystery that remains rooted in modernism and still not uprooted by postmodernism.

This sketch began with the confident rebuilding of certainty in a new episteme during the Renaissance. But a classical medium of linear narration, similar to the newer rational models of discourse, was not the only product of the critical drive of the Renaissance. Eventually the ambitious Renaissance project of reconstituting knowledge and the late Renaissance invention of a "method" that internalized self-reflection promoted an analysis of the self that challenged the traditional role of the self. Using further discoveries about the self as a fiction-making "subject," romanticism prepared the collapse of the self as a stable entity. By high modernism, Joyce felt free to treat the self as an overly edited palimpsest, as everything it has been in the cultural record. Today the individual self still exists as a legal concept, enshrined in the older terms of religion and kinship and the newer terms of the Enlightenment. But there is no clear indication yet in which direction imaginative literature will carry the sense of selfhood.[36] It remains to be seen whether the nihilistic deconstruction of the self in so-called postmodern writing will give way to a renewal of narrative structures in analogy to further newly perceived structures of consciousness.

35. E.g., the endorsement of Santayana's words (Borges's italics), *"Vivir es perder tiempo: nada podemos recobrar o guardar sino bajo forma de la eternidad,"* in Jorge Luis Borges, *Historia de la Eternidad* (Buenos Aires: Emecé Editores, 1953), 34f.

36. It is striking how the abundant modernist literary interest in questions of identity still plays only a disproportionately minor role in studies oriented to philosophic treatments of the matter, such as in Raymond Martin and John Barresi, *The Rise and Fall of Soul and Self: An Intellectual History of Personal Identity*, 2 vols. (New York: Columbia University Press, 2006).

1. Reconsidering and Retelling

The dreaming Proustian narrator plumbs the deeper core of human consciousness in the overture to the "Combray" section of *Swann's Way* before he comes back to the historical surface, the Mannian authorial voice imaginatively evokes even prehuman stages of evolution in the "Prelude" to the *Joseph* tetralogy, and the Joycean demiurgic mind opens *Finnegans Wake* by introducing us to the flow of being which the human story expresses, eternal fall and rebirth. These initiations into texual labyrinths start us on pathways of seeking and discovery which sometimes are directly represented by lead protagonists, for example, Hans Castorp whose interest in the arts, sciences, philosophy, and life is rekindled in *The Magic Mountain* and Stephen Dedalus who ponders aesthetic, psychological, and metaphysical questions in *Ulysses*. Despite their important differences, both stand closer to the figure of an educational protagonist like Proust's Marcel who, speaking in the first person and sometimes demonstrably obtuse, as he often recognizes in retrospection, conducts us through the unfolding of modernism and the crisis of World War I. These characters serve not only as vehicles for the authorial exposition of bodies of knowledge and experience, but also as comforting shadows for us readers. Whether as individuals inhabiting a world that was once partly contemporaneous to the novels written by Proust, Mann, and Joyce, or finding ourselves today in a world decidedly posterior to them, we readers too are invited to cope with a heritage. The heritage as the novelists construe it requires us—as it does fictional avatars internalized in their works—finally to reach through the multiple temporal and spiritual registers and probe below the surface of the life of the human race. Proust, Mann, and Joyce employ an extraordinary range of means to convey the explicit record and implicit challenge of human existence to us—straight narration of episodes of *Bildung,* interpolated chunks of history or scientific lore, meditation at the authorial level or the level of characters, parodies of bodies of materials or approaches to them, phantasmagoric and oneiric passages spiked with cultural references, and more. Proust's *ro-*

man fleuve and the later novels of Mann and Joyce are constituted in considerable measure, and in many ways, of thematically interlaced chains of essays.

This is a logical outcome in narrative works of ambitious design that aspire to render a "totalizing" picture of the human estate and follow in the tradition of the serial novel (Balzac, Galdós) and/or of the encyclopedic novel (Rabelais, Cervantes, Sterne). What renders this essayism more potent in the works of Mann and Joyce, and to a lesser extent in Proust (in part because of his artistic temperament), is awareness that the human record is a continuous rewriting, a palimpsest that has emerged from archaic and prehistorical strata. A corollary which the novelists explore (in the train of the romantics) is that history therefore in some respects must evidence a mythic structure. I shall consider this latter proposition in some illustrative detail in the following subchapter.

We encounter an important stage in the twinning of the palimpsestial and essayistic principles in *The Magic Mountain*. Mann depicts Hans Castorp not only as a representative of his class, society, and era, but also as a parodic reenacter of many roles we know from works of art and mythology. We follow his "education" as he listens to the debates of Settembrini and Naphta, rival interpreters of values and forces that have shaped civilization over several millennia. This sequence is overlaid by Hans's observations of fellow patients and personnel at the international sanatorium, and of himself. Falling for Madame Chauchat, he discovers the Dionysian side of life, and this intensifies rather than displaces his accrual of historical and cultural insights into his familial roots and home world. Gradually Hans develops his own independent program to explore the human and natural sciences and experiences a rebirth of keen appreciation of the arts, especially music—a by-product for us readers, of course, being a wealth of scarcely disguised essays, controlled by the ironic outer narrator who openly engages in his own authorial meditations, of which perhaps the most notable is his stroll "By the Ocean of Time" ("Strandspaziergang"), the exordium to chapter seven probing the nature of narrative and the mysteries of time. Here Mann's meditator sounds momentarily close to Joyce's Stephen on the beach in "Proteus." The character Hans eventually gains the ability to assume personal positions vis-à-vis those of the disputants and to arrive at syntheses transcending their arguments. The novel's overarching framework of alchemical symbolism contains both Hans's human growth as a new "compound" and the world's tragic movement toward conflagration, a transformational moment.

Metamorphosis, Play, and the Laws of Life

The rightly celebrated "Snow" subchapter openly exhibits the palimpsestial principle in the form of an interpolated perspectival narrative. Fictional Hans becomes a special vessel through whose dreaming on the edge of death we are enabled to connect the countless layers of human experience and to grasp the doubleness of time, once human consciousness of time comes into play. His mind, activated as a channel for the human heritage in the hermetic space of the sanatorium, suddenly opens the surface of history for us and transports us all the way back to archaic humanity. In a privileged vision—one of the loftiest and most vivid epiphanies in modernist fiction—we witness the foundational steps in the development of religious consciousness. When Hans resolves not to surrender to the power of blackness that threatens to claim him, his act reinstates the sacramental understanding arrived at by early mankind who in the "dream" face the horror of nature as a blind circle and invent mythic structures to contain it—the first steps toward a higher spirituality. The deeply melancholic later subchapter "Fullness of Harmony" reminds of the miracle of love and courage in the steps taken. The needle of the record player moves in a circle, yet moves toward a goal as it elicits and thus rescues the human voice from death, confirming that voice's nobility. Mann clearly believes in narrative art as a kind of sacramental embodiment that both commemorates and asserts the human drive to break out of perverse enchantment.

In launching his project *Joseph and His Brothers* soon after *The Magic Mountain*, Mann exploited two subject matters widely popularized in modern poetry and fiction (e.g., by Stéphane Mallarmé and D. H. Lawrence), filmmaking (e.g., by D. W. Griffith and Cecil B. De Mille), and anthropological and psychological theorizing (e.g., by Sigmund Freud, Carl G. Jung, and Karl Kerényi): biblical stories and the Egyptian craze. Taking up the family romance available in the first book of the Old Testament, Mann granted himself ample license to combine traditional ideas of scriptural correspondences and figuration with newer psychology, myth studies, and biblical scholarship. Renaissance and baroque literature abounded in epical works which taught subsequent cultural periods how, simultaneously, to retell episodes from Greco-Roman and biblical antiquity, to allude to later or contemporary historical events and personages under antique garb, and to construct psychomachias and worldviews into the bargain. Thus there is nothing unusual in the fact that over the course of a decade the novelist of *Die Geschichten Jaakobs* (The Tales of Jacob, 1932), *Der junge Joseph* (Young Joseph, 1934), and *Joseph in Ägypten* (Joseph in Egypt, 1936) should end up in *Joseph der Ernährer*

(Joseph the Provider, 1942) suggesting, among other things, an arche-typal foreshadowing of President Franklin Delano Roosevelt through the mature Joseph's political craft. Both the ancient biblical hero who guid-ed Egypt through extraordinary crisis and his hinted-at modern shadow, the "savior" of modern American democracy, are, besides being Christ figures, also Hermes figures in Mann's repertory of types; and he re-stores the figure of the clever artist of life once again under a new guise in his very last novel as the charming fin-de-siècle confidence-man Fe-lix Krull. Felix, as will be noted briefly below, speaks in the first person for an important reason. In *The Magic Mountain* Hans expands his own knowledge and consciousness of this encyclopedic drive, while the nov-elist plays this progression against the already extant complexity of the actual world which, alongside hard-won moral values—so the authorial voice suggests to us—is what human beings need to learn about. In the 1930s the *Joseph* tetralogy reenergizes this paradigm by shifting our fo-cal point from the crisis of modern Europe to a remote but crucial junc-ture in antiquity when a transformational hero emerged whose story promised movement forward, a spiritual breaking out.

The paradigm is prefigured in the family history of Joseph's father Jacob who yearns to realize the mission of their restless great ancestor Abraham. Jacob concretely initiates the shift from paganism to mono-theism and sires the twelve Jewish tribes destined to carry the heritage forward. Jacob, in Mann's retelling of this strand of Genesis, already ex-hibits the habit of mythical association of ideas in his visions and medi-tations. Hence it comes as no surprise when his most beloved son Joseph continues the practice of grasping his own experiences in terms both of imitation and of succession. The channel is more distinctly marked around the pattern of his life by which the chosen people will elaborate the elements of a new religious direction. Just as Joseph understands his time in Egypt as fulfilling a pattern registered in the life of Abraham, so we are encouraged to interpret his triumphant rise in Egypt and re-turn to the Holy Land to bury the patriarch Jacob as foreshadowing the yet future Exodus under the leadership of Moses, an Egyptian prince of Hebrew origin. However, at the conclusion of *Joseph the Provider*, it is "prophesied" by Jacob that, rather than embody primarily the function of a good ruler, Joseph more importantly will play a special poetic role throughout history inspiring his people and humanity. Mann associates his hero with the power of the artist and confirms the high mission of narration to be a redemptive act.

Metamorphosis, Play, and the Laws of Life

Needless to say, Mann wants to recover and celebrate the critical foundational moment in the Bible as a counterweight to the Nazi's sick synthetic myth. But it is abundantly clear he does not choose this subject matter merely as a convenient way to champion the threatened Jews of contemporary Europe; he is genuinely fascinated by the grand narrative of the evolution of religious thought. He expends loving care in coaxing out and commenting on nuances in the Jewish experience prior to the existence of the more formally shaped religion brought forth in a later time by the steadfast heroism of Moses after the Exodus and recorded in the next books of the Old Testament. In addition, most notably in *Joseph in Egypt*, Mann lavishes a comparable degree of care on the different, but highly elaborated Egyptian religion, and—often with gentle humor—compares modes of Egyptian belief with those of the then contemporaries of the Egyptians and Jews. To this is added, especially in *Joseph the Provider*, foreshadowings of Christianity. At the same time, we occasionally detect in overripe Egypt something reminiscent of a latter-day decadent Europe to whose inhabitants the novelist is directing this tale retold. If in scrutinizing contexts the narrator comments ironically on curious aspects of ancient cultures and myths, the game of fluctuating identities is not intended to undercut religion but to explain the basis for the long evolution of spiritual striving and standards of decency as a heritage we can embrace. Ricardo Quinones has convincingly formulated Mann's success in taking religious development seriously, while celebrating its better fruits as a meaningful past for a modern secular culture to cherish.[1]

In the next subchapter I shall consider some central themes that Mann brings forward as part of a great code in the fourth volume of *Joseph*. In appreciating the stark tone of *Dr. Faustus*, published when Mann's own native cultural world of Germany was collapsing in ruins, it is helpful to contrast the distinct narrative modes of his major late novels. An outer narrator frames the entirety of *The Magic Mountain* and the *Joseph* tetralogy by means of several traditional devices—an authorial foreword, interventions to comment on conditions obtaining in the story and in characters' states of mind, direct allusion (especially in the tetralogy) to past instances or variants of story elements, sometimes a self-evident reminder of some motif in Mann's prior works, and on occasion

1. Ricardo Quinones, *Mapping Literary Modernism: Time and Development* (Princeton, N.J.: Princeton University Press, 1985), 203–12.

veiled or more or less open pointing to the views of "modern" thinkers relevant to Mann's own cultural milieu. Touches of authorial irony serve from time to time to tell us it is presumed we are cognizant of the matters being referenced, or ought to be. These latter kinds of allusion establish a larger network which is simultaneously intertextual and palimpsestial. In contrast, aside from a somber prefatory epigraph (lines from Dante's invocation of the muse in canto two of the *Inferno*), Mann opens *Doctor Faustus* with the voice of an internal first-person narrator, Serenus Zeitblom, who amidst the disaster for Germany in 1943, two years after the death the composer Adrian Leverkühn, recounts the story of this friend and that of their culture. In effect, Mann splits into two characters the twinned aspects of the confessional mode established in picaresque literature with which he was thoroughly familiar. In the classical picaresque tale of the Renaissance and baroque period, the first-person delinquent recounted his or her life, witnessing it as if it were unfolding *ab ovo,* but commenting on it from a moral plane attained only after profound existential trauma had occurred, with either religious conversion or surrender to societal rules. The pairing of Zeitblom and Leverkühn also faintly reenacts the juxtaposition of the characters Settembrini and Naphta in *The Magic Mountain,* in each of whom Mann bundles skeins of intertwining cultural memories and impulses. The full title, *Doktor Faustus: Das Leben des deutschen Tonsetzers Adrian Leverkühn erzählt von einem Freunde* (Doctor Faustus: The Life of the German Composer Adrian Leverkühn, Told by a Friend, 1947), displays the principle of doubling.

Eventually, in *Bekenntnisse des Hochstaplers Felix Krull: Der Memoiren erster Teil* (Confessions of Felix Krull, Confidence-Man, Part 1, 1954), the novelist felt ready to revert to the split-level, but "individual" picaresque voice. However, whether by design or because too soon overtaken by death (1955), in postponing the never added "part two" in which Felix would be expected to tell us of the trauma which made him into a confessional artist, Mann magically preserves his antihero's entertaining early obtuseness and suspends any retribution and setback for playing fast and loose in the game of life. To a considerable extent, the reader enjoys the luxury of being tacitly the moral authority who witnesses the rogue acting in the theater of the world and perceives the mythic identities at play. The "confession" of Felix Krull thus accomplishes a kind of compromise. The story restores the hope embodied in the hermetic protagonist Joseph and heals the terrible gap that later opened in history between the tragic modernist artist Leverkühn ("living boldly"), who knew demonic depths, and the inadequate humanist Zeitblom ("flowering of time"), who observed his struggles but could not intervene effectively and prevent or mitigate the destructive disease of his age.

The narrative framework of *Doctor Faustus* is more complex than that of the *Joseph* tetralogy in order to sustain a quantum leap in referential complexity. There is no simple equation of historical episodes, although the title does indeed alert us to anticipate allusions to the original late sixteenth-century German chapbook and to Goethe's *Faust: eine Tragödie*. Of course, Goethe's *Faust*, a cosmic drama encompassing many millennia of cultural history and interpolating references to such great poets as Homer and Shakespeare, already ranks—in Gérard Genette's sense of the term—as one of the crowning hypertexts of all European literature prior to Joyce's *Wake*.[2] This new version or continuation of the Faust story takes up once again, as a painful recapitulation of the great symposium in *The Magic Mountain,* the problem of cultural history itself when the destiny of humankind is being tested in the crucible. The deepest story line in *Doctor Faustus* is thus that of human history since its beginnings down to the present, and through the narrator Zeitblom, Mann leaves us wanting to know how the *grand récit* can or will continue. The longest narrated strand overlaid on the story of humanity is that of European civilization and its major turning points. Unfolding above that stratum Mann situates the development of Germany from the late Middle Ages and the twinned Renaissance and Reformation onward. Running in tandem with this early-modern-to-modern stratum are furthermore the parallelisms in the Old and New Testaments of which Mann reminds us, and the pattern of recapitulation itself which the sacred scriptures exhibit. The biblical doubling of the text is clearly analogized to the youth and the "second" childhood of Leverkühn, and his lifetime in turn is recounted against the background of the period leading to World War I and then the insidious recapitulation leading to World War II (dread of which Mann expressed in *The Magic Mountain*). These sequences are embraced in an internal framing of the total narration by Zeitblom who has outlived his friend and who as we learn in the prologue and confirm in the epilogue is witnessing the collapse of the Nazi realm.

The development of the narration involves a dualism, a parallelism,

2. Gérard Genette, *Palimpsestes: La littérature au second degré* (Paris: Editions du Seuil, 1982). Gerald Gillespie, "Classic Vision in the Romantic Age: Goethe's Reconstitution of European Drama in *Faust II*," in *Romantic Drama*, ed. Gerald Gillespie (Philadelphia: John Benjamins, 1994), 379–98.

and a mirroring of what in effect amounts to a cobiography.[3] Ostensibly Zeitblom, the vehicle of Apollonian attributes, commemorates and struggles to understand Leverkühn, the vessel of Dionysian forces. But Zeitblom desperately craves to understand his own role and thus is also confessing to us; and in the process, a double polarity manifests itself which we see additionally in the development of modernism in its various alternatives, notably in such pairings as Nietzsche and Wagner. Through their own cultural roots, behaviors, and temperaments, the school friends Zeitblom and Leverkühn represent the overlay of stages of German development and the crucial need for a resynthesis of these. Tragically, a rebalancing of impulses exhibited in the two friends fails to achieve completion in the first half of the twentieth century, and malign forces epitomized by the Nazis rush into the gap. An heir of Erasmus and Reuchlin, Zeitblom—describing himself in chapters one and two—is a Catholic humanist of bourgeois background who feels positively connected to Judaism. He has studied the ancient classics, loves Italy and Greece, as a scholar combines philology with theology, believes in human dignity and reason, integrates elements of Enlightenment and romantic sentiment, and accepts the rise of liberal and democratic principles as beneficial. His successful marriage to Helene Oelhafen doubtlessly is an underground Faustian parody and an advance signal of looming failure to readers; sadly, at the novel's end the only honest way he can continue to bear witness is to curse his own sons who have embraced the Hitler cause. In contrast, as related in chapters three and four, Leverkühn's family still bears characteristics from the rebellious first Protestants and a proclivity toward the natural sciences and experimentation, married with a tendency toward melancholy. Through the names of persons associated with Leverkühn's early and later life, Mann indicates lingering traits associated with medieval mysticism, fear of witchcraft and magic, anxiety over discovering the secrets of nature, and the Faustian drive for a key to understanding the world. The author likewise signals Leverkühn's mixed heritage through the mother who is a

---

3. Starting from the pair Erasmus and Luther in his book *Dualisms: The Agon of the Modern Age* (Toronto: University of Toronto Press, 2007), Ricardo Quinones deals with a series of rival, yet complementary, historical figures in whom we see variations on a recurrent polarity and cultural dialectic which down to the present remains unresolved. Like Thomas Mann in his fictions and in essays on major cultural figures, in these pairings Quinones discerns bundled complexes of belief, temperament, social ties, and the stimuli of historical events—particular actual cases that exhibit the rhythms and metamorphoses of Western culture.

brunette with "Roman blood," and the composer's own strange blue-gray-green eyes with metallic sprinkles and rust-colored rings—a kind of identification that echoes earlier works of Mann (e.g., the artist-elect Tonio's mixed traits in the novella *Tonio Kröger*) and thus links the author Mann implicitly to Leverkühn as well as to Zeitblom as a scion of a "divided" heritage.

As in *The Magic Mountain,* so too in *Doctor Faustus* the myriad details woven into the fictional cobiographies of Zeitblom and Leverkühn are connected to Mann's modernist geocultural map of Europe and the world—a framework that chapter four ("Prime Coordinates") of the present book has treated. The essential compass in Mann's works places Germany in the contested center of evolving Europe. Among the major axes are the southeast to northwest migration of civilization over the centuries, from the Greek-Levantine region by way of Italy to the French and Dutch facing on the Atlantic. Another alignment in Mann's map juxtaposes the purer Germanic North, earlier barbaric, in tension with the Mediterranean South, which itself was once pagan, but adopted Christianity and matured earlier. The most advanced Western tendency, manifested in liberal, democratic Britain and in its vital extension to America, is countered by a reactionary, backward Russia to the east, the dubious buffer between Europe and Asia. In Mann's lifelong play with the legacy of Nietzsche and Wagner, this map moreover presents a complicated field of crisscrossing Dionysian and Apollonian attributes; mixtures abound, and either polarity may appear encapsulated or hidden where the other seems to prevail. In *Doctor Faustus,* Mann grapples once again with the mysterious Donysian power of music in German culture, a power that during the later nineteenth century invaded and devastated the family in the novel *Buddenbrooks* and in the early twentieth preoccupied but also heightened the life of Hans Castorp in *The Magic Mountain.* Thus, in making a modern composer and the crisis of modern music the core of *Doctor Faustus,* Mann grapples with a dangerous, perplexing subject matter. But as Susan von Rohr Scaff has shown, Leverkühn's anguish as a creator who has been destined to wrestle with demonic forces ultimately restates a message of redemption *in extremis.*[4]

Mann piles up developmental strata in a multilevel palimpsest so that certain symptomatic traits emerge from his and our correlation of

---

4. Susan von Rohr Scaff, *History, Myth, and Music: Thomas Mann's Timely Fiction* (Columbia, S.C.: Camden House, 1998).

the layers. He simultaneously engages in a searching examination of these traits, a massive essay on culture which he writes "indirectly" both through the observations of Zeitblom and through recurrent favorite numerological, psychological, and anthropological motifs. Mann, Joyce, and Proust share a fascination for "doubling" associated with androgynic patterns in humanity. In addition, Joyce and Mann show an obsession with certain numbers, each having his own favorite combinations. The numerological coding that Oskar Seidlin demonstrated in the case of *The Magic Mountain* certainly applies to *Doctor Faustus* as well.[5] Mann is obsessed by patterns of 3 and 4, resulting in the important 7 and the magical squaring of the Chaldean series in 49. He is also drawn to combinations that yield 10, a dangerous number containing both unity (the 1) and nothingness (the 0), and by their interaction infinity (1 × 0). It is his own private numerological system that Mann ruminates on in addition to exploiting the twelve-tone system of musical composition which he "borrows" from Arnold Schönberg for its symbolic values. The numerological system also appears connected to the brooding of the early modern period, exemplified in the fixation of artists like Albrecht Dürer on the problem of melancholy; this thematic cluster recurs in the distress of the modern mind as it grapples with the puzzles in nature and the cosmos in Mann's novel. If we try to erect some sort of analytical scaffolding to grasp how Mann guides us in our reading of *Doctor Faustus,* we find ourselves constrained to imagine something like a multidimensional chess board through which our minds can move in a variety of directions, thereby generating another quality of time experience. In each separate rereading our appreciation of the novel discovers new interconnections as if we are listening once again to a great symphony and deepening our awareness of its themes.

The late Renaissance, notably in its mannerist and baroque phases, brought forth the awareness that a work of art could be a multidimensional construct, and often sought to impart to viewers and readers the understanding that they as members of an audience were experiencing involvement in a special realm. We see this impulse, for example, in Maurice Scève's long poem *Délie, objet de plus haulte vertu* (Délie, Object of Supernal Virtue, 1544) written in ten-line strophes, with fifty interspersed emblemata whose mottoes are drawn from the final line of pre-

---

5. Oskar Seidlin, "The Lofty Game of Numbers: The Mynheer Peeperkorn Episode in Thomas Mann's *Der Zauberberg*," *PMLA* 86 (1971): 924–39.

ceding poetry. In the manneristic mental game, we can read both across each line, line by line in a traditional flow, and at times among lines vertically or obliquely; and we can slip in and out of the alternate visual language of the *picturae*. Cervantes famously introduces his readers to the game of literature in *Don Quixote* (1605, 1615); after training us to critique its forms and to posit their roots in the human mind, he goes so far as to hold a living symposium on literary art at the end of part 1 and to spawn metaphysical puzzles regarding the seeming reality of fictional figures throughout part 2. Mann's deliberate "musicalization" of his narrative *Doctor Faustus* depends, of course, on the fact of his readership's thorough prior training in the Wagnerian revolution and our ability to appreciate the echo effect of motivic repetitions and thematic development. Joyce parlays his particular kind of multidimensionality to dizzying heights in *Finnegans Wake* and famously caps the creation of his alternate universe by allowing it to demonstrate its own self-enclosure through the circular tie that joins ending and beginning. If we rightly think of the *Wake* as one of the most hypertrophic of palimpsests in all literature, nonetheless it is manifestly, over many and often large stretches, also a container of innumerable "essays." Sometimes a piece of history may be examined by Joyce under the guise of an allegorical fairytale, sometimes the novel may veer into what amounts to speculation on a question such as the origin of language, sometimes the authorial mind self-indulgently sports with contemporary references such as to modern schools of psychiatry or to religious systems, and so forth—there is a rich variety in Joyce's rambling, intermittently essayistic pieces toward an encyclopedia.

Mann engaged in an important demonstrative kind of doubling when, in 1949, he published *Die Entstehung des "Doktor Faustus": Roman eines Romans* (The Genesis of Doctor Faustus: The Novel of a Novel). As Rüdiger Görner has shown cogently, Mann was concerned over his own relationship to trends in the modern novel toward self-referentiality.[6] This went beyond the poetological discussion of literary structures and reception as a subject matter of literature in the tradition from Cervantes and Sterne. It included increasingly the use of narration for authorial self-reflection and historicizing, and the encompassing of authorial reflections on the world and humankind very close to philosophic discourse.

6. Rüdiger Görner, *Thomas Mann: Der Zauber des Letzten* (Düsseldorf and Zürich: Artemis und Winkler, 2005). See especially the chapter "Adrian Leverkühns Musik des Letzten," 139–59.

As Görner points out, Mann was particularly upset to learn from critics like Harry Levin about the radical avant-gardist leap which Joyce had completed in 1939 with the *Wake*.[7] On the one hand, he wondered whether his own reliance on the split between a partly obtuse first-person voice (Zeitblom) and a third-person creative actor (Leverkühn) might make his work seem outmoded. On the other hand, he was irritated that some negative reviewers could not distinguish between the dangerous forces which beset the world as depicted in his novel and his own authorial purposes and perspective. The fact he had also come through a difficult time, surviving an operation for lung cancer, as well as having been heavily engaged in social and political efforts as a leader of the exile community in America, also impelled him to tell the story of the storyteller—to hold up his own mirror to the artifice he had wrested from time, lest his public be misled and fail to associate him with the serious contemporary artists whose works were a kind of narrated theory, and psychograms revealing the deepest essence of the age.

When Mann sought a free mental space away from the urgent questions of the postwar situation in his novella *Der Erwählte* (The Holy Sinner, 1952), contemporary criticism by and large was not disposed to follow gladly, even though the work enjoyed considerable acclaim. Its central themes of androgyny and incest returned to basic subject matter since Mann's earliest works, but unlike *Wälsungenblut* (The Blood of the Walsungs, 1906), in which he tied the story line of headstrong brother-sister mating in modern Berlin directly to a travesty of Richard Wagner's popular *Ring* cycle, *The Holy Sinner* was set less familiarly in the Middle Ages and drew on the medieval poet Hartmann von Aue's verse romance *Gregorius*. The biblical plot elements of the Joseph saga were far better known and the *Joseph* tetralogy was completed before the horrors of World War II radically altered the expectations of Mann's public. Faced with the cold war, the broader initial readership was unable to focus well on the sense and spirit behind his treatment of the legend of a young nobleman, the offspring of brother-sister love, who by tragic mischance marries his widowed mother, seeks to expiate their sin by withdrawal in holy hermitage, and becomes a great pope, nor to appreciate the author's unmistakable delight in aspects of the long past medieval world. However critics currently may rank *The Holy Sinner* in some qualitative hierarchy of Mann's writings, the realization has gradually taken

7. Görner, *Thomas Mann: Der Zauber des Letzten*, 154.

hold that it, too, attempts to retrieve a paradigm of human purposefulness from an old inspiring story of fall and recovery. It is a scarcely disguised essay in cultural history that deliberately turns back to a period in which a Europe of many parts and peoples shared a common ethos antedating nationalism—the wise, benign Pope Gregory of our tale envisions a reasonable community in the spirit of this hypothesis and hope. The stages whereby the story of incest unfolds picture allegorically a progression from narcissism to moral self-consciousness and finally to enlightened awareness of community. Once again we can detect the influence of the romantic philosopher Novalis in Mann's manner of portraying the happy reunion of mother and son-husband on a higher plane of loving kindness after all the travails of life. Contrary to Freudian pessimism, the violence of Oedipal struggle dims away in the course of suffering and learning.[8] *The Holy Sinner* lends special force to Mann's avowal of the erotic nature of irony. The gambit of employing an internal medieval narrator, the Irish monk Clemens, who can relate to the world of Gregorius, in a work that is openly a modernist palimpsest, only underscores that principle.

Partly because of its tighter narrative form echoing the density of Hartmann's poem, Mann's novel is never pulled into the kind of vortex of historical detail, the pageantry, occasionally ribaldry, and roving disorder which we see in a later work like Umberto Eco's *Baudolino* (2000). By first exhibiting supposed samples of Baudolino's error-laced writing as if from a chrestomathy of the Italian language and then switching to a third-person version of his adventures supposedly redacted by some unknown later editor-author, Eco "doubles" the ploy of pretending that we are following a medieval narrator, the picaro-like title figure who swiftly rises into the currents of high politics in the disastrous Fourth Crusade. Adventurous Baudolino is close cousin not to Mann's Gregorius, but to his Felix; we go on a grand tour of the strange, yet oddly enchantment-filled world of the early twelfth century with him. Eco strives to evoke for us many of the ancestral traits and proclivities which underlie our overconfident sense of distance from our own "exotic" past, whereas half a century earlier in *The Holy Sinner* Mann grasps for a hold on what he feels is the very threatened ideal of a meaningful modernity

---

8. Russell Berman has noted the demurrer from Freud and analyzed the multilevel story in his introduction to the reissued English translation by H. T. Lowe-Porter, *Thomas Mann: The Holy Sinner* (Berkeley and Los Angeles: University of California Press, 1992), vii–xxi.

and enlightened polity. Both a thesis of human development in its grander dimensions and the educational promise of the European experiment are projected by means of a medieval legend which Mann retrieves for us as something inhering in the palimpsest of the twentieth century.

The period surrounding World War II is replete with several strains of novels that reflect the felt reality of repeated epochal rupture, disorder and fragmentation, social pathologies, and the threat of irreversible loss of cultural values. In the broader class of allegorical narratives are works like the cultural conservative Ernst Jünger's apocalyptic vision of the attack on the foundations of Western culture by sinister new rebels (read: the Nazis, led by Hitler) in *Auf den Marmorklippen* (On the Marble Heights, 1939), the existentialist Albert Camus's depiction of the spreading totalitarian threat in *La Peste* (The Plague, written ca. 1942, published 1947), and the British humanist George Orwell's dystopic fable of life under totalitarian dictatorship in *Animal Farm* (1945). The nightmarish futuristic variation, drawing on contemporary historical details, is Orwell's *1984* (1949). The cultural conservative Alexander Solzhenitsyn, in such works as *The First Circle* (1968) and *The Gulag Archipelago* (1973), is preeminent among the numerous authors who have directly commented on the baleful reality of the Soviet brand of totalitarian rule. Honorable defenders of the liberal and social democratic traditions after World War I and again after World War II include figures as diverse as Aldous Huxley in early works like *Point Counter Point* (1925) and *Brave New World* (1932), André Malraux scrutinizing the political and cultural civil war preceding the world war in China in *La condition humaine* (Man's Fate, 1933), Ernest Hemingway on the Spanish civil war in *For Whom the Bell Tolls* (1940), and the American expatriate Richard Wright in his nonfiction book *Pagan Spain* (1957). A great deal of confusion about spiritual allegiances still lingers because writers of many different stripes were responding in an era when anarchic and nihilist attitudes and doctrines of decadence were in full bloom, and allegiances could shift over a lifetime. *Die Anarchisten: Kulturgemälde aus dem Ende des 19. Jahrhunderts* (The Anarchists: A Picture of Civilization at the End of the Nineteenth Century), the Scot-German John Henry Mackay's classic novel of 1891 set in working-class London, in addressing the tangle of anarchic and nihilistic impulses, contrasted the communist position as a deceptive new authoritarian threat, indicted syndicalism as criminal madness, and sought to resurrect the ideal of pure, absolute anarchism lifted from Max Stirner's remarkable treatise of 1844, *Der Einzige und sein Eigentum* (The Ego and

Its Own). *Die Anarchisten* reflected negatively on the rising tide of rationalizations of violence, rejecting by anticipation such classics as Georges Sorel's *Réflexions sur la violence* (Reflections on Violence) and *Les illusions du progès* (Illusions of Progress), both appearing in 1908. Oswald Spengler's *Der Untergang des Abendlandes* (Decline of the West, 1917) is one the more prominent works which formulates a sweeping theory of the collapse of Europe's grand narratives, thus an inevitable loss of cultural coherence and world status.

Against this backdrop, it seems futile today to repeat slogans such as "reactionary" and attempt to apply this term as a pejorative to an author like Mann who struggled decade after decade amid epochal disorder to analyze the cultural impulses at play and to construct an independent view of what is humanly desirable.[9] There is a plethora of Mann's contemporaries who more distinctly belong to some direction inimical to what he endorsed in the longer run or who develop inversely to him, moving from a liberal to an authoritarian or totalitarian persuasion. Mann pays attention to the vitalist strain the the early twentieth century, but in the final analysis finds it—like the spiritualist craze and other attractions—to be flawed and failed, as witness the Peeperkorn and séance sections of *The Magic Mountain*. The full-blown irrationalism of vitalism is not seen in the quondam decadent, later professing fascist, Gabriele D'Annunzio nor in the sorry case of the neoromantic, nationalistic Knut Hamsun who foolishly mistook Nazi propaganda about the folk as promising a chance for authentic Norwegian identity, in resistance to both British and Soviet imperialism. The truly flamboyant example is

9. The essay "Modernism and the Technologies of Insight" by Julian Nelson, in *Modernism* (Philadelphia: John Benjimns, 2007), 419–30, can be cited among innumerable illustrations of the persistent problem of critics who seek to be superior to the novelist Mann by the simple method of extracting motifs and themes with which Mann himself has constructed an intricate examination of processes and forces in his culture, and then employing the same materials as instruments to subject Mann to analysis, in order to find him implicated in all the ills of his age. A product of a generation of deconstructionist exercises, this debilitating habit entails ignoring both explicit statements of position over a long career and obvious strategies of valuation which the novelist has internalized in specific fictions and series of fictions. The predictable outcome is that the creative writer is permanently tainted with complicity, while the critic swans about majestically. As the young ironist Mann has the jealous, self-important critic think a century ago, on leaving the performance depicted in "Das Wunderkind": "Die Kritik ist das Höchste." One example of better critical practice: In "The End of the Millenium: Thomas Mann and the Last Romantic Generation" (Ph.D. diss., Stanford University, 1998), Jason Apuzzo meticulously compares and contrasts position statements by Mann and those of a large selection of prominent German intellectuals in the critical decade of decision when Hitler came to power, and clearly discriminates Mann's achievement measured against a range of responses to the dangers and ills of the age.

the medical doctor and powerful writer Louis-Ferdinand Céline, a rest-less wanderer and nihilistic anarch who yearned for an undefined trans-formational apocalypse that would cleanse Europe of its essential corrup-tion. Two of his major works, *Voyage au bout de la nuit* (Voyage to the End of Night, 1932) and *Mort à credit* (Death on the Instalment Plan, 1936), had already gained him notice before he veered fulsomely into paranoiac anti-Semitism as a way to rail against human degradation and collabo-rated with the fascist Vichy regime. Just as perplexing is the case of the enormously popular Maxim Gorky who appeared to be a champion of the poor and oppressed, was drawn to social democracy, was early and openly critical of Bolshevik censorship, but like an Italian futurist ad-mired Mussolini in the 1920s and excoriated American capitalist soci-ety as soulless. Actually an elitist, Gorky wanted urbanization and indus-trialization and he justified the terrible treatment of the peasants under collectivization, even while he encouraged Russian writers to translate major foreign works. Solzhenitsyn devotes an entire chapter of the *Gu-lag Archipelago* to condemning Gorky and his many collaborators who produced the notorious propaganda work, *Belomorsko-Baltiyiskiy Kanal imeni Stalina* (Stalin's Belomorsk-Baltic Canal, 1934), for being the only group of writers in modern times to glorify merciless slavery. The novel *La familia de Pascual Duarte* (1942) by the many-talented Galician fascist and Franco adherent Camilo José Cela seems equally bleak in depicting the horrific eruption of criminality on the part of a lower-class person, but it has an important subtext. Cela's work justifies benign authoritar-ian rule as a necessity.

2. Stories Profane and Sacred

Of our chief triumvirate of novelists Mann became the most en-gaged socially and politically as a participant in the monumental con-test that unfolded with the rise of totalitarian states in Europe and that was only partly resolved in World War II. He contrasts with Joyce inso-far as Joyce, although he made an impressive range of elements of his-tory into subject matter for fiction, programmatically avoided personal capture in history's toils as dangerous for the truth-telling artist. Proust seems closer than both Mann and Joyce in acting as a "straightforward" recounter of many strands of the life of his times. While he shares nu-merous traits with them such as a conviction in the essentially andro-gynic constitution of the psyche and in resemblances among patterns of life experience, narration, and music, he remains principally devoted to memory and history. In this sense the novelist draws closer to the historian. Mann and Joyce differ from Proust in the extent of their fluctuation between the polarities of history and myth as a higher or more primary order against which things should be measured. Joyce tended toward amalgamating and conflating archaic and historical episodes of humanity and placing his compounds within myth-based analytical and container structures, such as the loosely applied forms of the Odyssean epic in *Ulysses* or the Viconian paradigm of a succession of ages and *ricorso* or recycling in the *Wake*. Once Mann had worked through in his own mind to a resolution of the question of the claims of German tradition as against the developmental logic of the modernizing democracies by the end of World War I, his "problem" with history actually became more challenging insofar as his own humanist commitment to the cause of civilization entailed thereinafter the necessity of also acknowledging that the hope in the reality of progress, the higher Western goal, was constantly threatened. He recognized that residual older aspects of culture, however constructive and appropriate in the past, sometimes needed to be superseded or transformed. This painful realization informs the grief that Hans feels in *The Magic Mountain* when he must let go of his noble cousin Joachim, whose death in effect is the dying of a huge part of his own spiritual identity. Mann's passionate researches into psychological and mythological evidence posed its own powerful counterattraction, the tempting glimpse into the abyss rather than the renewed resolution to struggle toward the difficult future. His endeavor to reconstitute a meaningful relationship between the pathway of history as a humane story and the spell of mythic identity, which attained a comforting outcome in *Joseph and His Brothers,* almost led over the brink of despair in *Doctor Faustus.*

There are some prominent analogies between the figurations which Mann in the *Joseph* tetralogy and Joyce in the *Wake* employ in setting out the basics in the evolution of the family romance and for a human typology. Both artists start from the well-known anthropological facts of myths of creation in which an intramundane divine couple, usually twinned brother and sister, bring forth the cosmos and humankind. The arrival of humankind entails consciousness which releases awareness of the creation mysteriously as a Fall. Once the vital process is launched, conflict appears in the contest between brothers as in the story of Cain and Abel in Genesis. Consonant with the examples given in sacred scripture and many myths, being a channel of revelation or insight is often assigned to one protagonist type or kind of brother in the works of Mann and Joyce. But it can be fashioned as a perplexed aspect of multiply split male roles. In *Ulysses,* Stephen Dedalus feels his deeper identity with Thoth, the Egyptian god of writing, numbers, and magic, and this is a crucial aspect of Shem the penman in the *Wake,* while his brother Shaun the postman usurps and delivers the message which Shem brings forth as revelation. Joseph is explicitly connected with Thoth in the opening chapter of *The Young Joseph* well before his important career in Egypt. As a beautiful ephebe, the shepherd boy Joseph also represents the attractive savior figure who is destined to appear in human affairs. Mann expands on the implication in Genesis that the special family who carry the capacity for insight is many generations deep, even though the layers of spiritual development seem copresent as if in an eternal moment of potential creative breakthrough. The contest between the chosen vessel, as Isaac, and his brother Esau is replicated in the opposition of the brothers, led by Reuben, to their father's favorite Joseph. The promise of redemption, the reconciliation of the heirs (the people of Israel and ultimately mankind at large), is pictured in the loving bond between Joseph and the youngest son Benjamin. Mann dotes on the parallelism between going down into Egypt and returning, of being consigned as a victim to the pit as Joseph is and being rescued from it, and the future Christian story of a resurrected savior who is the son of God and champion of the human race.

Like so many poets since the Renaissance, Mann and Joyce readily exploit resemblances found in Near Eastern and Egyptian religions in the stories of handsome gods such as Osiris who are sacrificed and then reconstituted and reborn. But there is a significant difference between Joyce's interest in the rebirth of the "husband" or "father" as "son" and the way Mann introduces the theme in the Joseph novels. There it is elaborated in conjunction with the first appearance in history of an extramundane godhead whose nature and purposes must and will be puzzled out over untold generations. This occurrence of a world-altering intuition of the existence of a sole supreme God qualifies how we should regard the gradual metamorphosis of the sacrificial hero figure who will become central in the Judeo-Christian tradition. The favorite son Joseph is already present, as if foreordained, in the opening pages of *The Tales of Jacob* and possesses a luster which internalizes the beauty of his mother Rachel, before we read on and get to know his father Jacob and her. The master "Preface" has already informed us that Jacob was capable of discovering the "real world-navel" and envisioning "the umbilical cord between heaven and earth" (Lowe-Porter 21).[10] For the ladder to heaven in Scripture, Mann suggests a literal marriage or bonding of heaven and earth; the umbilical cord more boldly states God's mothering of the world He marries. The next novel, *Der junge Joseph*, deepens the import of this mystery by taking us back to Jacob's and Joseph's remote ancestor Abraham who in a sense invented God by changing His relationship to the world. Mann attributes to Abraham a radical move, the biblical idea of man being made in God's image as the opening of Genesis states, whereby a new human-divine mirroring emerges, an I-Thou relationship that simultaneously reveals God as more than nature, as extramundane: "They were two, an I and a Thou, both of whom said 'I' and to the other 'Thou.' [. . .] But after all God remained a powerful Thou, saying 'I,' independent of Abraham and independent of the world" (Lowe-Porter 287).[11]

Mann depicts the development of ancient Hebrew monotheism in minute steps. The aim of this gradualism is to evoke the naturalness of the achievement, while respecting its epochal significance. The removal of the father figure into a supreme status as a heavenly father has the consequence of elevating the hero or protagonist as destined divine child, a masculine heir of God, a representative of the chosen people with whom God forms a covenant, a champion eventually to be reinterpreted in the Christian phase of revelation as the redeemer of all mankind. By absorbing the qualities of his mother Rachel, the moon-oriented Joseph replaces or rather represents her function and the Astarte principle vis-à-vis the sun or father principle. George Bridges is one of the first critics to argue in great detail that Mann portrays in the origins of monotheism a shift toward a patriarchal, phallocentric concept of being which sidelines or subordinates the feminine.[12] Bridges regards the special and reciprocal love of Jacob for Joseph, as portrayed by Mann, to be rooted in a homoerotic transference. This paternal affection exhibits both the new relationship of God to his "son" and, therefrom de-

---

10. References, henceforth, are by page number to the translation by H. T. Lowe-Porter, Thomas Mann: *Joseph and His Brothers* (New York: Alfred A. Knopf, 1974). The original German is drawn from the paperback edition, *Joseph und seine Brüder*, vol. 1: *Die Geschichten Jaakobs; Der junge Joseph* (Frankfurt: Fischer Taschenbuch Verlag, 1971): "den wahren Weltnabel"; "das Mutterband Himmels und der Erde" (29).

11. "Sie waren Zwei, ein Ich und ein Du, das ebenfalls 'Ich' sagte und zum andren 'Du'. [. . .] Darum blieb Gott aber ein gewaltig Ich sagendes Du außer Abraham und außer der Welt" (*Joseph*, 1.321).

12. George Bridges, *Thomas Mann's "Joseph und seine Brüder" and the Phallic Theology of the Old Testament* (New York: Peter Lang, 1995).

rivative, a heightening of human community and solidarity, which we also see in the biblical story of the covenant. Joseph's escape from Potiphar's wife, in Mann's very entertaining expansion in *Joseph in Egypt* upon the succinct biblical mention, certainly maintains the theme of his chasteness and escape from the trammels of potentially negative sexual involvement with women. There is material with which to construct the case that Mann gives the romance of the soul a homosexual coloration through his hero Joseph. But I doubt Mann wanted the biblically founded, oft repeated fact that Joseph is winsome and charms men and women, old and young alike—though thereby he also excites jealous animosity in ill-favored persons—to distract us from the grander saga of cultural discovery and fulfillment in Egypt. Rather, as a hermetic figure, Joseph plays a broader role that is generally analogous to that of John the Baptist in the dream of the "Snow" chapter in *The Magic Mountain:* There John foreshadows the divine child and champion Christ and stands at a juncture in the destiny of mankind. He enables Hans to reach back to the primordial mothers and the first cultic shaping of worship and he points forward to later positive "avatars" such as the Madonna with baby Jesus, a new relationship on the necessary pathway of human education. Mann does not have to name the mythic figures in Hans's dream: we know them as precious cultural memories.

It is useful to think of broad analogies with Joyce's treatment of Stephen. In *Ulysses,* despite all manner of overt control on Joyce's part, Stephen still possesses strong traits of a fictionalized educational protagonist in whom we can invest our desire to encounter a quasi-factual or "biographical" person. We enjoy following his discoveries and thought processes just as, despite varying degrees of authorial intrusion or limitation of access to the minds of characters, we consider the adventures of Mann's Hans, Joseph, or Felix in their respective fictions. Stephen's search for authentic paternity and the fact his youthful quest requires his psychological separation from his mother do not determine the whole picture. Joyce's major theme of the consubstantiality of father and son in *Ulysses,* partly played out in the symbiosis of Stephen and Bloom, in no way annuls the reality of the mother or of womanhood portrayed more extensively in Molly but also in a variety of other girls and women. Similarly, we receive food for thought through encounters in *Joseph in Egypt* with fictionally "living" religious phenomena that are loaded with psychosexual contents. We modern readers know mainly as exotic items in scholarly works what the hero witnesses as actual practices or relationships in an ancient society. For example, Joseph's observations on such matters as the acceptance in Egypt of aspects of the worship of Baal and Astharte are explicitly distanced and critical. He feels a kind of pitying sympathy for the elderly brother-sister couple Huia (Huij) and Tuia (Tuij), who have attempted to live in emulation of the androgynic sacred marriage, but he is truly dismayed by their sacrifice of their son whom they castrate as a high offering. (Momentarily and eerily, Mann almost seems to be latching onto a Kafkan insight regarding the sacrificial son.) Nothing indicates that their love for each other is not genuine, but they represent an earlier stage of matriarchal consciousness; and knowing the story of his own ancestor Abraham's sparing of Isaac, Joseph recognizes the profound difference, the human advance in the nascent Jewish religion. In *Joseph the Provider,* Mann not only elaborates further on the Egyptian world but switches our attention back to the hardy chosen people whose larger story augurs a renewal of human affairs. His portrait of the resolute, tenacious Tamar, who is determined to make a mark in history and who gazes forward, suggests a companion feminine strain of greatness, the line of heroines worthy to stand alongside and win the respect of the biblical heroes.

It was only natural that Mann would reexamine in *Doctor Faustus* the deep perplexity he already felt in *The Magic Mountain.* Both novels not only treat the historical record linked to epochal crisis but also attempt to elaborate a cosmological and metaphysical understanding of the drama played out in the crisis. We encounter the "mountain" in 1924 as a paradigm for the soul, as the Venusberg where spiritual captives languish, a purgatory and hell, yet also an intimation of eternity and the unconscious, and of the secrets of hermetic-alchemical transformation, both descent and heightening. We sense something more arcane lurking behind all the dialectical oppositions: health/sickness, barbarism/civilization, progress/decadence, literature/music, ways now humanist-bourgeois, now aristocratic-folk, and so forth, in an impressive array. The "fall" of the cosmos and man, recurring in the disaster of World War I, is puzzling insofar as it also reveals the mystery of a redemptive counterforce. The novel intimates that matter is a decay of the void, spirit a decay of matter, and love a decay of spirit, but it also asserts that the human yearning for form, that is, in its higher aspect through art, emerges from love. Hence art claims a high mission when it speaks out of the ruins and defies despair. That is the essential message still in *Doctor Faustus* when in his terrible isolation the modern artist Leverkühn arrives at the extremity where he may annul the great breakthroughs of the human spirit achieved by predecessors of the romantic age, may cancel the "Ode to Joy" of Beethoven's *Ninth Symphony* and fail to follow the light which attracts Goethe's Faust onward despite all failure. Ultimately, Leverkühn's love for his little nephew Nepomuk produces the musical reaching for an answer that expresses the tenuous survival of the human spirit in the midst of anguish.

The history and nature of music is the master complex in *Doctor Faustus* because Mann believes music has played and plays an ambiguous central role in German culture. His far-flung network of references converges here in a major intersection; music is the guide that leads us through the longer range cultural story to the metaphysical mystery behind it. Some themes are recognizably Mannian concerns about the modern era recycled from *Buddenbrooks* and *The Magic Mountain,* for example, the worrisome judgment that Wagner's *Tristan and Isolde* exhibits "theatrical mysticism robust in its corruption" (DF 143).[13] We grow increasingly anxious when Leverkühn makes a trip to Pressburg, Hungary, the border zone between Europe and Asia, symbolically from the Apollonian to the Dionysian side of life, and there, in a tacit imitation of Nietzsche, contracts syphilis in order, like the Faust of the chapbook, to satisfy his "longing for demonic conception [. . .] mysteries, magic formulas, charms" (DF 155).[14] In *Doctor Faustus* the growing malaise in early twentieth-century society is correlated with artistic dissatisfaction and worry over a dead end, but Mann never draws any crude parallel between Leverkühn's restless experimentation and the paired collapse of liberal humanism and rise of reactionary totalitarianism. Rather, the suffering composer is more like a fine instrument tuned to receiving currents of his times for good or ill. The novelist takes us back to the Renaissance and Reformation because he wants us to grasp how dialectic reversals, interactions, and metamorphoses of cultural impulses occur over long stretches of time. For example, he has us consider the magic square in Albrecht Dürer's depictions of *Melancholia* and the Pythagorean theo-

---

13. References to the English translation by page number after the abbreviation DF follow the edition, *Doctor Faustus: The Life of the German Composer Adrian Leverkühn as Told by a Friend,* translated by H. T. Lowe-Porter (New York: Alfred A. Knopf, 1948). In the original, "einer in der Verderbtheit robusten Theatermystik"; Thomas Mann, *Doktor Faustus: Das Leben des deutschen Tonsetzers Adrian Leverkühn erzählt von einem Freunde* (Frankfurt: Fischer Taschenbuchverlag, 1990), 193.

14. "Verlangen nach dämonischer Empfängnis"; "Heimlichkeiten formel- und sigelhafter Art" (*Faustus,* 207, 208).

ry of the universe as involving the play of number whose concert brings about harmony (DF, chapter 12). The interchanges which Mann suggests between his sketching of a metaphysical plotline and his analyses of moments in the German past are so numerous that no just summary is possible here.

The point is that Mann does perceive a baleful connection among several tendencies of the twentieth century. He borrows the twelve-tone system of Arnold Schoenberg as a means to elaborate a master metaphor, not to indict modern artists. Leverkühn's struggle in the novel is to create a strict composition that is "indifferent to harmony and melody," that is like "a magic square," and achieves "emancipation of dissonance from its resolution" and is "progressive and regressive in one" (DF 192–93).[15] In contrast to the individualism and freewheeling subjectivity of the Beethoven era, every note would now be governed by "its function in the whole structure. There would no longer be a free note" (DF 191).[16] The system would preempt even "the freedom of the composer" (DF DF 193).[17] This extended metaphor of the return of polyphony serves as an objective correlative to the epochal story of the drift away from modern liberalism into totalitarianism. Much in the style of the devil and the Grand Inquistor who speak to the fevered Ivan in Fyodor Dostoyevsky's *Brothers Karamasov*, and simultaneously echoing the original Faust chapbook, the devil discourses eventually with the diseased Leverkühn; that is, the composer's inner reservations and misgivings are reproduced by a wary Zeitblom. For example, asserting that the artist could play with dead forms to regain a lost freedom, Leverkühn tries to counter the devil's view that expansion of technique cripples artistic vitality. But the devil answers, this is "melancholy in its aristocratic nihilism" (DF 241).[18] The composer's "rediscovery of music as an organization of time" (DF 321) makes him a companion to the time-oriented novelist, but so too is Zeitblom who shares Mann's conviction that "democracy of the western lands [is] essentially in the line of human progress" (DF 340).[19] Zeitblom

15. "Indifferenz von Harmonik und Melodik"; "Ein magisches Quadrat"; "die Emanzipation der Dissonanz von ihrer Aufklärung"; "progressive und regressive in einem" (*Faustus*, 260, 261).

16. "in der Gesamtkonstruktion seine motivische Funktion erfüllte. Es gäbe keine freie Note mehr" (*Faustus*, 258).

17. "wäre er nicht mehr frei" (*Faustus*, 260).

18. "trübselig [. . .] in ihrem aristokratischen Nihilismus" (*Faustus*, 324).

19. "Wiederentdeckung der Musik selbst als Organisation der Zeit"; "die Demokratie der Westländer [ist] wesentlich doch auf der Linie des menschlichen Fortschrittes" (*Faustus*, 428, 453).

is the mirror in which Mann catches the glimpses of his society's intellectual complacency, irresponsibility, perverseness in rejecting the historical gift of freedom and a democratic republic, the resurgence of lust for absolute power and the "old-new world of revolutionary reaction" and "deliberate rebarbarization" when the political Right and Left fuse (DF 368–70).[20] The course of Leverkühn's artistic development and anguish reflects the paradoxes and conflicts which Zeitblom registers as the agon of the age, but Mann makes it clear through the internal observer Zeitblom that it is in circles like the Kridweiss group that the intellectual and spiritual betrayal is incubated.

One of the pleasures of reading Joyce is to discover yet another point in his narratives where he alludes to a figure from myth or legend. Readers must skirt the corresponding danger. It is tempting to become so enthusiastic over a new or prominent figure as to deem it to be a governing factor, rather than "just" one instance in an intertextual-and-palmipsestial web; or, conversely, it is tempting to dismiss less familiar or less frequent figures as merely incidental associations or even trivial freight. The fact that some allusions undergo their own metamorphoses internally within Joyce's life work complicates the matter. The novels of both Mann and Joyce finally yield their own internal intertextuality over time that is a worthy subject in its own right. We may well not notice the presence of certain references in specific conditions of occurrence and shifts in their import, or only notice upon a rereading. A rewarding case in illustration of the need to let our reading evolve with the development of a figure is the sporadic appearance of the god Manannán mac Lír in *Ulysses* and *Finnegans Wake*.[21] The Celtic scholar Charles W. MacQuarrie has contributed important background on Manannán's roles in Irish and Manx lore predating his resurgence in the new wave of Anglo-Irish literature when the young Joyce came on the scene.[22] Without the efforts of Celtic scholars who were editing and translating mate-

20. "alt-neue, eine revolutionäre rückschlägige Welt"; "intentionelle Re-Barbarisierung" (*Faustus*, 489, 491).

21. In concerning ourselves with an allusive strand, we do no more than supplement or slightly adjust the early encyclopedic responses to an encyclopedic author, such as that by James K. Atherton, *The Books at the Wake: A Study of Literary Allusions in James Joyce's "Finnegans Wake"* (1959; expanded and corrected edition, Mamaroneck, N.Y.: Paul P. Appel, 1974) and Adaline Glasheen, *Third Census of "Finnegans Wake": An Index of the Characters and Their Roles* (original *Census*, 1954; Berkeley and Los Angeles: University of California Press, 1977).

22. Charles W. MacQuarrie, *The Biography of the Irish God of the Sea from "The Voyage of Bran" (700 A.D.) to "Finnegans Wake" (1939): The Waves of Manannán* (Lewiston, N.Y., Queenston, Ontario, Canada, and Lampeter, Wales: Edwin Mellin Press, 2004).

rials from Old, Middle, and Early Modern Irish, and the receptivity of a considerable number of authors of the Irish literary renaissance in the nineteenth century, it would have been far less likely Joyce would have joined in as he did with his uses of Manannán.[23] Joyce's start in the "Proteus" chapter seems consonant with the mixture of interest and skepticism, dependency and rivalry which Stephen Dedalus feels vis-à-vis the major writers William Butler Yeats and AE (George Russell) who themselves took up the tradition of Manannán from Samuel Ferguson's epic poem *Congal* (1872) and histories and historical novels of the popularizer Standish James O'Grady. Enrico Terrinoni has documented the significant ambivalent relationship of Joyce to AE and to Yeats, and the younger writer's initial fascination for the Irish sea god (unmentioned by Terrinoni) may well have sprung from the same complex habit of noticing what his seniors were doing.[24] In *The Candle of Vision* (1919) the theosophist AE conflated the Celtic lore with his own mix of world religions, with the result that, Brahma-like, Manannán's father Lír represents the primordial undifferentiated cosmos and the son Manannán a Vishnu-like Logos. The advantages of applying his own authorial control and exploiting the extant contemporary interest certainly would not have escaped Joyce.

In any event, he began reinventing Manannán in his own fashion by having the god capture Stephen's attention as he broods about fleshly incarnation and the mystery of "the divine substance wherein Father and Son are consubstantial." Then, with a dramatic flourish worthy of Neptune or Poseidon (the association is partly triggered in Stephen's mind by the deprecatory phrase, "a Greek watercloset," applied to Arius, the heresiarch who in effect demoted Christ, the son), the sea god impinges on his imagination: "Airs romped round him. They are coming, waves. The whitemaned seahorses, champing, brightwindbridled, the steeds of Mananaan" (U 32).[25] Something of the strange power of a Poseidon-like divinity inheres in "those therrble prongs" (W 628) of the father whom the weary Liffey yearns to rejoin in the *Wake*'s coda.[26] Stephen's sense of a father in the watery depths precedes the remarkable passages of chap-

---

23. See especially ch. 13, "The Old God Rises Up: Manannán mac Lír and the Irish Literary Renaissance," and ch. 14, "'My Cold Feary Father': Manannán in *Ulyssses* and *Finnegans Wake*" (MacQuarrie, 337–83).

24. Enrico Terrinoni, *Occult Joyce: The Hidden in "Ulysses"* (Cambridge, U.K.: Cambridge Scholars Publishing, 2007).

25. References to *Ulysses: The Corrected Text*, ed. by Walter Gabler et al. (New York: Vintage Books, 1986) by page number after the abbreviation U.

26. References to *Finnegans Wake* (New York: Penguin Books, 1976) by page number after the abbreviation FW.

ter five of *Ulysses* where Joyce draws together the motifs of ritual cleansing (a kind of rebaptism) and the Eucharist.[27] We have been eavesdropping on Leopold Bloom's thoughts a long while by the time he enters the bath to wash away, in addition to all else, the somber experience of his attending Paddy Dignam's funeral. While paying his respects at the graveyard, in his fashion, he has been analyzing the Eucharist in his own mind and musing on its likely origins in ritual cannibalism and has simultaneously been feeling great distaste for the grim testimonials of death and decay. It is worth repeating some of Bloom's inner voice as the chapter of cleansing closes:

> [. . .] Always passing, the stream of life, which in the stream of life we trace is dearer thaaan them all.
>
> Enjoy a bath now: clean trough of water, cool enamel, the gentle tepid stream. This is my body.
>
> He foresaw his pale body reclined in it at full, naked, in a womb of warmth, oiled by scented soap, softly laved. He saw his trunk and limbs riprippled over and sustained, buoyed lightly upward, lemony-yellow: his navel, bud of flesh: and saw the dark tangled curls of his bush floating, floating hair of the stream around the limp father of thousands, a languid floating flower. (U 71).

As in some measure we slip away from the words surfacing in Bloom's mind to a more indirect narrative voice conveying his thoughts, it is not crystal clear whether Bloom himself, rather than the narrator on his behalf, analogizes his penis to the lotus flower and brings in its symbolic values too. But Bloom's repetition of Christ's words from the Last Supper and the Mass, "This is my body," suffices for the reader as yet one more reason to link "father" Bloom (Flower), who has lost his beloved teenage son Rudy, to the "body" which is ritually made manifest in the Eucharistic sacrament. Musing in the bathtub as in a ciborium or chalice, Bloom momentarily becomes in his own mind, and in the reader's, a sacramental embodiment that can nourish, like a tin of *"Plumtree's Potted Meat"* (U 61). An ad for this homey product, with its hints at the return to paradise (plumtree), hermetic conservation of life sustenance beyond the grave (potted), and its vital embodiment (meat), has flashed across his and our field of vision earlier. Bloom's bath is significant also because in

27. Several of the following paragraphs on Joyce are drawn from my wider treatment of a number of relevant authors, including Proust and Kafka, in an essay entitled, "Swallowing the Androgyne and Baptizing Mother: Some Modernist Twists to Two Basic Sacraments," *The Comparatist* 33 (2009): 63–85.

his own exhibition of the sacramental body there is a clear emphasis on the fact it is laved by the feminine element par excellence: water. He feels as if he is harbored in placental bliss ("in a womb of warmth"), restored to the promised land (oil and lemon motifs). This return to the core by way of ritual ablution is one of many Judeo-Christian analogies to his role as Odysseus returning home.

The Telemachus figure and prospective symbolic surrogate for the role of son, the promising intellectual Sephen Dedalus, is hydrophobic yet fascinated by the mystery of the sea, as is obvious in the "Proteus" chapter. Stephen, an exile on many levels, is suffering doubly the anguish of separation and broods over the difficulty of return and integration. On the one hand, he is sorting out the problem of searching for a genuine, creative fatherhood, something beyond the all-too-human biological connection to his actual legal father. On the other hand, as a young male rebel he is trying to assert his own identity and by necessity is struggling against the hold of his pious mother. The trouble is, so Gian Balsamo argues, Stephen actually feels profound guilt and grief over her death, because his mother's love for him, however threateningly possessive it might have been or seemed as he sought to strike out on his own into life, constituted an absolute that he simply cannot rationalize away.[28] Her love was an absolute gift. The image haunts him of her sinking into the watery depths, with the trail of bile testifying to her final agony, and this comes back in the "Circe" chapter in horrific form when she appears as a green crab with claws who tries to snatch him. Reference by the antagonist Buck to the sea as "a great sweet mother" and to the "snotgreen sea" leads directly into the theme of Stephen's loss and anguish—"Pain, that was not yet the pain of love, fretted his heart"—and to the flow of terrible memories of his dead mother visiting him in dream (U 4–5). A peculiar linkage of motifs occurs starting from the mention of "poor dogsbody" (U 5) by way of Stephen's inner sympathetic memories of his mother as an ordinary human being (U 8) which mutate into terror over the possibility she will reclaim him, that he will be suffocated by nature (U 9). With his mother still on his mind in "Proteus," Stephen encounters an actual "poor dogsbody's body" on the beach (U 39), and analogizing himself to Hamlet his mind rambles in thoughts of women of every guise from harlots to midwives and of his own desires (U 38–41).

28. Gian Balsamo, *Joyce's Messianism: Dante, Negative Existence, and the Messianic Self* (Columbia: University of South Carolina Press, 2004).

Among the wealth of things which his meditation weaves together for us is the mysterious appearance of the father in the watery depths of death, via Shakespeare ("Full fathom five thy father lies"), and the eternal transformations of being and sacrificial nourishment, pictured in the half-eaten corpse (U 41–42). Joyce intimates a mysterious connection between drowning and being baptized. Stephen dreams of the trail of green bile oozing from his mother's corpse like some horrifying reminder of decaying life; yet, as noted, strangely this thought suggests a relationship to the "snot-green sea," or the odd Irish equivalence to the more robustly ancient Mediterranean as Homer's wine-dark sea. The sea as "sweet mother" has morphed into "Old Father Ocean," but what this means still eludes and torments Stephen. Oddly enough, Joyce scholarship has failed to notice that already in "Proteus," thus relatively early in *Ulysses*, we are introduced to this momentous possibility that the father and mother can blend into and out of each other.

"Water" is the feminine element par excellence, and its importance in Joyce's later fiction has long been a commonplace for criticism. O Hehir (1967) documents how Joyce put his knowledge of Irish to work quite expansively in *Finnegans Wake* and had a special interest in associating water, the river Liffey, and the originally marshy site of Dublin in variants of the name of the mother protagonist.[29] Glasheen's (1977) listing of the profuse occurrences of variant names of Anna Livia Plurabelle and of her initials illustrates just how thoroughly "she" permeates the novel.[30] One of the longer term thematic continuities in Joyce's fiction that has not received adequate attention is the transposition whereby "sacramental" Bloom reappears in an ancient Irish avatar who, in the *Wake*, as we move deeper into the *ricorso*, exemplifies the mystery of being totally laved in the flow of the feminine element. Nor have commentators as yet paid due attention to a remarkable fact that is confirmed by the ending of the *Wake* when the tired mother becomes a girl again. Readers experience nothing less at the end of the *Wake* than the first significant attempt in world literature to baptize "her," to baptize the Mother. She is reborn forever. This extraordinary conclusion occurs in the same passages which conduct us by narrative magic into an eternal rebeginning as the novel's last words rejoin its first, the ever-flowing "riverrun." Joyce

29. Brendan O Hehir, *A Gaelic Lexicon for "Finnegans Wake" and Glossary for Joyce's Other Works* (Berkeley and Los Angeles: University of California Press, 1967); supplementary note on "Anna," 355–59.
30. Adeline Glasheen, *Third Census*.

brings us to the experience of rebirth and baptism despite the situation of our having slogged our way, with the narrator, through the piled-up debris of the human story in the unfolding of the Viconian ages—despite our encounter with the sordid and weird aspects of our bodily and mental life, despite the burden of having admitted every wretched impulse or aberration which resides stubbornly collected in the midden of the unconscious.

Like a deepest memory floating up from some lost Edenic stage of earthly being, the miracle of spring and dawn appears in the story of Saint Kevin close to the novel's very final pages which bring us the Liffey's farewell musings. The novel locates the innocent discovery of the mother's redemptive grace and of her own salvation in the heart of the world, before any fall, that is, right in the green motherland, Ireland. This Liffey we meet is pristine, long before she has to accept the sewage spewed out by a future dear dirty Dublin. The Kevin passages, starting from "Of Kevin, of increate God the servant, of the Lord Creator a filial fearer [. . .]" ("fearer" plays on the Irish word fear = man), and leading to the affirmation-laden cry of someone dipping into exhilarating cool water or addressing mankind in the plural, "Yee" (FW 604–5), count among the most lyrical and charming of the *Wake*. Unlike hydrophobe Stephen Dedalus, Kevin is hydrophile. Joyce discards some of the legends associated with him as the founder of the monastery at Glendalough (Irish = Valley of Two Lakes), such as his banishing of a monster, and concentrates entirely on his peculiar behavior as an anchorite. The story line is fairly simple, but it reads almost like something out of an Indic imagination. Two rivers come together at the lakes to form the headwaters of the Liffey. The saint takes a portable altar and bath (ostensibly to serve as a baptismal fount) onto the island in the center of the "circumfluent watercourses." In the earth of his enclosure on the island he digs a small pond one seventh of a fathom deep, fills it from the river, and sits in it reverently. It is worth dipping into the passage at this point:

> [. . .] and with ambrosian Eucharistic joy of heart as many times receded, carrying that privileged altar *unacumque* bath, which severally seven times into the cavity excavated, a lector of water levels, most venerable Kevin, then effused thereby letting there be water where was theretofore dry land, by him so consecrated, who now, confirmed a strong and perfect christian, blessed Kevin, exorcised his holy sister water, perpetually chaste, so that, well understanding, she should fill to midheight his tubbathaltar, which handbathtub, most blessed Kev-

in, ninthly enthroned, in the concentric centre of the translated water, whereamid, when violet vesper vailed, Saint Kevin, Hydrophilos, having girded his sable *cappa magna* as high as to his cherubical loins, at solemn compline sat in his sate of wisdom, that handbathtub, whereverafter, recreated *doctor insularis* of the universal church, keeper of the door of meditation, memory *extempore* proposing and intellect formally considering, recluse, he meditated continuously with seraphic ardour the primal sacrament of baptism or the regeneration of all man by affusion of water. Yee. (FW 605–6)

The mythic and religious dimensions of Kevin's story as retold by Joyce are extraordinary. He can be seen as a surrogate for the author, as *doctor insularis*, that is, learned in the matter of the island (Ireland), or as a learned Hibernian, or as being himself an island in some sense. He postfigures Bloom as a body in a tub and explicitly feels "Eucharistic joy of heart" in performing his pious act of creating a baptismal pond in analogy to the natural lakes at Glendalough. Kevin simultaneously celebrates a rite of marriage (reconstitutes the androgyne) and pictures a new Eucharist in which the male body and the female sacred fluid bond into a higher thing. Kevin, like an island, sits in water on an island, and around that island flows water which courses through an island (Ireland) and merges into a greater water. Finally we realize we cannot divorce the maternal and paternal aspects of being; we discover both together, discover them as what we are contained in and what we contain. It is tempting to speculate that Joyce may be allowing Saint Kevin to anticipate by many centuries Saint Francis's loving appreciation of the feminine elements in "The Canticle of the Sun" where he addresses "sister earth" and "sister water." In any event, "she" is essential for Kevin in the "primal sacrament." The logic is clear: humankind depends on the maternal foundation of life.

The larger progression from Bloom, the body in the bathtub, to Kevin who communes with his "holy sister water" as he laves himself in the altar-tub of the *Wake* prepares us as privileged initiates to enter into the spirit of a profound mystery made explicit in the novel's coda when the flowing feminine element "talks" of her own course and yearning. The Catholic Church eventually recognized that the Virgin Mary should enjoy an apotheosis that was a fitting parallel to the ascension of her divine Son, but according to Scripture even she, the Queen of Heaven, was never baptized, in contrast to her Son. As if making good this omission in the religious tradition, now twenty centuries later Joyce permits Anna

Livia Plurabelle to find her way into the cosmic and ontological depth of the father. In the aspect of the Liffey, the river which in our human springtime washed around and through the soul of Kevin, the tired mother at the end of the *Wake* seeks rest in the father and babbles about the myriad forms in which she has known him, brought him forth, in many eras, many places. These manifestations always include by implication the reciprocal innocence of the ever falling, fallen father: "[. . .] a youth in his florizel, a boy in innocence [. . .] The child we all love to place our hope in forever. All men has done something. Be the time they come to the weight of the old fletch" (FW 621). The mother's role and gift is to make our incarnation possible (body as temple) before, in the pull or pulse of time, death intervenes; her assignment is to be the water of baptism, to wash us clean, to absorb all our transgressions in love, to enable our movement toward absolution and reconciliation: "We'll lave it. So. We will take our walk before in the timpul they ring the earthly bells" (FW 621). Departing into death (lave, dialect pronunciaton for "leave"), all mankind passes through the "time pool" or "temple" (timpul) and is washed by it. The mother knows she is bound to the laws of the world, yet she is confident in her high origin and understands she is capable of rebirth:

> For she'll be sweet for you as I was sweet when I came down out of me mother. My great blue bedroom, the air so quiet, scarce a cloud. In peace and silence. I could have stayed up there for always only. It's something fails us. First we feel. Then we fall. And let her rain now if she likes. Gently or strongly as she likes. Anyway let her rain for my time is come. I done me best when I was let. Thinking always if I go all goes. A hundred cares, a tithe of troubles and is there one who understands me? One in a thousand of years of the nights? (FW 627).

Love, the mother's principle too, causes her to fall in harmony with the fall of the father (who "falls" by means of the creation he brings forth, being mother to the mother and loving the world). I think we can see Joyce standing in the wings as "one who understands" and who invites the reader to the love feast which Stephen Dedalus missed in *Ulysses* because he could not yet unabashedly kiss his mother. *Finnegans Wake* expiates Stephen's immature failure to grasp the essential innocence of the mother, although he draws toward that deep knowledge, for example, by following the clues in Shakespeare's life and plays. Something of the real, historically determined mother who dies in actual time and something of the grief of a loving husband or child is commingled in the plaintive utterances of the "loonely" Liffey when she is "passing out" into the vast sea (FW 627).

The pain of departure and the anguish of closure of the vision of the book chime together. Yet the mother also clearly is yearning to rush into the arms of her "cold mad feary father" (FW 628; in "feary" again an echo of Irish *fear* = man). The yearned-for beloved presents a *tremendum*, a reality so powerful that it seems scary, a threat of total surrender. The final lines of the *Wake* are remarkable poetry. The Liffey feels both apprehension, the thrill of final encounter, yet tender affection and confidence; she becomes a trusting child again, in total affirmation: "Yes. Carry me along, taddy, like you done through the toy fair!" "He" calls, and "she" responds: "Far calls. Coming, far." Here "far" echoes the Danish word for father, as well as conjures the strangeness of our distance from the origins. God, the father principle, is oceanic, the unfathomable which Stephen probed in the "Proteus" chapter of *Ulysses*. Nature, the mother, flows into and out of the father. In her life cycle she pictures the redemptive element of baptism on the eternal level of a return "home," a wonderous anticipation of being with God, Love which "falls" because it is an absolute gift. The mystery resides in the fact that for us simple participants in the world the cosmic or total soul cannot be separated from her flow, although it envelopes and blesses her, even while she is coursing as the sacred fluid, the "riverrun." In an important essay, Benjamin Boysen explores the theme of the redemptive acceptance of the other as woman (mother, wife), and juxtaposes Bloom as the matured protagonist and Stephen as the still conflicted striver who resists any contingency or dependency.[31] I would add that Joyce's understanding of the "togetherness" of the father and mother challenges our minds to grasp a kind of involution that only mystics can approach, and this capacity reaches a new acme in the *Wake*. Elsewhere I have discussed Joyce's ability to resurrect the late medieval concept of a coincidence of contraries such as Cusanus formulated (Gillespie 2006, ch. "Entering Echoland").[32] Here I hope to have underlined another remarkable feat: how Joyce relates the sacred meaning of marriage, the union of male and female, to the meaning of baptism.

In my estimation, many notable existentialist and apophatic writ-

31. Benjamin Boysen, "'I Call That Patriotism': Leopold Bloom and the Cosmopolitan Caritas," *The Comparatist* (2008).

32. Gerald Gillespie, chapter "Entering Echoland," in *Echoland: Readings from Humanism to Postmodernism* (Bruxelles: Presses Interuniversitaires Européennes-Peter Lang, 2006).

ings—for example, Jean-Paul Sartre's encounter with threatening noth-ingness in *La nausée* (Nausea, 1938) and the novels and plays of Samuel Beckett—differ categorically from Joyce's intermittent lyrical epiphanies in the *Wake*. The latter amount to a modern mysticism embedded in Joyce's cosmic encyclopedism. The remarkable novels by Flann O'Brien, *At Swim-Two-Birds* (1939) and *The Third Policeman* (written 1939–1940, published posthumously 1967) epitomize the move into textuality itself as a ludic realm. Through its brilliant mixture of linguistic elements, time periods, myths, and ontological puzzles, *At Swim-Two-Birds* stands closer to Joyce, whereas *The Third Policeman* seems almost to commem-orate Kafka in an Irish setting and to anticipate Beckett. Its uncanny events in what otherwise appears to be an ordinary, even a banal world and its strange symbols, such as the ever recurrent bycicle pump, also qualify it as belonging to the larger repertory of surreal fantasy. In the mid-twentieth century, Anna Balakian made a strong case that the radi-cal features of the new surrealist mode, whose deeper roots were in ro-manticism, reflected attempts to respond, by creative acts of negation, to the felt shattering of the known world.[33] Surrealism, too, as a response to nothingness was a kind of modern mysticism—in her view qualitative-ly diverging from dada which was more a channel for nihilist respons-es. As the preceding chapter fourteen ("Structures of the Self and Nar-rative") has shown in some detail, many leading writers and thinkers of the twentieth century—for example, Miguel de Unamuno, Fernando Pessoa, Hermann Hesse, Carl Gustav Jung—experimented with possi-ble consequences of a breakdown of the classical view of personal and collective identity. The manner in which literary artists regard the onto-logical question and frame various historical-developmental contexts for it covers a very broad spectrum in modernism. This demonstrable fact should urge caution. Not only is it important to avoid any sweeping judg-ment about the amazingly rich profusion of creative writing in the times of Proust, Mann, and Joyce; it is likewise to our gain if we pay careful at-tention to the lasting worth of their particular messages.[34]

33. Anna Balakian, *Literary Origins of Surrealism: A New Mysticism in French Poet-ry* (New York: New York University Press, 1947) and *Surrealism: The Road to the Absolute* (New York: Noonday Press, 1959).

34. Although she does not refer to Mann or Joyce, Margaret Topping's *Supernatural Proust: Myth and Metaphor in "À la recherché du temps perdu"* (Cardiff: University of Wales Press, 2007) serves to demonstrate how much the French author shares with them in de-veloping a repertory of allusions to ancient classical, scriptural, medieval, and later in-stances and uses of myth, and in relating these to fairytales, legends, rituals, and beliefs, as well as to art media (painting, opera, etc.), so as to achieve epiphanic syntheses and sug-gest a modern visionary mode of questing for identity and understanding.

The Artifice of Eternity

Modernist obsession with time and modernist attempts to master its dimensions in fictional artifices have provided an abiding topic for criticism for most of the twentieth century. I do not propose to return here
to the perennial debate in cultural theory about the significance of these
powerful drives; instead I want to revisit a few specific examples of modernist practice of larger structural girth that eventually furnished new
staple assumptions about narrative means and substance—including a
number of assumptions that survive a rejection of modernism itself.

For example, it was by looking with the demiurgic narrator over the
shoulder of Joyce's artist figure in *Ulysses* that readers gradually grew
capable of walking imaginatively, as Stephen Dedalus eventually does,
through the multiple selves of a diverse humanity as roles in a timeless
drama. Moments when Stephen distances himself from his own troubling ego-fiction and becomes a chamber for multiple fictions bear an
analogy to a reader's suspension of a bounded personal fiction by reception of the universe of identities suggested by the novel. When Stephen's
"contemporary," the title hero of Hesse's *Steppenwolf* (1927), leads readers
(as he is being led) through the psychedelic fragmentation of identity in
that novel, they learn to juxtapose rival models by which we can, even today, still experiment in constructing inner or outer reality and possible
supra- or superrealities. The ostensibly Eastern and Western metaphysical viewpoints in Hesse's novel merge in an art that is sometimes sur-
realistic for long stretches and that draws heavily on such psychological
theories as Jung's.

By slightly turning the modernist kaleidoscope from decade to decade, we arrive at John Barth's *Lost in the Funhouse* and many another intricate cultural memory puzzle. Although we have become palimpsestial
in our own awareness, we readers of today nonetheless remain conscious
of ourselves in the Joycean act of looking "over a shoulder, rere regardant"; thematically, among other things, we are looking at the eternal,

ghostly arrival of the ship or sperm "homing, upstream"[1] for Ithaca (U 42). The infinite regression contained in "rere," Joyce's favorite reduplicative particle, fuses the ontological planes of his artifice in the thematized "now" or "yes" of rebirth—whether we think of this reattained moment as a celebration of procreative life, or as an affirmation of creative breakthrough by the human spirit, or as both simultaneously.

Two years after *Ulysses*, the authorial voice speaking in an oracular statement of design, the supreme narrator of the "Vorsatz" or "Foreword" (MM xi) to Mann's *The Magic Mountain*, teases us about the necessary doubleness of time and narration.[2] The novelist openly confronts the strangeness of telling a story that, just a few years later, lies on the other side of a chasm separating historical ages, an abyss that ripped open with the roar of World War I. The story Mann tells,

> does not actually owe its pastness to time—an assertion that is itself intended as a passing reference, an allusion, to the problematic and uniquely double nature of that mysterious element. (MM xi)[3]

On spiritual stilts in the final paragraph of *Time Regained*, Proust's narrator Marcel wonders whether, in order to capture in an artifice his insights about being in time, he will have the strength to remain attached long enough to a past that has revealed itself in his own experience as possessing vertiginous depths. The shore of the world ocean, upon which Mann's narrator and Joyce's Stephen meditate, is strewn with shells, one emblem of those "envelopes" (here I invoke a favorite term of Proust's) that have housed a message that moves ever into new containers. The mortal remembering artist too belongs among those fellow creatures he observes:

> occupying so considerable a place, compared with the restricted place which is reserved for them in space, a place on the contrary prolonged

1. James Joyce, *Ulysses*, ed. Hans Walter Gabler with Wolfhard Steppe and Claus Melchior (New York: Vintage Books, 1986); henceforth abbreviated as U followed by the page number.

2. Thus in the translation by John E. Woods: Thomas Mann, *The Magic Mountain* (New York: Vintage Books, 1996); henceforth abbreviated as MM followed by the page number. Ordinarily the exact German cognate for "Foreword" would be "Vorwort"; "Vorsatz" conveys the sense of "design, purpose, intention, deliberation, premeditation."

3. Thomas Mann, *Der Zauberberg* (Frankfurt: Fischer Taschenbuch Verlag, 1987), henceforth abbreviated as Zb followed by page number: "verdankt den Grad ihres Vergangenseins nicht eigentlich der Zeit,—eine Aussage, womit auf die Fragwürdigkeit und eigentliche Zwienatur dieses geheimnisvollen Elementes im Vorbeigehen angespielt und hingewiesen sei" (Zb, 5).

past measure, for simultaneously, like giants plunged into the years, they touch the distant epochs through which they have lived, between which so many days have come to range themselves—in Time (SLT 6.531–32).[4]

By the end of the *In Search of Lost Time* we readers have explored sufficiently with Marcel to understand we are giants of all time in the limits of our present time. The rekindling of fascination for knowledge of every kind in *The Magic Mountain* on the part of that parodic Faustus, Hans Castorp, causes the novel's enchanted space to expand exponentially, so that the chapters acquire the growth pattern of a widening spiral in proportion as we rediscover the heritage of millennia hidden in the moment. The circularity of Proust's closing for what the reader has already experienced—by having progressed through the extant volumes of *In Search of Lost Time*—resonates in spiritual affinity with the overtly hermetic metaphors that constantly point us to the idea of sealed or hidden sources in Mann and Joyce.[5] The descent into primordial evolutionary strata by the tormented consciousness that is represented by an as yet unnamed authorial voice in the overture to *Swann's Way*, and the rising back of this voice to the marked surface in the modern world, establishes the paradoxical doubleness of human identity. It too is signed with specific attributes in the aspect of its permanent becoming. Similarly, appearing sealed or masked in the hermetic past tense, the literary heritages of Marcel, Stephen, and Hans mark the surface of this present tense of history.

Certain signatures already enfolded in the evolving human story come into appearance out of the phenomenal flux to Proust's and Joyce's readers, much as they do to their lead figures. Not just the Thoth-like scribe Stephen amid the books of the living and the dead in the National Library in Dublin, but also the All-Father surrogate Leopold Bloom, who

4. English citations are from Marcel Proust, *In Search of Lost Time*, trans. C. K. Scott Moncrieff and Terence Kilmartin, rev. by D. J. Enright, 6 vols. (New York: Modern Library, 1998); references are indicated by the abbreviation SLT with volume and page number. French citations are from Marcel Proust, *A la recherche du temps perdu*, Pléiade Edition, 4 vols. (Paris: Editions Gallimard, 1987); henceforth abbreviated as R followed by the page number. The passage reads in the original: "occupant une place si considérable, à côté de celle si restreinte qui leur est réservée dans l'espace, une place au contraire prolongée sans mesure—puisqu'ils touchent simultanément, comme des géants plongés dans les années, à des époques, vécues par eux si distantes, entre lesquelles tant de jours sont venus se placer—dans le Temps" (R, 4.625).

5. On the importance of "hermetic" metaphoricity, see chapter eleven, "The Ways of Hermes in the Works of Thomas Mann."

in the bathtub resembles a tin of Mrs. Plumtree's Potted Meat, point us toward the notion of a sacramental order to life. That theme appears everywhere in Mann's novel, too, as when Hans listens to the gramophone, the updated sarcophagal model of the soul. The ubiquitous symbol of the hermetic wand, appearing in chapter seven as a gramophone needle, moves inexorably from start to finish in a circle, unlocking the treasures imbedded on the surface of a record; and the opera music released from its hermetic container, from the realm of death, affirms the connection of all life to the psychohistorical drama that the novel records. The modern gadget mimics the lofty hermetic activity of the epical rememberers of pasts lost and regained. Acting in the Cervantine spirit, Mann finally awards his educational protagonist Castorp a diploma for his alchemical-hermetic development.

Of course, it is the reader who actually earns the diploma through the effort of recognizing or acquiring the signaturae of the seven-year ("actually" seven-chapter) symposium. In such representative elements of the human record, Proust, Joyce, and Mann exhibit a will for totalization or universality that can be traced from such great Renaissance and baroque antecedents as Rabelais and Cervantes, over their protoromantic followers such as Sterne. The main title *A la recherche du temps perdu*, and its realization in the continuous probing of being in time in Proust's masterwork, such Mannian subchapter titles as "Enzyklopädie," "Humaniora," and "Forschungen" in *Der Zauberberg*, and the plethora of Joycean omnium gatherum displays and assemblies in *Ulysses* resonate to a core understanding about their authorial acts of cultural anamnesis as recognition of the human "intertext" (I use the term here cautiously to mean both the remains of actual texts, the collective residue of innumerable texts still labeled or lost and untagged, and the strands of tradition in which they are implicated). By their gestures of parody and play, not just with isolated motifs and themes, but with generic structures and finally with the nature of literature in general, the modernist masters, like their notable predecessors, reconstitute the human intertext in new simulacra.

As early as in the brooding painting *La tempesta*, by the Venetian artist Giorgione (ca. 1478–1510), we can see the emergence of a new imaginative capacity that depends on complex temporal perspectivism and synthesis. By the eighteenth century, notably in such works by the Venetian Piranesi (1720–1778) as *Le antichità romane* (Roman Antiquities), *Le vedute di Roma* (Views of Rome), and *I carceri d'invenzione* (Imaginary Prisons), we can confirm that the twinned polarities of a spatiotemporal imagination, nourished by and continuing to nourish the Western historical mind, are imbedded in ways that not the Enlightenment, but romanticism and modernism would fully exploit. Crucial, I believe, is that the theatricalization of art, mightily advanced by a temporal perspectivism that saturated all media from the late Renaissance onward, quite naturally prepared the ground for a second enormous perceptual sea change between romanticism and high modernism. This was the ability to amalgamate architectonic metaphors, fluctuating spatiotemporal optics, and historical perspectivism with perception of the fascinating internal rhythms of the human mind. When literary artists riveted their attention on the mind's perceived perspectival operations, and the interplay among memory, feeling, and the mysterious layers of subconscious life, they were predisposed to use techniques from any art that abetted our capturing flux, process, and fusion. The further romantic step of linking associational, rather than rational, procedures in poetry with musical principles was important in helping to bring about a far-reaching internalization of perspectival rhythms and structures from painting and architecture as a potent weapon in the artist's arsenal. We can readily illustrate the move to a synaesthetic intermedic union in prose fiction in the nineteenth century that occurs from Novalis to Huysmans. This happens simultaneously with the move, starting with the romantics, to break down generic boundaries and to promote a mutually enriching interchange among fictional and discursive modes.

The juncture where the spatial-architectonic, the temporal-musical, the historical, anthropological, and the psychological converge appears in the brilliant opening paragraph of the overture to the "Combray" section of *Swann's Way*. The self of the dreamer who has just slipped from wakeful reading, his dreaming and dream state, and the human story in his depths interact: "it seemed to me that I myself was the immediate subject of my book: a church, a quartet, the rivalry between François I and Charles V" (SLT 1).[6] The distant sound of trains, which in another kind of fiction might more emphatically reestablish the fact of his presence in the late nineteenth century, becomes interwoven as part of the obscure dreamscape of a possible "existence antérieure" that lives beneath the existential debris burdening him. The narrative will go on to explore the roots of his world, as he encounters the guiding Vinteuil theme, as the church unfolds for him into the complex organism arising

6. "il me semblait que j'étais moi-même ce dont parlait l'ouvrage: une église, un quatuor, la rivalité de François Ier de Charles Quint" (R, 3).

and decaying in time, and as he discovers his grounding in the history of France. We find this perspectival organicism that is transformed into lyrical values in contemporary poems by Rilke such as "Die Kathedrale." Proust spins together in a nodular cluster the creature who is having the particular dream or text and the dreaming through him that gradually proves to be connected to a greater text. Thomas Mann lets Castorp arrive at such a moment in the "Snow" subchapter of *The Magic Mountain* when, near death, he is carried by remembered music into an archaic world where he walks backwards through the religious evolution of mankind to witness the horror of nature before human shaping. Through an explicitly communal dreaming and anamnesis (Zb 517, 521), he discovers the "dream-poem" ("Traumgedicht," "Traumwort," Zb 523) of humanity born in response to the harsh laws of life.

Although they are entertaining, the moments of mere pastiche in *In Search of Lost Time*—like the imitation of the manner of the Goncourt brothers, inserted close to the beginning of *Time Regained* in mock illustration of an alternative way the work could have been written (R 4.287–95)—are relatively simple means by which Proust builds up the texture of the times of Time. They are elements subordinate to a larger scale mimetism of human experience that includes spirituality. Besides situating the new consciousness of being in time in his experiencing narrator, Proust mimics or parodies entire structures of narration as enormous subtexts generic in scope and subsumed in him and his book. Within *In Search of Lost Time*, the narrator offers us alternate kinds of narration through which to measure our own altered awareness of our world, such as the sudden switch to the Flaubertian third-person treatment in the book-length section "Swann in Love." Drawing upon the humoristic-encyclopedic tradition, Mann's narrating voice uses an educational protagonist as the medium through whom we reacquire and consider, in ironic partnership with the narration itself, the vast repertory of "our" endangered, multifarious civilization.[7] Joyce juxtaposes eighteen stylistically disparate chapters into which a multitude of literary echoes are gathered, sometimes in cubistic, musical, or other transformations. Parodic tours-de-force, such as the mock review of the evolution of English over the course of nine centuries in the "Oxen of the Sun" chapter, a parodic chrestomathy, all subserve evocation of the depersonalized "inter-

---

7. On the connection between the encyclopedic-humoristic tradition and the educational novel, see chapter nine, "Educational Experiment in Thomas Mann."

text" that *Ulysses* seeks to reinstantiate in its own right and which intimates an "Urtext" in *Finnegans Wake*.

To a limited extent, we can compare Proust's probing into innumerable areas of psychological, cultural, and historical discovery in *In Search of Lost Time* with *The Notebooks of Malte Laurids Brigge,* published in 1910. After many dazzling shifts of focus and topic, Rilke has Malte expound his own theory—a theory directly descended from Huysmans's in *A rebours*—that he is writing a new kind of novel that attempts the overcoming of time in the form of a modernist "mosaic" assembled out of intervibrating fragments.[8] It is simultaneously a musical and an architectonic construct mobilizing perceptions gleaned from various centuries and arranged in the narrator's consciousness like jewelry. The encyclopedic potential of the modern novel, which is already huge in Proustian or Rilkean recollection, is realized even more copiously in Mann's explicit symposium on European and human evolution in *The Magic Mountain*. Mann's narrator openly conducts a symposium about the crisis of World War I in a "hermetic" time out of time, into and through which a myriad of elements of the evolutionatory story flow. In its narrative technique and use of the "quotational" principle, Mann's novel thus stands somewhere between the *In Search of Lost Time* and *Ulysses*. Rilke's "mosaic" points toward the leitmotivic, multidimensional palimpsest in *Ulysses,* but *The Notebooks* is still centered on an identified, representative consciousness, whereas Joyce's narrator is reconditely beyond any unifying individual. Joyce converts the carnivalesque fecundity of language into a perpetually rediscoverable source of creativity, just as he compacts all time into the modernist eternity of a day in Dublin.

One of the most intense responses at midcentury to the supreme mimetism of Joyce is Borges's two-page story "El Hacedor," or, as the translated title in English underscores, the Renaissance "Maker." "El Hacedor," in creating a parodic pseudobiography of Homer, is simultaneously the hypertextual imitation of hypertextual parody: repotentiated hypertext. It compresses dozens of Joyce's motifs and ideas into a mirrorlike crystal that of course reflects not only the mirror-of-mirrors *Ulysses,* but also Borges's own realization of a strange destiny, the conversion of his own life comparable to the transformation of Saul into St. Paul.[9] Blind-

---

8. R. M. Rilke, *Die Aufzeichnungen des Malte Laurids Brigge,* in *Sämtliche Werke* (Frankfurt: Insel-Verlag, 1992), 895.

9. For the Borgesian impersonal immortality and the Joycean palimpsest, see D. Jullien, "Biography of an Immortal," *Comparative Literature* 47 (1995): 136–59.

ness (in some measure also the threat determining Joyce's pathway) is mirrored in epiphany. As in Borges's story "El inmortal," the mortal individual becomes the ghostly Everyman, who eventually loses his own identity to the narrating voice of Borges's "Hacedor." This "first person" gives a paradoxical metaphysical depth of simultaneous temporality and atemporality to the pronominal surface or label, the "I," commenting: "The story which I have narrated seems irreal because the affairs of two distinct men are mixed in it."[10]

In a radical moment of truth, a blind character discovers himself to be Homer. But it is the Homer whom Joyce parodies via such predecessor intermediaries as Wagner, Shakespeare, and Virgil, and symbolic figures such as the Wandering Jew and the Flying Dutchman, Sindbad and Hamlet. The story is implicitly told in any and every language throughout time, Borges agrees, and therefore authorial consciousness is inherently cosmopolitan. Authorship involves a paradoxical innovative freedom from fixedness of role, because universality brings the condition of the impersonal validity beyond the ego-fiction, hence marginality in the eyes of all those with a less fluid sense of human identity. The twentieth-century author Borges, in the wake of Joyce, Rilke, and more, accepts that identity has crumbled into a mosaic of literary fragments that he reassembles, bits out of time. The spiritual leap to immortality is thus acceptance of a kind of death in the work of art: "I have been Homer; shortly I shall be nobody, like Ulysses; shortly I shall be everybody; I shall be dead."[11]

It goes without saying that in any adequate eternity there will always be Venice, under some name or other (such as Dublin), the archetypal city that is the Proustian and Mannian and Joycean juncture or crossroads. It is not only the transactional place where all realms meet, as in the novella *Death in Venice*. Near the very end of *Ulysses*, Molly thinks of Venice in recollecting the promises of youth: "but I saw through him telling me all the lovely places we could go for the honeymoon Venice by moonlight with the gondolas" (U 630). Proust's mature Marcel will explore and meditate in subtle detail on Venice, but it is already among the manic names the mere mention of which causes him to get ill from overexcitement as a teenager. Venice is one of those complex works evolving

10. "La historia que he narrado parece irreal porque en ella se mezclan los sucesos de dos hombres distintos" (H, 543). J. L. Borges, "El Hacedor," in *El Hacedor*, vol. 2 of *Obras completas* (Barcelona: Emecé Editores, 1989); hereafter abbreviated as H followed by the page number.

11. "Yo he sido Homero; en breve, seré nadie, como Ulises; en breve, seré todos; estaré muerto" (H, 543–44).

through time, like a cathedral, and thus getting to know it can be associated with the resonating experience of the Vinteuil sonata. Venice by whatever name unfolds like the madeleine in the condition of time, because it has evolved in art in particular history as a hypertextual juncture that suggests the intertext finally out of time. Eventually the experiences in the condition of time insist on the status of "resurrections" within the framework of a usually victorious present, and the "momentary appearances of the Combray or the Balbec or the Venice which invaded only to be driven back" constitute the mosaic of "an indescribably beautiful vision"—"fragments of existence withdrawn from Time" that intimate "eternity" (SLT 6.267–68).[12] Whoever reads Proust also learns that the invisible essence of the beauty of the finest works comes last to us as deeply known truth and lasts longest. Whether as Sindbad-like comparatists or just homebound tourists, we readers are always returning to Venice, or Combray, or Ithaca, that place we cannot relinquish.

---

12. "ces résurrections-là," "moments [. . .] à faire réapparaître [. . .] Ce combray, ce Venise, ce Balbec envahissants et refoulés," "une vision ineffable"; "des fragments d'existence soustraits au temps," "d'éternité" (R, 4.453–54).

Listed below are two main categories of works: editions from which I cite passages, and critical writings from which I cite or to which I draw special attention. This listing of sources does not include all authors and works I mention in connection with particular topics. Especially in the absence of any direct quotation from a work, I may list it only in the index. The reader should check the index to find a fuller repertory of names and titles. Books and articles appear below by authors' names in alphabetical order. Since the reader can garner a wider selection of relevant critical commentary from the bibliographical pointers in books listed under "Secondary Literature," I dispense with any attempt to reference the huge number of works that could be adduced and to which I may owe some general debt.

Primary Literature

Adams, Henry. *Mont-Saint-Michel and Chartres*. Boston: Houghton Mifflin, 1930.

AE (George Russell). *The Candle of Vision*. London: Macmillan, 1918.

Almqvist, Carl Jonas Love. *Törnrosens bok*. In *Samlade Skrifter: Forsta fullständiga upplagan, med inledningar, varianter och anmärkningar: Törnrosens bok*, edited by Frederk Böök, vols. 5–7. Stockholm: Bonniers, 1921.

Anon (probably August Klingemann). *Die Nachtwachen des Bonaventura: The Night Watches of Bonaventura*. Translated by Gerald Gillespie. Edinburgh, U.K.: Edinburgh University Press, 1972.

Antonioni, Alessandro. *L'eclisse*. Interopa Film-Cineriz, Paris Film Production, 1962. Irvington, N.Y.: Criterion Collection, 2005.

Barth, John. *The End of the Road*. Garden City, N.Y.: Doubleday, 1967.

———. *Giles Goat-Boy; or, the Revised New Curriculum*. New York: Doubleday, 1966.

———. *Lost in the Funhouse*. New York: Bantam, 1969.

———. *The Sot-Weed Factor*. New York: Grosset & Dunlap, 1966.

Baudelaire, Charles. *Les fleurs du mal*. Edited by Jacques Prepet and Georges Blin. Paris: José Corti, 1950.

Beckett, Samuel. *En attendant Godot, pièces en deux actes*. Paris: Éditions de Minuit, 1952.

———. *Waiting for Godot: Tragicomedy*. Translated by Samuel Beckett. New York: Grove Press, 1954.

———. *Watt*. Paris: Olympia Press, 1953.

Beckett, Samuel, et al., eds. *Our Exagmination round his Factifications for Incamination of Work in Progress*. London: Faber & Faber, 1972.

Behn, Aphra. *Oroonoko; or, The Royal Slave.* Edited by Lore Metzger. New York: Norton, 1973.

Benét, Stephen Vincent. *John Brown's Body.* New York: Holt, Rinehart and Winston, 1968.

Blasco Ibáñez, Vincente. *Los cuatro jinetes del apocalipsis.* Valencia: Promoteo, 1919.

Borges, Jorge Luis. "El Hacedor." Vol. 2 of *Obras completas.* Barcelona: Emecé Editores, 1989.

———. *Historia de la eternindad.* Buenos Aires: Emecé Editores, 1953.

Bowles, Paul. *The Sheltering Sky.* New York: New Directions, 1949.

Brentano, Clemens. *Werke.* Edited by Wolfgang Frühwald et al. Darmstadt: Wissenschaftliche Buchgesellschaft, 1968.

Butor, Michel. *L'emploi du temps.* Paris: Les Editions de Minuit, 1957.

———. *Passing Time.* Translated by Jean Stewart. London: Faber & Faber, 1961.

Byron, George Gordon, Lord. *The Poems and Dramas of Lord Byron.* New York: Arundel, n.d.

———. *The Poetical Works of Lord Byron.* London: Oxford University Press, n.d.

Camões, Luís de. *Os Lusiadas.* Vols. 4 and 5 of *Obras completas.* Edited by Hernâni Cidade. 3rd ed. Lisbon: Sá da Costa, 1968.

Camus, Albert. *La peste.* Paris: Gallimard, 1947.

Carpentier, Alejo. *El siglo de las luces.* Introduction by Carlos Fuentes. Caracas: Biblioteca Ayachuco, 1979.

———. *Explosion in a Cathedral.* Translated by John Sturrock. Boston: Little, Brown, 1963.

Cela, Camilo José. *La familia de Pascual Duarte.* 4th ed. Barcelona: Ediciones del Zodiaco, 1946.

Céline, Louis-Ferdinand (Louis-Ferdinand Destouches). *Mort à credit.* 13th ed. Paris: Gallimard, 1952.

———. *Voyage au bout de la nuit.* Paris: Denoël et Steele, 1932.

Cooke, Ebenezer. *The Sot-Weed Factor.* London, 1708.

Cooper, James Fenimore. *The Leatherstocking Tales.* 2 vols. New York: Literary Classics of the United States, 1985.

Cortázar, Julio. *Rayuela.* Buenos Aires: Editorial Sudamericana, 1963.

D'Annunzio, Gabriele. *La Leda senza cigno.* In *Romanzi e conti,* 2 vols., edited by Ezio Raimondi and Niva Lorenzi, vol. 1. Milan: Arnaldo Mondadori Editore, 1989.

———. *"Nocturne" and "Five Tales of Love and Death."* Translated by Raymond Rosenthal. Marlboro, Vt.: Marlboro Press, 1988.

Defoe, Daniel. *The Life and Adventures of Robinson Crusoe.* Edited by Angus Ross. Harmondsworth, U.K.: Penguin Books, 1965.

Döblin, Alfred. *Berlin Alexanderplatz: Die Geschichte vom Franz Biberkopf.* Düsseldorf: Artemis und Winkler, 2001.

Donoso, José. *El obsceno pájaro de la noche.* Barcelona: Seix Barral,1970.

Doyle, Arthur Conan. *"A Study in Scarlet" and "The Sign of Four."* New York: Berkeley Books, 1975.

Eco, Umberto. *Il nome della rosa.* Milan: Bompiani, 1985.

————. *Baudolino*. Milan: Bompiani, 2000.

Eisenstein, S. M. "Literature and Cinema." In *Selected Works*, vol. 1: *Writings, 1922–34*, edited and translated by Richard Taylor. Bloomington: Indiana University Press, 1988.

Eliot, Thomas Stearns. *The Complete Poems and Plays, 1909–1950*. New York: Harcourt, Brace & World, 1971.

Faulkner, William. *Absolom, Absolom*. In *Novels, 1936–1940*. New York: Library of America, 1990.

Ferguson, Samuel. *Congal: A Poem in Five Books*. 3rd ed. Dublin: Sealy, Bryers, and Walker, 1907.

Flaubert, Gustave. *L'éducation sentimentale: Histoire d'un jeune homme*. Paris: G. F. Flamarion, 1985.

Fuentes, Carlos. *La muerte de Artemio Cruz*. Madrid: Cátedra, 1995.

García-Márquez, Gabriel. *Cien años de soledad*. Buenos Aires: Editorial Sudamericana, 1967.

Gide, André. *L'immoraliste: Roman*. Paris: Henri Jonquières, 1925.

Goethe, Johann Wolfgang von. *Die Faustdichtungen: Urfaust, ein Fragment, Faust, eine Tragödie, [. . .]*. Edited by Ernst Beutler. Zürich: Artemis-Verlag, 1950.

————. *Die Wahlverwandtschaften*. Edited by Franz Muncker. Jubiläumsausgabe 21. Stuttgart and Berlin: Cotta, 1809.

————. *Wilhlem Meister's Appenticeship and Travels*. Translated by Thomas Carlyle. 2 vols. New York: Burt, n.d.

Gorky, Maxim (Alexei Maximovich Peshkov), et al., eds. *Belomorsko-Baltiyskiy Kanal imeni Stalina*. Moscow, 1934.

————. *The White Sea Canal, Being an Account of the New Canal between the White Sea and the Baltic Sea*. London: John Lane, 1935.

Hamsun, Knut. *Mysterier*. Gyldendal: Norsk Førlag, 1992.

————. *Mysteries*. Translated by Gerry Bothmer. New York: Carroll & Graff, 1971.

Hawthorne, Nathaniel. *Novels: "The Scarlet Letter," "The House of the Seven Gables," "The Blithedale Romance," "The Marble Fawn."* Edited by William Charvat, Roy Harvey Pearse, et al. Columbus: Ohio State University Press, 1982.

Hemingway, Ernest. *For Whom the Bell Tolls*. New York: Charles Scribner's Sons, 1940.

————. *The Short Stories of Ernest Hemingway*. New York: Charles Scribner, 1953.

————. *The Sun Also Rises*. New York: Charles Scribner's Sons, 1926.

Herder, Johann Gottfried. *Journal meiner Reise im Jahre 1769*. In *Sturm und Drang: Eine Auswahl theoretischer Texte*. Edited by Erich Löwenthal. Heidelberg: Lambert Schneider, 1972.

Hérédia, José-Maria. *Les trophées*. Edited by W. N. Inee. London: Athlone Press, 1979.

————. *Sonnets from "The Trophies" of José-Maria de Hérédia*. Translated by Edward Robeson Taylor. 5th ed. San Francisco: Taylor, Nash, & Taylor, 1913.

Hesse, Hermann. *Der Steppenwolf*. Vol. 4 of *Gesammelte Dichtungen*. Berlin: Suhrkamp, 1958.

———. *Steppenwolf.* Translated by Basil Creighton; revised by Joseph Mileck. New York: Bantam Books, 1969.

Hoffmann, E. T. A. *Die Lebens-Ansichten des Katers Murr nebst fragmentarischer Biographie des Kapellmeisters Johannes Kreisler in zufälligen Makulaturblättern.* Edited by Hartmut Steinecke. Stuttgart: Reclam, 1986.

Howells, William Dean. *A Hazard of New Fortunes.* New York: New American Library, 1965.

Hume, David. *A Treatise of Human Nature* [selections]. In *The Age of Enlightenment: The Eighteenth Century Philosophers,* edited by Isiah Berlin. New York: New American Library, 1956.

Huxley, Aldous. *Brave New World.* New York: Harper, 1932.

———. *Point Counter Point.* Garden City, N.Y.: Doubleday, Doran, 1928.

Huysmans, Joris-Karl. *A rebours.* Vol. 7 of *Oeuvres complètes.* Geneva: Slatkine, 1972.

Joyce, James. *Finnegans Wake.* New York: Penguin Books, 1976.

———. *A Portrait of the Artist as a Young Man.* New York: Modern Library, 1944.

———. *A Portrait of the Artist as a Young Man.* Edited by Hans Walter Gabler with Walter Hettche. New York: Vintage Books, 1993.

———. *Stephen Hero.* Edited by John J. Slocum and Herbert Cahoon. Rev. ed. London: Jonathan Cape, 1956.

———. *Ulysses.* New York: Vintage Books, 1961.

———. *Ulysses: The Corrected Text.* Edited by Hans Gabler, with Wolfhard Steppe and Claus Melchior. New York: Vintage Books, 1986.

Kafka, Franz. *Der Prozeß: Ein Roman.* Edited by Max Brod. Frankfurt: S. Fischer Verlag, 1953.

———. *The Trial.* Translated by Willa and Edwin Muir; revised by E. M. Butler. New York: Schocken Books, 1984.

Keats, John, and Percey Bysshe Shelley. *Complete Poetical Works.* New York: Random House, n.d.

Mackay, John Henry. *The Anarchists: A Picture of Civilization at the Close of the Nineteenth Century.* Translated by George Schumm. New York: Autonomedia, 1999.

Mallarmé, Stéphane. *Oeuvres complètes.* Edited by Henri Mondor and G. Jean-Aubry. Paris: Gallimard, 1945.

Malraux, André. *La condition humaine.* Rev. ed. Paris: Gallimard, 1946.

Mann, Thomas. *Bekenntnisse des Hochstaplers Felix Krull: Der Memoiren erster Teil.* Frankfurt: S. Fischer Verlag, 1957.

———. *Confessions of Felix Krull, Confidence Man: The Early Years.* Translated by Denver Lindley. New York: Vintage Books, 1969.

———. *"Death in Venice" and Other Stories by Thomas Mann.* Translated by David Luke. New York: Bantam Books, 1988.

———. *Der Erwählte: Roman.* Frankfurt: S. Fischer, 1951.

———. *Der Zauberberg: Roman.* Frankfurt: Fischer Taschenbuch Verlag, 1987.

———. *Die Entstehung des "Doktor Faustus": Roman eines Romans.* Amsterdam: Bermann-Fischer, 1949.

———. *Doktor Faustus: Das Leben des deutschen Tonsetzers Adrian Leverkühn erzählt von einem Freunde*. Frankfurt: Fischer Taschenbuch Verlag, 1990.

————. *Doctor Faustus: The Life of the German Composer Adrian Leverkühn as Told by a Friend*. Translated by H. T. Lowe-Porter. New York: Knopf, 1948.

————. *Gesammlte Werke in Einzelbänden*. Edited by Peter de Mendelssohn. Frankfurt: S. Fischer Verlag, 1980.

————. *The Holy Sinner*. Translated by H. T. Lowe-Porter. Berkeley and Los Angeles: University of California Press, 1992.

————. *Joseph and His Brothers*. Translated by H. T. Lowe-Porter. New York: Knopf, 1974.

————. *Joseph und seine Brüder*. 4 vols. Frankfurt: Fischer Taschenbuch Verlag, 1991.

————. *The Magic Mountain*. Translated by H. T. Lowe-Porter. New York: Modern Library, 1952.

————. *The Magic Mountain*. Translated by John E. Woods. New York: Vintage International, 1996.

————. *Reflections of a Nonpolitical Man*. Translated by Walter D. Morris. New York: Ungar, 1987.

————. [Self-commentary.] In *Dichter über ihre Dichtungen*, vol. 14, part 1 (Thomas Mann: Teil 1: 1889–1917), edited by Hans Wysling. Munich: Ernst Heimeran, 1975.

Mann, Thomas, and Karl Kerényi. *Mythology and Humanism: The Correspondence of Thomas Mann and Karl Kerényi*. Translated by Alexander Gelley. Ithaca, N.Y.: Cornell University Press, 1975.

Manzoni, Alessandro. *I promessi sposi*. Edited by Dante Isella. Milan: Casa del Manzoni, 2006.

Melville, Herman. *The Confidence-Man: His Masquerade*. Edited by H. Bruce Franklin. Indianapolis and New York: Bobbs-Merrill, 1967.

Meyer, Conrad Ferdinand. *Die Versuchung des Pescara*. Vol. 13 of *Sämtliche Werke: Historisch-Kritische Ausgabe*. Berne: Benteli-Verlag, 1962.

————. *The Tempting of Pescara*. Translated by Clara Bell. New York: W. S. Gottsberger, 1890; rpt. New York: Howard Fertig, 1975.

Miller, Henry. "The Universe of Death." In *The Best of Henry Miller*. London: Heinemann, 1960.

Musil, Robert. *Der Mann ohne Eigenschaften*. In *Gesammelte Werke*, edited by Adolf Frisé, vol. 1. Frankfurt: Rowolt, 1978.

Nietzsche, Friedrich. *"The Birth of Tragedy" and "The Case of Wagner."* Translated by Walter Kaufmann. New York: Vintage Books, 1967.

————. *Die Geburt der Tragödie aus dem Geiste der Musik*. In *Nietzsche: Werke*, edited by Giorgio Colli and Mazzino Montinari, vol. 3, part 1. Berlin and New York: Walter de Gruyter, 1972.

Novalis (Friedrich von Hardenberg). *Hymnen an die Nacht; Heinrich von Ofterdingen*. Munich: Wilhelm Goldmann Verlag, n.d.

O'Brien, Flann (Brian O'Nolan). *At Swim-Two-Birds*. Normal, Ill.: Dalkey Archive Press, 1998.

————. *The Third Policeman*. New York: Walker and Company, 1967.

Ortega y Gasset, José. *La rebelión de las masas*. Madrid: Editorial Castalia, 1998.

General Bibliography

———. *The Modern Theme.* Translated by James Cleugh. New York: Harper & Row, 1961.

Orwell, George (Eric Arthur Blair). *Animal Farm.* London: David Campbell, 1993.

———. *Nineteen Eighty-Four.* New York: Knopf, 1992.

Pater, Walter. *Walter Pater: Three Major Texts ("The Renaissance," "Appreciations," and "Imaginary Portraits").* Edited by William E. Buckler. New York: New York University Press, 1986.

Pérez Galdós, Benito. *El amigo Manso.* Madrid: Perlado, Paez y ca., 1910.

Potocki, Jan. *Le manuscrit trouvé à Saragosse.* Edited by René Radrizzani. Paris: J. Corti, 1989.

Pound, Ezra. *Cantos.* New York: New Directions, 1998.

Proust, Marcel. *A la recherche du temps perdu.* Edited by Jean-Yves Tadié. 4 vols. Paris: Gallimard, 1987–1989.

———. *In Search of Lost Time.* Translated by C. K. Scott Moncrieff and Terence Kilmartin; revised by D. J. Enright. 6 vols. New York: Modern Library, 1998–1999.

———. *Remembrance of Things Past.* Translated by C. K. Scott Moncrieff and Terence Kilmartin. 3 vols. New York: Random House, 1981.

———. *Time Regained.* Translated by Andreas Mayor; revised by D. J. Enright. New York: Modern Library, 1992–1993; paperback, 1998–1999.

Pynchon, Thomas. *Gravity's Rainbow.* New York: Viking Press, 1973.

———. *V, a Novel.* Philadelphia: Lippencott, 1983.

Rilke, Rainer Maria. *The Complete French Poems of Rainer Maria Rilke.* Translated by A. Poulin Jr. Saint Paul, Minn.: Graywolf Press, 1986.

———. *Die Aufzeichnungen des Malte Laurids Brigge.* Vol. 6 of *Sämtliche Werke.*

———. *The Notebooks of Malte Laurids Brigge.* Translated by M. D. Herter Norton. New York: W. W. Norton, 1964.

———. *Sämtliche Werke.* Edited by Ruth Sieber-Rilke and Ernst Zinn. 6 vols. Wiesbaden: Insel-Verlag, 1955–1966.

Sayers, Dorothy. *Gaudy Night.* New York: Harper & Row, 1964.

Scève, Maurice. *Délie: Object de plus haulte vertu.* Edited by Gérard Defaux. 2 vols. Genève: Droz, 2004.

Schlegel, Friedrich. *Friedrich Schlegel's "Lucinde" and the Fragments.* Translated by Peter Firchow. Minneapolis: University of Minnesota Press, 1971.

———. *Kritische Schriften.* Edited by Wolfdietrich Rasch. Munich: Carl Hanser, 1964.

Schopenhauer, Arthur. *Die Welt als Wille und Vorstellung.* In *Sämtliche Werke,* edited by Paul Deussen, vol. 1. Munich: Carl Hanser, n.d.

———. *The World as Will and Representation.* Translated by E. F. J. Payne. 2 vols. New York: Dover Books, 1969.

Scott, Walter. *The Heart of Midlothian.* Edited by David Hewitt and Alison Lumsden. Edinburgh: Edinburgh University Press, 2004.

———. *A Legend of the Wars of Montrose.* Edited by J. H. Alexander. Edinburgh: Edinburgh University Press, 1995.

Sebald, Winfried Georg. *Austerlitz.* Munich: C. Hanser, 2001.

General Bibliography

Shelley, Percy Bysshe. *The Poetical Works of Shelley*. Edited by Newell F. Ford. Boston: Houghton Mifflin, 1975.
Solzhenitsyn, Alexander Isaevich. *The First Circle*. Translated by Thomas P. Whitney. Evanston, Ill.: Northwestern University Press, 1997.
———. *Archipelag GULAG, 1918–1956: opyt khudozhestvennogo issledovannia.* Moscow: "Vagrius," 2008.
———. *The Gulag Archipelago, 1918–1956: An Experiment in Literary Investigation.* 3 vols. Translated by Thomas P. Whitney and H. Willets. New York: Harper & Row, 1974–1978.
———. *V kruge pervom: Roman.* Moskva: Nauka, 2006.
Spengler, Oswald. *The Decline of the West.* 2 vols. 1: *Form and Actuality.* 2: *Perspectives of World-History.* Edited and translated by Charles Francis Atkinson. New York: Alfred A. Knopf, 1926, 1928.
———. *Der Untergang des Abendlandes.* 2 vols. 1: *Gestalt und Wirklichkeit.* 2: *Welthistorische Perspektiven.* Munich: C. H. Beck'sche Verlagsbuchhandlung, 1918, 1922.
Stendhal (Henri Beyle). *Le rouge et le noir.* Edited by Henri Martineau. Paris: Garnier, 1957.
Sterne, Laurence. *The Life and Opinions of Tristram Shandy, Gentleman.* New York: Modern Library, n.d.
Stifter, Adalbert. *Witiko, eine Erzählung; mit Bruchstücken früherer Fassungen.* Edited by Max Stefl. Augsburg: A Kraft, 1953.
Stirner, Max (Johann Kaspar Schmidt). *Der Einzige und sein Eigentum.* Edited by Ahlrich Meyer. Stuttgart: Reclam, 1972.
———. *Max Stirners kleinere Schriften [. . .].* Edited by John Henry Mackay. Berlin: Schuster & Loeffler, 1898.
Strindberg, August. *By the Open Sea.* Translated by Mary Sandbach. London: Secker & Warburg, 1984.
———. *A Dream Play.* In *August Strindberg: Selected Plays,* translated by Evert Sprinchorn. Minneapolis: University of Minnesota Press, 1986.
———. *Ett Drömspel.* In *Samlade Skrifter,* 55 vols., 36.213–330. Stockholm: Albert Bonniers, 1912–1921.
———. *I Havsbandet.* In *Skrifter,* 14 vols., 2.207–343. Stockholm: Albert Bonniers Förlag, 1946–1953.
Walcott, Derek. *Omeros.* New York: Farrar, Straus & Giroux, 1990.
Woolf, Virginia. *Mrs. Dalloway.* New York: Harcourt Brace Jovanovich, 1953.
———. *Orlando, a Biography.* New York: Harcourt, Brace, 1928.
Wright, Richard. *Pagan Spain.* New York: Harper, 1957.

Secondary Literature

Adorno, Theodor W. "Freudian Theory and the Pattern of Fascist Propaganda." In *The Essential Frankfurt School,* edited by Andrew Arato and Eike Gebhardt. New York: Urizen Books, 1978.
Agheana, Ion T. *The Prose of Jorge Luis Borges: Existentialism and the Dynamics of Surprise.* New York: Peter Lang, 1984.
Alldritt, Keith. *Modernism in the Second World War: The Later Poetry of Ezra*

Pound, T. S. Eliot, Basil Bunting, and Hugh MacDiarmid. New York: Peter Lang, 1989.

Andriopoulos, Stefan. *Possessed: Hypnotic Crimes, Corporate Fiction, and the Invention of Cinema.* Chicago and London: University of Chicago Press, 2008.

Apuzzo, Jason Alexander. "The End of the Millennium: Thomas Mann and the Last Romantic Generation." Ph.D. diss., Stanford University, 1998.

Atherton, James S. *The Books at the Wake: A Study of Literary Allusion in James Joyce's "Finnegans Wake."* New York: Viking Press, 1960.

Auerbach, Erich. *Mimesis: The Representation of Reality in Western Literature.* Translated by Willard R. Trask. Princeton, N.J.: Princeton University Press, 1953.

Bailey, Helen Phelps. *Hamlet in France from Voltaire to Laforgue.* Geneva: Droz, 1964.

Balakian, Anna. *Literary Origins of Surrealism: A New Mysticism in French Poetry.* New York: New York University Press, 1947.

———. *The Snowflake on the Belfry: Dogma and Disquietude in the Critical Arena.* Bloomington and Indianapolis: Indiana University Press, 1994.

———. *Surrealism: The Road to the Absolute.* New York: Noonday Press, 1959.

Balsamo, Gian. *Joyce's Messianism: Dante, Negative Existence, and the Messianic Self.* Columbia: University of South Carolina Press, 2004.

Beja, Morris. *Film and Literature: An Introduction.* New York, London: Longman, 1979.

———. *Epiphany in the Modern Novel.* Seattle: University of Washington Press, 1957.

Benda, Julien. *La trahison des clercs.* Paris: Editions Grasset et Fasquelle, 1975.

Benjamin, Walter. *Reflections: Essays, Aphorisms, Autobiographical Writings.* Edited by Peter Demetz; translated by Edmund Jephcott. New York: Schocken Books, 1986.

Berger, Willy R. *Die mythologischen Motive in Thomas Manns Roman "Joseph und seine Brüder."* Cologne and Vienna: Böhlau, 1971.

Bertens, Hans, and Douwe Fokkema, eds. *Literary Postmodernism: Theory and Practice.* Philadelphia: John Benjamins, 1997.

Beugnet, Martine, and Marion Schmid. *Proust at the Movies.* Aldershot, Hampshire, U.K., and Burlington, Vt.: Ashgate, 2004.

Binder, Hartmut. *Kafka-Kommentar zu den Romanen, Rezensionen, Aphorismen und zum Brief an den Vater.* Munich: Winkler, 1976.

Black, Joel D. *The Reality Effect: Film and Culture and the Graphic Imperative.* New York: Routledge, 2001.

Block, Haskell M. "The Myth of the Artist." *Yearbook of Comparative Criticism* 9 (1980): 3–24.

———. "Theory of Comedy from Dante to Joyce." In *Comparative Literary Dimensions: Essays in Honor of Melvin J. Friedman,* edited by Jay L. Halio and Ben Siegel, 19–30. Cranbury, N.J.: Associated University Presses, 2000.

Boheemen, Christine. *The Novel as Family Romance: Language, Gender, and Authority from Fielding to Joyce.* Ithaca, N.Y.: Cornell University Press, 1987.

General Bibliography

Bowen, Zack. "Joyce and the Epiphany Concept: A New Approach." *Journal of Modern Literature* 9 (1981–1982): 103–14.

Bowen, Zack, and James F. Carens, eds. *A Companion to Joyce Studies*. Westport, Conn.: Greenwood Press, 1984.

Bowie, Malcolm. *Freud, Proust and Lacan: Theory as Fiction*. Cambridge, U.K.: Cambridge University Press, 1987.

Boysen, Benjamin J. "'I call that patriotism': Leopold Bloom and the Cosmopolitan Caritas." *The Comparatist* 32 (2008): 140–46.

Bradbury, Malcolm. *The Modern World: Ten Great Writers*. New York: Penguin Books, 1988.

Brady, Patrick. Introduction to "Chaos in the Humanities." Inaugural issue of *Synthesis: An Interdisciplinary Journal* 1, no. 1 (1995): 5–17.

Braudel, Fernand. *The Structures of Everyday Life: The Limits of the Possible*. Vol. 1 of *Civilization and Capitalism*. Translated by Siân Reynolds. New York: Harper & Row, 1981.

Bridges, George. Thomas Mann's *"Joseph und seine Brüder" and the Phallic Theology of the Old Testament*. New York: Peter Lang, 1995.

Brivic, Sheldon. *Joyce between Freud and Jung*. Port Washington, N.Y.: National University Publications/Keenikat Press, 1980.

———. *The Veil of Signs*. Urbana: University of Illinois Press, 1979.

Bruford, W. H. *The German Tradition of Self-Cultivation: "Bildung" from Humboldt to Thomas Mann*. Cambridge, U.K.: Cambridge University Press, 1975.

Brunel, Patrick. *Le rire de Proust*. Paris: Honoré Champion, 1997.

Bulson, Eric. *Novels, Maps, Modernity: The Spatial Imagination, 1850–2000*. New York and London: Routledge, 2007.

Burton, Stacy. "Bakhtin, Temporality, and Modern Narrative: Writing 'the Whole Triumphant Murderous Unstoppable Chute.'" *Comparative Literature* 48 (1996): 39–64.

Calinescu, Matei. *Five Faces of Modernity: Modernism, Avant-garde, Decadence, Kitsch, Postmodernism*. Bloomington: Indiana University Press, 1995.

Calinescu, Matei, and Douwe Fokkema, eds. *Exploring Postmodernism*. Philadelphia: John Benjamins, 1987.

Campbell, Joseph. *The Hero with a Thousand Faces*. 2nd ed. Princeton, N.J.: Princeton University Press, 1968.

Cardinal, Roger. *Figures of Reality*. London: Croom Helm; Totowa, N.J.: Barnes & Noble, 1981.

Carnell, Simon. "*Finnegans Wake*: The Most Formidable Anti-Fascist Book Produced between the Two Wars?" *European Joyce Studies* 4 (1994): 139–63.

Carpenter, William. *Death and Marriage: Structural Metaphors for the Work of Art in Joyce and Mallarmé*. New York: Garland, 1988.

Carter, William C. *The Proustian Quest*. New York: New York University Press, 1992.

Chadwick, George F. *The Park and the Town: Public Landscape in the Nineteenth and Twentieth Centuries*. New York and Washington, D.C.: Frederick A. Prager, 1966.

Chatman, Seymour. *Story and Discourse: Narrative Structure in Fiction and Film*. Ithaca, N.Y.: Cornell University Press, 1978.

Cheng, Vincent John. *Joyce, Race, and Empire*. Cambridge, U.K.: Cambridge University Press, 1995.

———. *Shakespeare and Joyce: A Study of "Finnegans Wake."* University Park: Pennsylvania State University Press, 1984.

Chiaromonte, Nicola. *The Worm of Consciousness and Other Essays*. Edited by Miriam Chiaromonte; preface by Mary McCarthy. New York: Harcourt Brace Jovanovich, 1976.

Clark, Hilary. *The Fictional Encyclopedia: Joyce, Pound, and Sollers*. New York: Garland, 1990.

Cléder, Jean, and Jean-Pierre Montier, eds. *Proust et les images: Peinture, photographie, cinema, video*. Rennes: Presses Universitaires de Rennes, 2003.

Cohn, Robert G. *Vues sur Mallarmé*. Paris: Nizet, 1991.

———. *The Writer's Way in France*. Philadelphia: University of Pennsylvania Press, 1960.

Colum, Mary. "Review of Ulysses." *The Freeman*, 19 July 1922.

Cope, Jackson I. *Joyce's Cities: Archaeologies of the Soul*. Baltimore: Johns Hopkins University Press, 1981.

Corngold, Stanley. *The Fate of the Self: German Writers and French Theory*. New York: Columbia University Press, 1986.

Coupe, W. A. *A Sixteenth-Century German Reader*. Oxford, U.K.: Clarendon Press, 1972.

Davidson, Michael. "Ekphrasis and the Postmodern Painter Poem." *Journal of Aesthetics and Art Criticism* 42 (1983): 69–79.

Dench, Alfred Ernest. *Making the Movies*. 2nd ed. New York: Macmillan, 1919.

D'haen, Theo. "From Fantastic to Magic Realist," in Bertens and Fokkema, eds., *International Postmodernism*, 283–93.

Dierks, Manfred. *Studien zu Mythos und Psychologie bei Thomas Mann: An seinem Nachlaß orientierte Untersuchung zum "Tod in Venedig," zum "Zauberberg" und zur "Joseph"-Tetralogie*. Berne and Munich: Francke, 1972.

Dijkstra, Bram. *Idols of Perversity: Fantasies of Feminine Evil in Fin-de-Siècle Culture*. New York: Oxford University Press, 1986.

Dowden, Stephen D. *Kafka's "Castle" and the Critical Imagination*. Columbia, S.C.: Camden House, 1995.

———. *Sympathy for the Abyss: A Study in the Novel of German Modernism; Kafka, Broch, Musil and Thomas Mann*. Tübingen: Niemeyer, 1986.

Dresden, Sam. "Thomas Mann and Marcel Proust: On Myth and Anti-Myth." *Yearbook of Comparative Criticism* 9 (1980): 25–50.

Dyck, Joachim. *Athen und Jerusalem: Die Tradition der argumentativen Verknüpfung von Bibel und Poesie im 17. und 18. Jahrhundert*. Munich: Beck, 1977.

Edel, Leon. *The Modern Psychological Novel*. New York: Grove Press, 1955.

Ellenberger, Henri F. *The Discovery of the Unconscious: The History and Evolution of Dynamic Psychiatry*. New York: Basic Books, 1970.

Engelberg, Edward. "The Displaced Cathedral in Flaubert, James, Lawrence, and Kafka." *Arcadia* 21 (1986): 245–62.

Eysteinsson, Astradur, and Vivian Liska, eds. *Modernism*. 2 vols. Amsterdam and Philadelphia: John Benjamins, 2007.

General Bibliography

Feldman, Burton, and Robert Richardson. *The Rise of Modern Mythology, 1680–1860*. Bloomington: Indiana University Press, 1972.

Fernández-Morera, Darío. *American Academia and the Survival of Marxist Ideas*. New York: Praeger, 1996.

Figueira, Dorothy M. *Aryans, Jews, and Brahmins: Theorizing Authority through Myths of Identity*. Albany: State University of New York Press, 2002.

Firchow, Peter Edgerly. *Strange Meetings: Anglo-German Literary Encounters from 1910 to 1960*. Washington, D.C.: The Catholic University of America Press, 2008.

Foster, John Burt. *Heirs to Dionysus: A Nietzschean Current in Literary Modernism*. Princeton, N.J.: Princeton University Press, 1981.

Foucault, Michel. *L'archéologie du savoir*. Paris: Gallimard, 1969.

———. *Les mots et les choses: Une archéologie des sciences humaines*. Paris: Gallimard, 1966.

———. *The Order of Things: An Archaeology of the Human Sciences*. New York: Pantheon Books, 1970.

Frank, Arnim Paul, and Kurt Mueller-Vollmer. *The Internationality of National Literatures in Either America: Transfer and Transformation*. Vol. 2, part 1, of *British America and United States, 1770s–1850s*. Göttingen: Wallstein Verlag, 2000.

Frank, Joseph. *The Widenening Gyre: Crisis and Mastery in Modern Literature*. New Brunswick, N.J.: Rutgers University Press, 1965.

Fraser, Robert. *Proust and the Victorians: The Lamp of Memory*. London: Macmillan, 1994.

Freedman, Ralph. *The Lyrical Novel: Studies in Hermann Hesse, André Gide, and Virginia Woolf*. Princeton, N.J.: Princeton University Press, 1963.

Frye, Northrop. *The Anatomy of Criticism: Four Essays*. Princeton, N.J.: Princeton University Press, 1957.

———. *The Great Code: The Bible and Literature*. New York: Harcourt Brace Jovanovich, 1982.

Gelley, Alexander. *Narrative Crossings: Theory and Pragmatics of Prose Fiction*. Baltimore: Johns Hopkins University Press, 1987.

Gennette, Gérard. *Palimpsestes: La littérature au second degré*. Paris: Editions du Seuil, 1982.

Gillespie, Diane. "Through Woolf's 'I's': Donne and *The Waves*." In *Virginia Woolf: Reading the Renaissance*, edited by Sally Greene. Athens: Ohio University Press, 1999.

———, ed. *The Multiple Muses of Virginia Woolf*. Columbia: University of Missouri Press, 1993.

Gillespie, Gerald. "Classic Vision in the Romantic Age: Goethe's Reconstitution of European Drama in *Faust* II." In *Romantic Drama*, edited by Gerald Gillespie, 379–98. Philadelphia: John Benjamins, 1994.

———. "Disembodied Voice, Disinherited Mind: 'Development' in Pre-Romantic and Romantic Fiction." In *Proceedings of the 7th Congress of the International Comparative Literature Association*, 1.479–86. Stuttgart: Kunst und Wissen-Erich Bieber, 1980.

———. "Domesticating Don Juan." *Dedalus* 6 (1996): 207–20.

———. *Echoland: Readings from Humanism to Postmodernism*. Brussels: Presses Interuniversitaires Européennes-Peter Lang, 2006.

———. "Estebanillo and Simplex: Two Baroque Views of the Role-Playing Rogue in War, Crime, and Art (with an Excursus on Krull's Forebears)." In *Garden and Labyrinth of Time: Studies in Renaissance and Baroque Literature*. New York: Lang, 1988.

———. "From 'Baroque' Michael Drayton to 'Enlightened' Ebenezer Cooke: (Re-) Debunking the American Golden Age." In *Erkennen und Deuten: Essays zur Literatur und Literaturtheorie, Edgar Lohner in memoriam*, edited by Walter Lohnes. Berlin: Erich Schmidt, 1983.

———. "The Incorporation of History as Content and Form: Anticipations of the Romantic and Modern Novel." In *Proceedings of the 9th Congress of the International Comparative Literature Association*, 4.29–34. Innsbruck: Innsbrucker Gesellschaft zur Pflege der Geisteswissenschaften, 1982.

———. "In Search of the Noble Savage: Some Romantic Cases." *Neohelicon* 29, no. 1 (2002): 89–95.

———. "Novella, Nouvelle, Novelle, Short Novel? A Review of Terms." *Neophilologus* 51 (1967): 117–27, 225–30.

———. "Peripheral Echoes: 'Old' and 'New' Worlds as Reciprocal Literary Mirrorings." *Comparative Literature* 59 (2006): 339–59.

———. "Schopenhauer's Shadow: Stephen as Philosophic 'Superman.'" In *Bloomsday 100: Essays on "Ulysses*,*"* edited by Morris Beja and Anne Fogarty. Gainesville: University Press of Florida, 2009.

———. "Swallowing the Androgyne and Baptizing Mother: Some Modernist Twists to Two Basic Sacraments." *The Comparatist* 33 (2009): 63–85.

Gillespie, Gerald, Manfred Engel, and Bernard Dieterle, eds. *Romantic Prose Fiction*. Amsterdam and Philadelphia: John Benjamins, 2008.

Glasheen, Adaline. *Third Census of "Finnegans Wake": An Index of the Characters and Their Roles*. Berkeley and Los Angeles: University of California Press, 1977.

Godeau, Florence. "Peindre l'éphémère: Marcel Proust, Virginia Woolf et l'impressionisme," in Cléder and Monier, eds., *Proust et les images*.

Görner, Rüdiger. *Thomas Mann: Der Zauber des Letzten*. Düsseldorf and Zürich: Artemis and Winkler, 2005.

Gose, Elliott B. Jr. *The Transformation Process in Joyce's "Ulysses."* Toronto: University of Toronto Press, 1980.

Gray, Margaret E. *Postmodern Proust*. Philadelphia: University of Pennsylvania Press, 1992.

Grözinger, Karl Erich. *Kafka und die Kabbala: Das Jüdische im Werk und Denken von Franz Kafka*. Frankfurt: Eichborn Verlag, 1992.

Harrison, John R. *The Reactionaries: Yeats, Lewis, Pound, Eliot, Lawrence: A Study of the Anti-Democratic Intelligentsia*. New York: Schocken Books, 1967.

Hayman, David. *Joyce et Mallarmé*. 2 vols. Vol. 1, *Stylistique de la suggestion;* Vol. 2, *Les éléments mallarméens dans l'oeuvre de Joyce*. Paris: Les Lettres Modernes, 1956.

General Bibliography

———. *Re-Forming the Narrative: Toward a Mechanics of Modernist Fiction.* Ithaca, N.Y.: Cornell University Press, 1987.

Hayot, Eric. *Chinese Dreams: Pound, Brecht, Tel Quel.* Ann Arbor: University of Michigan Press, 2004.

Henke, Suzette A. *James Joyce and the Politics of Desire.* New York: Routledge, 1990.

Henriksen, Line. *Ambition and Anxiety: Ezra Pound's "Cantos" and Derek Walcott's "Omeros."* Amsterdam and New York: Rodopi, 2007.

Hopper, Keith. *A Portrait of the Artist as a Young Post-modernist.* Cork: Cork University Press, 1995.

Humphrey, Robert. *Stream of Consciousness in the Modern Novel.* Berkeley and Los Angeles: University of California Press, 1958.

Jameson, Fredric. *The Political Unconsciousness: Narrative as Socially Symbolic Act.* London: Methuen, 1981.

———. *Postmodernism; or, the Cultural Logic of Late Capitalism.* Durham, N.C.: Duke University Press, 1991.

Jennings, Lee B. "Keller's Epiphanies." *German Quarterly* 55 (1982): 316–23.

Jullian, Philippe. *Dreamers of Decadence: Symbolist Painters of the 1890s.* Translated by Robert Baldick. New York and Washington, D.C.: Praeger, 1971.

———. *Esthètes et magiciens.* Paris: Librairie académique Perrin, 1989.

Kaes, Anton, Martin Jay, and Edward Dimendberg, eds. *The Weimar Republic Sourcebook.* Berkeley and Los Angeles: University of California Press, 1994.

Karthaus, Ulrich. "'Der Zauberberg'—ein Zeitroman (Zeit, Geschichte, Mythos)." *Deutsche Vierteljahrsschrift für Literaturwissenschaft und Geistesgeschichte* 44 (1970): 269–305.

Kearney, Richard. *The Wake of Imagination.* London: Hutchinson, 1988.

Kenner, Hugh. *Ulysses.* Rev. ed. Baltimore: Johns Hopkins University Press, 1987.

Kern, Stephen. *The Culture of Time and Space, 1880–1918.* Cambridge, Mass.: Harvard University Press, 1983.

Koelb, Clayton. *Legendary Figures: Ancient History in Modern Novels.* Lincoln: University of Nebraska Press, 1998.

Kracauer, Siegfried. *Theorie des Films.* Frankfurt am Main: Suhrkamp, 1996.

Kristeva, Julia. *Proust and the Sense of Time.* Translated by Stephen Bann. London: Faber & Faber, 1993.

———. *Time and Sense: Proust and the Experience of Literature.* Translated by Ross Guberman. New York: Columbia University Press, 1996.

Langer, Suzanne K. *Philosophy in a New Key: A Study in the Symbolism of Reason, Rite, and Art.* 3rd ed. Cambridge, Mass.: Harvard University Press, 1963.

Lindsay, Vachel. *The Art of the Moving Picture.* New York: Macmillan, 1916.

Lodge, David. "The Language of Modernist Fiction: Metaphor and Metonymy." In *Modernism,* edited by Malcolm Bradbury and James McFarlane. Harmonsworth, U.K.: Penguin Books, 1976.

Lotman, Yury. *Semiotics of Cinema.* Edited and translated by Mark E. Suino. Ann Arbor: Department of Slavic Languages and Literatures, University of Michigan, 1976.

General Bibliography

MacKenzie, Robin. *The Unconscious in Proust's "A la recherche du temps perdu."* Oxford, U.K.: Peter Lang, 2000.

MacQuarrie, Charles W. *The Biography of the Irish God of the Sea from "The Voyage of Bran" (700 A.D.) to "Finnegans Wake" (1939): The Waves of Manannán.* Lewiston, N.Y., Queenstown, Ontario, Canada, and Lampeter, Wales: Edwin Mellen Press, 2004.

Mains, John William. "Literary Impressionism: A Study in Definitions." Ph.D. diss., University of Washington, 1978.

Manganiello, Dominic. *Joyce's Politics.* Boston: Routledge & Kegan Paul, 1980.

Marcus, Laura. *The Tenth Muse: Writing about Cinema in the Modernist Period.* New York and Oxford: Oxford University Press, 2007.

Marcuse, Herbert. "Repressive Tolerance." In *A Critique of Pure Tolerance,* edited by Herbert Marcuse, Robert P. Wolff, and Barrington Moore Jr. Boston: Beacon Press, 1965.

Martin, Raymond, and John Barresi. *The Rise and Fall of Soul and Self: An Intellectual History of Personal Identity.* New York: Columbia University Press, 2006.

McDougal, Stuart Y. *Dante among the Moderns.* Chapel Hill: University of North Carolina Press, 1985.

Meyer, Herman. *The Poetics of Quotation in the European Novel.* Translated by Theodore and Yetta Ziolkowski. Princeton, N.J.: Princeton University Press, 1968.

Moeller, Hans-Bernhard. "Thomas Mann's venezianische Götterkunde, Plastik und Zeitlosigkeit." *Deutsche Viierteljahrsschrift für Literatur wissenschaft und Geistesgeschichte* 40 (1966): 184–205.

Mommsen, Katharina. *Goethe und die arabische Welt.* Frankfurt: Insel, 1988.

Moretti, Franco. *The Way of the World: The Bildungsroman in European Culture.* London: Verso, 1987.

Moses, Michael Valdez. *The Novel and the Globalization of Culture.* Durham, N.C.: Duke University Press, 1995.

Münsterberg, Hugo. *The Photoplay: A Psychological Study.* New York: Appleton, 1916.

Murphy, Jonathan Paul. *Proust's Art: Painting, Sculpture and Writing in "A la recherche du temps perdu."* Oxford, U.K.: Peter Lang, 2001.

Nalbantian, Suzanne. *Aesthetic Autobiography: From Life to Art in Marcel Proust, James Joyce, Virginia Woolf, and Anaïs Nin.* New York: St. Martin's Press, 1994.

Nelson, Donald F. *Portrait of the Artist as Hermes: A Study of Myth and Psychology in Thomas Mann's "Felix Krull."* Chapel Hill: University of North Carolina Press, 1971.

Nemoianu, Virgil. "Hating and Loving Aesthetic Formalism: Some Reasons." *Modern Language Quarterly* 61 (2000): 41–57.

———. *Postmodernism and Cultural Identities: Conflicts and Coexistence.* Washington, D.C.: The Catholic University of America Press, 2009.

Noon, William T., S.J. *Joyce and Aquinas.* New Haven, Conn.: Yale University Press, 1957.

Northcote-Bade, James. *Die Wagner-Mythen im Frühwerk Thomas Manns.* Bonn: Bouvier, 1975.

General Bibliography

O Hehir, Brendan. *A Gaelic Lexicon for "Finnegans Wake" and Glossary for Joyce's Other Works.* Berkeley and Los Angeles: University of California Press, 1967.

O'Sullivan, Michael. *The Incarnation of Language: Joyce, Proust and a Philosophy of the Flesh.* London and New York: Continuum, 2008.

Palencia-Roth, Michael. *Myth and the Modern Novel: García Márquez, Mann, and Joyce.* New York: Garland, 1987.

Perloff, Marjorie. *The Poetics of Indeterminacy: Rimbaud to Cage.* Princeton, N.J.: Princeton University Press, 1981.

Polhemus, Robert M. *Comic Faith: The Great Tradition from Austen to Joyce.* Chicago: University of Chicago Press, 1980.

Prier, Raymond A. "Joyce's Linguistic Imitation of Homer: The 'Cyclops Episode' and the Radical Appearance of the Catalogue Style." *Neohelicon* 14, no. 1 (1988): 39–66.

Quiñones, Ricardo J. *Mapping Literary Modernism: Time and Development.* Princeton, N.J.: Princeton University Press, 1985.

———. *Dualisms: The Agon of the Modern Age.* Toronto: University of Toronto Press, 2007.

Rabaté, Jean-Michel. "'Alphybettyformed Verbage': The Shape of Sounds and Letters in *Finnegans Wake.*" *Word and Image* 2 (1986): 237–43.

Rather, L. J. "The Masked Man(n): Felix Krull Is Siegfried." *Opera Quarterly* 2 (1984): 67–75.

Reed, Terence J. *Thomas Mann: The Uses of Tradition.* Oxford, U.K.: Oxford University Press, 1974.

Rice, Thomas Jackson. *Joyce, Chaos, and Complexity.* Urbana and Chicago: University of Illinois Press, 1997.

Richardson, Robert. *Literature and Film.* Bloomington: Indiana University Press, 1969.

Ricoeur, Paul. *History and Truth.* Evanston, Ill.: Northwestern University Press, 1965.

Roberts, David. *The Indirections of Desire: Hamlet in Goethe's "Wilhelm Meister."* Heidelberg: Carl Winter, 1980.

Robertson, Ritchie. *Kafka: Judaism, Politics and Literature.* Oxford, U.K.: Clarendon Press, 1985.

Rolleston, James. *Kafka's Narrative Theater.* University Park: Pennsylvania State University Press, 1974.

Rorty, Richard. *Contingency, Irony, and Solidarity.* Cambridge, U.K.: Cambridge University Press, 1989.

Salm, Peter. "The Reflected Text: Kafka's Modern Inferno." In *Countercurrents: On the Primacy of Texts in Literary Criticism,* edited by Raymond A. Prier. Albany: State University of New York Press, 1992.

Sanulescu, C. George, and Clive Hart, eds. *Assessing the 1984 "Ulysses."* Totawa, N.J.: Barnes & Noble, 1986.

Scaff, Susan von Rohr. *History, Myth, and Music: Thomas Mann's Timely Fiction.* Columbia, S.C.: Camden House, 1998.

Scheel, Charles W. *Réalisme magique et réalisme merveilleux: Des théories aux poétiques.* Paris: L'Harmattan, 2005.

General Bibliography

Schmeling, Manfred. *Der labyrintische Diskurs: Vom Mythos zum Erzählmodell.* Frankfurt: Athenäum, 1987.

Scholem, Gershom G. *Major Trends in Jewish Mysticism.* New York: Schocken Books, 1961.

Schutte, William H. *Joyce and Shakespeare: A Study of the Meaning of "Ulysses."* New Haven, Conn.: Yale University Press, 1957.

Seidlin, Oskar. "Laurence Sterne's *Tristram Shandy* and Thomas Mann's *Joseph the Provider." Modern Language Quarterly* 8 (1947): 101–18.

———. "The Lofty Game of Numbers: The Mynheer Peeperkorn Episode in Thomas Mann's *Der Zauberberg." PMLA* 86 (1971): 924–39.

———. "Picaresque Elements in Thomas Mann's Work." *Modern Language Quarterly* 12 (1951): 183–200.

Senn, Fritz. *Joyce's Dislocutions: Essays on Reading as Translation.* Edited by John Paul Riquelme. Baltimore: Johns Hopkins University Press, 1984.

Shaffer, E. S. *"Kubla Khan" and The Fall of Jerusalem: The Mythological School in Biblical Criticism and Secular Literature.* New York: Cambridge University Press, 1975.

Shaffner, Randolph P. *The Apprenticeship Novel: A Study of the "Bildungsroman" as a Regulative Type in Western Literature with a Focus on Three Classic Representatives by Goethe, Maugham, and Mann.* New York: Peter Lang, 1984.

Shattuck, Roger. *Proust's Binoculars: A Study of Memory, Time, and Recognition in "A la recherche du temps perdu."* Princeton, N.J.: Princeton University Press, 1962.

———. *Proust's Way: A Field Guide to "In Search of Lost Time."* New York: W. W. Norton, 2001.

Sicher, Efraim. "Art as Metaphor, Epiphany, and Aesthetic Statement: The Short Stories of Isaak Babel." *Modern Language Review* 77 (1982): 387–96.

Simmel, Georg. "Die Großstädte und das Geistesleben." In *Die Großstadt, Jahrbuch der Gehe-Stiftung zu Dresden* 9 (1903): 185–206.

Spanos, William V. "The Detective and the Boundary: Some Notes on Postmodern Literary Imagination." *boundary 2* 1, no. 1 (1972): 147–68.

———. "Rethinking the Postmodernity of the Discourse of Postmodernism." In *International Postmodernism,* edited by Hans Bertens and Douwe Fokkema, 65–74. Philadelphia: John Benjamins, 1997.

Strauss, Walter. *Descent and Return: The Orphic Theme in Modern Literature.* Cambridge, Mass.: Harvard University Press, 1971.

Swales, Martin. *The German Bildungsroman from Wieland to Hesse.* Princeton, N.J.: Princeton University Press, 1978.

Terrinoni, Enrico. *Occult Joyce: The Hidden in "Ulysses."* Cambridge, U.K.: Cambridge Scholars Publishing, 2007.

Thacker, Christopher. *The Park and the Town: Public Landscape in the Nineteenth and Twentieth Centuries.* Berkeley and Los Angeles: University of California Press, 1979.

Thorton, Weldon. *Allusions in "Ulysses": An Annotated List.* Chapel Hill: University of North Carolina Press, 1968.

Tindall, William York. *A Reader's Guide to "Finnegans Wake."* New York: Farrar, Strauss & Giroux, 1969.

General Bibliography

Togornov, Mariana. *Gone Primitive: Savage Intellects, Modern Lives*. Chicago: University of Chicago Press, 1990.

Topping, Margaret. *Supernatural Proust: Myth and Metaphor in "À la recherché du temps perdu."* Cardiff: University of Wales Press, 2007.

Tratner, Michael. *Modernism and Mass Politics: Joyce, Woolf, Eliot, Yeats*. Stanford, Calif.: Stanford University Press, 1995.

Treip, Andrew. "'As per Periodicity': Vico, Freud and the Serial Awakening of Book III, Chapter 4." *In Finnegans Wake: "teems of times,"* edited by Andrew Treip. Amsterdam and Atlanta, Ga.: Rodopi, 1994.

Tuveson, Ernest Lee. *The Avatars of Thrice Great Hermes: An Approach to Romanticism*. Lewisburg, Pa.: Bucknell University Press, 1982.

Vaget, Rudolf. *Seelenzauber: Thomas Mann und die Musik*. Frankfurt: S. Fischer Verlag, 2006.

Verstraete, Ginette. *Fragments of the Feminine Sublime in Friedrich Schlegel and James Joyce*. Albany: State University of New York Press, 1998.

Vitoux, Pierre. "L'esthétique de Joyce: De l'épiphanie à la déconstruction de l'objet." *Cahiers Victoriens et Edouardiens* 14 (1981): 89–101.

Wachtel, Albert. *The Cracked Looking Glass: James Joyce and the Nightmare of History*. Selingsgrove, Pa.: Susquehanna University Press, 1992.

White, Hayden. *Figural Realism: Studies in the Mimesis Effect*. Baltimore: Johns Hopkins University Press, 1999.

White, John J. *Mythology in the Modern Novel: A Study of Prefigurative Techniques*. Princeton, N.J.: Princeton University Press, 1971.

Williams, Trevor L. *Reading Joyce Politically*. Gainesville: University Press of Florida, 1997.

Zamora, Lois Parkinson. *The Usable Past: The Imagination of History in Recent Fictions of the Americas*. Cambridge, U.K.: Cambridge University Press, 1997.

Zilcosky, John. "Kafka Approaches Schopenhauer's Castle." *German Life and Letters* 44 (1990–1991): 353–69.

———. *Kafka's Travels: Exoticism, Colonialism, and the Traffic of Writing*. New York: Palgrave/St. Martin's Press, 2002.

Zischler, Hanns. *Kafka Goes to the Movies*. Translated by Susan H. Gillespie. Chicago: University of Chicago Press, 2003.

Zumthor, Paul. *Oral Poetry: An Introduction*. Translated by Kathryn Murphy-Judy. Minneapolis: University of Minnesota Press, 1990.

SELECT INDEX OF NAMES AND SUBJECTS

This index covers writers, artists, thinkers, and critics (whether in their own right or as subjects in modernism), but passes over most ancient, biblical, and later historical figures if these are not referenced primarily as writers, artists, thinkers, or critics. A few biblical and mythological figures are referenced as subjects in modernist writing. Names and subjects selected from the footnotes are indicated by the page where the footnote begins. Translators and editors incidental to full bibliographical citation in the bibliography and footnotes are omitted here. In the case of authors known by their pen name, the legal name follows in parentheses.

Select Index of Names and Subjects

Select Index of Names and Subjects

Select Index of Names and Subjects

Select Index of Names and Subjects

Select Index of Names and Subjects

Select Index of Names and Subjects

Select Index of Names and Subjects

253, 269–70; time as montage, strata, intersections, 34, 37, 51, 58, 61, 139, 303; time as problem, enigma to explore, 15, 190, 198, 221, 269.
Tindall, William York, 208
Tirso de Molina (Gabriel Téllez), 233
Topping, Margaret, 338
Torgovnick, Mariana, 102
Trakl, Georg, 17
Tratner, Michael, 16
Treip, Andrew, 248
Tuveson, Ernest Lee, 214

Unamuno, Miguel de, 290–91, 338
unconscious, 6, 63, 69, 73, 79, 96, 149, 177, 194, 218, 220, 225, 236, 241, 243, 284, 289
Ungaretti, Giuseppe, 17

Valéry, Paul, 17, 231
Vasari, Giorgio, 277
Vega Carpio, Lope Félix de, 127
Verdi, Giuseppe, 149, 193
Verstraete, Ginette, 300
Vico, Giovanni Battista, 204, 207, 211, 248, 322, 334
Vigny, Alfred de, 288
Villiers de l'Isle-Adam, Auguste, 72–73
Viollet-le-Duc, Eugène-Emmanuel, 36
Virgil (Publius Vergilius Maro), 103, 192, 232, 242, 346
Visconti, Luchino, 132
Vitoux, Pierre, 66
Voltaire (François-Marie Arouet), 89
Vondel, Jost van den, 234

Wachtel, Albert, 246
Wagner, Richard (Wagnerian), 46, 51, 55, 64, 74, 81, 84, 95, 130, 132, 134, 145, 159, 170, 185, 187, 193, 220, 226, 240, 242, 313–14, 316–17, 327, 346
Walcott, Derek, 121
Weber, Carl Maria von, 223
Wedekind, Franz, 149
Welles, Orson, 144
Weston, Jessie L., 84
Wharton, Edith, 19, 148
White, Hayden, 8
White, John J., 249
Wickram, Jörg, 98, 103–4, 147, 278, 280
Wieland, Christoph Martin, 280
Wiene, Robert, 140
Williams, Trevor I., 13
Winckelmann, Johann Joachim, 224
Wolfe, Tom, 10
Wolfe, Thomas, 150
Woolf, Virginia, 1, 4, 17, 20, 51–52, 62, 133, 138–40, 164, 293–94
Wotan (Zeus), 142, 145, 226, 235, 242
Wright, Richard, 319

Yeats, William Butler, 4, 17–18, 78, 231, 330

Zamora, Lois Perkinson, 114
Zilcosky, John, 14, 266
Zischler, Hanns, 131, 135
Zola, Émile, 19, 86, 130, 148, 160
Zumthor, Paul, 204

Proust, Mann, Joyce in the Modernist Context was designed in Scala
by Kachergis Book Design of Pittsboro, North Carolina. It was
printed on 50-pound Natural and bound by Versa Press
of East Peoria, Illinois.